Zikrullah Khadem

With love

Champion Builder Books are a series of biographies about individuals who have been instrumental in helping the North American Bahá'í community fulfill its destiny—in the words of Shoghi Effendi, the Guardian of the Bahá'í Faith—as "the champion builders of Bahá'u'lláh's rising World Order."

Other Champion Builder Books:

To Move the World: Louis G. Gregory
and the Advancement of Racial Unity in America
by Gayle Morrison

Martha Root: Lioness at the Threshold
by M. R. Garis

Zikrullah Khadem
The Itinerant Hand of the Cause of God

With Love

by Javidukht Khadem

Bahá'í Publishing Trust
WILMETTE, ILLINOIS 60091

Bahá'í Publishing Trust, Wilmette, IL 60091
Copyright © 1990 by the National Spiritual Assembly
of the Bahá'ís of the United States
All rights reserved. Published 1990
93 92 91 90   4 3 2 1

Library of Congress Cataloging-in-Publication Data

Khadem, Javidukht.
    Zikrullah Khadem : itinerant hand of the cause of God : with love
/ written and compiled by Javidukht Khadem.
       p.   cm. — (A Champion builder book)
    ISBN 0-87743-224-4. — ISBN 0-87743-225-2 (pbk.)
    1. Khadem, Zikrullah, d. 1986.   2. Bahais—United States-
-Biography.   I. Title.   II. Series: Champion builder books.
    BP395.K46   1990
    297'.93'092—dc20   90-264
    [B]   CIP

Photograph Credits: All photographs provided by the author, except for
the following: p. 59, courtesy of the Bahá'í World Center; pp. 96, 107,
courtesy of the National Bahá'í Archives; pp. 50, 108, 109, 130, 131,
135, 136, 146, 169, 171, courtesy of Bahá'í Periodicals; p. 213, courtesy
of Riaz Khadem; pp. 167, 223, courtesy of Ramin Khadem

Design by John Solarz

With sorrowful hearts announce passing indefatigable fearless defender Faith deeply loved Hand Cause Zikrullah Khadem. His sterling services to the Cause, his total consecration to tasks assigned to him by beloved Guardian, his outstanding efforts as member National Spiritual Assembly cradle Faith, his valuable soul-uplifting stimulation imparted body believers North America, particularly United States Bahá'í Community, his untiring endeavors through his talks and writings in safeguarding Covenant and in instilling appreciation love for Shoghi Effendi shed undying luster over period his admirable stewardship Cause God. Offering prayers holy shrines progress his radiant soul Abhá Kingdom. Urge hold befitting memorial gatherings his name at all Houses of Worship as well as in all local Bahá'í communities.

UNIVERSAL HOUSE OF JUSTICE

To my husband,
who kindled the fire,
with love

Contents

ILLUSTRATIONS / xv
FOREWORD / xix
PREFACE / xxi
INTRODUCTION / xxv

Part 1 / *A LIFE OF SERVICE*
     / *Recollections by Javidukht Khadem*

1   MY HUSBAND / **3**
      Early Life / **3**
      First Pilgrimage / **7**
      His Career / **12**
      Courtship / **13**
      Marriage Partnership / **16**
      Family Ties / **18**
      Spiritual Guidance / **21**

2   EARLY SERVICE / **23**
      Mentor / **23**
      Traveling through Iran / **27**
      Photographing the Resting-Places of the Martyrs / **28**
      Praying for Assistance / **30**
      Dream or Reality? / **31**
      The Prayer-Answering God / **31**
      Mission to Egypt / **33**
      The Spirit of Pioneering / **34**

The Future Hand of the Cause of God Abu'l-Qásim
  Faizí / 37
Centenary of the Declaration of the Báb / 40

3 APPOINTMENT AS A HAND OF THE CAUSE OF
    GOD / 45
    A Cable Arrives / 45
    Another Cable Arrives / 46
    "With a Look He Granteth a Hundred Thousand
      Hopes" / 48

4 INTERNATIONAL SERVICE—EUROPE / 52
    Itinerant Hand / 52
    His Suitcase / 54
    Europe / 55
    Ireland / 60
    God-Intoxicated Souls / 62

5 INTERNATIONAL SERVICE—AFRICA / 68
    Preparation for the Holy Year / 68
    Africa / 69
    First Bahá'í Intercontinental Teaching Conference—
      Kampala / 71
    Kenya / 74
    Ethiopia / 76
    Back to Kenya / 76
    Tanzania / 76
    Zambia / 77
    South Africa / 78
    Belgian Congo / 79
    Angola / 82
    Back to the Belgian Congo / 82
    Liberia / 83
    Sierra Leone / 84
    Morocco / 89
    Tunisia / 90

6   INTERNATIONAL SERVICE—WEST AND EAST / 92
        Dedication of the Mother Temple of the West / 92
        Intercontinental Conferences / 97
        Ella Bailey / 98
        Munír Vakíl / 99
        Spiritual Preparation / 101
        India / 103
        Japan / 105
        Burma / 110
        Tonga / 112
        Bountiful Blessings from the Threshold of the
            Beloved / 113

7   THE IMPACT OF THE PASSING OF THE
        GUARDIAN / 115
        Devastating Dream / 115
        Devastating News / 117
        Despair / 118
        Take Off Your Mourning Coat / 119

8   LATER SERVICE / 122
        A New Beginning / 122
        The Light That Cannot Be Concealed / 122
        Hand of the Cause of God for the Western
            Hemisphere / 125
        Election of the Universal House of Justice / 127
        Bahá'í Schools / 129
        Green Lake / 134
        The Lovers of the Cause / 137
        The Martyrs and the Lords / 138
        Kindling "the Fire of the Love of God" / 140
        Edifying "the Souls of Men" / 143
        The Bounty of Ḥuqúqu'lláh / 144

9   MR. KHADEM'S PASSING / 148

10 MEMORIALS / **155**
   Memorial Gathering in the Holy Land / **155**
   Memorial Services in Wilmette / **157**
   Encompassing Love / **169**

Part 2 / OUR FATHER
   / *Reminiscences by Zikrullah Khadem's Five Children*

1 "ALL IS THE BELOVED, THE LOVER IS A VEIL" / **175**
   by Mozhan Khadem

2 IN MEMORY OF MY PRECIOUS FATHER / **185**
   by Jena Khadem Khodadad

3 THE POWER OF EXAMPLE / **200**
   by Riaz Khadem

4 GLIMPSES OF AN ENDEARING FATHER / **214**
   by Ramin Khadem

5 WITH GRATITUDE / **232**
   by May Khadem Czerniejewski

Part 3 / A SAMPLING OF ARTICLES
   / *by Zikrullah Khadem*

INTRODUCTION / **243**

1 PILGRIMAGE TO THE SCENES OF THE BÁB'S
   CAPTIVITY AND MARTYRDOM / **246**
   an article by Zikrullah Khadem, *translated by* Marzieh Gail

2 FROM BADA<u>SH</u>T TO SAINT LOUIS: AN EVALUATION
   OF THE FIRST BAHÁ'Í CONFERENCE AND THE
   LARGEST / **266**
   an article by Zikrullah Khadem

3   CARMEL: THE MOUNTAIN OF GOD AND THE
    TABLET OF CARMEL / **279**
    an article by Zikrullah Khadem

4   BAHÁ'U'LLÁH AND HIS MOST HOLY SHRINE / **301**
    an article by Zikrullah Khadem

    APPENDIX / **329**
       REMEMBRANCES OF COLLEAGUES AND FRIENDS / **329**
    NOTES / **349**

Illustrations

Mírzá Naṣru'lláh / 5

Radyyih Khánum with Zikrullah Khadem and Sháhin Khadem / 6

Zikrullah Khadem's 1925 passport photograph / 9

Javidukht and Zikrullah Khadem's wedding photograph, 1933 / 17

The Khadem family, 1951 / 19

Keith Ransom-Kehler with Zikrullah Khadem
and Salím Nounou / 25

The Khadems and other Bahá'í pilgrims, 1940 / 35

The National Spiritual Assembly of the Bahá'ís of Iran, 1948 / 41

Delegates to the centenary celebration of the Declaration of the
Báb, Shiraz, 1944 / 43

The Hand of the Cause of God Zikrullah Khadem,
Rome, 1952 / 49

Zikrullah Khadem and Counselor Peter McLaren / 50

Zikrullah Khadem and Counselor Angus Cowan / 50

A Bahá'í in Barcelona, Spain, with the Khadems, 1952 / 56

The Bahá'ís of Stuttgart, West Germany, with the
Khadems, 1952 / 56

Honor Kempton and students in Geneva, Switzerland, with the
Khadems, 1952 / 57

The Bahá'ís of Luxembourg with the Khadems, 1952 / 57

Participants in the 1952 Benelux teaching conference, Brussels,
Belgium / 59

Marion Little and the Khadems, Italy, 1952 / 63

Nine Hands of the Cause of God at the First Intercontinental
  Teaching Conference, Kampala, Uganda, 1953 / 73

Bahá'ís at the First Intercontinental Teaching Conference,
  Kampala, Uganda, 1953 / 74

Three Hands of the Cause of God and Bahá'í friends,
  Nairobi, Kenya, 1953 / 75

Zikrullah Khadem at the dedication of the Mother Temple
  of the West, 1953 / 96

Knight of Bahá'u'lláh Munír Vakíl, c. 1954 / 100

Zikrullah Khadem, the National Spiritual Assembly of the Bahá'ís
  of India, and others offering prayers at the site of the Indian
  Mashriqu'l-Adhkár, 1954 / 105

Participants in the Asia Teaching Conference,
  Nikko, Japan, 1955 / 107

The Bahá'ís of Taiwan, 1955 / 108

The Bahá'ís of Macao, 1955 / 109

The resting-place of Shoghi Effendi being visited by Zikrullah
  Khadem / 120

The Hands of the Cause of God and the Universal House of
  Justice, assembled at Bahjí / 123

Mr. Khadem celebrating Ayyám-i-Há with Bahá'í
  children, 1968 / 129

Mr. Khadem and children at a Bahá'í school / 130

Mr. Khadem and Bahá'ís, Potosi, Missouri / 131

Mr. Khadem and Bahá'ís, Frogmore, South Carolina / 133

Mr. Khadem and a Bahá'í youth, Green Lake,
  Wisconsin, 1973 / 135

Mr. Khadem and Jamaican Bahá'ís at the Caribbean
  Conference, 1971 / 136

Mr. Khadem addressing the Seventy-Fifth U.S. National Bahá'í
  Convention, 1984 / 146

The Hand of the Cause of God Zikrullah Khadem,
  c. 1904–1986 / 154

The graveside service held for Mr. Khadem,
   15 November 1986 / **159**

Zikrullah Khadem at a Native-American gathering, Wilmette,
   Illinois, 1980 / **164**

Mr. Khadem and participants in a Bahá'í school in Montreal,
   Quebec / **166**

Mr. Khadem and a group of Native-American Bahá'ís / **168**

Mr. Khadem and Bahá'ís in Dallas, Texas / **169**

The resting-place of the Hand of the Cause of God Zikrullah
   Khadem, Skokie, Illinois / **171**

Javidukht and Zikrullah Khadem and their son Mozhan / **176**

Javidukht and Zikrullah Khadem / **177**

The Khadem family, Teaneck, New Jersey, 1957 / **187**

Riaz Khadem at Oxford University / **208**

Zikrullah and Riaz Khadem, 1986 / **213**

Ramin and May Khadem at the resting-place of
   Shoghi Effendi / **219**

Zikrullah and Ramin Khadem / **223**

Zikrullah and May Khadem / **233**

The Hand of the Cause of God Abu'l-Qasím Faizí with May and
   Ramin Khadem, Geneva, Switzerland, 1952 / **235**

The Bahá'í community of Champaign, Illinois, the Khadems' first
   home in the Western Hemisphere / **237**

Foreword

The Hand of the Cause of God Zikrullah Khadem occupies a position of enduring prominence in the history of the North American Bahá'í community. When Mr. Khadem volunteered in 1959 to move to the United States, becoming one of the first Hands of the Cause of God allocated to the Western Hemisphere after the passing of Shoghi Effendi, the Guardian of the Faith, he was already distinguished for his outstanding work as a member of the National Spiritual Assembly of the Bahá'ís of Iran and for his service as a Hand of the Cause of God. Having traveled extensively in those capacities both in Iran and abroad, Mr. Khadem had made an indelible impression on the thousands of Bahá'ís whom he had met and befriended.

From 1960 to 1986—more than a quarter of a century—Mr. Khadem lived in the West and continued to distinguish himself through his dedicated service to the Cause of God, tirelessly working to fulfill the twin duties of his station as a Hand of the Cause—the protection and propagation of the Faith. During these years Mr. Khadem continued to travel, visiting Bahá'ís not only in the Western hemisphere but in many parts of the world, speaking at conferences, conventions, Bahá'í schools, and other gatherings. Frequently he was called upon to represent the Universal House of Justice at various Bahá'í events. Wherever he went, whatever he did, Mr. Khadem always brought his indomitable and contagious love and enthusiasm for the Faith.

An urbane and compelling Persian gentleman, Mr. Khadem became, in the finest sense, a North American. He dedicated enormous amounts of time and effort to educating and motivating the American Bahá'ís and had a special affinity for the Native Americans, for he excelled in communicating to them the spirit of the Bahá'í Faith.

Mr. Khadem infused the North American Bahá'í community with his penetrating knowledge of and reverence for the majestic significance of the station and person of Shoghi Effendi. Moreover, Mr. Khadem continually demonstrated his profound and undeviating respect for the institutions of the Bahá'í Faith.

The National Spiritual Assembly of the United States acknowledges, on behalf of the Bahá'ís of Alaska, Canada, and the United States, an immense debt that can never be repaid to Mr. Khadem for his wise counsel, his tremendous love, his vigorous inspiration, and his stalwart defense of the Faith. As the benefactor of Mr. Khadem's presence in the West, the North American Bahá'í community witnessed his exemplary consecration to whatever task he undertook, his thorough humility and complete selflessness in service to the Faith, and his fierce dedication to the protection of the Cause of God. Such qualities set a standard of service to the Cause that will undoubtedly inspire many generations to come.

NATIONAL SPIRITUAL ASSEMBLY OF
THE BAHÁ'ÍS OF THE UNITED STATES

Preface

A few months after the passing of the Hand of the Cause of God Zikrullah Khadem, I felt a longing to record my memories and to review many of the treasured moments I was blessed to share with him, my husband. I wished to review my sentiments and recollections with my precious Bahá'í family, who lovingly surrounded me at a time of great stress and captured my heart with love. I communicated this desire to the members of the National Spiritual Assembly of the Bahá'ís of the United States, who very lovingly and enthusiastically encouraged me in my project. Little did I appreciate at the time that I was embarking on a monumental task. I soon realized that it was impossible for me to record adequately his years of service to the threshold of Bahá'u'lláh. Therefore this book is not intended to be a complete biography of Mr. Khadem's life, nor is it an exact enumeration of his many accomplishments.

The material contained in *Zikrullah Khadem, The Itinerant Hand of the Cause of God: With Love* draws upon only a small fraction of a massive storehouse of valuable documents and meticulously collected memoirs detailing over sixty-one years of service to the Bahá'í Cause. When I decided to write about my husband, I had no idea of the magnitude of material I would discover. Researching this book has been an extremely enriching experience for me, for I have learned so much about my husband's life and services that I never knew. Much of the material I came across, I only had time to skim. Many documents, letters, and books of memoirs remain unexplored because of time constraints.

The first draft of the book was written without consulting the rich resources in Mr. Khadem's library. It was only through the numerous and persistent queries of my editor, Dr. Betty J. Fisher, that I was compelled to delve into the masses of papers, notes, and diaries. This

research more than doubled the length of the first part of the book. I
am deeply indebted to her for her meticulous attention to detail and
documentation as well as her ever-present loving cooperation at
every step. To answer her questions I had to conduct exhaustive
searches, sometimes agonizingly tedious and painful. Often I was at
a loss, having no idea where to look, tearfully beseeching God for
guidance. Then I would miraculously discover veritable treasures,
some of which I never knew even existed.

My story of love describes a part of Mr. Khadem's life that I
personally shared. Many trips that he took alone and recorded in his
diary are not included. In addition, a great many trips on which I
accompanied him—trips involving matters of protection of the Faith
—are also excluded. Surely in the future historians will do justice to
a life such as Mr. Khadem's that exuded sheer devotion and love for
Bahá'u'lláh's magnificent revelation.

My deepest appreciation goes to the Universal House of Justice,
whose guidance is our shelter. I give my tenderest love and appreciation to Mr. Khadem's co-workers, those standard-bearers who are
still serving our precious Cause in this world, those beloved Hands of
the Cause of God whom we pray will remain with us for a long time.
I extend very special thanks to the National Spiritual Assembly of the
Bahá'ís of the United States, who accepted my request that I be
permitted to share my written sentiments with the friends. I also
thank the thousands of Bahá'ís all over the world whose messages
and acts of love filled our home, both during Mr. Khadem's illness
and after his passing, even to the present day.

My heartfelt appreciation goes to all my children, who, each in his
or her own way, encouraged me to persist in recording my thoughts.
I feel compelled to acknowledge the bounties and blessings Bahá'u'-
lláh has showered upon this family, albeit undeservedly, through the
addition of our dear daughters-in-law, Jaleh, Linda, and Faraneh,
and sons-in-law, Manuchehr and Richard. My children have found
in their marriage partners gems who have mastered the love of this
Faith and served as instruments for passing on this precious Bahá'í
heritage to their children and future generations.

This book could not have been written without the assistance of
my daughter and son-in-law—May and Richard Czerniejewski—
both of whom helped in so many ways to shape it.

JAVIDUKHT KHADEM

Introduction

The Bahá'í Faith, in its essentials, is a mystical linking of hearts. Those with insight perceive traces of the awesome strength in this burgeoning unity, which, like the strength of an interlocked chain, is far greater than the sum of its parts. The links binding Bahá'ís together trace directly to the "Fashioner," our Creator. God's Manifestation, who in this age is Bahá'u'lláh, casts, as in former ages, links of love that lock together the hearts of God's near ones.

In the Bahá'í Dispensation we witness the unique, never-ending perpetuation of that process through "Bahá'u'lláh's peerless and all-enfolding Covenant."[1] After Bahá'u'lláh's passing, the mystical process was reinforced by 'Abdu'l-Bahá, the designated Center of that Covenant, "the Mainspring of the Oneness of Humanity," and later by Shoghi Effendi, the Guardian of that Covenant, whose "radiance . . . illumines all the horizons of the world."[2] With the Guardian's passing in 1957, it devolved upon the institution of the Hands of the Cause of God, acting completely "under the direction of the Guardian" and the unfailing guidance of his Ten Year Crusade, to steward the divine process.[3] Lastly, the Universal House of Justice, established in 1963 in accordance with Bahá'u'lláh's Covenant, emerged as His indestructible Institution forever securing the continuity of God's Plan for linking together the hearts of all humanity.

Zikrullah Khadem recounts the story of a remarkable figure who arose in loving service, was appointed a Hand of the Cause of God, and played an historic part in the mystic process. He was one of a few blessed souls to receive links cast from the heart of God's Covenant, forged by the transforming love of the Guardian of the Cause of God, Shoghi Effendi. The heat and light of that forging passed through Zikrullah Khadem and, as if focused in a ruby laser, burned brilliantly, welding many other hearts into that spiritual chain.

Mr. Khadem was, foremost, a lover, his heart bursting with spiritual attraction. As attested by so many within these pages, he carried out the assignment, given to the Hands of the Cause of God by 'Abdu'l-Bahá in His Will and Testament, to kindle "the Fire of the Love of God in the very hearts and souls of His servants."[4] The mystical reality of this process was revealed to me by Mrs. Khadem one day, several months after Mr. Khadem's passing. She movingly related, "Do you know what I'm missing so much? Yes, I miss him deeply, but what is missing most of all from my life is the beloved Guardian! Who is there now in this household to speak of him with such burning passion, to bring him so close? That is the greatest treasure I have lost." Thus did he kindle "the Fire of the Love of God" in his closest companion.

Zikrullah Khadem is a record, in my estimation, of the life story of one of "the treasures of the earth."* Some of the events of his life, some of his services, some remembrances and tributes from loved ones, are shared in this book. Virtually all of the quotations in these pages are from the notebook he always carried with him. A prayer he repeatedly chanted and, I feel, God fulfilled for him, is found at the beginning of chapter 2.§ Such remembrances, tributes, and quotations from passages that were important to him give one a sense of who Zikrullah Khadem was. But the reality of Mr. Khadem—his virtues, his station, his certitude, his love and the reasons for it—cannot be contained in any book.

How perfectly he fulfilled his given name, Zikrullah, which means "the mention of God," and Khadem, which means "servant." Perhaps the course of his life was foreshadowed in that name given at birth. Even to the last moments of his life, "*Yá Bahá'u'l-Abhá!* [O Thou the Glory of the Most Glorious!]," the Greatest Name of God, continually issued from his mouth. This he would say with great enthusiasm. Mr. Khadem was perpetually immersed in the sacred

---

*God promised, while Bahá'u'lláh was imprisoned in the Síyáh-Chál (Black Pit), to render Him victorious and to "raise up the treasures of the earth—men who will aid Thee through Thyself and through Thy Name" (Bahá'u'lláh, quoted in Shoghi Effendi, *God Passes By*, rev. ed. [Wilmette, Ill.: Bahá'í Publishing Trust, 1974], 101).

§See p. 23.

writings. They were his standard. He bathed in the Word of God, cleansed himself spiritually in it each day. The beloved Guardian's master work, *God Passes By*, was his unerring resource. His mind, his thoughts were chaste. He was unsullied by the pollution and decay that suffuse today's world. The average ten year old has already had corrupt thoughts and experiences that Mr. Khadem, in his eighty years, never permitted to enter his consciousness. His tongue never spoke curse, invective, or corruption. In essence, it was chaste, mentioning God.

And, oh, what an excellent "servant"! He was precise, meticulous. He demanded of himself that he fulfill his assignments to the letter, swiftly and completely. His travels, his classes, his deeply moving talks, punctuated, from a prodigious memory, with quotations from the Bahá'í writings, are well known. Many of his services, however, are not widely known. 'Abdu'l-Bahá, in His *Will and Testament*, paired protection of the unity of the Cause with propagation as twin duties assigned to the Hands of the Cause of God. How tenaciously this Hand of the Cause pursued unity. He invariably put aside his own wishes and concerns in favor of and in respect for the Bahá'í institutions and the protection of their stature. His achievement in this regard, the protection of the unity of the Cause, was, perhaps, his noblest and most historic service.

Mr. Khadem was also a scholarly resource, reviewing Bahá'í publications from around the world. To many correspondents he sent information culled from a vast library of source materials with which he was intimately familiar. He wrote many works in Persian and in English. Some of his English publications are included in this book.*

I feel certain that, however heartfelt the praise offered in these pages, we can retain no illusion that our treasured Hand of the Cause, Mr. Khadem, would humbly accept or proffer such loving adulation at the feet of his Lord. His humility about his accomplishments is an enduring standard for each of us who witnessed it.

Zikrullah Khadem is not intended to provide the definitive record of the Hand of the Cause of God Zikrullah Khadem. Rather, it is a

---

*See part 3 pp. 246—325.

love letter composed for one who consecrated his life to the Bahá'í Faith, who loved immensely and accepted willingly the pain and sorrow such love entails. It conveys some of his qualities and a glimpse of the depth of his love. The tender sentiments of some of those enkindled souls who have loved him, whose lives were linked with his, are also found here. The following pages testify to the role one outstanding soul played in the continuing mystical process whereby all humanity will become linked through God's Covenant. By this recounting, may solace and inspiration come to all who, as willingly and fearlessly as did Mr. Khadem, saddle the steed of the Valley of Love.[5] May it be God's providence that the links of love burnished by that sterling "servant," the unbounded "mention of God," never be tarnished, always be strengthened, and endure eternally.

RICHARD CZERNIEJEWSKI

Part 1 / *A LIFE OF SERVICE*
/ *Recollections by Javidukht Khadem*

1 My Husband

I desire distinction for you. . . . But this distinction must not depend upon wealth. . . . It is not an ordinary distinction I desire; not scientific, commercial, industrial distinction. For you I desire spiritual distinction. . . . In the love of God you must become distinguished from all else. You must become distinguished for loving humanity, for unity and accord, for love and justice. In brief, you must become distinguished in all the virtues of the human world— for faithfulness and sincerity, for justice and fidelity, for firmness and steadfastness, for philanthropic deeds and service to the human world, for love toward every human being, for unity and accord with all people, for removing prejudices and promoting international peace. Finally, you must become distinguished for heavenly illumination and for acquiring the bestowals of God. I desire this distinction for you.

—'Abdu'l-Bahá

Early Life

Zikrullah Khadem was born into a Bahá'í family in Tehran, probably in 1904.* He often expressed his profound indebtedness to his father, Mírzá Nasru'lláh, who had the bounty of serving 'Abdu'l-Bahá as His attendant and companion during a period of some four years, shortly after the passing of Bahá'u'lláh. While enjoying the special blessing of being in 'Abdu'l-Bahá's service, Mírzá Nasru'lláh became an excellent calligrapher under the tutelage of Mishkín-

---

*Although Mr. Khadem's passport says he was born in 1904, that date may be incorrect, as he was born in a time when births were often not recorded.

Qalam, the leading calligrapher of Persia.* He wished to continue all his life in his service to 'Abdu'l-Bahá, but he was instructed by the Master to leave the Holy Land and marry. Obediently, he returned to Persia and was married to a faithful Bahá'í, Rádyyih Khánum. The marriage produced six children, five of whom survived to adulthood. The second of the five was named Zikrullah, which means "the mention of God."§

'Abdu'l-Bahá bestowed the name "Khadem," which means "servant," on Mírzá Nasru'lláh in a tablet. In a tablet addressed to Mr. Khadem's paternal grandmother, surnamed Bíbí Ján, 'Abdu'l-Bahá praised Mírzá Nasru'lláh's services, saying, "Wert thou to know to what bounty he hath attained, and what great blessing he hath received, thou wouldst assuredly spread thy wings and soar in the heavens." He also predicted in the same tablet that "Erelong the clear evidences of these favors will be apparent and manifest, like unto the sun shining from the horizon of existence, and the bright light of this grace will enkindle the lamp of that family. Soon thou shalt rejoice at that which he will offer in servitude, and thy heart shall be gladdened at meeting him." Consequently, Rádyyih Khánum, Mr. Khadem's mother, always felt that a great blessing would come to her family.[1]

Thus Zikrullah Khadem was reared in a spiritual household and was trained in the love of God by a father who received his own lessons from the Center of the Covenant Himself, 'Abdu'l-Bahá. The family lived in Tehran at the Hayát-i-Bágh, an enclave of Bahá'í homes around a large garden, which had been purchased at the instruction of 'Abdu'l-Bahá and where the remains of the Báb had been secretly kept for some time. There great Bahá'í figures, such as

---

*One of our family treasures is a calligraphy of Mishkín-Qalam addressed to "His honor, Mírzá Nasru'lláh." For an account of Mishkín-Qalam, see 'Abdu'l-Bahá, *Memorials of the Faithful,* trans. Marzieh Gail (Wilmette, Ill.: Bahá'í Publishing Trust, 1971), 97–101.

§According to the Bahá'í system of transliteration, the name "Zikrullah Khadem" would be transliterated "Dhikru'lláh Khádim." In a letter dated 7 August 1972 to Mrs. Florence Avis, Mr. Khadem explained that, inasmuch as Shoghi Effendi wrote his name both as "Zikrullah" and "Dhikru'lláh," he used both spellings himself. For continuity I have used "Zikrullah Khadem" throughout the book, as Mr. Khadem most often spelled his name that way.

*MÍRZÁ NAṢRU'LLÁH KHÁDEM,
father of Zikrullah Khadem.
Zikrullah often expressed a profound
indebtedness for the spiritual training
given to him by his father, who served
as personal attendant and companion
to 'Abdu'l-Bahá for four years.*

the poets Nayyir, Síná, and Na'ím, could often be found teaching the Faith.

Mr. Khadem often spoke of the great teachers who traveled throughout Iran at a time when there were very few Bahá'ís. These early traveling teachers went from city to city to spread the message, attracting seekers wherever they went. Some immediately recognized the truth and were so enamored with their new discovery that they would accompany Nayyir and Síná on further journeys. Others, angered by what they considered to be heresy, stoned and beat them and whoever was with them. This is how the Bahá'í Faith was spread in those days.

The conditions under which the Bahá'ís lived in the early days of the Faith were very difficult. In a talk given in 1955, Mr. Khadem described the dangers and precautions the Persian believers had to take in those days:

> My father used to take my hand as we walked down the dark lanes. When we approached the house of the Bahá'í we were to meet, he would bump his shoulder against the door in passing, as if by accident. We would continue walking down the lane. Meanwhile, the owner of the house would open the door very carefully. When we were sure that no one was looking we would return and quickly slip into the house.
>
> In those days they used to bake bread in outdoor ovens. Sometimes

RAḌYYIH <u>KH</u>ÁNUM
(center) with Zikrullah,
the second of her five children, and
a daughter-in-law, <u>Sh</u>áhin Khadem

the friends would meet around these ovens. Light from a candle placed inside was well concealed so the people could not guess they were having a Bahá'í meeting. From the light of the candle, however, they would be able to read the Bahá'í writings and chant the prayers.[2]

Zikrullah was a very unusual child. His father, noticing Zikrullah's capacity, trained him to the best of his abilities and prepared him for great deeds in the future. Recognizing that Zikrullah was blessed with a fantastic memory, his father required him to memorize from the Bahá'í writings daily and to recite before breakfast every morning for a reward. Years later Shoghi Effendi, knowing of Zikrullah's capacity, also bade him memorize from the holy writings, for example, the Tablet of Carmel, the Tablet to Náṣiri'd-Dín <u>Sh</u>áh, and parts of other tablets to the kings and leaders of the

world.* Those who knew Mr. Khadem recall him effortlessly chanting Persian or Arabic writings from memory.

Zikrullah's father was a spiritual anchor and compassionate counselor to him. Once, in his youth, Zikrullah was not given a position
he dearly wanted. When he returned home, he tried to conceal his
disappointment from his father, who lay in bed quite ill. His father,
however, immediately perceived his son's bitter disappointment. Mr.
Khadem, misty-eyed, recalled that moment in these words:

> My father said, "O my dear, my heart! Why are you agonized with what
> happens in this world? Does not the Lord know our heart? He knows.
> And whatever is good, He plans for you!" Then he quoted from the
> Qur'án, "It may happen that you will hate a thing which is better for you;
> and it may happen that you will love a thing which is worse for you; God
> knows, and you know not."³ And in order to comfort me, he said, "Be
> happy with whatever God has planned for you." But at that moment, if
> the angels themselves came down to tell me that it was not good for me
> to join that office, I would not have believed it.

Years later the wisdom of the disappointment was revealed to Mr.
Khadem. He recalled the profound guidance his father had so often
given him and cherished the special blessing of having been his son.

FIRST PILGRIMAGE

Sometime after the passing of 'Abdu'l-Bahá, the Central Spiritual
Assembly of Iran had advised the Bahá'ís to convey their loyalty to
Shoghi Effendi.⁵ Zikrullah eagerly followed this recommendation

---

*For the Tablet of Carmel, see Bahá'u'lláh, *Tablets of Bahá'u'lláh Revealed after the
Kitáb-i-Aqdas,* comp. Research Department of the Universal House of Justice, trans.
Habib Taherzadeh et al. (Wilmette, Ill.: Bahá'í Publishing Trust, 1988), 3–5. For the
Tablet to Násiri'd-Dín Sháh and other tablets to the kings and leaders of the world,
see Bahá'u'lláh, *The Proclamation of Bahá'u'lláh to the Kings and Leaders of the World*
(Haifa: Bahá'í World Centre, 1967). For Mr. Khadem's discussion of the Tablet of
Carmel, see "Carmel: The Mountain of God and the Tablet of Carmel," reprinted in
part 3, pp. 279–300.

⁵The Central Spiritual Assembly of Iran was the Spiritual Assembly of the capital
city Tehran, which acted as a liaison between the Bahá'ís of Iran and the Bahá'í World
Center in Haifa until the National Spiritual Assembly of Iran was formed in 1934.

and wrote a letter to the beloved Guardian, pledging his love and devotion. In response he was honored with a letter from the beloved Guardian that enkindled his heart and created a fervent longing to attain the presence of his beloved.

After he received that first communication from the Guardian, little else occupied his thoughts. He often recounted to me the details leading to that first pilgrimage: the ardor, the unquenchable longing, the anguished waiting, the torrent of emotions when he finally attained his goal. He ardently prayed for the opportunity to attain the beloved Guardian's presence and to visit the holy shrines. Eager for any news, hoping to quench vicariously his burning thirst for contact with Shoghi Effendi, he sought the company of anyone going on or returning from pilgrimage.

One day, while passing through the customs office, he was drawn like a magnet into conversation with a European traveler whose suitcase bore a Haifa sticker, the land of his beloved. When had the man been in Haifa? Had he seen the Bahá'í holy places? Did he know of the Bahá'í Faith? The stranger did not know and had not heard; he brought no "trace of the traceless Friend."[4]

One night in a dream Zikrullah made his pilgrimage to the Holy Threshold and to the presence of the beloved Guardian.* During this dream he wept tears of joy so profusely that, when he awoke, his entire pillow was wet. He was subsequently able to live out that dream exactly as he had dreamt it.

Eager to be on his way, he first secured a passport with the help of one of the friends and packed his suitcase. But then he realized he did not have the necessary permission. Fortuitously, he encountered Jináb-i-Amín Iláhí, the trustee of Ḥuqúqu'lláh during the time of 'Abdu'l-Bahá. After much careful consultation with Zikrullah regarding his eagerness to visit the Guardian, this loyal, trusted companion of 'Abdu'l-Bahá composed a mild letter to Shoghi Effendi, requesting permission for Zikrullah to make pilgrimage. The humble request did not appease the ardent youth, who wanted a stronger, more urgent letter. This was done, but Zikrullah felt the language could be stronger yet. However, Jináb-i-Amín insisted that, if the request met with the Guardian's approval, permission would be

*The Holy Threshold refers to the Bahá'í sacred shrines in the Holy Land.

ZIKRULLAH KHADEM's
passport photograph from his first pilgrimage in 1925,
to the Bahá'í World Center and the presence of Shoghi Effendi,
the Guardian of the Bahá'í Faith. The trip made
a deep and lasting impression on Zikrullah.

granted. "If not, so much the better because the paradise of good pleasure is preferable to the paradise of pilgrimage. Since the beloved Guardian's choice is flawless, his decision, regardless of our own desires, is so much the better for us."* Zikrullah's father echoed this advice, saying, "Whatever he [the beloved Guardian] does is sweet." Though intellectually convinced, Zikrullah's heart had already taken flight. His patience ran out. To be closer to his heart's desire he went to Baghdad to await permission there. Yet even though he was closer, the waiting was agonizing.

His zeal and excitement were most touching. The Central Spiritual Assembly of Iraq consulted about his case and through a mes-

*From a tape of Mr. Khadem's.

senger advised him to be patient until he received an answer from the Holy Land.* He tried, but the fervor of his longing and the anguish of his separation from his beloved finally made him ill. Recognizing the gravity and urgency of his condition, the Central Assembly, accepting responsibility for its action, advised him to leave for Haifa at once.

Elated, he left Baghdad and traveled to Beirut via Damascus. From there he lost no time in finding a group of Europeans driving to Haifa. However, far from quelling his impatience, every passing minute, every mile, fueled his longing. He deluged his companions with questions about how much farther it was, finally so annoying them that, upon arriving in Haifa, they unceremoniously dumped him and his luggage in front of the house of 'Abdu'l-Bahá.

Abruptly, he was confronted by his own rashness. Though he was following the instructions of the Central Spiritual Assembly of Iraq, he did not have permission for pilgrimage in hand. As he stood there remorsefully, Dr. Esslemont and a Dutch pilgrim spotted him from the window in the Western Pilgrim House and quickly came out to welcome him. At the same time, one of the Bahá'ís recognized him and handed him the letter of permission that had been prepared that day and was about to be posted.

Among the many highlights of that most memorable trip and its manifold blessings was a special message to Iranian youth. Shoghi Effendi asked the ardent pilgrim, who was eager to perform any service, to convey to the youth of Iran his love and encouragement, to ask them to deepen themselves in the Faith and to study English, especially English literature. This request inspired Zikrullah to embark on a zealous study of the English language, a study he was to pursue the rest of his life. This was further reinforced during subsequent visits and through communications in which the Guardian asked him to translate Bahá'í articles from English to Persian.§

---

*The Central Spiritual Assembly of Iraq was the Spiritual Assembly of the capital city Baghdad, which acted as a liaison between the Bahá'ís of Iraq and the Bahá'í World Center in Haifa until the National Spiritual Assembly of Iraq formed in 1931.

§See the introduction to part 3, pp. 243–45.

Another highlight of that visit, according to Zikrullah's notes, was being present when the Guardian laid out the three-room addition to the Shrine of the Báb. The six original rooms that 'Abdu'l-Bahá had built were separated from the mountain slope by a wide path. Behind these, the Guardian planned to add three more rooms. One day during this pilgrimage, when Shoghi Effendi came into the gardens surrounding the Shrine of the Báb, he summoned the gardener, Áqá Raḥmatu'lláh, to ask for string and a handful of plaster. He instructed Zikrullah to hold one end of the string as he outlined the location of the addition by marking the ground with plaster along the line of the string. Anything that the beloved Guardian requested of this eager youth, no matter how small or insignificant it might be, became a precious treasure that Zikrullah would recall over and over again with gratitude throughout his life. Every event that included any interaction with the Guardian became an indelible and precious memory.

The crowning event of that pilgrimage was a gift of a picture of 'Abdu'l-Bahá holding a rose in His hand. Zikrullah had requested a photograph of the Guardian. In response, Shoghi Effendi gave him 'Abdu'l-Bahá's portrait, saying, "I give you a portrait of the beloved Master as a souvenir."[5] I cannot describe how deeply Mr. Khadem cherished such gifts from the Guardian. They were visible, tangible symbols of Shoghi Effendi's appreciation of Mr. Khadem's love and devotion.

Mr. Khadem has described his pilgrimages in greater detail elsewhere. Suffice it to say that, after that first pilgrimage, when he met his beloved Guardian for the first time in May 1925, Zikrullah Khadem was no longer the same person. His being was recreated with love. He was galvanized with a new purpose, propelled in a new direction, infused with a new passion. His only thought, his only desire after that was to please his beloved. That meeting with Shoghi Effendi, the spiritual center of the world, and five subsequent meetings, established a profound and unshakable devotion. That devotion was reinforced and strengthened by innumerable confirming experiences, especially when Mr. Khadem was carrying out assignments for the beloved Guardian. Over and over again, before Mr. Khadem would even have a chance to make his reports, Shoghi Effendi would somehow know of events as they came to pass, would anticipate Mr. Khadem's concerns and dilemmas, and would cable instructions for handling problems. Ceaselessly, the Guardian communicated encouragement, appreciation, and nurturing love via cables and letters.

His Career

Mr. Khadem's childhood mastery of the verities of the Faith, his memory, and his excellent Persian and Arabic all distinguished him. After completing the schooling available in Tehran, he taught briefly at the Tarbíyat School, a Bahá'í secondary school. He then went to the south of Iran to serve as an interpreter and language tutor for the Anglo-Persian Oil Company. He developed an accelerated method of teaching Persian to the English-speaking population and opened a language school that used this method. A certificate from this school was highly prized, as it obtained special privileges and promotions for the employees of the oil company. It meant that one had attained a level of proficiency in Persian. In this and many other ways Mr. Khadem swiftly distinguished himself and was eventually selected to be a personal assistant to the British general manager of the company.

While still in his twenties, Mr. Khadem reached a turning point. Should he continue with the oil company, or should he, as he desired, return to Tehran and set out on his own? He had a dream that 'Abdu'l-Bahá was beside a grindstone. The grindstone was working very slowly and was coming to a halt. The Master placed His finger on the mill, and the grindstone began to speed up. It turned faster and faster. From this dream Mr. Khadem knew that 'Abdu'l-Bahá would support him. He returned to Tehran and found work assisting Iraq to establish an embassy in Iran. His skill in scholarly Arabic and Persian, diplomatic French, and English, as well as his ability to accomplish the seemingly impossible swiftly, soon made him indispensible.

While Mr. Khadem lived in Tehran, he was able to transmit many items to Shoghi Effendi. The sword of Mullá Ḥusayn and Bahá'í documents were among the treasures of the Faith that he was able to send. He was also able to send a plaster model of the Wilmette House of Worship from Haifa to Tehran, and he was instrumental in helping to open the doors of pilgrimage to the Iranian believers. In

1940, while Mr. Khadem was on pilgrimage during the dedication of the monument of the Purest Branch, the beloved Guardian bade him to chant two prayers in the holy shrines.* Afterward, the Guardian indicated that these prayers had accomplished two purposes: the relief of the suffering of the believers in Iran and the reopening of the doors of pilgrimage to them. Shoghi Effendi then instructed Mr. Khadem to go back and "prepare the means" for these pilgrims to come. Mr. Khadem returned to Iran and ingeniously devised a plan that fulfilled his beloved Guardian's will.

Bahá'ís from Iran were soon able to travel to the Holy Land and to state on travel documents that they were Bahá'ís traveling to the holy shrines of the Bahá'í Faith. The flow of pilgrims to the holy shrines began again, fulfilling the dying supplication of the Purest Branch "that his life might be accepted as a ransom for those who were prevented from attaining the presence of their Beloved."[6]

Over the years Mr. Khadem prospered through wise investments and sound business enterprises. With Shoghi Effendi's approval, he left the Iraqi embassy for personal business ventures that allowed him more time for Bahá'í activities. In 1960 he began serving the Faith full time and was able to live on his savings for the remainder of his life.

COURTSHIP

Owing to the Persian Bahá'í practices in the time I grew up, young women did not have to suffer as much as they do today in

---

*The Purest Branch is a title that was given to Mírzá Mihdí, 'Abdu'l-Bahá's youngest brother. In 1870, at the age of twenty-two, the Purest Branch was praying on the roof of the barracks in Akka. Carried away by his meditations, he accidentally stepped through an open skylight and fell onto an open crate. Severely injured, he died less than a day later, on 23 June 1870.

For accounts of the final interment of the remains of the Purest Branch in 1939, see Shoghi Effendi, *God Passes By*, new ed. (Wilmette, Ill.: Bahá'í Publishing Trust, 1974), 347–48, and Shoghi Effendi, *Messages to America: Selected Letters and Cablegrams to the Bahá'ís of North America, 1932–1946* (Wilmette, Ill.: Bahá'í Publishing Committee, 1947), 31–33. See also the section on the dedication in 1940 of the twin monuments for the wife of Bahá'u'lláh and the Purest Branch in "Carmel: The Mountain of God and the Tablet of Carmel," reprinted in part 3 (see pp. 279–300).

order to find their mates. It was the parents' responsibility to help their daughters by suggesting the right suitors for them. This is not the same as arranged marriages, for according to the laws of Bahá'u'lláh, six persons must give their consent for marriage: the couple as well as the two sets of parents. This law provides a wonderful, moderating influence on the marriage practices of Eastern cultures, in which Muslim parents sometimes arrange marriage contracts for their children without consulting them.

When I was growing up, a young Bahá'í woman might have had a number of suitors who wished to marry her; however, the parents were vigilant. Because marriage could not take place without parental consent, parents waited for the right suitor to appear, one who had a spiritual upbringing, a high quality of character, intelligence, and the capacity to shoulder the responsibilities of life. When such a man came courting their daughter, parents could be sure that she would find happiness in the match. In many ways this relieved women of the burden of searching for a mate on their own without the mature judgment and experience that a wise choice requires. While women could follow the dictates of their hearts with suitable candidates, their emotions did not entrap them in unsuitable matches. For my part, I probably was not aware of all my suitors. If they did not match the high standards of my parents' expectations, I never heard of them.

In my case, courtship took place in an extraordinary fashion. I was young, still in school, and eager to finish my education. I had no interest in marriage. However, because Bahá'u'lláh permits marriage at a young age if the consenting parties agree, my youthfulness was not a problem to my father. If the suitor had the qualities my parents wanted, my parents would be ready to give their consent.

On 10 September 1933, as I was preparing to go to school, my father joyously and enthusiastically announced, "A young man with magnificent qualities has asked to marry you. He is of a noble family. His father served 'Abdu'l-Bahá and raised him in the love of God. He has a very bright future. He is intelligent, educated, and has the ability to make you happy in every way. I watched him grow up. He is very special!" Then he added with a mischievous laugh, "He is very handsome, too! Wouldn't you like to meet him?"

"No!" I declared emphatically, worried at the thought of having to interrupt my education and hopes of a career. Marriage was the last thing on my mind, and I began to cry at the thought of having to give up my dreams.

My father tenderly tried to console me. "Don't cry. According to the laws of the Bahá'í Faith you must be willing and happy with the decision. I can't force you to marry." He suggested gently, "But wouldn't you just like to see him?"

"No!" I said again, unmoved.

"Anyway," he concluded casually, "he is coming over tonight."

That whole day I cried and agonized over this terrible shattering of my hopes. I could not wait to get the whole ordeal over with. I would find my mate when I was ready.

That evening, as I watched through the window facing the court-yard of my grandmother's house, my suitor arrived with several members of his family and an elegant Western woman, Mrs. Keith Ransom-Kehler, who was holding onto his arm.* Immediately my heart was touched, and my weeping stopped. I was drawn to him as if by a magnet. My father entered the room, sensed the change, and teased, "Well, why don't you cry? Where are the tears?"

"I have to be obedient," I replied, trying to hide my true feelings.

But he was not fooled. He scolded, "Why did you make yourself miserable all day and cry so much for nothing? Now look at you! Your eyes are red, puffy, and ugly! Hurry! Go and wash your face! Then come into the living room to receive him and his friends. They are guests!" Hospitality to guests is very important in Eastern cultures.

Our first meeting occurred when I entered the room to serve refreshments. I served each guest. When I came to Mrs. Ransom-Kehler, she greeted me very warmly and asked me about my studies. She was very interested in determining whether I was a good match for Zikrullah. Even in that brief meeting, I could sense the bond of genuine concern and mutual affection between them. After that day, my doubts and fears evaporated.

---

*Mrs. Ransom-Kehler, at Shoghi Effendi's request, was in Iran as a representative of the American Bahá'í community, appealing to the Iranian government to remove a ban on the entry of Bahá'í literature into that country. She was posthumously appointed a Hand of the Cause of God. See chapter 2, pp. 23–27.

MARRIAGE PARTNERSHIP

Mr. Khadem later told me that he had felt the same magnetic attraction that I had felt when we had first met. We were married, heart and soul, on 3 October 1933, three weeks after we met. Mrs. Ransom-Kehler had gone to Isfahan and could not be present at our wedding, but she cabled a tender message of congratulations and love.

After our marriage, our very first conversation was on the subject of our spiritual life. I had been trained in a Bahá'í family, but I was no match for Mr. Khadem's depth and devotion. He said, "You do not have the obligation to perform the customary household duties. Don't worry if you don't know how to cook and keep house. These are not important to me and can be done by others. I want only two things from you. First, I want you to love God as I do."

"How do you love God?" I asked, eager to learn.

"God should be the center and pivot of our life. Second, I want you to love the beloved Guardian as I do."

I said I would try. Soon I learned that the Guardian was everything to him, dearer than his own life. I tried very hard to live up to his standards, but I could never match his depth of love and devotion.

How lucky I was to be married to a man of such quality, how lucky even to have been introduced to him. My father, who had recognized his strength of character and his spiritual nature, loved him deeply and was truly joyous when we were married. The first magnetic attraction between us continued as the years passed, deepening into a love so strong it was as if we were one soul.

The bond that joined us together so tightly was the Faith, in which he deepened my understanding and educated our children. Our personalities were very different; nevertheless, we were united. We disagreed over many mundane things in our daily life, but in the essentials we were always united. Before each day was over, we resolved our differences and returned to the same appreciation for each other.

Mr. Khadem truly believed in and practiced the teaching of the equality of men and women. To appreciate how liberated he was, one has to be aware of the practices and customs in Iran at that time, conventions that have again been revived today. Women did not

JAVIDUKHT AND ZIKRULLAH KHADEM
on their wedding day, 3 October 1933

freely associate in mixed company, nor did they have the liberty to speak openly. Many were denied education, and those who pursued it were usually discouraged. All were expected to wear the veil.

Although Bahá'í women were more liberated than the general population and did not wish to wear the veil, they sometimes had to, depending on where they lived. It was easier to ignore such customs in Tehran than in the smaller towns and villages. Neither my father nor my husband accepted the custom of the veil. The freedom of choice in personal appearance with which I had grown up continued in marriage. Mr. Khadem's progressive attitude extended to all areas of life. He had only one standard—the Bahá'í standard—the words and teachings of Bahá'u'lláh and nothing else.

After we were married, I was still eager to continue my education. I had my husband's full support and encouragement, for he felt education was very important in my development and role as a mother. He wished for me to develop to my fullest potential. When we were married, I had not yet finished high school. He assisted and encouraged me until I completed a Liberal Arts degree at the University of Tehran. Later, when we were living in the United States, I enrolled in a commercial course in order to help him with his voluminous correspondence as a Hand of the Cause of God in the Western Hemisphere.

Mr. Khadem upheld the same standard of achievement for his sons and daughters. He encouraged all of them to pursue excellence, and he supported them in furthering their education.

Mr. Khadem was also very hospitable and loved to have guests. I entertained our friends, men and women, as an equal, expressing my opinions as though we were living in a Bahá'í society. Since all of his friends, Bahá'ís and non-Bahá'ís alike, loved him deeply and admired his views, they grew to respect his attitude toward women. The complete trust and mutual respect we shared influenced our children, who grew up expecting equal partnership in their own marriages.

FAMILY TIES

Mr. Khadem placed great emphasis on the importance of family life and family unity. He worked very hard and assumed the responsibility of providing for us. At the same time he had a great appreciation and respect for the role of motherhood and the education of children. Learning from his attitude, I, too, developed a great appreciation for that role and experienced true fulfillment as a mother. We were blessed with five children: Mozhan, Jena, Riaz, Ramin, and May. The birth of each brought great joy to our hearts, and we held a special celebration for each one's arrival, thanking Bahá'u'lláh for bestowing upon us another gift who could be reared in the bosom of the Faith and become, in turn, a servant to humanity.

Our mornings began with the sound of Mr. Khadem chanting the long obligatory prayer before breakfast. He usually followed this with chanting (from memory) from tablets of 'Abdu'l-Bahá. What beautiful music transformed the atmosphere of our home every morning!

The first draft of this manuscript was written during the Nineteen Day Fast, a special period that makes Mr. Khadem's absence so much more acute because he loved to chant the long fasting prayer, some-

THE KHADEM FAMILY, Naw-Rúz 108, 21 March 1951.
Front row, left to right: Riaz, Javidukht, May, Zikrullah, Ramin;
back row, left to right: Mozhan, Jena. Shoghi Effendi kept a copy
of this picture when the Hand of the Cause of God
Amelia Collins showed it to him in 1952.

times twice a day. The whole family would join in on the refrain:

> Thou seest me, O my God, holding to Thy Name, the Most Holy, the
> Most Luminous, the Most Mighty, the Most Great, the Most Exalted,
> the Most Glorious, and clinging to the hem of the robe to which have
> clung all in this world and in the world to come.[7]

He always remarked that there was a special potency in this prayer.
During our son Ramin's very first Fast away from home, he tele-
phoned one morning at 5:00 A.M. and begged his father to chant it.
As Ramin listened to this prayer over the phone, he was deeply
moved.

Recognizing the crucial importance of our children's education,
particularly in the Bahá'í Faith, we always consulted on the best
means of training them. Mr. Khadem set very high standards and
believed that the spiritual education of the children must be balanced by excellent academic education. He quoted the beloved
Guardian, who told him while he was on pilgrimage that there must
be moderation in every area of life. He felt that the Guardian
emphasized this so much because, "I wasn't moderate, and he
wanted to educate me."

Mr. Khadem believed in inspiring excellence through praise and
encouragement. He, like all Bahá'ís, tried to follow the example of
'Abdu'l-Bahá, who never failed to shower love and encouragement
on everyone and would never criticize, coerce, or belittle their
efforts. Likewise, the beloved Guardian always showered love, appreciation, and encouragement upon all the friends, especially the
Hands of the Cause of God. They responded to this magnetic, divine
love with increasingly devoted services.

My husband utilized the same philosophy in training our children
as well as in his talks with the believers throughout the world. His
attitude and words conveyed joy and appreciation for their efforts
and accomplishments, whether great or small. He expressed confidence in and lofty expectations for the ability of his listeners. This
concept was one of the foundations of parenting as we practiced it in
our home.

Mr. Khadem was joyful, exuberant, cheerful, optimistic, and full
of life. He loved his children and treated each of them as a priceless
gem. He played with them, swinging them around, telling them
rhymes and playful endearments. However, after the passing of the

Guardian in 1957, he became taciturn, whether in the company of family or friends. The only thing that brought him out of his introverted silence was the name of the beloved Guardian, which would animate him and bring him to life. He would sparkle, and words would flow with such devotion, attraction, and reverence that his sentiments would penetrate the hearts of those who heard him.

He was well known for his love of Shoghi Effendi. This is the love he wanted to implant in his children, who basked in an atmosphere of love. This is the love that he asked me, beseeched me, to acquire when he married me. Our life as a family brimmed with this love. Through it, we became deepened in the revelation of Bahá'u'lláh and in the station of the Master, 'Abdu'l-Bahá, and we truly came to love the Guardian.

SPIRITUAL GUIDANCE

Mr. Khadem was always guiding our family in the service of the Cause, injecting the love of the Faith into our very beings. The names of the Central Figures of the Faith were music in our ears. Our children learned at a very young age that reverence and love for the Faith are essential to one's existence. They all tried to emulate their father, who nurtured so effectively their love for 'Abdu'l-Bahá and the Guardian. We learned from his example that all of our affairs—whether they concerned marriage, family life, finances, or career—would be successful when we put the love of God at the center of our lives.

However, in spite of his total dedication to the Faith and his strong ideas about individual responsibilities, Mr. Khadem did not impose his views on his children or on others. When our children were very young, he would carefully instruct them. However, once they were of age, he never monitored their spiritual activity, never chastened them, never coerced them or interfered in their right to conduct their own spiritual lives.

He stood behind them financially until they finished their education, supporting them just enough for them to continue, but was never lavish with them. The moment they were able to work on their own, he no longer supported them. He felt they should find their own destiny, experience their own successes and setbacks, and become mature through becoming accustomed to hardship, as 'Abdu'l-

Bahá taught. He thought parents should not give children whatever they want, nor should they cushion their falls financially. Otherwise, they will lack determination and ambition to acquire excellence. Mr. Khadem wanted our children to be victorious in life through their own efforts and accomplishments.

Until the passing of the Guardian in 1957, our children received a most precious gift upon turning fifteen years of age: they could go on their own for a visit to the Guardian and the holy shrines. We would get a box of chocolates and place the permission of the Guardian (which we acquired ahead of time) and a ticket to Haifa on top. This was their birthday gift and a symbol of their lifelong spiritual journey. I can never forget the change that was apparent when each returned. They had been timid; they became fearless. They had been shy; they became bold. They were transformed from children into adults, from adolescents into individuals with purpose and direction.

It was not our instruction or influence that changed our children. The transformation was due to the overwhelming creative power of the Faith. We noticed a dramatic change in every returning pilgrim. The qualities of self-discipline, love, and devotion were among the gifts with which they returned. Three of our children were among the lucky ones to make such a pilgrimage before the Guardian's passing.

2 Early Service

He is the Compassionate, the All-Bountiful! O God, my God! Thou seest me, Thou knowest me; Thou art my Haven and my Refuge. None have I sought nor any will I seek save Thee; no path have I trodden nor any will I tread but the path of Thy love. In the darksome night of despair, my eye turneth expectant and full of hope to the morn of Thy boundless favor and at the hour of dawn my drooping soul is refreshed and strengthened in remembrance of Thy beauty and perfection. He whom the grace of Thy mercy aideth, though he be but a drop, shall become the boundless ocean, and the merest atom which the outpouring of Thy loving-kindness assisteth, shall shine even as the radiant star.

Shelter under Thy protection, O Thou Spirit of purity, Thou Who art the All-Bountiful Provider, this enthralled, enkindled servant of Thine. Aid him in this world of being to remain steadfast and firm in Thy love and grant that this broken-winged bird attain a refuge and shelter in Thy divine nest that abideth upon the celestial tree.

—'ABDU'L-BAHÁ

MENTOR

During his youth, Mr. Khadem was greatly influenced by his association with Mrs. Keith Ransom-Kehler. In her, he encountered the same depth of love for the Faith and the same desire to serve the threshold of the Beloved that burned in his own heart. He was impressed by the refinement and quality of her character, the generosity of her spirit, the completeness of her obedience to the beloved Guardian, and the total dedication of her life to the Cause. It was these qualities that welded the bond of friendship between a very young Eastern man and a middle-aged Western woman.

In the early 1930s Mrs. Ransom-Kehler had traveled for two years throughout China, Japan, and India as a Bahá'í teacher. In 1932, upon instruction from the beloved Guardian, she went to Iran on a special mission as an ambassador representing the North American Bahá'í community in its appeal to the Iranian government to remove the ban on the entry of Bahá'í literature into Iran.

Mr. Khadem met her when she first arrived and felt an immediate kinship. He greatly admired her services and became so devoted to her that he was ready to serve her at all times. He used to transcribe her talks and type all of her reports to Shoghi Effendi. She reciprocated the affection and admiration, which can be gleaned from her many letters to him. The following letter dated 9 May 1933 is typical of her communications to him, which mingle love, encouragement, and instruction:

> Dearest Zikr'u'lláh—
> Your service to the Cause of God is exemplary. No one, but you has ever done this routine work for me so diligently.
>
> Of course I am terribly pleased over the news from the girl's father. I feel that God would abundantly bless such a union.
>
> Yes, darling, I want you to type the English. I only write by hand to the Sháh. Of course it will have to be returned to me for my signature.
> . . .
> With unutterable thanks for all your splendid services of which I have often spoken to the Guardian.
>
> > Yours in El Abhá
> > Keith

Mrs. Ransom-Kehler's insights and opinions were so important to him that he had asked her to accompany him when he came to ask for my hand in marriage. After we were married, he frequently spoke about her. The following is what he recounted to me of his precious moments with her:

> I could not wait to finish my work each day so that I could serve her. Every day there was something to do. We would go to visit either a group of Bahá'ís or the authorities. I acted as her translator and personal

KEITH RANSOM-KEHLER with
ZIKRULLAH KHADEM (right) and SALÍM NOUNOU.
Mrs. Ransom-Kehler is holding a picture of Shoghi Effendi,
whom she and Zikrullah both served with exemplary devotion.

secretary. I would type her reports. Sometimes I would accompany her to the bazaar and other places she wished to visit.

She taught me so much! I learned about generosity and the appreciation of human dignity. When we went to the bazaar, she would seek out the vendors who were especially honest and hard-working and would reward them with large purchases or generous tips. She would take some of these people gifts during their holidays. Our trips to the bazaar were usually for this purpose. When she noticed those in need of love and compassion, she would visit them more frequently. People would cluster around her, drawn by her sincerity and love, and would appreciate her in the most lavish ways. They would ask God's blessings for her and shower praise on her. They would thank God for her presence among them. Oh how they loved her!

Mr. Salím Nounou, Mr. Khadem's closest friend, would occasionally accompany them to the bazaar. He, too, loved Mrs. Ransom-Kehler and served her in many ways.

Mr. Khadem once told me that Mrs. Ransom-Kehler was the most stylish woman he had ever met. She had a beautiful and elegant mink coat cut in the latest fashion. Her dresses were so exquisite they would attract the attention of onlookers. Yet they were also very dignified and tasteful. Once there was a memorial gathering at the Iraqi embassy for an Iraqi government official. Mr. Khadem was greeting the guests who came to offer their condolences. Suddenly, among all the men present, he noticed Keith Ransom-Kehler. Women did not customarily appear at such events, but there she was, dressed elegantly in mourning black with a beautiful matching broad-brimmed hat. She was stunning, he told me later.

Noticing Mr. Khadem's concern, she approached him and whispered, "Don't worry. I came today to introduce myself as a Bahá'í. I came for the sake of the dignity of the Faith." Indeed, the ambassador, as well as the rest of the embassy staff, were very impressed by her bearing and conduct.

Though she had a regal bearing and never failed to impress all who encountered her, she was also a lesson in humility. She once told Mr. Khadem, "When you look back on these times, you will be astonished at how Bahá'u'lláh chose an old, weak, and ordinary woman like me to come to Persia and serve Him in this manner. Who am I?"

Yet the beloved Guardian called her "the sign of eloquence." Mrs. Ransom-Kehler carried out his instructions with precision and devotion. She demonstrated to Iranian authorities the universal scope, the unity, and the integrity of the Faith in Bahá'í communities all over the world.

In 1933, while in Isfahan, she contracted smallpox and died on 23 October. Shoghi Effendi conferred upon her the double distinction of martyr and Hand of the Cause of God. In a message dated 30 October, the Guardian eulogized her as follows:

> Keith's precious life offered up in sacrifice to beloved Cause in Bahá'u'lláh's native land. On Persian soil, for Persia's sake, she encountered, challenged and fought the forces of darkness with high distinction, indomitable will, unswerving, exemplary loyalty. The mass of her help-

less Persian brethren mourns the sudden loss of their valiant emancipa-
tor. American believers grateful and proud of the memory of their first
and distinguished martyr. Sorrow stricken, I lament my earthly separation from an invaluable collaborator, an unfailing counselor, an esteemed
and faithful friend. I urge the Local Assemblies befittingly to organize
memorial gatherings in memory of one whose international services
entitled her to an eminent rank among the Hands of the Cause of
Bahá'u'lláh.[1]

Keith Ransom-Kehler remained for Mr. Khadem an inspiration
and an example of dignity, devotion, and service. Over the years he
frequently recalled his fondness for her and his respect and admiration for the fearless and obedient manner in which she served the
beloved Guardian.

TRAVELING THROUGH IRAN

A few years later, when Mr. Khadem had the blessing himself of
carrying out assignments from the beloved Guardian, he brought
Keith Ransom-Kehler's same eagerness and enthusiasm to the work.
When he traveled throughout Iran in 1938 and 1939 to visit the
friends, I often went with him. In order to reach all the distant
centers of Iran efficiently, we traveled every weekend, leaving Thursday evening and returning Friday evening (Fridays are holidays in
the Muslim world). We would usually have to drive all night,
arriving early Friday morning. Mr. Khadem would visit the friends
all day Friday and drive home Friday night. In this manner we
missed two nights' sleep every weekend.

Most of the roads in Iran at that time were unpaved and very
narrow and often traversed difficult mountainous terrain. Such dangers and difficulties never deterred my husband. Because the beloved
Guardian had requested something, the response had to be quick
and complete. There was no time to stop or rest. My function on
these trips was to talk so that Mr. Khadem would not fall asleep at
the wheel. Once, I remember, both of us began to doze. I was
awakened by a sudden lurch. When I opened my eyes, I discovered
that we were driving only inches from the edge of a precipice. The
slightest movement sideways would have plunged us into the chasm.
I screamed for him to stop. We did not doze any more that night.

PHOTOGRAPHING THE RESTING-PLACES OF THE MARTYRS

One of our trips was to Nayríz, about an hour or so by car from Shiraz. Our beloved Guardian had asked Mr. Khadem to take pictures of the graves of the martyrs there. We had our son Mozhan with us. When we arrived in Shiraz, Mr. Khadem asked me to stay in the hotel with the baby while he left for Nayríz that afternoon. He said he would return late at night.

The hotel was crowded and not very safe, especially for an unaccompanied young woman. Hence I stayed in the room, afraid to wander out by myself, as none of the Bahá'ís knew I was in Shiraz.

When it became dark, I heard heavy footsteps pacing on the balcony outside my door. The balcony overlooked a courtyard where people were dining and enjoying themselves. I became worried because the pacing did not stop. I peeked out the window and saw a middle-aged man limping back and forth. From time to time he would look at the window as if he were checking on me. My worry changed into fear. I opened the door very slightly to ask if he wanted something. When he saw how worried I was, he told me gently that he just wished to look after my safety until my husband came back. He said that he was a Bahá'í and that I should not be afraid.

At the word "Bahá'í," my fear drained away, and my anxiety turned into calm. I invited him to dine with me on the balcony in front of my room, where a table was set. While we ate, he introduced himself and told me about his life. He said that his occupation had been robbing camels and that he had been very skilled at cutting the loads off the backs of camels without being detected. As I listened to his story, I became anxious again and regretted having invited him to dinner. He continued:

> I was a member of a band of robbers. For one of my business engagements [he referred to robbing as his business], I came to Shiraz, where I saw a crowd in the street, gathered around some object, cheering, dancing, and having a good time. I looked through the crowd and discovered that the object in the middle was a man sitting backward on a donkey with the tail of the donkey in his hands and his face painted with different colors. The crowd was poking and jabbing at him with sticks, throwing stones, and spitting at him. He just sat there serenely. I was so shocked that I pushed my way through and went to him. I asked him,

"What have you done?"

He replied calmly, "Nothing."

"Nothing?" I scoffed. "I am a highwayman, and they don't even do this to me. Why are they doing it to you, then?"

He replied, "I did nothing. It's just that I am a Bahá'í, and they want me to deny my Faith."

I told him, "Well, say you are not a Bahá'í!"

He said, "How can I deny God and His Revelation? It is my life—dearer than my life."

Then the crowd that was encouraging cruelty to an innocent man made the donkey run, taking him away. The next day, I heard the man had been killed. This incident inspired me to investigate the Faith. I became a Bahá'í and tried to live the Bahá'í life. I wrote a letter to the Master, 'Abdu'l-Bahá, and told him that I had accepted the Faith but was not worthy to call myself a Bahá'í.

His eyes filled with tears as he spoke:

'Abdu'l-Bahá wrote me a very personal message of forgiveness that penetrated and melted my heart. I learned I had been forgiven for all my past sins. That knowledge made me a new being. I was not the only one that day who saw that cruelty and witnessed the martyrs' spirit; there were many, many others who were also inspired to find out the truth and become Bahá'ís.

I was deeply moved. How often the Master had rescued souls who had seemed beyond redemption. How totally safe and comfortable I, a naive young woman, now felt with this blessed soul, a transformed highwayman.

The hour was getting later and later, however. Not having received any news from my husband, we became increasingly worried over his whereabouts and safety. Finally, at midnight, I received a phone call. It was my husband's voice, thank God. He said calmly, "I don't want you to worry. Everything is fine."

"What is it?" I asked anxiously. "What is it?"

He told me that he had been arrested for taking pictures and was now in the Nayríz prison.

Mr. Khadem in prison! God help us! After his reassuring words and voice calmed me down, he asked me to inform the Spiritual Assembly of Shiraz because he was only allowed one phone call. I

assured him this would be done with the help of the devoted Bahá'í
who happened to be in the hotel.

Well, at least my husband was safe. When I told my guest what
Mr. Khadem had asked, he left immediately, on foot (for there was
no transportation at night), to inform each of the members of the
Spiritual Assembly throughout the city of Shiraz. He implored me to
be patient because it would take him all night. He explained that, as
a punishment for stealing, the authorities had severed his Achilles'
tendons so that he would no longer be able to run or walk properly.
(That explained his heavy pacing.) He assured me that by morning
all the Assembly members would know, and Mr. Khadem would be
released.

That is exactly what happened. With the Bahá'ís' assistance, Mr.
Khadem was released. The camera and photographs were returned.
In the Nayríz court, a long indictment of Mr. Khadem's "crimes" was
drawn up and sent to Tehran for a hearing. There the incident led to
extensive publicity for the Faith because Mr. Khadem was able to
give public testimony to the truths of the Faith while demonstrating
his own innocence. He sent a complete report along with the court
indictment to the beloved Guardian.

God had freed both of these prisoners, the transformed robber
and Mr. Khadem, and used their services to assist His Cause. Were it
not for the martyrs—the steadfast Bahá'í the robber encountered on
a donkey and the Bahá'ís whose graves Mr. Khadem had set out to
photograph—neither victory would have occurred. What a time!
What victories!

PRAYING FOR ASSISTANCE

In late 1938, on another of these trips, Mr. Khadem and I were
accompanied by friends. We arrived in town, as usual, in the early
morning. Mr. Khadem looked in his notebook to find an address for
the Bahá'ís. He searched everywhere—in his suitcase, in the car—
but he could not find any information. We did not know where to go
or whom to see. We consulted about what we should do. One of our
companions suggested that we get out of the car and start praying.
He thought maybe a name would come to our minds or perhaps the
Bahá'ís would somehow find us.

"Let us concentrate and beseech Bahá'u'lláh to help us," he

advised. "Otherwise, this trip is wasted."

We stood on the corner and prayed fervently for guidance. When the prayer was over, we noticed our group was larger. Two had been added. The newcomers introduced themselves as Bahá'ís and directed us to the rest of the friends.

DREAM OR REALITY?

Once, as we arrived just before dawn in one of the towns in the provinces of Iran, a well-dressed man on the road beckoned us to stop. The man came forward eagerly, introduced himself, and greeted us lovingly with Bahá'í greetings.

He said that he had had a dream that same night that a blue car just like ours would be coming in the early morning, its occupants on a mission to bring the loving greetings of the beloved Guardian for the Bahá'ís of the town. He was so convinced of the reality of the dream that he ran to the road as soon as he was dressed. He had been standing for several hours, watching the road from Tehran so that he could receive us properly.

This electrifying occurrence amazed us. I will never forget the heavenly meeting there that day with the Bahá'ís. The man's dream, demonstrating the nearness and reality of the spiritual world, created loving, spiritual bonds that linked our hearts forever.

THE PRAYER-ANSWERING GOD

When I could not accompany Mr. Khadem on his trips, he traveled with a few of the Bahá'ís. One of them was Salím Nounou, his most loyal and dearest friend. I saw Mr. Nounou in Haifa, in early January 1986, after the dedication of the "Lotus of Bahapur" in India, the newest of the Houses of Worship circling the globe. The group returning from India was permitted to visit the holy shrines. It was there I renewed our close ties with dear Mr. Nounou. He reminded me of the following occurrence, which I recount in his honor the way I heard it told by Mr. Khadem:

It was early in the morning as we were entering the city of Tabríz. We were very tired. I had been driving all night. Perhaps I was driving too fast, or people were not expecting a car to pass so early in the morning. All of a sudden, although I did not see anything, I hit something. When we got out of the car, we discovered that the object I had struck was a man. He was motionless in the road. He was dead!

We decided to park the car, clear our minds, and consult on how to cope with this ghastly occurrence. Mr. Nounou argued that he wanted to introduce himself as the driver. "I do not have a wife and family yet. You have a family. Think of them! I can submit myself to the authorities. Surely this is not your fault! He must have darted into the road. In these provinces, you don't know what may happen. Someone may say it's your fault. You'd be put on trial and could be imprisoned. I'll submit myself!"

The two of us argued back and forth. Each of us was convinced of his point of view, and neither wanted the other to be in trouble. Mr. Aḥmadpúr-Mílání (one of the passengers on this trip, a Tabrízian by birth who was able to speak the local dialect) offered to investigate the accident scene to see what was happening and verify that the man was, indeed, dead. We waited in the car until he returned. He reported that the man was dead and that we had to hurry with our decision because the crowd was agitated.

I said, "Let's not waste any more time. I have to submit myself to the authorities as the driver and remain here as long as necessary to accept the punishment."

"Please, friends, let us pray!" we all said simultaneously. We sat in the car and prayed, "He is the prayer-hearing, prayer-answering God!"[2] The prayer was intense. I had never prayed so ardently in all my life. It was as if I were kneeling and taking the hem of the robe of the Blessed Beauty [Baháʼuʼlláh] and begging for His assistance. Our prayers were getting longer and longer until we realized we had to stop. It was time for me to submit myself for the necessary judgment.

Mr. Aḥmadpúr-Mílání again went to the scene of the accident. He quickly returned with the news, "He is alive! He is alive! There is some movement in him!"

The crowd was yelling, "Alláh-u-Akbar!" [God is great!] Our prayers were answered!

As it turned out, the victim maintained to the authorities that the accident was his fault, that he had not seen the car coming. All the friends that day generously offered to provide for his needs. He received much love, compassion, and help for himself and his family and recovered fully. Mr. Khadem remained in communication with him and his family for a long time.

MISSION TO EGYPT

Beginning in 1937, I was privileged to accompany Mr. Khadem on five pilgrimages to the presence of Shoghi Effendi. On each occasion he was favored with an assignment from the beloved Guardian. He recalled one of these in a talk he gave at the Ninth Annual Conference of the Association for Bahá'í Studies:*

On one assignment the beloved Guardian sent me to Egypt. Visiting in Haifa at the same time was an old resident of Egypt, Husayn Rúhí, who lived to be over one hundred years old. This man was truly wonderful. He received a knighthood from the British government and was an historic figure. The beloved Shoghi Effendi bade him to go with me to Jerusalem and obtain a visa for Egypt. Upon our return with the visa, the beloved Guardian said to me, "Go to Egypt, and tell the friends the glad tidings." Then the beloved Guardian turned to Mr. Rúhí and said, "And you translate for him into Arabic." Neither of us knew what the glad tidings were that I was to tell the friends. I did not dare ask the beloved Shoghi Effendi. So we went to Egypt and met the friends. In a packed hall in Cairo, I stood before the Bahá'ís, desperately wanting to tell them the glad tidings. But I couldn't think of anything. I prayed, "O God! *Yá Bahá'u'l-Abhá!* [O Thou the Glory of the Most Glorious!] What to tell them?"

A voice within me said that I should tell them about the sufferings of the Bahá'ís of Iran, although this did not seem to be glad tidings. But I started to tell them that I had been to the prison in Tehran and met the entire membership of the Assembly of Yazd, including two Afnáns (relatives of the Báb), while an officer stood guard. Two tall fences, about two meters apart, had separated us. The old Hájí Muhammad Táhir Malmírí, the great historian, then in his eighties, was in chains amidst the other prisoners.[5] His vision and hearing were both impaired. You can just imagine the state of our emotions.

---

*These pilgrimages occurred in 1937, 1938, 1939, 1940, and 1952. The Ninth Annual Conference of the Association for Bahá'í Studies, dedicated to the memory of Shoghi Effendi, was held in Ottawa, Canada, 2–4 November 1984.

[5] Hájí Muhammad Táhir-Malmírí was the father of Universal House of Justice member Adib Taherzadeh and of the well-known translator of Bahá'í texts, Habib Taherzadeh.

I said to the prisoners, "I came from the beloved. He sends his bounties, blessings, and greetings to you all." Upon hearing this, they started to dance!

But the aged Hájí Táhir could not hear, nor could he see me. He asked his companions, "What does he say?"

So I said louder, "I came from on high and brought the good pleasure of the beloved for you." This phrase, *"az fawq ámadam,"* is one that the Bahá'ís understand.*

Finally comprehending, Hájí Muhammad Táhir cried and raised his hands in thanksgiving to Bahá'u'lláh. He said, "This only shows the generosity of the beloved Guardian! Who are we to deserve such a bounty?"

These are the stories that came to mind when I met the Bahá'ís of Egypt.

After our meetings, we prepared to go back to the Holy Land, but I was so unhappy. I kept blaming myself for not asking the Guardian what were the glad tidings that I was to deliver to the friends in Egypt. I felt that I had failed to accomplish my assignment. When we arrived in the Holy Land, while I was still silently agonizing over this, the beloved Shoghi Effendi said to me, "The great glad tidings were the stories of the sufferings of the Bahá'ís of Iran that you have already told the believers in Egypt."

THE SPIRIT OF PIONEERING

In February 1940, we were again sent off from Tehran by many devoted friends, as was typical for Bahá'ís who were departing for pilgrimage. By this thoughtful and tender act, the Persians displayed their deep love for the Guardian and their longing to be in his presence. They sent with us their messages of homage and devotion.

On that visit the beloved Guardian gave Mr. Khadem two important missions. One was to arrange for Iranian pilgrims to obtain permission to visit the Bahá'í holy places, and the other was to encourage the Bahá'ís of Iran to go pioneering. When we went back to Iran, like all returning pilgrims, we were welcomed just as we had

---

* *"Az fawq ámadam"* means "I come from on high." To Bahá'ís it meant the Bahá'í World Center in the Holy Land. More specifically, at that time it meant the presence of the beloved Guardian.

*The Khadems and other Bahá'í pilgrims and residents of Haifa,
visiting Buq'at'ul-Hamrá, one of Bahá'u'lláh's favorite spots,
during the Khadems' 1940 pilgrimage. Back row, right to left:
Javidukht Khadem, Salím Nounou, Zikrullah Khadem;
front row, right: Jena Khadem*

been sent off—by a huge crowd of Bahá'ís, all of them eagerly
awaiting a full recounting of our experiences. For days and weeks afterward, visitors by the dozen flooded our home, wanting to hear
every detail of the events that had taken place, every word that had
been spoken. Mr. Khadem was only too eager to speak of the subject
closest to his heart: his beloved Guardian. He never tired of repeating
the stories day after day. He was especially eager to communicate the
Guardian's call for pioneers. He did this with such zeal, such magnet-
ism, that those who heard him could not help but feel moved
themselves. In this manner the spirit of returning pilgrims was
infused into the entire Bahá'í community. Those precious experiences, those incomparable bounties and blessings, were shared by the
entire body of believers.

In addition to these small, informal gatherings, larger meetings
were held throughout the country, to which the Bahá'ís were invited
to come and hear the message from the Holy Land. They flocked to
these meetings, eager to hear any news from the Guardian, ready to
obey his every wish. First, Mr. Khadem would communicate the
depth of his love for and devotion to the Guardian. Then he would

share with them the glad tidings that the Guardian was predicting
that the doors of pilgrimage would be reopened. Finally, he would
announce the Guardian's call for pioneers.

The response of the Bahá'ís to the call for pioneers was truly
impressive. They were so eager to please their Guardian, so eager to
carry out his wishes! Everyone was talking about this. Everyone
wanted to go, regardless of the hardships and sacrifices. Many families went immediately. Many youth, some still in their mid-teens,
were longing to go. Most, however, were adults.

As the Bahá'ís made their decisions to arise and answer the
Guardian's call for pioneers, Mr. Khadem did everything he could to
facilitate their departure. Between November 1941 and January
1942 he received numerous cables from the Guardian, expressing his
appreciation of Mr. Khadem's efforts and assuring him of his prayers.
Such communications only inflamed Mr. Khadem's ardor and inspired him to work harder. Those who arose to serve as pioneers
became the focus of his attention. He served them in any way he
could. The prospective pioneers, in their turn, transmitted that spirit
of love and self-sacrifice to others. The mood at that time in Iran is
indescribable. There was a contagious and raging pioneering fever.
Those who were infected, infected others, until the entire community was in the throes of a spiritual epidemic!

Never flinching, never hesitating, these pioneers pledged to open
new areas to the Faith. These stalwart believers went to their posts
and stayed. Most never returned to the land of their birth. They
remained faithful to their commitment. To this day, that spirit of
love and self-sacrifice still burns. Mr. Khadem felt a special fondness
for those who arose to pioneer. The bond that connected him with
them from the beginning only grew stronger with time. He loved
them with all his heart.

One group of pioneers repeatedly invited him to come and share
this special and mutual love. On each visit they did their utmost to
make him comfortable, hoping to prolong his stay. Whenever they
met, they were like magnets, instantly drawn to one another, forget-
ting the passage of time, drinking in their spiritual nourishment.

Often the meetings would end very late, sometimes after midnight. One night at 1:00 A.M. we were driven by one of the Bahá'ís to
where we were staying, an hour and a half away. As the others could
not bear to end the meeting, they followed us. The situation was

quite humorous but also educational and uplifting. Five cars accompanied us to our destination; we were in the middle car of the convoy. The friends in our car asked Mr. Khadem to speak about his experiences, about the Universal House of Justice, or about any topic he wished to share. They told us that they had placed speakers in the other cars so all would be able to hear him. They were so enamored that they did not wish to waste a moment of time together. So as we traveled, we communicated with the other cars. Every once in a while Mr. Khadem enjoyed asking a question that required an answer. If the answer was yes, they were to respond by flashing their headlights twice; if no, only once. The blinking lights of these enraptured souls was an impressive visual testimony to their love.

What a joyful, hilarious, never-to-be-forgotten evening that was. Mr. Khadem often recounted it with great fondness, saying, "We *enjoyed* it! Whenever I need spirit, I visit the lovers of the Cause."

THE FUTURE HAND OF THE CAUSE OF GOD ABU'L-QÁSIM FAIZÍ

One of the outstanding pioneers who arose as a result of the Guardian's call in 1940 was Mr. Abu'l Qásim Faizí.* Mr. Khadem and I first met Mr. Faizí when he came from Beirut to Tehran after finishing his education. There he obtained a very good job with a promising future working for the Anglo-Persian Oil Company. He had tremendous potential for advancing in an important career, but his heart was not in material distinction. He did not attach significance to fame, power, or wealth. He had been trained in the school of the love of God, and his only ambition was to demonstrate befittingly that love. The Guardian had told Mr. Khadem (during one of his pilgrimages) that he had singled out Faizí from among the students in Beirut for service to the Cause.

Shortly after initiating this promising career, we heard that Mr. Faizí had left his job to devote himself to educating the children in one of the villages of Iran. There were many Bahá'í schools all over Iran, including the well-known Tarbíyat Schools in Tehran (there

---

*Mr. Faizí was appointed a Hand of the Cause of God by Shoghi Effendi in October 1957.

was one for boys and one for girls). The Bahá'í schools were so highly regarded for their academic curricula and their moral standards that even non-Bahá'ís sent their children to them. Mr. Faizí had chosen to devote his time to the education of the children in the village of Najaf-Ábád, outside of Isfahan.

When Mr. Khadem, at Shoghi Effendi's request, was traveling throughout Iran to visit the Bahá'ís, we saw Mr. Faizí in Najaf-Ábád. When we arrived, we were greeted by the Bahá'ís, among whom was Mr. Faizí, dressed like the other villagers, his face beaming with joy. He devoted five extremely productive years to this work, training and educating the young Bahá'ís, preparing them for a life of service to humanity, and transmitting to them the same love that inspired and motivated him. His loving and painstaking care nurtured a number of spiritual giants who, in turn, arose to perform outstanding services to the Cause of God. Many are now scattered throughout the world as pioneers.

Mr. Faizí then went to Qazvín to continue his exemplary services to Bahá'í youth. He had been there for a year when the Guardian issued the call for pioneers. Upon receiving this news, he immediately left Qazvín and began to make preparations for the documents he needed in order to travel. Mr. Khadem met with him several times; as a result, these two future Hands of the Cause of God, eagerly working to fulfill the beloved Guardian's wishes, formed a tender bond that was rooted in their mutual love for Shoghi Effendi. When Mr. Khadem returned from these trips during which he met Mr. Faizí, he recounted the blaze of love that characterized Mr. Faizí's service to the Faith.

Other prospective Bahá'í pioneers, like Mr. Faizí, had to wait during World War II for visas so they could move to their pioneering posts. Most of them were families living together under very difficult conditions, waiting for an opportunity to move. Mr. Faizí was a symbol of patience among them, always full of humor and joy. He would tell the friends stories of the early believers and infect them with joy and love of service to the Cause. Through the inspiration these stories provided and through their own intense longing to perform heroic services to the Faith, these prospective pioneers later became examples for others to follow.

Before long, Mr. Faizí attained his goal and was able to move to his post with his family. In January 1955, Mr. Khadem and I visited Mr. Faizí, who had distinguished himself among the pioneers for his mode of life and his sacrificial efforts. Mr. Faizí welcomed us to his modest home with the overwhelming tenderness and love that were so characteristic of him. What a joyful occasion that was! There was constant laughter as he shared with us humorous stories about other pioneers who had waited for visas and about how they had finally entered their respective countries.

The weather was oppressively hot and humid, but this did not affect the spirit of the Faizí family. When Mr. Khadem asked for a glass of water, Mr. Faizí apologetically offered a glass of hot water, gently explaining that his family did not have a refrigerator. I later heard from another pioneer that Mr. Faizí received an adequate income from teaching English but that he refused to buy a refrigerator because other pioneers could not afford such luxuries. Everything he had was shared with others.

One day Mr. Faizí asked us to visit a family he had grown to love dearly. Mr. Khadem and I welcomed the occasion and accompanied Mr. Faizí to the home of his new friends. To get there, we had to pass through many streets until we reached a very poor and squalid area of town. We stopped in front of a big garage door. Mr. Faizí knocked and then pushed the door open, revealing a barren room furnished with a single wooden bed upon which lay a sick woman. Beside her were two children covered with dirt and dressed in scant rags. As soon as they saw Mr. Faizí, they exclaimed with joy, calling, "Uncle Faizí! Uncle Faizí!" With unbelievable gentleness and tender affection, Mr. Faizí swept them into his arms and embraced them. He washed their faces and gave them sweets. Then he attended the sick mother and fed her a bowl of soup that he had brought for the occasion. I cannot describe the emotions that surged within us as we observed that family's devastating poverty and the overpowering love and care that Faizí showered on them.

Many who knew Mr. Faizí personally had similar experiences and were transformed by the power and sincerity of his love. He was particularly attentive to children. Our children received tender love notes and calligraphy from him, as did so many other correspondents scattered across the globe. Our family was highly blessed to have such a close association with him throughout his noble life.

Centenary of the Declaration of the Báb

The year 1944 was one of great joy and excitement. The Bahá'í world was celebrating the one hundredth anniversary of the inauguration of the Bahá'í Cycle. In the spiritual world there was a vibration, an excitement. But in the material world, as the Second World War reached its climax, there was a frightening demonstration of the world's capacity for self-destruction and self-inflicted suffering.

Under such difficult conditions, with scarcities of food, machinery, and parts, with hazardous traveling conditions and difficult communications, the beloved Guardian asked the National Spiritual Assembly of the Bahá'ís of Iran to commemorate befittingly the centenary of the Declaration of the Báb at the House of the Báb in Shiraz, the very place where Mullá Husayn had attained the presence of his Lord. The delegates from all over Iran were to assemble there discreetly for this auspicious occasion. The beloved Guardian asked Mr. Khadem to carry his message by hand to that historic assembly. This message, the Centenary Tablet, was seventy pages long.*

The precious assignment brought great excitement to our household. I vividly remember when Mr. Khadem received the cable from Shoghi Effendi in early May saying that an "Important communication" had been mailed to the National Spiritual Assembly of the Bahá'ís of Iran through an intermediary, Daoud Toeg. The message was "to be read for" the centenary "celebrations." Mr. Khadem was to "ensure its safe prompt delivery."[3] What an honor, but what a weighty responsibility! Time was getting short. The message had been sent through Iraq but had not yet arrived in Tehran. Mr. Khadem was very anxious that he might fail to deliver the message

---

*From 1940 to 1957, Mr. Khadem was entrusted with the mission of receiving mail and cablegrams addressed from Shoghi Effendi to institutions and individual Bahá'ís in Iran. Being the Guardian's mailman was a priceless bounty and a source of great pride to Mr. Khadem. It blessed our home for seventeen years with a special excitement and sense of anticipation.

Before opening and reading communications from Shoghi Effendi, Mr. Khadem prayed to become spiritually aware and ready to carry out the Guardian's wishes with exact and complete obedience. He placed great importance on such preparation and obedience.

*Members of the National Spiritual Assembly of Iran,
on which Mr. Khadem served for many years, 104 B.E., 1948.
Clockwise, from lower left: Valíyu'lláh Varqá, Shu'á'u'lláh 'Alá'í, 'Abdu'l-
Hussayn Na'ímí, Ahmad Yazdání, 'Alí Akbar Furútan (holding the
Greatest Name), Jalál Kházeh, 'Alí-Muhammad Barafrúkhtih,
Zikrullah Khadem, Núriddín Fath-i-A'zam*

on time. He was in constant communication with the National
Spiritual Assembly of the Bahá'ís of Iraq, who reported to him step
by step the whereabouts of the message.

A Bahá'í pilot, Mr. Náfidh, was identified to help ensure the safe
delivery of the message.* Mr. Khadem approached him, explained
the problem, and asked if he wished to offer his services to

---

*Mr. Náfidh was the brother-in-law of Músá Bánání, who later became a Hand of
the Cause of God.

Bahá'u'lláh. Would he, despite the dangers of the war, fly to Iraq to pick up the precious message and bring it back to Tehran? Did he wish to "grasp this precious opportunity?"

"Yes, of course," was the reply.

Anxiety filled our household from the moment of the pilot's departure on the special mission until his return. When the message finally arrived, Mr. Khadem was overcome with joy and gratitude. Even the small children were caught up in the spirit of the occasion—they did not understand exactly what was going on, but they jumped up and down, cheering, knowing something wonderful had happened.

Although the message had arrived safely in Iran, it still had not reached its destination. The trip from Tehran to Shiraz was long and difficult; public transportation was not an option. What was needed was a reliable car and several spare tires—this was wartime, and good tires were just not available. Finally, Mr. Khadem found a solution. We had a fairly reliable car. Mr. Khadem contacted a friend whose car had broken down and asked to borrow his tires. He and his companions then set out for Shiraz with the precious message and the four spare tires. They arrived breathlessly at the House of the Báb two hours after sunset, exactly when the meeting was to start.

For many years after, Mr. Khadem was to cherish the bounty of having been an eyewitness and a participant on this blessed occasion, and he often referred to the Centenary gathering. It is significant that his most eloquent and scholarly piece of prose in Persian, an article entitled "The Blessed House of the Báb," was inspired by that occasion. In the article he conveys the spirit of awe that made such an impression on him:

> One hundred years ago, on this very night, upon the maturation of the human race, two hours and eleven minutes after sunset, the Declaration of the Lord of the Age was commemorated in the upper chamber of the House of the Báb through divine melodious chanting of the verses of the Qayyúmu'l-Asmá'. . . .
>
> From the very spot where the Blessed Báb first announced His historic mission, that spot designated by the silk carpet offering of the servant of His Threshold, Shoghi Effendi, anthems of praise and salutation from the Centenary Tablet of the beloved Guardian pealed out to echo throughout the rooms, the courtyard, and environs. . . .

Delegates to the centenary celebration of
the Declaration of the Báb, assembled in Shiraz on 28 May 1944.
Mr. Khadem is in the top row at the far right.

The following account from volume 10 of *The Bahá'í World* also captures some of the emotions that must have surged in the hearts of the participants:

It was a May evening in S͟híráz. Through the dusk, by twos and threes, at intervals, men were coming; unobtrusively, they went through the door of a house and joined the throng of persons inside. They were silent, too moved for speech; they had come here from all over Persia, in secret, at the risk, perhaps, of their lives. . . . They had come here to share in the joy of this night.

. . . The men, who included ninety Convention delegates and the members of the National Spiritual Assembly, poured rose water on their hands.* Silently, they took off their shoes and stepped into the court-yard of the sacred House next door. They circumambulated the House; through the shadows, they heard the chanting of the Visitation Tablet . . . . Then they climbed the stairway to the Threshold of the Room

---

*There were actually ninety-one delegates present.

where, one hundred years ago tonight, the Báb's disclosure had been received by His first disciple; where a message destined for the whole human race had blazed out before one man, leaving him dazzled and as if he had lost his mind. Here in the Declaration Chamber, Jináb-i-Varqá had spread out a precious carpet, the Guardian's gift.

At the exact moment when the hundred years were completed—that is, at two hours and eleven minutes after sunset—the members of the National Spiritual Assembly on behalf of the Guardian, and all the delegates, one after the other, knelt down and kissed the Threshold. Then a portion of the Guardian's new letter, beginning, "Greeting and glory rest upon His Herald, the Peerless One," and "O Holy night, upon thee of all praises be the best and most glorious!" was chanted, and afterward, very humbly and prayerfully, and bowing low, the men took leave of the sacred House, returned next door, and till dawn they listened to the chanting of prayers, the recitation of Bahá'í odes, and readings from Bahá'í history and from the new Centenary letter of the Guardian.[4]

The message was so awesome, so vehement, so majestic that it transformed the atmosphere of the meeting and transported the participants to a different plane. It seemed as though the words descended from the Abhá Kingdom itself. Then, as the sun began to rise, the Bahá'ís left in small groups of two or three, returning to their homes.

Upon his return to Tehran, Mr. Khadem, as well as the other participants, spoke of little else. Everywhere they went they tried to share with the friends the awesome spirit of that occasion. Mr. Khadem recalled those electrifying moments on many occasions, for he cherished the bounty of having been a participant. On 4 June 1944 he cabled the following joyful message:

Wellbeloved Guardian Shoghi Effendi Rabbani Haifa

Just returned praise thy holy threshold convention ninetyone present formed twentythird adjourned thirtyfirst May with continuous success divine tablet seventy pages received before departure Shiraz miraculously inspired whole gathering endeavoring worthy thy divine blessings will submit reports commanded humbly.

3 Appointment as a
Hand of the Cause of God

Light and glory, greeting and praise be upon the Hands of His
Cause, through whom the light of fortitude hath shone forth and the
truth hath been established that the authority to choose rests with
God, the Powerful, the Mighty, the Unconstrained, through whom
the ocean of bounty hath surged and the fragrance of the gracious
favors of God, the Lord of mankind, hath been diffused. We beseech
Him—Exalted is He—to shield them through the power of His
hosts, to protect them through the potency of His dominion and to
aid them through His indomitable strength which prevaileth over
all created things. Sovereignty is God's, the Creator of the heavens
and the Lord of the Kingdom of Names.
—BAHÁ'U'LLÁH

A CABLE ARRIVES

In December 1951 a cablegram brought the joyous news to our
home that Shoghi Effendi had appointed the first contingent of the
Hands of the Cause of God. 'Abdu'l-Bahá had given the institution
its mandate: "The obligations of the Hands of the Cause of God are
to diffuse the Divine Fragrances, to edify the souls of men, to
promote learning, to improve the character of all men and to be, at
all times and under all conditions, sanctified and detached from
earthly things."[1] Years earlier the beloved Guardian had educated
Mr. Khadem about the institution of the Hands and had instructed
him to announce to the Bahá'ís of Iran that it would soon be
established. Mr. Khadem had, therefore, anticipated this event and
was jubilant when it came to pass.

I vividly recall when that cablegram naming the first of the Hands
arrived. Mr. Khadem told me excitedly, "These are very special

people. They have been elevated to the rank of Hands of the Cause!"
He felt such love and respect for the newly appointed Hands that he
wanted to congratulate Mr. 'Alí-Akbar Furútan, one of that first
contingent, immediately.* He asked me to accompany him.

I reminded Mr. Khadem that the hour was very late and that Mr.
Furútan would undoubtedly already be in bed. "Can't it wait until
morning?" I asked.

"For this kind of news, he would be more than happy to get up,"
Mr. Khadem insisted, eager to deliver the cable immediately. "He
would prefer not to sleep in order to learn of his exalted station."

So, very late at night we went to Mr. Furútan's house. He came to
the door in his pajamas. He was quite surprised to see us, especially
me, dropping by unannounced that late at night. But in courteous
Persian style, he welcomed us in, acting as if our late-night visit were
not unusual and begged leave to get dressed. Mr. Khadem chuckled
with glee at Mr. Furútan's plight. When rituals of courtesy and
hospitality had delayed the joyous news for as long as Mr. Khadem
could stand, he delivered the cable. Mr. Khadem smiled as Mr. Furútan responded with stunned disbelief at the Guardian's choice.

Thus I was privileged to be an eyewitness to the inauguration of
the institution of the Hands of the Cause of God. Bahá'ís all over the
world were filled with great joy and excitement, as yet another stage
of Bahá'u'lláh's world order was unveiled.

ANOTHER CABLE ARRIVES

A few months later, on an early Friday morning during the Fast in
1952, Mr. Khadem returned to bed to rest after having breakfast and
saying prayers. The children were having their breakfast in the
dining room. While I was serving them, the doorbell rang. I opened
the door and took delivery of a cablegram. It was from the beloved
Guardian. Such cables were not unusual, except that this one was
addressed personally to Mr. Khadem. I knew he would be exultant. I
took the cable to the bedroom to inform him of its arrival.

---

*In addition to Mr. Furútan, the first contingent of Hands of the Cause of God
included Sutherland Maxwell, Mason Remey, Amelia Collins, Valíyu'lláh Varqá,
Tarázu'lláh Samandarí, Horace Holley, Dorothy Baker, Leroy Ioas, George Townshend, Hermann Grossmann, and Ugo Giachery.

"There is a cablegram from the Holy Land with your name on it," I said. "It's for you!"

He literally jumped out of bed. "Please don't touch it!" he said. "Leave it on my desk!"

I complied, knowing how precious and dear such a communication would be to him. Exhibiting his usual reverence, he began to prepare himself to open the message. Later I found him in the dining room, facing the window with his back to me. Holding the cable up to the light, he was reading and rereading the message. Even from the back he looked different, transformed somehow. He was trembling and sobbing. The effect of that cablegram amazed and worried me.

"Is there bad news?" I asked. He did not reply. I tried again. "Please, please tell me what has happened!" Still no answer. I approached him, begging him to share the tragic news.

He handed me the cablegram, dated 28 February 1952, which I read with wonder and excitement:

Zikrullah Khadem Teheran

Moved convey glad tidings your elevation rank Hand Cause. Appointment officially announced public message addressed all National Assemblies. May sacred function enable you enrich record services already rendered Faith Bahá'u'lláh.*

I jumped for joy and congratulated him. To my surprise, his expression of deep concern and anxiety did not change. Instead, he said very sternly, "This is a ruse. The enemies of the Faith are trying to trick me. I don't deserve this. The beloved Guardian knows that. He knows my spiritual capacity. I couldn't possibly be a Hand of the Cause. Besides, the Guardian always signs his cables 'Shoghi' or 'Shoghi Rabbani.' This one has no signature." Convinced of this explanation, he insisted that I keep it a secret. "Never, never tell anyone about this joke."

Taken aback, but respectful of his wishes, I acquiesced. I begged him, however, for permission to inform his mother because she was always telling me about the tablet she had from 'Abdu'l-Bahá stating that there would be glad-tidings for the family in the future. She

---

*Also appointed at the same time were Fred Shopflocher, Corinne True, Shu'á'u'lláh 'Alá'í, Adelbert Mühlschlegel, Músá Banání, and Clara Dunn.

used to tell me, "Someday there will be a great blessing from the center of the Faith for Dhikru'lláh, but I don't know what it is." With great reluctance, he agreed to inform his mother of the "joke."

That morning we went to her home. When Rádyyih Khánum opened the door, she immediately noticed how very pale and upset her son was. Distressed, she asked about his health and the health of the children. I assured her everyone was fine.

"Is there some tragic news, then? Tell me, what has happened?"

I told her about the cablegram and about Mr. Khadem's conviction that it must be a ruse. She smiled and turned to Zikrullah, tears welling in her eyes. She said, "I knew something great was in store for you. You, among all my children, deserve such a great station."

Mr. Khadem defended his conviction and insisted on secrecy. He was absolutely sure the cable was fake, that someone had tricked him. The idea that it might be true was even more devastating because he felt unable to assume such weighty responsibilities. He made his mother promise that she would not mention it to anyone, not even to members of the family. Unconvinced, but wishing to calm his anxiety, she promised.

The next day we received another cable, addressed to the National Spiritual Assembly of the Bahá'ís of Iran, announcing the appointment of the second contingent of Hands of the Cause of God and thereby confirming the news.

"WITH A LOOK HE GRANTETH A HUNDRED THOUSAND HOPES"[2]

As it happened, we were scheduled to leave on pilgrimage to Haifa a little more than a week after learning of Mr. Khadem's appointment; our eldest son, Mozhan, had received permission to accompany us. Before our departure Mr. Khadem learned of yet another blessing: He had been entrusted by the Guardian with carrying a very precious copy of the Kitáb-i-Íqán to the Holy Land.*

---

*The Kitáb-i-Íqán, Shoghi Effendi has written, sets forth "in outline the Grand Redemptive Scheme of God" (God Passes By, new ed. [Wilmette, Ill.: Bahá'í Publishing Trust, 1974], 139). See Bahá'u'lláh, Kitáb-i-Íqán: The Book of Certitude, trans. Shoghi Effendi, 2d ed. (Wilmette, Ill.: Bahá'í Publishing Trust, 1950).

ZIKRULLAH KHADEM
(second from right), the newly appointed Hand of the Cause of God,
attending a conference in Rome, Italy, Naw-Rúz 1952, as the
Guardian's representative. Javidukht Khadem is first from the right.

This book was a copy in 'Abdu'l-Bahá's handwriting and had notations by Bahá'u'lláh in the margins. It had long been in the possession of Fátimih Khánum Afnán, a Bahá'í living in Shiraz. In 1948 Shoghi Effendi had asked the Hand of the Cause of God Tarázu'lláh Samandarí to offer his assistance to her in transporting this treasure to a safe location until it could be sent to the Holy Land. Fátimih Khánum had lovingly acquiesced, and the book had been taken to Tehran, where it was placed in a safe by the National Spiritual Assembly of Iran.

Mr. Khadem had prayed intensely and persistently for the bounty of carrying the precious copy of the Kitáb-i-Íqán to the Holy Land. On 9 March 1952, two days before our departure, a cable arrived, saying, "Send original copy Íqán with pilgrims. Shoghi."

Words cannot describe Mr. Khadem's joy and gratitude. He was making his sixth pilgrimage to the presence of his beloved Guardian. He was carrying the precious copy of the Kitáb-i-Íqán (which he read in its entirety during our five-hour trip). He had just been elevated to the rank of Hand of the Cause of God, a position from which he would be able to serve his beloved even more than before.

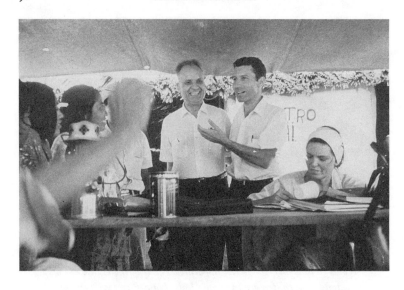

Top: The Hand of the Cause of God Zikrullah Khadem
and Continental Counselor for South America Peter McLaren
meeting with Bahá'ís in Honduras. Bottom: Mr. Khadem and Continental
Counselor for North America Angus Cowan
sharing a moment of humor.

For the rest of his life Mr. Khadem prayed fervently, night and day, to become worthy of his appointment as a Hand of the Cause of God. Soon afterward, he left his work at the Iraqi embassy in Tehran to be at the service of Shoghi Effendi at all times.

4 International Service–Europe

*O that I could travel, even though on foot and in the utmost
poverty, to these regions, and, raising the call of "Yá Bahá'u'l-Abhá"
in cities, villages, mountains, deserts and oceans, promote the
Divine teachings! This, alas, I cannot do. How intensely I deplore it!
Please God, ye may achieve it.*   —'ABDU'L-BAHÁ*

ITINERANT HAND

Although Mr. Khadem carried out assignments outside Iran before his appointment as a Hand of the Cause of God, his services
became increasingly international afterward. On 25 March 1952,
less than a month after Mr. Khadem learned of his new responsibilities, the beloved Guardian, in a cable to the European Bahá'ís,
referred to him as the "itinerant Hand"—a description that aptly
describes his services for the rest of his life.[1]

Beginning in 1952 he traveled constantly, especially during the
Ten Year Crusade.[§] The following list of places he visited and events

---

*Mr. Khadem always carried with him a copy of this passage from 'Abdu'l-Bahá's
Tablets of the Divine Plan (*Tablets of the Divine Plan,* rev. ed. [Wilmette, Ill.: Bahá'í
Publishing Trust, 1977], 39) because he found it especially inspiring. Known as the
charter for propagating the Bahá'í Faith, the fourteen tablets Tablets of the Divine
Plan convey to the North American Bahá'ís 'Abdu'l-Bahá's mandate for transmitting
the Faith around the world.

§The Ten Year World Crusade, the international teaching plan Shoghi Effendi
inaugurated in 1953, was the first global plan in which all national Bahá'í communities pursued their goals in a coordinated effort. It culminated with the first
election of the Universal House of Justice in 1963.

in which he participated between March 1952 and October 1961 suggests the scope of his travels during this period:

March–September 1952—Visited Bahá'í centers in Europe, including ones in Italy, Belgium, Switzerland, Germany, Austria, France, Spain, Portugal, England, Scotland, Ireland, Norway, Sweden, Denmark, the Netherlands, and Luxembourg

12–14 April 1952—Attended Benelux Teaching Conference, Brussels, Belgium

12–18 February 1953—Attended First Bahá'í Intercontinental Teaching Conference, Kampala, Uganda

25 February–16 April 1953—Visited Bahá'ís in Africa

3–6 May 1953—Attended All-American Bahá'í Intercontinental Teaching Conference, Chicago, Illinois

May–July 1953—Visited Bahá'í centers in Central and South America, including ones in Cuba, Jamaica, Haiti, Puerto Rico, Venezuela, Colombia, Panama, Costa Rica, Nicaragua, Honduras, El Salvador, Guatemala, and Mexico

July 1953—Visited Bahá'í centers in the United States, the Netherlands, Denmark, and Sweden

21–26 July 1953—Attended Third Bahá'í Intercontinental Teaching Conference, Stockholm, Sweden

August 1953—Visited Bahá'í centers in the Netherlands, Belgium, Luxembourg, and France

September–October 1953—Visited Bahá'í centers in Switzerland, Italy, Cyprus, Lebanon, and Pakistan

7–15 October 1953—Attended Fourth Bahá'í Intercontinental Teaching Conference, New Delhi, India

October–November 1953—Visited Bahá'í centers in India, Thailand, Hong Kong, Japan, Formosa (Taiwan), Macao, the Philippines, North Borneo (East Malaysia), and Malaya (West Malaysia)

December 1953—Visited Bahá'í centers in Thailand, Burma, India, Pakistan, Iraq, and Iran

December 1954–February 1955—Visited Bahá'í centers in India, Pakistan, and Iraq

September–December 1955—Visited Bahá'í centers in the Far East, including ones in Pakistan, Japan, Taiwan, Hong Kong, Macao, Thailand, Burma, and India

April 1957—Represented the Guardian of the Bahá'í Faith at the Central American convention in Panama City, Panama

April–November 1957—Visited Bahá'í centers in Italy, Switzerland, Denmark, the United States, Panama, Costa Rica, Nicaragua, Honduras, El Salvador, Guatemala, British Honduras, Mexico, Canada, Sweden, Finland, Norway, Holland, Belgium, Luxembourg, and France

March 1958—Attended Intercontinental Conference, Sydney, Australia

March–April 1958—Visited Bahá'í centers in Indonesia, Thailand, Burma, and India

July 1958—Attended Intercontinental Conference, Frankfurt, Germany

July–September 1958—Visited Bahá'í centers in Germany, Switzerland, Belgium, Italy, Yugoslavia

September 1958—Attended Intercontinental Conference, Djakarta-Singapore

October–December 1958—Served as a substitute member of the Body of Nine Hands of the Cause of God in the Holy Land

April 1959—Represented the World Center at the formation of the National Spiritual Assembly of Turkey

July–September 1959—Visited centers in Germany, Switzerland, England, Austria, and Yugoslavia

June 1960—Visited Bahá'í centers in Germany, Italy, Switzerland, England, and France, en route to the United States

August 1960—Transferred to the Western Hemisphere as a Hand of the Americas

November 1960—Visited Bahá'í centers in Germany

April–May 1961—Represented the World Center at conventions of Costa Rica and Panama

October 1961—Visited Bahá'í Centers in England, Holland, and Switzerland

HIS SUITCASE

As he traveled throughout the world, Mr. Khadem acquired so many stamps and visas that his small passport was soon filled. Accessory pages were added frequently to accommodate repeated visits to numerous countries. The result was a very bulky passport. Mr. Khadem jokingly called it his "suitcase."

After we moved to Champaign, Illinois, in 1960, he went to obtain a driver's license and was asked to show some identification. He offered his passport. The police officer was amazed at its bulk and asked how he was able to travel so much. Mr. Khadem answered that he had friends in all these places. The officer remained skeptical. Mr. Khadem proceeded to explain why he had so many friends. He introduced the teachings of the Faith, finally telling the man, "His Holiness Jesus Christ has returned!"

"What?" the officer exclaimed, surprised at this statement. "How could such a thing possibly be true?"

"Did not His Holiness Jesus say He would return?" Mr. Khadem replied.

"Where?"

"There are so many references in the Bible." He began explaining each one and answering the officer's questions. Then he finally said, "Doesn't the New Testament say that the Son of Man will come as a 'thief in the night'?[2] You, a policeman, should be the best one to catch a thief!"

The tension broke, and they both laughed. Mr. Khadem's quick wit often saved a tense moment and enabled him to teach the Faith in the process.

The Universal House of Justice now has Mr. Khadem's "suitcase" for safekeeping.

EUROPE

In 1937 Mr. Khadem had recorded while on pilgrimage that Shoghi Effendi told him, "I will send you to the West . . . to witness with your own eyes the secret, the mystery, the light of the Cause in those lands." Years later, in 1952, when Mr. Khadem was a new Hand of the Cause of God, the beloved Guardian asked him to visit the Bahá'ís in Europe. We set out on this trip with confident assurance of the Guardian's prayers. He cabled on 22 March 1952: "Loving prayers accompanying you."

During our trip we met many dedicated European Bahá'ís, but we were especially impressed by the pioneers. Mr. Khadem's special assignment on this trip was to visit the ten European goal countries that were the objectives of the second Seven Year Plan: Belgium,

Two of the Khadems' many stops during their 1952
tour of the ten European goal countries of the Second Seven Year Plan.
Top: A visit with one of the Bahá'ís of Barcelona, Spain. Bottom:
A meeting with the Bahá'ís of Stuttgart, West Germany.

*Other stops on the Khadems' 1952 tour of the ten European goal
countries. Top: The Khadems with Honor Kempton (top row, second from
right), one of the outstanding pioneers to Europe, and a group of
students in Geneva, Switzerland. Bottom: A meeting
with the Bahá'ís in Luxembourg.*

Denmark, Holland, Italy, Luxembourg, Norway, Portugal, Spain, Sweden, and Switzerland.* There he saw the sterling qualities of the pioneers and recalled the beloved Guardian's promise to send him to the West to witness the wondrous light of the Faith. Mr. Khadem experienced the fulfillment of that promise by seeing with his own eyes the audacity, integrity, and sincerity of those who were offering heart and soul in service to our beloved Faith. As victory was added to victory, Mr. Khadem repeatedly remarked about the fulfillment of the Guardian's promise and exclaimed, "O Lord! Increase my astonishment at Thee!"[3]

So many memories from that trip still give me strength when I recall them. Particularly memorable is the rejuvenating spirit we experienced in Belgium. After visiting some of the Bahá'í communities in Italy, we proceeded from Milan to Brussels on 11 April 1952 for the Benelux teaching conference to be held 12 through 14 April. Remembering the example of 'Abdu'l-Bahá, who often traveled third class, we had decided, after praying about it, to book the most economical travel arrangements. These were third-class train seats that required sitting all night and part of a day on hard wooden benches. Sleep, let alone rest of any kind, was impossible. After many hours in the same uncomfortable position, our legs became numb and swollen. We were in pain and totally exhausted.

When the train finally arrived at our destination, we were greatly relieved. However, when I stood up, I discovered I could barely walk. My feet felt like balls of fire. I took my shoes off, but every step was still excruciating. My husband helped me as I hobbled into the station. I do not know what portion of my agony was from lack of sleep and what portion from poor circulation during that inhospitable train ride, but I could not bear any more hardship. I begged him to find the closest available hotel room so we could lie down and rest. As we walked out into the street, we saw on a nearby building a sign that said, *"Chambre à Louer"* (Room for Rent). I felt as if I had just been given the most wonderful gift in the world; I envisioned myself lying on a bed. When we saw the room, it did not matter that it was tiny and extremely noisy because of its proximity to the train

---

*The Second Seven Year Plan was an international teaching plan pursued by the Bahá'ís of the United States and Canada from April 1946 through April 1953.

station. It had a bed, and that was all I cared about. To me it was heaven. I immediately lay down and closed my eyes.

Mr. Khadem went to telephone the local Bahá'ís to inform them of our arrival and to find out details about the conference. Just as I was starting to relax and enjoy what I thought would be a few blissful hours of uninterrupted rest and sleep, I sensed a shadow across my bed. I opened my eyes to discover my husband looking at me tenderly. "What's wrong?" I asked. "Why aren't you resting?"

"I can't. They are waiting for us to start the conference. We have to go right now."

"Surely they can start without us. Don't you think we will be more useful after a little rest?"

"Don't forget," he replied, " I am the representative of the beloved Guardian. How can I delay even for a minute? We have to leave immediately."

Participants in the Benelux teaching conference held at the Brussels, Belgium, Bahá'í Center, 12–14 April 1952. Mr. Khadem (in the center, wearing a dark suit), Shoghi Effendi's representative to the conference, delivered a message on his behalf. Mrs. Khadem is seated in the front row, second from the right.

"Of course, you are right. But I can't walk!" I cried, feeling very sorry for myself.

"I will help you." Gently he helped me to stand up. "Just lean on me, and don't wear your shoes." I followed my husband out of the building and into a taxi in a painful daze.

As we approached the conference site, we witnessed a spectacular scene. Upon receipt of the news that we were coming, the Bahá'ís had assembled in front of the building to watch for us. Words of welcome and Bahá'í greetings echoed as we arrived. We were escorted to the conference hall to the sound of clapping and cheering.

In this manner the dear friends received the representative of their Guardian. Suddenly, inexplicably, we were filled with renewed strength and exhilaration. It was as if a drain had been unplugged, and the weariness had receded. The overwhelming and enveloping love and enthusiasm of that conference had such a soothing effect that no trace of fatigue or discomfort remained for either of us. The swelling in my feet subsided, and the color returned to my face. We had miraculously tapped into a spiritual source of strength and did not return to our hotel room until two o'clock in the morning. Through this experience we received a glimpse of how spiritual nourishment can, indeed, cure all the ills of humanity.

The conference was truly heavenly. It was opened with praise of Bahá'u'lláh, the Redeemer of humankind. The Guardian's message of love and admiration for the Belgian Bahá'ís was a powerful magnet that touched and firmly united the hearts of the entire assemblage.

The same love and spirit was manifested in one way or another in all the conferences held in Europe in 1952. They all opened with prayers, and all ended with a solemn pledge to spread the Bahá'í Faith throughout Europe. All of the attendees seemed transformed by the Guardian's love and their desire to please him.

IRELAND

In August 1952, a few months after our trip to Brussels, we traveled to Ireland to visit the Irish Bahá'ís. A special bonus of this trip was meeting the illustrious Hand of the Cause of God George Townshend, who was among the first contingent to be named a Hand of the Cause by the Guardian.

When we arrived at our hotel, the first item on Mr. Khadem's agenda was to call Mr. Townshend to schedule a meeting. They agreed to meet for tea in the hotel lobby. Mr. Khadem was so eager to meet Mr. Townshend that he stood by the door to greet him when he arrived. As soon as he spotted Mr. Townshend, he approached him, shook his hand, and embraced him. Mr. Khadem expressed his happiness and gratitude for the opportunity of meeting Mr. Townshend and went on to share his feelings about him. Mr. Townshend, in his great humility, interrupted the effusive praise and asked him not to say such things. When they went to tea, he insisted that Mr. Khadem be served first because he was a guest in Dublin. Mr. Khadem was deeply touched by this meeting and developed a profound admiration and love for George Townshend. He was very impressed by this wonderful man's quality of character, integrity, spirituality, and unrivaled scholarship. Many years later, in 1984 in Ottawa, at the Ninth Annual Conference of the Association for Bahá'í Studies, Mr. Khadem paid tribute to Mr. Townshend:

> George Townshend, oh, that great person! The Cause of God has not yet produced another like him. The beloved Shoghi Effendi once said, "The best scholar we have in Persia is Abu'l-Fadl, and the best in the West is George Townshend." To my mind, he had the greatest honor showered upon him by the beloved Guardian, who asked him to write the preface for *God Passes By* and for *The Hidden Words*. Nobody else has been given that kind of task. Just imagine! 'Abdu'l-Bahá said that His writings and the writings of Bahá'u'lláh should not be compiled in one volume. Who are we to write a preface to be compiled with the words of the beloved Guardian? Who is it that the beloved Shoghi Effendi chose from among the Bahá'ís to do that job?
>
> I had the honor to be at the Townshend grave in Ireland. When you go to his grave, there is a small chapel, and on top of it is a sign which, when seen from afar, appears as the ring symbol of the Greatest Holy Name.* The stone on his grave shows an open Bible with the phrase, "I saw a new heaven and a new earth." The chapel cemetery wouldn't accept anything more, but this was perfect.

---

*The ring symbol, designed by 'Abdu'l-Bahá and used on Bahá'í rings, is a calligraphic rendering of the Greatest Name, the name "Bahá'u'lláh" (meaning "the Glory of God") and its various forms.

Mr. Townshend's passing affected Mr. Khadem deeply. He and the other Hands of the Cause found great comfort in the following eulogy, which Shoghi Effendi cabled on 27 March 1957 to the National Spiritual Assembly of the Bahá'ís of the British Isles:

> Deeply mourn passing dearly loved much admired greatly gifted outstanding Hand Cause George Townshend. His death morrow publication his crowning achievement robs British followers Bahá'u'lláh their most distinguished collaborator and Faith itself one its stoutest defenders. His sterling qualities his scholarship his challenging writings his high ecclesiastical position unrivaled any Bahá'í Western world entitle him rank with Thomas Breakwell Dr. Esslemont one of three luminaries shedding brilliant luster annals Irish English Scottish Bahá'í communities. His fearless championship Cause he loved so dearly served so valiantly constitutes significant landmark British Bahá'í history. So enviable position calls for national tribute his memory by assembled delegates visitors forthcoming British Bahá'í convention.* Assure relatives deepest loving sympathy grievous loss. Confident his reward inestimable Abhá Kingdom.[4]

Beginning with that memorable visit in 1952 when we met Mr. Townshend, Mr. Khadem harbored a deep love for Ireland and the Irish Bahá'ís that only grew more intense with subsequent visits. He repeatedly praised their contagious spirit of sacrifice and dedication to the Cause of God.

GOD-INTOXICATED SOULS

The pioneers we visited in Europe were distinguished, hardworking, and dedicated. Many first arose to serve the Faith when 'Abdu'l-Bahá raised the call for pioneers in the Tablets of the Divine Plan. They persevered in that arena of sacrifice and went from one pioneering post to another as each new plan was announced. They

---

*The crowning achievement referred to was the publication in 1957 of *Christ and Bahá'u'lláh* (Oxford: George Ronald, 1966), one of George Townshend's best-known books. The high ecclesiastical position he attained was that of Canon of Saint Patrick's Cathedral, Dublin, and Archdeacon of Clonfert. The forthcoming British Bahá'í convention was the annual national convention held at Riḍván 1957.

diligently carried on their work with complete self-abnegation, fully expending their energies and resources in their adopted countries. Those God-intoxicated souls put their whole trust in God, relying completely on the power of prayer. This was the secret of their success. For example, I particularly recall Marion Little, a pioneer in Italy, who, when acting as our guide, paused at the front door of those whom we visited and said, "Let's pray for God's assistance."

MARION LITTLE
(center), a steadfast pioneer to Italy, with
Mr. and Mrs. Khadem in Florence during their
1952 tour of the ten European goal countries
of the Second Seven Year Plan

Another especially dedicated pioneer to Europe whom we met in 1952 was Dagmar Dole. Born into an illustrious family, she received the message of Bahá'u'lláh from Marion Holley Hofman in the United States. After accepting the Faith immediately, she became a very active Bahá'í, supporting local spiritual assemblies and serving on committees. Later, in response to the Tablets of the Divine Plan, she went to Alaska and made valuable contributions toward consolidating the Bahá'í community there and working with great love and devotion among the Eskimos. She then responded to the call for pioneers during the Second Seven Year Plan and went to Denmark, where she was instrumental in bringing into the Faith forty-seven people.[5]

Mr. Khadem and I met Dagmar at a Nineteen Day Feast in Copenhagen.* She sat in the corner of the room, her face radiant as she surveyed her spiritual offspring among the other participants. The three parts of the Feast (devotional, consultative, and social) were conducted beautifully by the Local Spiritual Assembly of Copenhagen, completely in accord with the Bahá'í writings.

We had learned a little about Dagmar's teaching style through one of her spiritual offspring, Mr. Jean Deleuran, a young architect, who spent some time with us before the Feast at which we were to meet Dagmar. He and his wife, Tove, who were among the first people of Denmark to accept the Faith, met us at our hotel and walked us to their home. He related the following story:

> It is strange to think back now that, had it not been for the feeling Tove and I had at that time that our life did not seem to have much meaning or a real goal, that it was an existence in relative comfort without much satisfaction either intellectually or spiritually, we would not have decided to move to another part of Denmark when I was offered an interesting job for one year in my field as hospital planner.
>
> As a result of this decision, Dagmar Dole and Eleanor Hollibaugh got to know, through the United States embassy, that we wanted to let our flat and so entered our life at the end of June 1947.
>
> We had not been looking for a new religion. Rather, on the contrary, we had freed ourselves from the religion we were born into, not finding any spiritual uplift in it and no relation to daily life. Our sense of spirituality was the base we had got in our respective families from our parents' attitude toward uprightness and honesty.
>
> Tove's family was rooted in the traditional Lutheran faith, and my father's family, being Calvinists, had come as refugees to Denmark during the religious wars in France.
>
> We were both baptized and registered in the community of the Danish State Church (Lutheran) as normal procedure in Denmark in

---

*The Nineteen Day Feast is a Bahá'í institution inaugurated by the Báb and incorporated by Bahá'u'lláh in the Kitáb-i-Aqdas into His Faith. It is held on the first day of every Bahá'í month, each consisting of nineteen days and bearing the names and attributes of God. The Feast is the heart of Bahá'í community life at the local level and consists of devotional, consultative, and social elements.

our childhoods. Our feeling was that, if God existed, He would know our problem of not being able to accept religion in the form it was presented by the Danish State Church.

This was our religious background when Dagmar Dole and Eleanor Hollibaugh came to see our flat. When we asked them why they had come to Denmark, they answered that it was because they were Bahá'ís and that they wanted to introduce to the Danish population a new and universal religion based on unity and justice. This released so many questions on our part that they did not leave until two o'clock in the morning, without having made any arrangement for a contract or going through the inventory. The same thing happened the next evening and the following, which was the last one before our leaving for the new job. So we handed over the keys and embraced each other feeling very sad that a whole year had to pass before we should see each other again.

However, we did get to see them a few times when we came to Copenhagen on short visits, and they gave us some books to study. Eleanor paid us a visit in the village where we had our temporary home, and we arranged a meeting for her with a group of the local people, headed by the priest, where she told about Bahá'u'lláh and His revelation.

When we returned the next year and took over our flat, a wonderful friendship began which motivated us to begin methodical study of the Faith. After six months with the patient and loving guidance of Dagmar and Eleanor, we realized that we had to identify ourselves with this unique Faith, which removed our previous conception of religion and could stop the fanaticism, superstition and misinterpretation religions had caused through the ages. This was a religion, we felt, where feelings and intelligence could work together, so one could be honest with oneself.

We signed our membership cards on 14 February 1949. It felt like getting a visa to a bright yet unknown world.

Dagmar Dole and Eleanor Hollibaugh, these two precious and gifted pioneers, followed to the letter the advice of the beloved Guardian on how to introduce and teach the Faith, and we shall be eternally indebted to them for the gift they offered us, and we thank and praise God for having guided them to our door.[6]

As Jean finished his story, we arrived at his home for a rest before walking to the Feast. His home was exquisite and tastefully decorated. The furniture was all new and of very high quality, except for one wobbly desk in the corner of the room, which caught my attention because it did not match the rest of the furniture. Noticing my interest, he said, "This desk is very precious because twenty-five people have signed their declaration cards on it. It is my treasure."

In 1953 this wonderful man, his wife, and his daughter participated in the Fourth Intercontinental Teaching Conference in New Delhi. I was very moved to see the entire family on the platform when the call for pioneers was raised. When he addressed the audience, his words about pioneering touched me so deeply that I can still remember them:

> The gardener plants seeds in a small container until they germinate into stems and leaves. He then separates these and replants them into the ground, where they will have room to grow, blossom, and bear fruit. If the gardener does not do this, the roots of these small plants will destroy each other. They will either die or be stunted and fruitless.
>
> Our divine gardener, Shoghi Effendi, asked us to disperse so that we can grow, develop, and bear luscious fruit, thereby beautifying the garden of humanity.

Today we can witness the results of the sacrifices made by pioneers such as Dagmar Dole, Eleanor Hollibaugh, Marion Little, Elsa Steinmetz, Fritzi Shaver, Honor Kempton, and Virginia Orbison. They have brought blessings to us all by their examples as well as through their tireless labors. Others who received the message of Bahá'u'lláh from Dagmar Dole must have been similarly affected by her love and example. How grateful we must all be to such heroes and heroines.

After a rich and enviable life of service, Dagmar Dole passed away in Switzerland on 12 November 1952 at a medical clinic where she received treatment for the last two months of her life. On 16 November Shoghi Effendi telexed the Bahá'í world: "Grieve passing distinguished, consecrated pioneer Dagmar Dole outstanding record unforgettable reward bountiful. Praying progress soul Kingdom."[7] He further immortalized Dagmar by saying that "'She died in "battle dress"; it is wonderful to die in active service.'" He also noted that "'Her spiritual station is very high'" and that "'Her grave will be a great blessing to Switzerland—to all Europe. She is the first to give her life for the Cause in the European project. Her resting-place is important.' "[8]

The victories the God-intoxicated pioneers achieved in Europe were joyously celebrated at the end of the Second Seven Year Plan by a conference held in Luxembourg from 30 August to 7 September 1952. Participating in the glorious celebration were Hands of the Cause of God Mr. Khadem, bringing greetings from Iran, the Cradle of the Faith, and Dr. Ugo Giachery, bringing fragrances from the Holy Land. The guests of honor were the stalwart pioneers to the ten goal countries and their spiritual offspring. The inspiration and spiritual energy stimulated by their exemplary achievements, combined with the Guardian's transforming love, which radiated from the two Hands, transported that gathering to a heavenly dimension. This was no ordinary victory celebration. The awesome vision of the future's glorious possibilities, however briefly unveiled to those participants, brought tremendous joy and provided the impetus for many heroic deeds and signal victories yet to come.

5 International Service–Africa

Release yourselves, O nightingales of God, from the thorns and brambles of wretchedness and misery, and wing your flight to the rose-garden of unfading splendor. O My friends that dwell upon the dust! Haste forth unto your celestial habitation. Announce unto yourselves the joyful tidings: "He Who is the Best-Beloved is come! He hath crowned Himself with the glory of God's Revelation, and hath unlocked to the face of men the doors of His ancient Paradise." Let all eyes rejoice, and let every ear be gladdened, for now is the time to gaze on His beauty, now is the fit time to hearken to His voice. Proclaim unto every longing lover: "Behold, your Well-Beloved hath come among men!" and to the messengers of the Monarch of love impart the tidings: "Lo, the Adored One hath appeared arrayed in the fullness of His glory!"

—BAHÁ'U'LLÁH

PREPARATION FOR THE HOLY YEAR

As the Holy Year 1953—the centenary year of the birth of Bahá'u'lláh's mission—approached, the frequency of the Guardian's messages to the Bahá'í world increased in preparation for a change from a regional to a more global perspective.* On 8 October 1952 he cabled the Bahá'í world:

---

*The Holy Year 1953 commemorated the year in which Bahá'u'lláh received the first intimation of His prophetic mission while in Tehran's Síyáh-Chál dungeon. The exact time of this first intimation is unknown; thus, the entire year from October 1952 to October 1953 (corresponding, according to the Báb's writings, to the Holy Year Nine—October 1852–October 1853) was regarded as holy.

Hail feelings humble thankfulness unbounded joy opening Holy Year commemorating centenary rise orb Bahá'u'lláh's most sublime revelation. . . . Feel hour propitious proclaim entire Bahá'í world projected launching occasion convocation approaching intercontinental conferences four continents globe fate-laden soul-stirring decade-long world-embracing Spiritual Crusade. . . .[1]

The "world-embracing Spiritual Crusade" to which Shoghi Effendi referred was a new phrase in the Bahá'í vocabulary. The Bahá'ís of Persia celebrated the occasion. Shoghi Effendi's joyous proclamation gave all the believers hope, inspiration, and encouragement to rededicate themselves to the Faith they loved so dearly. The cable evoked visions of a global spiritual army ready to conquer the world with the weapon of the love of God. It gave them a new self-image, a new identity, and a new vision. It broadened their scope and offered a new glimpse of the universal nature of the Faith, which had yet to be realized.

AFRICA

On 8 September 1952 Mr. Khadem had received the following cable from the Guardian: "Deep-felt appreciation magnificent historic services Europe advise prepare similar visit Africa Holy Year after attendance Kampala."[2] Messages such as this gave Mr. Khadem the zeal with which he carried out the Guardian's instructions. The beloved Shoghi Effendi was so kind to Mr. Khadem that he even sent messages of love and encouragement to him through others. In a letter dated 19 October 1952, Dr. Lutfu'lláh Ḥakím conveyed a message on behalf of the beloved Guardian, saying that Shoghi Effendi had instructed him to write to Mr. Khadem and tell him his letter had been received and that Shoghi Effendi was very happy with Mr. Khadem's services in so many centers in Europe. Dr. Ḥakím also conveyed the Guardian's hopes that Mr. Khadem's trip to Africa would be as beneficial to the Cause as was the trip through Europe. Shoghi Effendi wanted to assure Mr. Khadem and his family of prayers.

When Mr. Khadem received the Guardian's instruction about Africa, he shared it with the Africa Committee of the National Spiritual Assembly of the British Isles. They responded by giving him the addresses of all known believers in Africa and by suggesting an itinerary.

In accordance with the Guardian's instructions and the suggested itinerary, we started on a tour of Africa on 31 December 1952. Mr. Khadem was to have the joy of communicating the beloved Guardian's love and appreciation to virtually every Bahá'í in Africa. First we took several weeks to visit the friends in Iraq, Egypt, and Sudan. Then in February we went to the Intercontinental Teaching Conference in Kampala, Uganda.

We boarded a plane from Khartoum to Kampala. Curious to know whether we would be traveling with other Bahá'ís, we went through the list of passengers before boarding the plane but could not identify any familiar names. When we boarded, there were only two vacant aisle seats, one in the front of the plane, the other in the back. We took these two seats, but we talked so much with each other that the passengers decided it would be more peaceful if we sat together. The gentleman sitting across the aisle from my husband was willing to change his seat with me. Therefore, I moved to the front of the plane and sat next to Mr. Khadem.

We were very excited about the Kampala conference and most eager to share the priceless gift of the Faith with someone. We whispered together about how we could teach on the plane. I discreetly pointed to the lovely and receptive-looking woman next to me, by the window.

"Okay," my husband whispered, "but how will you start?"

"Easy. I'll admire her shoes. They *are* beautiful. I have never seen such lovely slippers." He thought it would be worth a try, so I proceeded to tell the woman how much I liked her slippers.

"Do you really like them?" she asked.

"Oh yes! Where did you buy them?"

"In America," she said.

"I'm going to America soon, and maybe I will be able to find similar ones," I said, trying to steer the conversation to the subject of why we were going to America (a Bahá'í conference), or why we were going to Kampala (another Bahá'í conference), or anything that would lead to mentioning the Faith.

"Do you have friends in Kampala?" she asked.

"Yes, we do. How about you?" This was perfect. Soon we would get around to the subject of the Faith. I was very confident.

"Yes!" she said a little too eagerly. "I am going to a conference."

"That's strange," I said. "I am going to a conference too, a Bahá'í conference."

"Are you a Bahá'í?" Her enthusiasm was mounting, and mine with it.

"Yes, of course!" I said.

"So am I!" she said.

"What is your name?"

"I'm Marguerite Sears."

I suddenly realized with whom I was speaking. I had been trying to teach the Faith to a well-known American Bahá'í. William and Marguerite Sears had pioneered to Africa and were honored and loved by many who knew of their services.* I had heard wonderful things about them. I was surprised and delighted. With tears in our eyes, we jumped from our seats to embrace each other in spiritual friendship. The passengers, especially those who knew we had never met before, sensed that something very unusual was happening, but they could not have guessed the sentiments that had overwhelmed my heart.

In late April, when Mr. Khadem and I arrived in Chicago to attend the dedication of the Bahá'í House of Worship in Wilmette and the All-American Bahá'í Intercontinental Teaching Conference,§ we found that our correspondence had been forwarded to our hotel room with loving greetings from the National Spiritual Assembly of the United States. Among the items of mail was a treasured gift from my new friend: a pair of those same lovely slippers.

First Bahá'í Intercontinental Teaching Conference—Kampala

Our trip to Kampala in February 1953 was our first introduction to the heart of Africa. Indeed, the large number of native African participants who came to the teaching conference was truly impressive. The Guardian's description of them as "pure-hearted" was vividly demonstrated to all who were present.[3] I recall one of the

---

*William Sears was named a Hand of the Cause of God in October 1957.
§The dedication was held 1–2 May 1953; the conference, 3–6 May 1953.

native African believers addressing the audience in the following manner: "We have received the fire of the love of God. We will take this fire back with us and set the jungles ablaze." When asked to identify himself, the man refused, saying, "My name is not important. It is the message of Bahá'u'lláh that is important." He was asked again to please state his name for the sake of the conference participants. Again he refused, saying, "It doesn't matter who I am. There are many of us dedicated to this Cause. I am only acting as a representative." This kind of purity and selflessness touched our hearts. We had visited Egypt, where our experience had been deeply moving, but our experience in "the heart" of Africa was unparalleled. For the remainder of our travels in Africa, Mr. Khadem repeatedly mentioned the singular experience of this conference, which had been the recipient of an overwhelming measure of love from Shoghi Effendi. How profusely and warmly the Guardian embraced this continent with his words. His loving message to the African Intercontinental Teaching Conference was presented by the Hand of the Cause of God Leroy Ioas, who was acting as the Guardian's representative. In that message, Shoghi Effendi welcomed "with open arms the unexpectedly large number of representatives of the pure-hearted and the spiritually receptive Negro race, so dearly loved by 'Abdu'l-Bahá, for whose conversion to His Father's Faith He so deeply yearned and whose interests He so ardently championed."[4]

As the Guardian's representative at this conference, Mr. Ioas had been entrusted with the mission of embracing, on behalf of the Guardian, every black Bahá'í he met. With great eagerness he had begun fulfilling this precious assignment as soon as he arrived at the airport. In turn, Mr. Khadem and the eight other Hands of the Cause who were present—Músá Banání, Valíyu'lláh Varqá, Shu'á'-u'lláh 'Alá'í, Mason Remey, Horace Holley, Tarázu'lláh Samandarí, Dorothy Baker, and 'Ali-Akbar Furútan—whether meeting Bahá'ís individually or addressing the conference, communicated their own love for and devotion to the Guardian, thereby bringing the participants closer to that storehouse of spiritual power and attraction.

The Hands of the Cause of God fulfilled a very special function at these intercontinental conferences and in their travels during the Holy Year. They served as spiritual catalysts in transmitting a new global spirit and vision to the Bahá'ís. Both collectively and indi-

Nine Hands of the Cause of God attending the
First Intercontinental Teaching Conference in Kampala, Uganda, 1953.
Back row, left to right: Leroy Ioas, Dorothy Baker, Músá Banání,
Horace Holley, Zikrullah Khadem, Shu'á'u'lláh 'Alá'í, Valíyu'lláh Varqá.
Front row, left to right: Tarázu'lláh Samandarí, 'Alí Akbar Furútan

vidually they received specific assignments from the Guardian to
participate in the intercontinental conferences and, between conferences, to visit Bahá'í centers.

The palpable love and appreciation conveyed to participants at
the Kampala conference through the Guardian's message, combined
with Mr. Ioas' acts of tenderness, released a potent spirit that permeated the conference, transformed it, and gave rise to a new level of
unity and dedication that welded a diverse representation of races,
nations, and backgrounds into one entity. To see such unity among
the races in Africa in 1953 was not only unique. It was miraculous!
Words cannot adequately describe our experience, but it seemed as
though God, in His great generosity, had permitted us a glimpse of
the true meaning of the unity of mankind. For years afterward Mr.
Khadem often spoke of that historic conference in Kampala.

Bahá'ís gathered at the First Intercontinental Teaching Conference,
Kampala, Uganda, 1953. Mr. Khadem is in the second row, far right;
Mrs. Khadem is in the front row, center.

KENYA

After the spiritually energizing Kampala conference, Mr. Khadem
and I continued our African tour on 25 February 1953. The beloved
Guardian had asked the Hand of the Cause of God Músá Banání,
who was a pioneer in Kampala and one of the first to bring the Faith
to Africa, to accompany Mr. Khadem on as many trips as possible.
Thus I had the opportunity to share the company of not only my
husband but also of Mr. and Mrs. Banání. For this, I consider myself
very fortunate.

Our first stop with the Banánís was Nairobi, Kenya. We met
many dear friends there who were also passing through. Among
them were the Hand of the Cause of God Dorothy Baker, Mr.
William Foster (who was a pioneer to Liberia), Mr. Ḥasan Ṣabrí
(another pioneer, who is now serving at the Bahá'í World Center),
and many others.[5] It was especially heartwarming to meet with our

*Hands of the Cause of God DOROTHY BAKER (top row, fourth from left),
JALÁL KHÁZEH (far right), and ZIKRULLAH KHADEM
(bottom row, second from right) gathered with Bahá'í friends in
Nairobi, Kenya, February 1953. Irene Bennett (holding the
picture of 'Abdu'l-Bahá), who became a Bahá'í
during the Khadems' visit, especially touched
Mr. Khadem's heart with her spirit and sincerity.*

dearest friends, Mr. and Mrs. 'Aziz Yazdí, who were pioneers in
Nairobi. We found it exciting to encounter so many familiar and
distinguished friends thousands of miles from home. We came upon
such friends everywhere. Some we already knew; others we met for
the first time. Over and over again, wherever we went, we learned
that there are no strangers and no strange lands.

During our visit in Kenya we met a lovely English woman named
Irene Bennett. Mr. Khadem was especially touched by her spirit and
sincerity. She had been seriously studying the Faith for a long time
and decided, while we were there, to become a Bahá'í. After her
declaration she cried continuously for two days. I became concerned
and asked Mrs. Baker's help in calming and comforting Irene.

"Darling, don't worry," the Hand of the Cause told me. "The
crying is good for her; she needs it. She is getting a baptism of the
heart." That beautiful image of tears washing away the dross and
baptizing the heart still moves me.

ETHIOPIA

On Saturday, 28 February, the Banánís, Mr. Khadem, and I went from Kenya to Addis Ababa, Ethiopia, where we spent five days. Because the Ethiopian community was one of the more established Bahá'í communities in Africa, we met many Bahá'ís there. Our days were filled with firesides, public meetings, and other Bahá'í gatherings and with greeting Bahá'ís who came to our hotel. Among those who came to visit were Mr. Muḥammad Muṣṭafá, chairman of the National Spiritual Assembly of Egypt; Mr. Gila Bata, one of the first Bahá'ís in Ethiopia; and Mr. and Mrs. Sabri Elias, who had been pioneers in Africa since 1933.

BACK TO KENYA

We returned to Nairobi on the fifth of March. Mr. Khadem was ill and confined to bed for a few days. Mr. Banání stopped at the Yazdís' house, which is where we were having our mail forwarded. In our mail we found a letter from the National Spiritual Assembly of the Bahá'ís of the United States. Enclosed was Mrs. Marzieh Gail's translation of an article Mr. Khadem had written about his trip to the prison cell of the Báb in Azerbaijan. The article was going to be printed in volume twelve of *The Bahá'í World.* * This news made Mr. Khadem very happy and consoled him when he was unable to join us that evening to listen to the Hand of the Cause of God Dorothy Baker talk about her recent pilgrimage to the Holy Land. However, I related to him every detail of the evening when I returned, because I knew how heartbroken he was at missing any opportunity to hear of the beloved Guardian.

TANZANIA

On the seventh of March Mr. Khadem, the Banánís, and I left Kenya, via Mombasa, for a week's stay in Dar es Salaam, Tanganyika (now Tanzania). Dar es Salaam, like Addis Ababa, was an established Bahá'í community with many pioneers from Iran, Egypt, England,

---

*For the text of the article entitled "Pilgrimage to the Scenes of the Báb's Captivity and Martyrdom," see part 3, chapter 1, pp. 246–65.

and India. Because of its sizable Bahá'í community, there were constant meetings, firesides, deepenings, and other events.

We were very busy attending the many functions and renewing friendships with old acquaintances. While there, we saw many pioneers, including Mr. and Mrs. Jalál Na<u>kh</u>javání, Mr. and Mrs. Muḥammad (Mammad) Yazdání, Mr. and Mrs. Ḥasan Ṣabrí, and Mr. and Mrs. Manú<u>ch</u>ihr Farhúmand. It was a special treat to see Mr. Matula (who had translated Dr. Esslemont's book, *Bahá'u'lláh and the New Era,* into Swahili), for we had met only weeks before at the Kampala conference.[6]

The firesides were very well attended; usually ten to twelve seekers came. In the short time we were there, several of these seekers became Bahá'ís. I was impressed with Mrs. Banání's generosity. She seemed to have an endless supply of Bahá'í rings and gave them away to new believers. Among the new believers we met was a Mr. Hooper, from England, who had been a clergyman. At one meeting he was visibly moved when he spoke about his spiritual search and expressed his joy at having recognized Christ in His second coming.

Dar es Salaam was oppressively hot during the Fast.* For this reason we frequently sought refuge on the beach and often met the Bahá'ís there, once for a pre-sunrise picnic. At dawn we would say prayers while we watched the sun color the horizon with its brilliance.

ZAMBIA

On the fifteenth of March we continued our trip, our next stop being Blantyre, which was then part of the Federation of Rhodesia and Nyasaland and is now in the Republic of Malawi. Mrs. Banání and I stayed in Blantyre while Mr. Khadem and Mr. Banání rented a car and drove to Zomba to see Mr. Dudley Smith Kuntendele, the first Bahá'í in Dar es Salaam and the first Zambian Bahá'í. The two men spent a great deal of time trying unsuccessfully to find his home, for they only had a post office box number to go by. Having

---

*The Nineteen Day Fast (2–21 March) is a period of spiritual renewal and development during which Bahá'ís abstain from food and drink from sunrise to sunset. A symbol of self-restraint, the Fast is a time of meditation, prayer, and spiritual recuperation and readjustment.

heard they were coming, Mr. Kuntendele had sent his son to find them. In the middle of the search, Mr. Kuntendele and the two Hands of the Cause stumbled upon each other. Mr. Kuntendele had been riding home on his bicycle, about eight miles from the hotel where Mr. Khadem and Mr. Banání were staying, and had immediately identified the two Persian men in the street as his expected visitors.

The meeting was a joyous occasion. Mr. Khadem and Mr. Banání told Mr. Kuntendele about the progress of the Faith and shared with him pictures from the Kampala conference. Spiritually stirred, Mr. Kuntendele told them about his devotion to the Faith and his efforts at promoting the Bahá'í message. He also introduced them to his brother who had become a Bahá'í. Mr. Kuntendele had taught the Faith to two people in Blantyre and was also doing his utmost to serve in Zomba. As they were parting he announced: "In the future you will hear of the victories we will win in promoting this Cause."

South Africa

Our next stop during the African tour was to be Johannesburg, South Africa. But on the way there, the Banánís, Mr. Khadem, and I had a layover in Salisbury, Rhodesia (now Harare, Zimbabwe), on 16 March. Mr. Khadem recorded in his diary the impressive view of the Zambezi River from ten thousand feet while we traveled at a "plane speed of 140 miles per hour." Salisbury was so charming that Mr. Khadem and I wished we could stay, but since no Bahá'ís were there, we left for Johannesburg the next day to visit Mr. Reginald Turvey, the only Bahá'í in South Africa. When we arrived in Johannesburg, we contacted him, got his address, and went to meet him at his studio. The studio was quite large, and Mr. Turvey's artwork was displayed all over its walls. His young assistant greeted us. Mr. Turvey was not there, but we asked if we could wait for him. The young man was very gracious, perhaps thinking that we were four potential customers.

It was not long before Mr. Turvey arrived. The two Hands of the Cause introduced themselves and said they had come to South Africa specifically to see him and to bring him the love and greetings of the Guardian. This very devoted believer had spent fourteen years completely isolated from the rest of the Bahá'í world. He was so overcome with emotion and gratitude that he began trembling and had to steady himself against the wall to keep from falling. For all those years, despite his isolation and loneliness, he had kept alive the spirit of his faith and had promoted the Bahá'í teachings.

Mr. Khadem and Mr. Banání invited him for dinner at the hotel, then to the Banánís' room to show him pictures of the Kampala conference. Mr. Turvey was overwhelmed to see so many Bahá'ís—a large percentage of whom were native Africans—gathered in one spot. He had been a lone Bahá'í in the south of this vast continent for many years and had had no idea that others, too, had found his treasure and dedicated their lives to it. He was not alone after all, far from it! The beloved Guardian had even sent two Hands of the Cause of God to bring his personal love and encouragement!

On the nineteenth of March we were invited to dinner at the home of a German family to whom Mr. Turvey was teaching the Faith. We spent most of the evening discussing Bahá'í principles and teachings. There were many with whom Mr. Turvey had spoken and who had shown some interest in the Faith. He was very excited to be able to introduce his friends to other Bahá'ís and demonstrate in this manner that there is, in fact, a Bahá'í world community.

In just a few days a powerful bond developed between the two Hands of the Cause and Mr. Turvey. To celebrate the coming Naw-Rúz (the Bahá'í New Year), the three men decided to demonstrate their unity in a cable of greetings to the Guardian, to which the Guardian promptly and briefly responded, "Loving remembrance Shrines," signing it "Shoghi."[7] I remember how we all prayerfully gathered in the Banánís' room to open this cable. It provided enough spiritual nourishment to energize Mr. Khadem and Mr. Banání for the rest of the trip through Africa.

BELGIAN CONGO

On 25 March 1953 we left Johannesburg and headed toward Elisabethville, Belgian Congo (now Lumbumbashi, Zaire) but had to make a stop in Bulawayo because of stormy weather. When we arrived in Elisabethville, we were to search for a Mr. Vaḥdat, one of two Bahá'ís in the Belgian Congo. He lived in Kamina, about six hundred kilometers from Elisabethville; planes were scheduled to fly there only about once a week. Because Mr. Khadem could not get any assurance about when the next flight would be, we could not make the trip to Kamina. Instead, Mr. Khadem cabled the Guardian's love and greetings to Mr. Vaḥdat and invited him to join us in Léopoldville (now Kinshasa) if possible, in care of Mme. Marthe Molitor, the other pioneer in the Belgian Congo.

We arrived in Léopoldville on Friday, 27 March. Before contacting Mme. Molitor, we needed to secure hotel rooms, but we learned, to our surprise, that all of the hotels except one were fully booked. The Hotel Regina had two rooms available for only one night. After making sure that we understood this condition, the hotel manager registered us. Mr. Khadem accepted the stipulation, believing that he and Mr. Banání would be able to visit Mme. Molitor and deliver Shoghi Effendi's message within one day. However, Mme. Molitor lived in the town of Matadi, which, they soon discovered, was quite a distance from Léopoldville. Furthermore, when they tried to telephone her, they kept getting a wrong number. One day would clearly be too short a time in which to accomplish the mission.

The next morning Mr. Khadem informed the hotel manager that we needed the rooms for a few more nights, as unforeseen circumstances prevented us from leaving as planned.

"It is absolutely impossible!" the manager exclaimed, unyielding. "Two generals in the Belgian army booked these rooms months ago!"

Mr. Khadem was equally firm. "Either you find us other accommodations, or we cannot vacate the rooms."

Unmoved, the manager insisted that, as previously agreed, the rooms must be vacated for the generals who were coming. Having, indeed, made that agreement, Mr. Khadem relented.

Then he obtained tickets to Matadi before coming to inform us of the manager's refusal to accommodate us. However, before he had a chance to tell us that we would have to leave for Matadi, we learned that Mr. Banání was feeling sick. I, too, was in bed with an upset stomach and a headache. The room was oppressively stuffy, as there were no windows, and a heavy, fishy odor intensified the stagnant air. Gradually, I began to feel so sick that I was dizzy and could not walk straight. Seeing how ill we were, Mr. Khadem had no choice but to return to the manager and explain our predicament.

Exasperated, the manager angrily replied, "They should go to the hospital, then. I will call a doctor to visit them right away."

The doctor was summoned and came to see me first. After

carefully examining me, he said that I was, indeed, very sick and certainly could not be moved, even from my bed. When he visited Mr. Banání, to our surprise, he came to the same conclusion. The frustrated hotel manager was obliged to let us stay where we were.

After the doctor had made his report and our rooms were confirmed, miraculously, I began to feel better. I moved around without feeling dizzy. When we called Mr. Banání we were surprised to discover that he, too, was beginning to feel better. As our condition improved, we realized we were very hungry. We consulted about whether to obey the doctor and endure the hunger or to go to the restaurant, risk our health, and risk facing the poor, harassed manager, who would, no doubt, find our story incredulous. We finally decided that we had to regain our strength for the long journey ahead. We needed good food more than we needed rest. As we entered the restaurant, you can imagine the manager's total exasperation and the onlookers' amazement, as well as their gossip about our "miraculous recovery" from death's door. Maybe we were just hungry and tired all along. Perhaps the doctor's intervention was planned by God so that we could stay and accomplish our mission. It is still an incredible and comical reminiscence today.

Since Mr. Banání and I were not fully recovered, Mr. Khadem decided to go on to Matadi alone. But, to our surprise, Mme. Molitor arrived while he was in the process of arranging to leave. Through a hotel attendant, she sent a message to our room on her personal card: "May I come? The phone is broken. I am downstairs." While Mr. Khadem was preparing to leave for Matadi, I had gone out into the hall and was walking down a ramp in order to get some fresh air. A woman approached me, asking, "Are you Mrs. Khadem? I sent a message to your room. I am Marthe Molitor." The coincidence was unbelievable; the person we were looking for was right there, in the hotel. I rushed to inform my husband, but he had already received Mme. Molitor's message in our room and was getting ready to go downstairs and greet her.

There she was, this lovely, dedicated woman, through whose sacrifices generations of Bahá'ís would come to the Faith in the future. She was a mature woman with a very attractive disposition. A talented artist who had embraced the Faith in Belgium, this devoted soul used the money she earned from selling her paintings to promote the message of Bahá'u'lláh. She did this because her husband was not a Bahá'í; she did not wish to use his funds for this purpose. She was deeply touched by the love of the Guardian, a love that had sent two Hands of the Cause of God to visit her in such a remote corner of the world.

ANGOLA

On 29 March we made a side-trip to Luanda, Angola. The following day, one of the two Portuguese pioneers there (Exma Senora Dama Gugdes DeMelo Rocha and Exma D. Laura Rodrequez) came to our hotel to greet us. Mr. Khadem and Mr. Banání shared with her news of the First Bahá'í Intercontinental Teaching Conference in Kampala and showed her their pictures from it. She was very excited to see evidence of the growth of the Faith and to see Bahá'í principles being realized at such events, as her father-in-law had been the first Bahá'í pioneer to Angola.

News of the worldwide expansion of the Faith created renewed hope and a fresh spirit in isolated centers such as Luanda. A fireside was held the next night. Among those who attended was the Belgian consul. There were many questions and much animated discussion. The non-Bahá'í husband of one of the pioneers said that he intended to declare his belief in Bahá'u'lláh when he returned to Lisbon. He and his wife were going home to Portugal for a visit. When we saw this couple off on their ship the next day, the husband reiterated his desire to embrace the Faith and continued to discuss the matter with us until their departure.

BACK TO THE BELGIAN CONGO

In order to derive the maximum benefit from the presence of two Hands of the Cause of God, Mme. Molitor had used the time while we were in Angola to organize a public meeting to be held when we returned to the Belgian Congo. The meeting was not outwardly successful, since few came. However, we had a wonderful time together, talking about the progress of the Faith in all parts of the world under the divine guidance of "the beloved of all hearts, Shoghi Effendi," as Mr. Khadem often referred to the Guardian. There were also other public meetings to which a number of seekers came, including M. Molitor, who was helping his wife with the meetings. He said he was very interested in promoting the principles of the Faith.

During the few days we were there, Mme. Molitor attempted in every possible way to take advantage of our presence in order to promote the Faith. On 2 April I went with her to Brazzaville, French Congo (now the People's Republic of the Congo), which was across the river and only a short distance from our hotel. She asked me to go into a bookstore where Bahá'í books were on sale and to buy them all. She wanted to impress the shop owner so that he would order more.

In 1953 there were very few Bahá'ís in the Belgian Congo and the French Congo. Could this dedicated woman who labored so devotedly, grasped every opportunity, and persisted in her lonely attempts to teach the Faith ever have imagined that today there would be thousands of believers? How could she have known that her lonely labors—pioneering with a non-Bahá'í husband, lacking funds, and being out of communication with the rest of the Bahá'í world—would bear such fruit?

After I returned from Brazzaville, the Banánís, Mr. Khadem, and I went to the airport and left for Monrovia, Liberia. M. and Mme. Molitor, together with a friend of theirs and an English general, came to see us off, bearing a beautiful bouquet of red flowers. We were deeply touched by this gesture of affection and offered to take those beautiful roses to the Bahá'ís of Liberia as a symbol of love. That love, transported from one part of Africa to another in the form of fragrant roses, brought great joy to the hearts of the Liberian Bahá'ís.

LIBERIA

Our flight to Monrovia, Liberia, took us through some extremely stormy weather that was particularly turbulent over Accra, Ghana. When we finally landed, we discovered that our tickets had been written incorrectly and that we had been taken to Robertsport, about fifty miles up the coast from Monrovia. We needed to find a way to Monrovia, but there was no public transportation available, and there were no cars for rent. As we consulted about how to remedy our unfortunate situation, an American resident stepped forward and graciously offered to drive us to Monrovia. We were most grateful and eagerly accepted his offer. However, when we got to Monrovia, he could not find a place to leave us, as all the hotels were booked up. Finally, through the police, we found two rooms in adjacent homes belonging to two Americans living in Monrovia.

We separated from the Banánís, each couple staying in one of the homes. The American with whom Mr. Khadem and I stayed, Mr. Clifton S. Hardy, was very hospitable and gracious. His house was quite spacious. However, our room on the second floor was tiny and had no ventilation. Still, we were grateful to have a place to stay.

There were two American pioneers in Monrovia, Mr. William Foster and Miss Valerie Wilson, whom we were to visit. Mr. Khadem had acquired their addresses through the American embassy, which is where we headed next. But it was difficult to accomplish anything that day because it was Good Friday. All the stores were closed, and most of the embassy's staff were absent.

Mr. Khadem finally discovered through a series of inquiries that Mr. Foster had gone to Haifa on pilgrimage and had not yet returned. One of the embassy personnel whom he was able to contact kindly agreed to escort us to Valerie Wilson's house. We thoroughly enjoyed meeting this delightful woman, who agreed to join us at a restaurant for dinner. Later that evening we returned to her house to meet her father and a woman, both of whom were investigating the Faith. Valerie's father held a very high position in one of the Christian churches and asked many questions. Although he was very skeptical, he was sincere and honest. When an answer made sense, he accepted it as the truth.

On the following day, we went with Valerie and her roommate to a church where the Liberian Prime Minister was speaking. We had a chance to meet him and tell him of the Faith. He said he had known a wonderful Bahá'í, Mr. Matthew Bullock, and felt a great fondness and admiration for the Faith as a result.

SIERRA LEONE

The following Tuesday, 7 April, Mr. Khadem attempted to schedule us for a flight to Freetown, Sierra Leone. He discovered, however, that only one flight a week went to Freetown. Since the next scheduled flight could not be confirmed, he arranged to charter a tiny taxiplane that seated four. All four seats had to be occupied "for proper balance," the pilot declared. I volunteered to accompany Mr.

Khadem if Mr. Banání was tired. Initially, he accepted my offer.

Mr. Khadem and I learned that the trip would be a treacherous one because of the heavy rainfall and the stormy weather that are usual at that time of year; flying in such a small plane over the ocean would be dangerous. We needed to find one more passenger to balance the weight of the plane, but we had no idea of where we would find someone to accompany us to Sierra Leone on such short notice and for such a hazardous journey. Mr. Khadem and I packed our bags, sat by the window of our room in Mr. Hardy's house, and started to pray, beseeching God to send us someone to fill the plane. In the middle of our prayers for assistance, Mr. Hardy interrupted us to ask if it would be at all possible for him to accompany us on this journey. We jumped up from our prayers. "Of course!" we said. "With pleasure! We would be delighted to have you accompany us! How wonderful!" Surely he had never had such an enthusiastic and eager invitation from anyone.

Our number was now complete. We needed only to hear from the pilot. As we waited, Mr. Banání arrived. His heart was like a mirror that concealed nothing; I could see that he was quite agitated.

I hurried to him. "What's the matter, Mr. Banání? Is something wrong? Please tell me."

"Yes! Something is very wrong. Why are *you* going?"

"I am going because they need four people to occupy the seats for balance. Besides, this is a dangerous trip, and I don't want to leave my husband alone. If something bad happens, we will die together."

"You can't go! You must stay! I will go instead."

I acquiesced because Mr. Banání was a Hand of the Cause. "I'll do as you wish."

Soon the pilot appeared, and the four men left. They flew out on Thursday, April ninth, at four o'clock in the afternoon, and were planning to return at ten the next morning. I stayed with Mrs. Banání in her room. In spite of my efforts to remain optimistic, I could not quell the dread in my heart. I feared for our husbands' safety. Such a small, light plane flying over the ocean in unpredictable weather—it just did not sound safe. But the orders of the Guardian had to be carried out exactly, according to the Hands of the Cause, no matter what.

Mrs. Banání shared my worry, especially when our husbands did not return at the appointed time the next day. Our anxiety escalated with every passing minute. By four o'clock in the afternoon, we were sure there had been some problem. We started to pray.

Mrs. Banání, a strong, wonderful person, was very submissive to the will of God. After many prayers, she finally said, "I think we should say the Prayer for the Departed."

"What?" I could not contain my shock.

She calmly tried to comfort me. "Look, they haven't returned yet. I'm afraid they must have crashed. Don't you accept the Will of God?" I was speechless and did not know how to react. I was not ready to give up hope just yet. But the later it got, the more likely that horrible possibility seemed.

Mrs. Banání, with her lovely voice, chanted many prayers for the departed. She then asked me very gently, "What are you going to do now? Are you going to the conference and the dedication?" She was referring to the upcoming dedication of the Bahá'í House of Worship in Wilmette.

"Are you serious?" I responded, amazed at her strength and resignation. "Are you suggesting that I could go alone?"

"No, we'll go together."

"How can I possibly do that?" I was beginning to feel panicked.

"I'm surprised at you, Javidukht! Our husbands have given their lives in the path of service. What greater glory is there? As for us, we have work to do. A new teaching plan is being given to the Bahá'í world. A House of Worship is being dedicated. This Bahá'í House of Worship was initiated with a petition by devoted Bahá'ís who were longing to realize this dream and worked so hard and sacrificially to construct it. His Holiness 'Abdu'l-Bahá laid the cornerstone with His own blessed hands. How can we miss it?"

I was not as experienced, nor was I as strong and detached as Mrs. Banání. I wished desperately that I had taken the chance to be with my husband, no matter where, even if the plane had crashed. I did not even want to think of the future without him.

But, of course, our husbands did return about an hour later, completely exhausted and totally drained. They told us the incredible story of their unique plane trip. The pilot was drinking alcohol while he was flying. Each time he finished a bottle, he rolled the plane to the side and dropped the bottle into the sea. The shaky craft rolled and wobbled and bounced around in the air. Mr. Banání held onto the hanging strap and, with each sudden movement, exclaimed *"Yá Bahá'u'l-Abhá!* [O Thou the Glory of the Most Glorious!]." Mr. Khadem continuously chanted "The Remover of Difficulties."[8] When the plane finally landed, it went off of the runway. The four of them got out and literally lifted the plane back onto the runway.

When they arrived in Freetown, the passport officer wanted to know their business. They explained that they were looking for Aaron "Arthur" B. Wellesley Cole at such and such an address.

"There is no such place in Freetown. But don't worry; I'll help you. You see, he is my cousin. I will write his correct address for you." He wrote "31 Pultney Street, Freetown."

They were grateful to have run into Mr. Cole's cousin, of all people. Armed with the correct address, they went to a hotel. Mr. Hardy, still quite shaken by the experience on the plane, was only too glad for a chance to rest.

After securing hotel rooms, Mr. Khadem showed the new address to the hotel manager.

The manager slowly shook his head. "There is no such street in Freetown."

"How can that be? The passport officer is Mr. Cole's cousin. He wrote it for me." Mr. Khadem was feeling a little battered. That the whole trip might be in vain, after the extraordinary airplane trip, was too much for him to contemplate. "There has to be such a street," he insisted.

"Listen," the manager said, "I have lived here all my life! There is no such street."

"But you don't understand. I came such a long distance over the ocean on a small, chartered plane just to see Mr. Cole. Surely he must live here!"

"Have you been here before?" the manager asked.

"No."

"How do you know him, then?" the manager asked.

After some reflection, Mr. Khadem replied, "He is a Bahá'í."

"So what?"

Realizing the hotel manager could not possibly understand the special bond that links all Bahá'ís, Mr. Khadem did not answer. The manager, in turn, was beginning to doubt the sanity of his guest. He, too, remained silent.

Meanwhile, an English gentleman of great compassion who had heard about the horrors of the trip from Mr. Hardy and had overheard the exchange with the hotel manager, came forward.

"Maybe I can help," he said. "I overheard your conversation. If your friend lives here, surely you will be able to find him. Why don't you just begin a systematic search? Perhaps he lives out of the way on an unknown road that he himself named."

"It's possible," the manager conceded. "There are some new residences that are out of the way."

"Please permit me to put my car and driver at your disposal," the Englishman generously offered. "Why don't you begin with the newly constructed homes?"

During Mr. Khadem's exchange with the hotel manager, Mr. Banání had been praying "The Remover of Difficulties." His prayers were answered. After a short search in the car, they discovered that Mr. Cole had, indeed, recently built a house on top of a very high hill and had himself named the rough road, which was more like a path. They would have to climb this steep path to get to the house. The driver very kindly offered to accompany them and wait to drive them back to the hotel. They set out on their journey up the hill to the house, which turned out to be much farther away than they had thought. Mr. Banání became exhausted, and Mr. Khadem, with the driver's assistance, helped him to the house.

By this time it was quite late. The servant, expecting his employer and surprised to see three strangers instead, was not very welcoming. However, Mr. Khadem explained their difficult trip up the mountain and insisted that they rest in the living room while waiting for the master of the house.

Soon Mr. Cole arrived with his wife. He was extremely surprised and suspicious to discover three strangers in his home. However, his momentary irritation was quickly replaced by awe and wonder as Mr. Khadem approached him and said, *"Alláh-u-Abhá!* [God is Most Glorious!]."* Mr. Banání and I are Bahá'ís sent by the beloved Guardian especially to visit you and tell you how pleased he is with you."

---

* *"Alláh-u-Abhá"* is a form of the Greatest Name that was adopted as a greeting among Bahá'ís during the period of Bahá'u'lláh's exile in Adrianople.

Those words transformed Mr. Cole. Deeply moved, he began to tremble and replied, "Who am I that the Guardian of the Cause of God sent you especially to see me?"

"You are a Bahá'í," they replied. A warm exchange followed as they invited Mr. Cole to join them at the hotel.

When they returned to the hotel they showered their appreciation on the wonderful Englishman for his generosity. They spent most of that night and the next day visiting with Mr. Cole, who had been completely isolated from the rest of the Bahá'í world for a long time. This visit gave him the courage and vitality to set goals of action and to undertake the responsibility of conveying the message of Bahá'u'lláh to the people of Freetown.

Both Mr. Khadem and Mr. Banání were very pleased about this visit and were awed by the vision of the Guardian, who recognized the need and infused into this lonesome believer his love and encouragement. Mr. Cole was like a fish deprived of water who had finally been immersed in the ocean. He submerged himself in news about his beloved Faith and its astounding progress. He could not be quenched. Witnessing how the Guardian's love brought him to life deeply moved the Hands.

Though they thoroughly enjoyed Mr. Cole's company, Mr. Khadem and Mr. Banání dreaded the return plane trip, which turned out to be every bit as nerve-wracking as the first flight—Mr. Khadem resumed his praying and Mr. Banání his exclamations of *"Yá Bahá'u'l-Abhá,"* both beseeching God's protection. Mr. Hardy regretted ever having gone on that trip. I still do not understand why he went.

That evening, back in Liberia, we went to a Bahá'í meeting where we met again with our newfound friends and had another chance to share stories. On behalf of the Bahá'í community, Mrs. Banání and I were each presented with a beautiful fan as a memento of our stay in Monrovia.

The next morning, after we wrote thank-you letters to our kind hosts, Valerie Wilson accompanied us to the airport and bid us a loving and tender good-bye.

Morocco

On 11 April we departed for Casablanca, Morocco, with stops on the way at Conakry, French Guinea (now Guinea), and Dakar,

Senegal. We were met in the Casablanca airport by the pioneers who had arranged accommodations for us at the Hotel Sally, where we were able to rest after the very long trip. We met with the Bahá'ís the following morning, some having come from Rabat, Morocco. As usual, Mr. Khadem and Mr. Banání communicated to them the Guardian's love and greetings and shared with them pictures of the conference in Kampala.

In each of these locales the scene was familiar. Whether there was one Bahá'í or a well-established community, the simple message of love and greetings from the Guardian inspired the Bahá'ís to rededicate their efforts. Over and over again we witnessed the magical power of Shoghi Effendi's love.

TUNISIA

Because we so often traveled by plane, many memorable experiences occurred in the air. On the trip to Tunis on 15 April, I was sitting on the aisle while Mr. Khadem had the window seat. He was very tired and soon fell asleep. Two Tunisian gentlemen across the aisle began to converse with me in French. They realized, because of my accent and my conversation with Mr. Khadem in Persian, that we were not Tunisians and asked whether this was the first time we were going to Tunisia.

"Yes," I said.

One of the gentlemen asked, "Do you have accommodations in Tunisia? I am Tunisian and would be happy to help you. I know of a very good hotel with excellent accommodations."

I knew that the Bahá'ís of Tunisia must have secured a place for us to stay. "Thank you very much," I replied, "but we have many friends in Tunisia. I am sure they have made satisfactory arrangements."

"I don't understand. You just told me this is the first time you are going to Tunisia."

"That's right."

"How could you possibly know so many people there without ever seeing them?" Then he asked a bit mockingly, "Are they young or old?"

Of course, I did not know any of them in person. Hence I said, "They are from all classes and both sexes, young and old."

He chuckled and made a gesture to his friend that meant I was crazy.

I was offended. Trying to regain my dignity, I told him, "I'll know them when I see them." This remark, of course, made matters worse, and I prayed that he would see our Bahá'í friends at the airport.

When the plane landed, we deplaned ahead of the two Tunisians. Behind a fence bordering the area for arriving passengers, more than thirty Bahá'ís waited. They knew Mr. Khadem from his photographs, and we recognized them by the picture of 'Abdu'l-Bahá that they were holding. They cheered and shouted words of welcome. I heard one of the Tunisians behind me say, "It's incredible! She *does* have Tunisian friends from all classes, men and women, old and young."

We spent two very productive days in Tunis, meeting all of the Bahá'ís and their friends. The spirit of that Bahá'í community and their efforts to promote Bahá'u'lláh's message of peace touched us deeply. My bold announcement to our fellow-travelers that we had many friends in Tunisia was not vain imagining. In the short period of two days we were to form bonds that I cherish even to this day.

Our trip through Africa ended after the visit to Tunisia, but the joy of meeting so many dear friends and early believers in that vast continent was permanently planted in our hearts. As the years passed, our memories of the 1953 tour of Africa were to become a source of continued inspiration and renewal. We ended this tour with deep gratitude to the beloved Guardian for such a precious and, we felt, undeserved blessing. We now eagerly looked forward to a trip to North America and especially to participating in the historic dedication of the Mother Temple of the West in Wilmette, Illinois.

6 International Service—West and East

*Hear Me, ye mortal birds! In the Rose Garden of changeless splendor
a Flower hath begun to bloom, compared to which every other
flower is but a thorn, and before the brightness of Whose glory the
very essence of beauty must pale and wither. Arise, therefore, and,
with the whole enthusiasm of your hearts, with all the eagerness of
your souls, the full fervor of your will, and the concentrated efforts of
your entire being, strive to attain the paradise of His presence, and
endeavor to inhale the fragrance of the incorruptible Flower, to
breathe the sweet savors of holiness, and to obtain a portion of this
perfume of celestial glory.*

—BAHÁ'U'LLÁH

DEDICATION OF THE MOTHER TEMPLE OF THE WEST

When we arrived in Chicago for the joyous occasion of the
dedication of the Mother Temple of the West in Wilmette, Illinois,
the National Spiritual Assembly of the Bahá'ís of the United States
had graciously secured rooms at a hotel for the Hands of the Cause
of God. In each room was a cordial note of welcome, a beautiful
bouquet of flowers, and a package containing correspondence.
Among the various items of mail, Mr. Khadem found a revision of
the program for the dedication, including instructions from Shoghi
Effendi saying that Mr. Khadem should chant a selection from the
writings of the Báb. The text for the selection was handwritten by the
Guardian; Mr. Khadem immediately recognized it. During his pilgrimage in 1952 Mr. Khadem had been asked by Shoghi Effendi to
chant those very pages in his presence. As Mr. Khadem chanted, the
Guardian corrected him. Mr. Khadem often recalled that memorable occasion. He used to tell me:

Those pages written in the beloved Guardian's own handwriting were so very precious. I wished with all my heart that I could have them. How I would have treasured such a gift! But of course I didn't say anything. I begged Bahá'u'lláh to fulfill this fervent wish. Alas, it was not to be granted then. As I finished chanting, the beloved Guardian reached for those precious pages.

Imagine, then, Mr. Khadem's overwhelming joy and gratitude when he found, attached to the amended program, those very same pages penned by Shoghi Effendi. Bahá'u'lláh had answered his fervent plea. He kept that treasure with him for the rest of his life. Mr. Khadem's awe at receiving this priceless gift was further heightened by the fulfillment of a promise made to him by the beloved Guardian in 1937, sixteen years earlier. Shoghi Effendi had told him that he would chant at the dedication of the House of Worship in Wilmette. Not only had he known that Mr. Khadem would be present, but he had also known Mr. Khadem's deepest heartfelt wish.

On that same pilgrimage in 1937 when Shoghi Effendi met with the Eastern women, he told me the same thing: "You will accompany your husband when he chants at the dedication of the House of Worship."

The private dedication for Bahá'ís was held on the afternoon of 1 May 1953. It was a simple, moving event, a celebration of the opening of the doors of the Mother Temple of the West and a commemoration of 'Abdu'l-Bahá's historic visit to America during which He laid the cornerstone for the Temple.* On the following day, 2 May, the public dedication was held. So many people attended the ceremony that it had to be held in three shifts, each filling the 1,191-seat auditorium. Hundreds of people had to be turned away. We entered quietly and reverently—some of us even tearfully—for our hearts were overwhelmed with gratitude for being able to witness such an historic event.

As we entered the "holiest House of Worship," many events in the history of the Faith flashed through my mind: the sufferings of

---

*'Abdu'l-Bahá visited the United States and Canada from 11 April through 5 December 1912. During that visit, he laid the cornerstone for the Wilmette House of Worship in a dedication and groundbreaking ceremony held on 1 May 1912.

Bahá'u'lláh; 'Abdu'l-Bahá's visit to America, a land upon which He abundantly showered His love and blessings; the sacrifices Bahá'ís the world over had made to contribute toward the construction of the magnificent edifice; and, most of all, the dynamic and inspiring spiritual leadership of our beloved Guardian, under whose direction we were now witnessing the dedication of this sacred spot.*

Thirteen of the eighteen living Hands of the Cause of God—the "standard-bearers" of Bahá'u'lláh's revelation—were present.[5] Several of them—Amatu'l-Bahá Rúḥíyyih Khánum, Paul Haney, Zikrullah Khadem, and Tarázu'lláh Samandarí—participated in the program. Prayers from the Bahá'í writings, the Qur'án, and the Bible were offered. Mr. Haney majestically and eloquently introduced Amatu'l-Bahá Rúḥíyyih Khánum as the beloved Guardian's representative at the dedication of this holy edifice for the worship of God.[#] After greeting and welcoming the participants on behalf of Shoghi Effendi, she said: "May I now request you all to rise while I read on behalf of the Guardian of the Faith these words of prayer written by the Author of the Bahá'í Revelation [Bahá'u'lláh]: 'O God, Who art

---

*Shoghi Effendi referred many times to the Bahá'í House of Worship in Wilmette as "the holiest House of Worship ever to be built" and "the holiest House of Worship in the Bahá'í world." See, for example, Shoghi Effendi, letter dated 5 June 1947, *Citadel of Faith: Messages to America, 1947–1957* (Wilmette, Ill.: Bahá'í Publishing Trust, 1965), 8; Shoghi Effendi, letter dated 25 April 1946, *Messages to America: Selected Letters and Cablegrams Addressed to the Bahá'ís of North America, 1932–1946* (Wilmette, Ill.: Bahá'í Publishing Committee, 1947), 88; and Shoghi Effendi, letter dated 4 May 1953, *Messages to the Bahá'í World: 1950–1957*, rev. ed. (Wilmette, Ill.: Bahá'í Publishing Trust, 1971), 149.

[5]The Hands of the Cause of God present at the dedication were Rúḥíyyih Khánum, Shu'á'u'lláh 'Alá'í, Dorothy Baker, Músá Banání, Amelia Collins, 'Alí-Akbar Furútan, Horace Holley, Zikrullah Khadem, Tarázu'lláh Samandarí, Siegfried Schopflocher, George Townshend, Corinne True, and Valíyu'lláh Varqá. Also present were Paul Haney and William Sears, who were later appointed to serve as Hands of the Cause. Shoghi Effendi referred to the Hands as the "standard-bearers" of the Bahá'í Cause. See Shoghi Effendi, letter dated 4 May 1953, *Messages to the Bahá'í World*, 153.

[#]Amatu'l-Bahá Rúḥíyyih Khánum (née Mary Maxwell), the wife of Shoghi Effendi, was appointed by him as a Hand of the Cause of God in 1952.

the Author of all Manifestations, the Source of all Sources, the Fountain-Head of all Revelations, and the Well-Spring of all Lights! . . .' "[1]

Everyone rose with reverence and humility. There was a feeling of complete dedication. Hearts were electrified with the love of God, and the many tears that were shed testified to an intense longing to serve Bahá'u'lláh's blessed Cause. It seemed that everyone present was rapt in communion and meditation; it was as if the words were descending from the Abhá Kingdom itself.*

Mr. Khadem was among those present who chanted from the Bahá'í writings, his heart filled with gratitude as he chanted the very same selection from the Qayyúmu'l-Asmá' that he had chanted a year earlier for the Guardian's approval.[5]

The readings from the holy texts, the first of the endless paeans that are to echo in that sacred spot, moved me deeply. But I was carried to new heights by the electrifying message of the beloved Guardian that was conveyed by Rúhíyyih Khánum. Mr. Samandarí concluded the readings with a Persian chant, and the majestic presentation ended with singing from the choir. But the crowning blessing of this historic event was to come the following day, 3 May.

The most exciting moment, the unforgettable event that we all awaited breathlessly was the unveiling of the portraits of the Báb and Bahá'u'lláh. It was an opportunity to delight in what may have been the blessing of a lifetime. One by one, each Bahá'í began a personal spiritual journey. Every precious detail had been carefully and lovingly planned. Rúhíyyih Khánum personally anointed each of us with attar of roses. We proceeded quietly, in single file, toward the tables where the two portraits rested.

Some glanced at the portraits quickly and moved on, while others, reluctant to leave, lingered to prolong the precious moment. Some knelt reverently; others wept.

The Hands of the Cause of God, particularly Rúhíyyih Khánum,

---

*The Abhá Kingdom, meaning literally "the Most Glorious Kingdom," is the spiritual world beyond this world.

[5]The Qayyúmu'l-Asmá' is the Báb's commentary on the Súrih of Joseph.

*The Hand of the Cause of God
ZIKRULLAH KHADEM
at the dedication of the Mother Temple of the West,
Wilmette, Illinois, 1953. He chanted from the
writings of the Báb, fulfilling a promise the
Guardian had made sixteen years earlier.*

were the guiding lights and precious gems among us. Mr. Khadem was highly excited throughout the program. His gratitude, his reverence, his demeanor, and especially his love and appreciation for his fellow Hands of the Cause were a great lesson to me. His reverence for and deference to Amatu'l-Bahá, the wife of the Guardian, was very moving. This sacred occasion is etched in my memory, for it taught me what reverence is all about.

INTERCONTINENTAL CONFERENCES

After the dedication of the House of Worship in Wilmette, we attended the All-American Bahá'í Intercontinental Teaching Conference in Chicago, 3–6 May 1953. Four such conferences were held around the world to consult about the goals of the Ten Year International Teaching and Consolidation Plan, or Ten Year Crusade, a plan the Guardian called the ninth part of "the majestic process, set in motion at the dawn of the Adamic cycle."[2] The Hand of the Cause of God Amatu'l-Bahá Rúhíyyih Khánum opened the Chicago conference as Shoghi Effendi's representative while the audience sat spellbound with emotion. Eyes were full of tears, and hearts were overflowing with love and longing to please the beloved Guardian. The goals he had set were bold and audacious, for implicit in them was the promise that the Cause of God would, in fact, encompass the planet.

The Guardian's message energized the audience. In it he summarized the glorious achievements of the first Bahá'í century and outlined the awesome goals to be achieved in the next decade. In 10 years the Bahá'ís were to spread throughout the world and double the accomplishments of the past 110 years! In his beautiful, majestic prose the Guardian addressed us:

> Let there be no mistake. The avowed, the primary aim of this Spiritual Crusade is none other than the conquest of the citadels of men's hearts. The theater of its operations is the entire planet. Its duration a whole decade. . . . Its driving force is the energizing influence generated by the Revelation heralded by the Báb and proclaimed by Bahá'u'lláh. Its Marshal is none other than the Author of the Divine Plan. Its standard-bearers are the Hands of the Cause of God appointed in every continent of the globe. Its generals are the twelve national spiritual assemblies participating in the execution of its design. Its vanguard is the chief executors of 'Abdu'l-Bahá's master plan, their allies and associates. Its legions are the rank and file of believers standing behind these same twelve national assemblies and sharing in the global task embracing the American, the European, the African, the Asiatic and Australian fronts. The charter directing its course is the immortal Tablets that have flowed from the pen of the Center of the Covenant Himself. The armor with

which its onrushing hosts have been invested is the glad tidings of God's own message in this day, the principles underlying the order proclaimed by His Messenger, and the laws and ordinances governing His Dispensation. The battle cry animating its heroes and heroines is the cry of Yá Bahá'u'l-Abhá, Yá 'Alíyu'l-A'lá.[3]

ELLA BAILEY

When Shoghi Effendi's divine vision, the Ten Year World Crusade, was first unveiled to the Bahá'ís from all over the world in October 1952, when they were given a glimpse of the priceless and unique opportunity to participate in the establishment of the Kingdom of God on earth, they could not hesitate. Many responded instantly and volunteered their services. Ella Bailey was among those pure souls who heard the call of the beloved Guardian and resolved to arise for service.[4] At the age of eighty-eight she vowed to go to Africa as a pioneer. She longed to serve and was determined to follow her heart's desire, regardless of the obstacles. Though she was quite ill and was eventually confined to bed in New York City at the home of Dr. Fazly Melany, she would not change her mind. Nothing could shake her iron resolve.

When Mr. Khadem heard about this very ill and elderly woman who was planning to pioneer to Africa, he wanted to meet her. Hence we went to Dr. Melany's. Because of Ella's serious condition, there were strict orders that no one could visit her, but an exception was made for Mr. Khadem, as he was a Hand of the Cause. When we reached her bedside, her eyes were closed. Mr. Khadem took her hand in his and tenderly asked her about her health.

"I will be all right," she said. "I just pray that God will give me enough time to reach Africa. Did you hear the comment that the old people can take their bones and bury them in the goal areas? This is my most cherished desire." Mr. Khadem was so moved by her noble deed, her exemplary spirit of detachment, her unflagging devotion, and her complete reliance on God that for the rest of his life he shared with others the inspiring story of her sacrifice.

Ella Bailey's heart's desire was fulfilled. Shortly after she arrived in Africa, she died and was buried there. The beloved Guardian cabled his tribute to her:

Irresistibly unfolding Crusade sanctified death heroic eighty-eight-year-old Ella Bailey elevating her rank martyrs Faith shedding further luster American Bahá'í Community consecrating soil fast awakening African Continent.[5]

Munír Vakíl

The Eastern Bahá'ís, as well as the Western ones, were inspired by the universal view of the Faith revealed at the intercontinental conferences in 1953. The Eastern Bahá'ís sought out the Persian Hands of the Cause for guidance and advice. Mr. Munír Vakíl, one of the Bahá'ís of Iraq, asked Mr. Khadem for counsel. Mr. Vakíl and Mr. Khadem knew each other well because of Mr. Khadem's repeated visits to Iraq on behalf of Shoghi Effendi. Munír Vakíl was a well-to-do, middle-aged man who was serving as a general in the Iraqi army. His heart was so moved by the call of the beloved Guardian that he was eager to leave his prestigious position and his material comforts to serve Bahá'u'lláh as a pioneer. He longed to open one of the virgin areas to the Faith. Mr. Khadem told him that all the places mentioned in the plan were goals, that all of them were close to Shoghi Effendi's heart.

"You can choose the place yourself," he advised.

"How can I choose the place if I don't know anything about any of these places?" asked Mr. Vakíl.

"All right, just close your eyes and put your finger randomly on the goals and see where you end up," suggested Mr. Khadem. Mr. Vakíl did this. His finger pointed to Kuria Muria, a rocky group of islands in the Arabian Sea.

"Where is that?" he wondered aloud.

"I don't know," Mr. Khadem responded.

"Don't worry. I will find it," replied this devoted lover of Bahá'u'lláh.

A few months later Mr. Khadem received a letter from Mr. Vakíl.

"I am searching the Indian Ocean but cannot find Kuria Muria. I won't give up until I find it!"

More time passed until another letter arrived.

"I've found it!" Mr. Vakíl wrote. "I am on an isolated and desolate island in the Indian Ocean with very few inhabitants.* There is no

---

*I believe he mentioned that the population was fifty-nine.

Knight of Bahá'u'lláh MUNÍR VAKÍL
in front of his small hut on one
of the Kuria Muria Islands in
the Arabian Sea, circa 1954.

sign of civilization here. There are no houses, huts, or facilities of any
sort. Our food is fish from the ocean. We catch the fish and bake
them on hot rocks in the sun."

After a few other comments about the appalling conditions of life
in Kuria Muria, he went on to describe the day an eggplant washed
ashore. He had been very excited about it because it gave him an
opportunity to cook a delicacy and share it with the people. They
were so amazed by his knowledge and experience that they asked
him, "If you are used to these delicacies, why did you come here?"

"I came because I love you," was his reply. Then he wrote about
how he was building a small hut for shelter and privacy because there
was no shelter from the rain anywhere on the island. In another letter
he said, "I've lost a lot of weight. I am not well, but I won't leave my
pioneering post."

The British government became very concerned when they heard a general of the Iraqi army was living in Kuria Muria, which was a British territory. When the British officials made a special trip to visit Munír and investigate his activities, it became a fortuitous opportunity for this devoted pioneer to proclaim the Faith to them. A picture showing Mr. Vakíl standing with his fellow islanders and the British authorities documents the event.

Mr. Vakíl's health continued to decline. When his condition became serious, Shoghi Effendi encouraged him to leave his pioneering post and go back to his home country. Mr. Khadem told me about his return to Iraq:

> I was in Baghdad on assignment for the Guardian when Munír arrived. He was frail, exhausted, and very ill. The friends asked him about his pioneering experiences at a meeting one night. Munír described his search for the island and the condition of life there. After he finished, one of the friends got up and said, "Munír did not know where he was going. Now I know where Kuria Muria is and what it's like. I am prepared to replace him. We cannot leave a pioneering post vacant."

What lovers of the Cause! Their consuming love now permits us to boast that "there are Bahá'ís everywhere." What sacrifice, what selflessness crowned those devoted Knights of Bahá'u'lláh.*

Spiritual Preparation

After the Intercontinental Teaching Conference in Chicago in May 1953, Mr. Khadem went to South America to visit the Bahá'ís while I went to spend some time with the Hand of the Cause of God Dorothy Baker in Lima, Ohio.[6] She lost no time in putting me to work. Though I was not fluent in English and was inexperienced at public speaking, she scheduled talks for me every night in public meetings in the Lima and Cleveland areas. Every afternoon Mrs.

---

*The Bahá'ís who were the first to settle and open a virgin territory to the Bahá'í Faith during the Ten Year World Crusade were named "Knights of Bahá'u'lláh." Most of the names appear in a "Roll of Honor" included in cables from Shoghi Effendi. Two such cables appear in Shoghi Effendi, *Messages to the Bahá'í World*, 50–53, 57–58. See also *The Bahá'í World: An International Record, Volume XIII, 1954–1963*, comp. the Universal House of Justice (Haifa: The Universal House of Justice, 1970), 449–571.

Baker assigned one of the Bahá'ís to pick me up, take me to my speaking engagement, and return me to the home of the Bakers afterward. My reticence did not discourage her in the least. How could I refuse a Hand of the Cause? I learned so much from her. I learned that the key to accomplishing any goal is taking the first step and relying on God's assistance. I witnessed a deeply moving example of love in her devotion, her reverence, her unusual intensity in prayer, and her absolute obedience to the beloved Guardian's wishes.

After I had been in Lima for two weeks, Mrs. Baker had to attend a meeting of the National Spiritual Assembly in Chicago. I drove with her in order to visit my brother. On that trip I asked her how she was able to concentrate consistently on the long obligatory prayer and prevent her mind from wandering.

"You must wait until you are feeling ready and spiritual before you say the obligatory prayer. Every morning I say many prayers before my obligatory prayer so that my mind is freed from everyday concerns, and I can concentrate."

Her reverent preparation for the obligatory prayer touched my heart. In the short time I had with her, I grew to love and respect her deeply. I recognized those special qualities in her that Mr. Khadem had always praised. He identified with her profound love for Shoghi Effendi and her eagerness to obey him.

One evidence of her obedience was her decision to pioneer. She told me on that trip that she was planning to resign from the National Spiritual Assembly of the Bahá'ís of the United States and pioneer for the Ten Year Crusade. I was shocked when I heard this.*

I thought to myself, she is a member of the National Spiritual Assembly of the United States. She is serving on such an august body. She is already promoting the progress of the Cause in such a responsible capacity. She should continue and not forfeit this special opportunity.

She looked deeply into my eyes, recognizing my confusion, and said, "Didn't the beloved Guardian call for pioneers to open the

---

*Four other members of the National Spiritual Assembly of the Bahá'ís of the United States resigned from their positions in 1953 in order to go pioneering: Elsie Austin, Matthew Bullock, Mamie Seto, and Dr. William Kenneth Christian.

virgin territories? How can we deprive ourselves? I have consulted with my husband. We have agreed to leave the United States and go pioneering to the West Indies. We have to be obedient to our beloved Guardian. Who knows what awaits us. We may be much more useful there, anyway."

The Hand of the Cause of God Dorothy Baker, that moving example of spirituality and obedience, never made it to the island of Grenada, which she had chosen as her pioneering post. She died when the airplane that was taking her from Karachi to London via Beirut and Rome went down in the Mediterranean Sea near the island of Elba on 10 January 1954. However, her illustrious husband, Frank Baker, carried out her heart's desire and went to Grenada, where he was instrumental in teaching many people the Faith. Because the first draft of this book was written in Grenada, I am especially moved by his example. The spirit of the Bakers is still very much alive there. Many of the Bahá'ís of Grenada recognized Bahá'u'lláh through his teaching efforts and remember him fondly. The Baker home, cared for by a radiant Bahá'í couple, is still a center for teaching and deepening.

India

In addition to his travels in Africa and the Western world, Mr. Khadem also traveled extensively throughout the East. He made several trips to India at the behest of Shoghi Effendi. One that began on 30 October 1953 took him to Delhi, Akra, Bombay, Poona, Panchgani, and Calcutta on the way to Bangkok and Tokyo. On 19 December 1954 he was to visit Delhi and Bombay again.

In a letter dated 9 September 1954 on behalf of the Guardian, the Persian Hands of the Cause of God had been asked to send a delegate to India to consult with the National Spiritual Assembly of the Bahá'ís of India, Pakistan, and Burma and urge it in person to take prompt action to purchase the site for the House of Worship that was to be built in India. This they were to do in order to accomplish the objectives given to that National Spiritual Assembly as its share of the Ten Year Plan.

On 10 October news arrived that Mr. Ardashír Rustampúr, one of the Bahá'ís of Hyderabad, had contributed one thousand rupees toward the purchase of the land for the House of Worship in New Delhi. Though this accomplished the Guardian's wish that a Temple site be purchased, his wish for a Persian Hand to go to India remained unfulfilled. Mr. Khadem eagerly volunteered, preparing for a 12 December departure. He cabled the Guardian for approval, saying he was ready to visit Delhi and Baghdad during the Indian National Spiritual Assembly's next session, on 27 December.* The Guardian replied: "Highly approve urge both Assemblies energetically prosecute tasks particularly purchase Ḥaẓíras Colombo Djakarta Rangoon identification sacred graves Najaf Karbilá fervent prayers surrounding you."[7] My husband left on 19 December with a one-week stopover in Karachi, where he met with the Bahá'ís. On 23 December, with several of the Karachi Bahá'ís, he took a side-trip to Hyderabad by train. There he met the devoted Mr. Rustampúr, whose name will be forever linked with the House of Worship in India.

On 27 December Mr. Khadem met with the Indian National Spiritual Assembly and encouraged them to work energetically on their assigned goals. The National Assembly immediately cabled the Guardian, assuring him that the Ten Year Crusade objectives that had been given to India—which included purchasing Bahá'í centers in Djakarta and Colombo and beginning construction of the Rangoon Bahá'í center—would be aggressively pursued. That entire trip to India was devoted to encouraging and inspiring communities to arise in service and make the sacrifices necessary for meeting the objectives of the Plan.

On 30 December Mr. Khadem visited the temple site in Bahapur with members of the Indian National Spiritual Assembly. Heartfelt, grateful prayers were said, for the acquisition of the temple site was a joyous, significant victory, and much of the funds needed to purchase the various Bahá'í centers had already been donated.[5]

---

*Mr. Khadem had been assigned by the Guardian to assist the National Spiritual Assembly of the Bahá'ís of Iraq in locating the grave of the father of Bahá'u'lláh, which was one of the objectives of the Ten Year Crusade. He made several trips to Iraq for this purpose.

[5]In 1986 the National Spiritual Assembly of the Bahá'ís of India asked Mr. Khadem to participate in the dedication of the Indian House of Worship. However,

The Hand of the Cause of God Zikrullah Khadem (center),
members of the National Spiritual Assembly of the Bahá'ís of India,
and other friends offering prayers at the newly purchased site of the
Indian Ma<u>sh</u>riqu'l-A<u>dh</u>kár of Bahapur in New Delhi, India,
30 December 1954.

As Mr. Khadem was preparing to leave Delhi on 9 January, a
precious gift—a cable from the beloved Guardian—arrived: "Deeply
appreciate services urge friends . . . concentrate objectives Plan assure loving prayers."[8] Periodic infusions of love and appreciation
such as this sustained and encouraged my husband.

JAPAN

Ten months later Mr. Khadem went to Japan as the Guardian's
representative. The United States Asia Teaching Committee and the
Tokyo Spiritual Assembly had organized an Asia Teaching Conference for 23–25 September 1955 in Nikko, Japan. This conference, it
was hoped, would lead to an increase in the number of local spiritual
assemblies and provide the foundation for the formation in 1957 of

---

his death on 13 November 1986 prevented his seeing the completion of his earlier
labors. My children and I recorded some of the thoughts he wished to convey on the
occasion, and I presented them in a talk given on his behalf at the dedication.

the National Spiritual Assembly of North East Asia. The Conference was held in a lovely building belonging to the Emperor of Japan. It was located atop a hill and had a magnificent view. Representatives had come from many countries: the Caroline Islands, Guam, the Marianas, Hong Kong, Korea, Formosa (now Taiwan), the United States (represented by Charlotte Linfoot, a member of the National Spiritual Assembly of the United States and secretary of the United States Asia Teaching Committee), and Macao. It was especially moving to meet Mr. Harry Yim, a Bahá'í from Macao who brought such great joy and enthusiasm to the conference. Indeed, all the participants were so moved by the Guardian's love and vision and so enthusiastic that at Riḍván 1956 six new local spiritual assemblies were formed in Japan and at Riḍván 1957 the National Spiritual Assembly of the Bahá'ís of North East Asia was elected.

It is one thing to accept the concept of the unity of mankind, but it is an entirely different and spiritually overwhelming discovery to experience it firsthand. Nearly every Bahá'í conference Mr. Khadem and I attended testified to this fundamental spiritual principle, but the Asia Teaching Conference, at which I felt so foreign at first, became, in the course of three days, like a gathering of friends at home. The love, the spirit, and the warmth of that gathering bespoke a unity that knows no boundaries of nation, race, or culture. The Oriental Bahá'ís were our precious brothers and sisters. Those three days were so memorable that Mr. Khadem recalled them frequently and for many years maintained correspondence with pioneers in Japan.

After the conference in Nikko, Mr. Khadem and I toured Japan, Taiwan, Macao, Hong Kong, Thailand, Burma, Singapore, the Philippines, and Vietnam for three months. Of all the cities we stopped in, and of all the trips we made in the Far East, the most unforgettable place we visited was Hiroshima. To get there, we traveled by train, which was a remarkable experience itself. There probably were no trains in the world that equaled those of the Japanese for cleanliness, beauty, and courteous service. Each row of seats was ornamented with hanging, fragrant flowers. Each seat was adorned with magnificently embroidered white, starched linen. The beautiful and immaculately coiffed hostesses, who wore fresh, white, embroidered aprons, served the passengers with an exemplary sweetness and courtesy. We were joined in Kyoto on this luxurious trip by

*Participants in the 1955 Asia Teaching Conference in
Nikko, Japan, a conference that Mr. Khadem found particularly memorable.
Charlotte Linfoot (top right), member of the National Spiritual
Assembly of the Bahá'ís of the United States and secretary of
the U.S. Asia Teaching Committee, was representing
the United States at the conference. Mr. Khadem is in
the front row, left; Mrs. Khadem, in the back row, left.*

the Hand of the Cause of God Agnes Alexander, who was then a
pioneer in Japan.* Traveling with her was a great honor for me, one
that I will always cherish.

When we arrived in Hiroshima on 10 October we learned that
there was an English class at the local Y.M.C.A. conducted by a Dr.
Robinson. At these classes each participant had to give a five-minute
talk in English. As this seemed to be an ideal opportunity for

---

*Agnes Baldwin Alexander (1875–1971) was appointed by Shoghi Effendi a
Hand of the Cause of God on 27 March 1957. She spent thirty-two years pioneering
for the Bahá'í Faith in Japan.

The Bahá'ís of Taiwan, 12 November 1955, during Mr. Khadem's
three-month tour of the Far East. Mr. Khadem is in the top row,
third from the right; Mrs. Khadem is in the second row,
third from the left.

meeting some Japanese people without having to struggle with the
language barrier, we agreed to attend this event. There were four of
us—Mr. Khadem; Agnes Alexander; Mr. Momtazi, a pioneer in
Japan; and myself—which meant that, between us, we had a full
twenty minutes to talk. We decided the time would be put to best
use if we gave it all to Mr. Khadem so that he could talk about the
Faith. After all, what could be more appropriate than delivering the
message of peace and brotherhood brought by Bahá'u'lláh? While
Mr. Khadem spoke with confidence, courage, and conviction, the
rest of us prayed that there would be hearing ears for this message.

As Mr. Khadem concluded his remarks, a young man, Mr.
Michitara Honkawa, a resident of Hiroshima, stepped forward. He
was a student at Hiroshima University, majoring in chemistry and
English. During his five-minute speech, he continued the discussion
Mr. Khadem had started, emphasizing the desperate need for a new
revelation to give us guidance at this time in our history. These
remarks, coming from a native of Hiroshima, added greatly to the

The Bahá'ís of Macao, 17 November 1955,
during Mr. Khadem's three-month tour of the Far East. Harry Yim,
who brought such enthusiasm to the Asia Teaching Conference,
is seated in the front row, center. Mr. Khadem is in
the top row, second from the right.

impact of Mr. Khadem's message. After Mr. Honkawa spoke, many asked for reading material on the Bahá'í Faith.

Mr. Honkawa and Mr. Shoji were the first two native Bahá'ís of Hiroshima. They joined us the next day (11 October) for lunch and accompanied us on a visit to the site of the atomic explosion and the peace memorial. Over a period of five days spanning two brief visits to Hiroshima (10, 11, and 21 through 23 October), Mr. Shoji and Mr. Honkawa were Mr. Khadem's companions and spent many hours discussing with him the significance of the Bahá'í revelation both for Japan and for world peace. They were especially interested in the Bahá'í fulfillment of Buddhist prophecy about the coming of Amitabha. Strong bonds of friendship and unity were created during these two visits to Hiroshima. On 23 October Mr. Honkawa and Mr. Shoji came to our hotel to say good-bye. Their sentiments of love and devotion were deeply moving; they tearfully asked to be

remembered to the beloved Guardian. That same day Mr. Khadem
cabled the Guardian: ". . . Hiroshima opened to Faith two first
believers Honkawa Shoji beseech beloved's blessings confirmation. . . ." To this message the Guardian lovingly replied: "Assure
Honkawa Shoji loving prayers. . . ."[9]

Our experience in Hiroshima was different from that of most
other places we visited. We found there more than the usual number
of sincere seekers among the people we met. During each of our two
short visits to that city, we were engaged in teaching and giving the
message of Bahá'u'lláh from the moment we arrived until the moment we left.

The reason the people of Hiroshima—especially the young
people—were so keenly interested in the Bahá'í message was obvious. They had suffered greatly in World War II, and its horror was
still alive. We visited Old Hiroshima and its ghastly ruins created by
the atomic bomb. The old town, with the signs of devastation and
human suffering the colossal explosion had caused, had been preserved by the government, forever reminding the world of the
horrors of atomic warfare. In its stead a new Hiroshima, a beautiful
city with modern conveniences, wonders, and facilities, was built
next to the old one. It was impossible for me to visit Hiroshima and
be unmoved by the experience. The chilling contrast, one part of
town symbolizing and celebrating life and the miracles of human
achievement, the other, a perpetual reminder of death and man's
formidable capacity for destruction, left an indelible impression on
me. Undoubtedly, this acute contrast helped to maintain the local
people's awareness of the need for a solution to the world's problems.

Burma

After our three-month tour of Japan, Mr. Khadem and I visited
the Bahá'ís in Burma. When we arrived in Rangoon on 23 November 1955, the Bahá'ís of that city and of the surrounding areas
gathered at the Rangoon Bahá'í center to meet Mr. Khadem and to
hear him speak. In his talk he discussed many topics; in everything
that he said his devotion to the Guardian was evident. He emphasized the importance of translating our devotion to the Faith into
obedience to the Guardian and the Bahá'í Administrative Order.
The Bahá'ís were deeply moved by his words of love and encourage-

ment. Some were in tears. It was obvious that many were taking his words to heart and resolving to better prepare themselves for service.

The trip to Burma was special for two reasons: the exemplary dedication of the Bahá'ís of Burma and the numerous opportunities we were given to contact high officials and obtain favorable publicity for the Faith. On Thursday, 24 November, Mr. Khadem went to the embassies of Singapore, Ceylon, and Australia to obtain visas for visiting those countries. At each embassy he had an opportunity to speak of the Faith. He had an especially prolonged discussion of Bahá'í principles with the ambassador from Ceylon.

The highlight of our trip to Burma, however, was visiting the village of Daidanaw in the township of Kungyangoon, which was six hours away from Rangoon by boat. When we arrived in Daidanaw, we were enthusiastically welcomed as we were docking by about a hundred Bahá'ís who came to meet us, crying, *"Alláh-u-Abhá!* [God is Most Glorious!]."* Most had come by rickshaw, a sort of bicycle with a side-chair for carrying a passenger. This means of transportation was still customary at that time in many parts of the Far East. Mr. Khadem climbed into one such passenger seat while I got into another, and we rode to the Bahá'í center of Daidanaw. We saw there a beautiful sign over the entrance that said "Bahá'í World Religion."

Across the street from the Bahá'í center was the grave of Siyyid Muṣṭafá Rúmí, who had been murdered in Daidanaw during World War II. The Bahá'ís told us that the Faith had been brought to this village by Siyyid Muṣṭafá, who had learned of the Faith from Jamál Effendí in Madras, India, when he was a young man.⁵ Siyyid Muṣṭafá was so elated to have discovered this truth and so enamored with the Bahá'í revelation that he accompanied Jamál Effendí and traveled with him throughout India and Burma to help spread the message. He never could be still after becoming a Bahá'í. He served the Faith with great audacity and total dedication. When he was older, he was invited by the head of the village of Daidanaw (who had had positive interactions with the Bahá'ís) to teach the Faith to

---

* *"Alláh-u-Abhá"* is a form of the Greatest Name that was adopted as a greeting among Bahá'ís during the period of Bahá'u'lláh's exile in Adrianople.

⁵Jamál Effendí (also known as Sulaymán Khán Ilyás) was the first Bahá'í pioneer sent to India, circa 1872–73, by Bahá'u'lláh.

all of the villagers. Siyyid Muṣṭafá not only taught the people of Daidanaw about the Baháʼí Faith; he also made Daidanaw his home and served the Cause there for the rest of his life. He translated many of the Baháʼí writings into Burmese, and, in 1899, helped to transfer to the Holy Land the marble casket that was to hold the remains of the blessed Báb. We are told, also, that "He was received by ʻAbduʼl-Bahá most graciously and was the recipient of special favours."[10]

During World War II, a period of great nationalistic fervor and hostility toward foreigners, a mob of three thousand people surrounded the village to purge it of all foreign influence. Discovering that Siyyid Muṣṭafá was not from Burma, the mob burned his home, beheaded him, and chopped his body to pieces. Earlier, the Baháʼís had tried to help him escape from the village, but he had told them, "I am old. I will not leave the place that I chose to serve." The Baháʼís later gathered the pieces of his body and buried him in front of the Baháʼí center. Beautiful flowers now frame his grave.[11] He was posthumously named a Hand of the Cause of God by the beloved Guardian, who greatly praised him and his noble services.[12]

After some of the Baháʼís told us the moving and tragic story of Siyyid Muṣṭafá, they wanted to cheer us up. They asked us to visit the others in the village, the majority of whom were Baháʼís. They told us that the Baháʼí Faith had such a wonderful reputation in Daidanaw that even the non-Baháʼís referred their problems to its spiritual assembly. We truly enjoyed our visit to this lovely Baháʼí village and had the good fortune to commemorate the Ascension of ʻAbduʼl-Bahá with the villagers while we were there.

Tonga

During his travels in the early part of the Ten Year World Crusade, Mr. Khadem met Mr. Dudley Blakely, who was longing for any news of the Guardian and was most eager to please him. Mr. Khadem encouraged Mr. Blakely, saying, "If you wish to cheer the heart of the Guardian, pioneering is 'the prince of all goodly deeds.' "[13]

Taking this advice to heart, Mr. Blakely decided to pioneer to Tonga. Like so many pioneers who had been ignited by the leadership and vision of the Guardian, he sacrificed his lifelong career and, mindless of the consequences, set out to enter and stay in his chosen post. He could not find employment in his regular field in Tonga.

Undeterred, he searched for any possible means of entering Tonga and discovered that the government wanted to grow tea because it was in great demand and would benefit the island economy. Mr. Blakely suggested to the Tongan government that his friend, Mr. Khadem, could arrange for them to receive tea seeds. Mr. Khadem, always eager to aid a pioneer, immediately contacted Mr. 'Alízádeh Rástání in Láhíján, Iran, a town known for its fine tea. Thus on the basis of helping the Ministry of Agriculture, Mr. Blakely was able to enter Tonga in order to serve as the Officer in Charge of Agriculture. He was to supervise personally the planting and care of the tea.

In our household there was always a lot of talk about pioneers and pioneering, so I had already heard quite a bit about Mr. Blakely and his situation. However, I was unaware that tea seeds would be sent to him through us; hence I was not expecting them. I also did not know what tea seeds look like. One day a large package arrived at our home in Tehran. It contained an unusual sort of nut that I had never seen before. They resembled beautiful almonds. I took one and tried to bite open the shell, but after several unsuccessful attempts, I had to give up. I decided to wait for Mr. Khadem to come home; surely he would be able to crack one open.

To my surprise, when Mr. Khadem heard my story, he laughed. He explained to me that these were not choice almonds but tea-plant seeds destined for Dudley Blakely in Tonga. Although I am not certain, I believe that none of that tea survived, probably because of climate differences between Iran and Tonga. However, Mr. Blakely's pioneering efforts did help to establish the Faith in Tonga. The tea plants may not have lived, but the Cause of God is thriving there with a National Spiritual Assembly and a multitude of adherents to the Cause of Bahá'u'lláh.

BOUNTIFUL BLESSINGS FROM THE THRESHOLD OF THE BELOVED

Throughout his period of service to the Guardian, Mr. Khadem was showered with appreciation from the pen of Shoghi Effendi. More than a decade after the Guardian's passing, Mr. Khadem's heart was touched when the Universal House of Justice shared with him several passages from letters written on behalf of the Guardian, which they had recently found:

16 January, 1970

Hand of the Cause of God
Dhikru'lláh Khádem

Beloved Friend,

In the course of our research in the writings of the beloved Guardian, we have come across two letters written on his behalf which make reference to your visits in different parts of the world, and to the deep love and appreciation of the Guardian towards you and Mrs. Khádem.

We quote herewith pertinent quotations from these letters, in case you have not seen them previously:

"The Guardian has received many messages such as yours, telling of the happiness and the spirit of rededication brought to the friends in different lands by the visit of the dear Khadems; and of the deep feeling of nearness to the Spiritual Center of their Faith, which Mr. Khadem, in his zeal and his longing to make happy the heart of the Guardian, gave them. These devoted Bahá'ís are indeed rendering the Faith a most great and far-reaching service in their travels." (To the Bahá'ís of Copenhagen, c/o Miss Britta Poulsen, October 19, 1952).

"The honored Hand of the Cause of God, Zikrullah Khadem, is very dear to the heart of the beloved Guardian; and from every city or town he visited messages of deep gratitude are received from the believers for the spiritual joy and the greater sense of nearness to the Guardian which he imparts." (To Mrs. Louise Caswell, September 26, 1953).

We feel sure that these loving sentiments of the beloved Guardian will bring a wave of joy to your heart, and we share in this joy.

Please convey to Mrs. Khádem our warmest greetings, and be both assured of our fervent prayers at the Holy Shrines on your behalf, and on behalf of your dear family.

With loving Bahá'í greetings,
The Universal House of Justice

Mr. Khadem's response to this letter was one of humble gratitude. In a letter of thanks to the Universal House of Justice, he said that he felt unworthy of receiving such bountiful blessings. As always, he attributed this precious treasure to the "all glorious, all gracious, all generous and kind" Shoghi Effendi.[14]

7 The Impact of the Passing of the Guardian

The community of Bahá, whether in the East of the world or the West, are lamenting like orphans left destitute; fevered, tormented, unquiet, they are voicing their grief. Out of the depths of their sorrowing hearts, there rises to the Abhá Horizon this continual piercing cry: "Where art thou gone, O torch of tender love? Where art thou gone, O source of grace and mercy? Where art thou gone, O symbol of bounty and generosity? Where art thou gone, O day-spring of detachment in this world of being? Where art thou gone, O trust left by Bahá among His people, O remnant left by Him among His servants, O sweet scent of His garment, shed across all created things!"

—SHOGHI EFFENDI*

DEVASTATING DREAM

In 1957 we were traveling in the United States, Canada, and Europe on a mission of protection at the instruction of the Guardian. On 21 September, while in Geneva, Switzerland, Mr. Khadem received a cable of instructions from Shoghi Effendi that began, "Heartfelt appreciation historic services advise visit Scandinavian

---

*The passage is from a letter dated 3 Kalimát 89 (15 July 1932 A.D.) to the Bahá'ís of the East in which Shoghi Effendi laments the passing of Bahíyyih Khánum, the Greatest Holy Leaf. See Shoghi Effendi, in Bahá'u'lláh, 'Abdu'l-Bahá, Shoghi Effendi, and Bahíyyih Khánum, *Bahíyyih Khánum: The Greatest Holy Leaf,* comp. Research Department at the Bahá'í World Centre (Haifa: Bahá'í World Centre, 1982), 24–25.

Benelux friends on way Persia visit also Beirut. . . ." This proved to be his last communication from the beloved Guardian. After visiting the various countries, he was to attend the Benelux Conference in late October as well as the dedication of the Bahá'í center in Luxembourg on 3 November, before returning via Beirut to Iran.

One morning after receiving the cable, Mr. Khadem awoke from a very disturbing dream. He had dreamed that the Greatest Name fell to the floor and that he was participating in a great funeral.* In the dream he felt quite sick and was completely helpless with grief. That morning he remained agitated and distraught.

"What a dream! What a devastating dream!" he kept repeating as he paced the room.

Trying to calm him, I said, "Well, a dream is a dream. Not all dreams are true."

"This is a true dream," he insisted. "Some great personality in the Bahá'í world has passed away."

"Well, let's see," I said, trying to allay his fears. "Who is a prominent personality?"

"Maybe the Hand of the Cause of God Mr. Samandarí," he suggested.

"Well, yes, he *is* a very prominent personality. But he has had such a magnificent life, and he is quite old. Certainly it would be a loss to the Bahá'í world, but we must accept that he will soon pass away."

"You're right," he conceded.

"Why, then, are you so agitated?"

"I don't know why I am so upset. But I am! I can't help it."

"Maybe it's your mother," I said, trying to understand his anxiety. "Maybe it's your concern for her, as she is so close to your heart."

"Perhaps. But I can't get this out of my mind. It is so disturbing. What do I do now? How can I visit the Bahá'ís and talk to them in this terrible state of mind?" he lamented.

I volunteered to shorten my stay and go back to Iran to see his mother and verify her well-being. He accepted my offer in the hope

---

*The Greatest Name of God, according to Bahá'ís, is *"Bahá"* (glory). A calligraphic rendering of a derivative of *Bahá—Yá Bahá'u'l-Abhá* (O Thou the Glory of the Most Glorious)—can be found in many Bahá'í homes as a wall hanging.

that it would calm his distress. When I arrived in Tehran, I contacted Mr. Khadem's mother and was assured that she and everyone in the family were fine. I immediately cabled him and conveyed the news through Mr. Nounou.

Mr. Khadem proceeded as Shoghi Effendi had instructed and went to each place on his itinerary. But he had no relief from his anxiety. Every time he appeared on the platform to speak, he began to cry. He was not able to sleep at night. He would pace his room and cry. He told me that once the people in the neighboring rooms complained to the hotel manager and requested that his room be changed.

During the previous three decades of his life, with the exception of the day he learned of his appointment as a Hand of the Cause of God, I had rarely seen Mr. Khadem shed even a single tear. He had always been lighthearted and full of laughter and jokes. Whenever he would return from the office, the neighbors would always know he had arrived because of his laughter and the children's shrieks of joy as they were tossed to the ceiling. Yet, because of that dream, wherever he went he would begin to cry in the middle of his talks. The Bahá'ís were naturally very concerned and asked him what was troubling him. He did not have an answer.

Devastating News

After the dedication of the National Bahá'í Center in Luxembourg, Mr. Khadem left for Frankfurt, Germany, to buy a car. He had arranged to drive back to Iran with one of his friends. On 4 November he was walking to a factory to take delivery of the car when he encountered a Bahá'í who had heard the news of the beloved Guardian's passing. Mr. Khadem later described to me that initial devastating shock:

> This Bahá'í ran up to me very abruptly. Without any tact, wisdom, or compassion, he suddenly said, "Have you heard the news?"
> "What news?" I asked.
> "The Guardian passed away."
> O my God! I felt all my strength drain away. Everything was finished! I didn't bother with the car or anything. I felt life itself had ended.

Mr. Khadem mustered what strength he had left to reach the
Bahá'í Center for accurate news. There he met the Hand of the
Cause of God Abu'l-Qásim Faizí, who confirmed the devastating
truth. Mr. Khadem became physically ill. He could not eat. He
could not sleep. Mr. Faizí lovingly nursed him. Mr. Khadem remained incapacitated during the journey to London for the funeral
and seemed so ill that his colleagues felt he would be unable to
attend the funeral, which was to be held on 9 November. This
experience exactly duplicated the illness and grief he had experienced
in his dream.

Afterward, those who attended the funeral told me about his
illness and his altered appearance. He was so ill that he could not eat.
He could not even move from his hotel bed. In desperation one of
his dear friends, told him, "All right, if you won't eat, you cannot
attend the services! Yes, you are a Hand of the Cause. However, if
you don't eat, we will hold your arms and legs, force your mouth
open, and pour chicken broth down your throat!" This stern yet
loving approach encouraged him to take a little sustenance.

At the Great Northern London Cemetery where the beloved
Guardian was to be buried, Mr. Khadem walked as if he were totally
drained and empty of life, for he had lost his mentor, his guide, his
heart's desire, and the source of his joy. He was barely able to
accomplish his wish of paying homage to his beloved.

Despair

In Iran, when I learned of the passing of Shoghi Effendi, I, too,
was stunned and heartbroken. The entire Bahá'í world had been or-
phaned. It seemed as though the light had gone out of our lives. Who
was there to take our hand and spur us on? I shuddered to think of
the absolute, utter devastation my husband must be experiencing. I
worried that he would not be able to endure and survive the loss. To
add to my great anxiety, I received no word at all about his condition.

For a long time I had no news. Then one day there was a knock at
the door of our house in Tehran. I opened the door and saw a man
with a severe, expressionless face, standing immovable, like a statue,
with all the weight of the world on his shoulders. This was my

husband. I could hardly recognize him. He was the picture of despair. Words cannot convey what a difficult time this was for us.

TAKE OFF YOUR MOURNING COAT

When I was trying to write about the passing of Shoghi Effendi, I was at a loss, for I had no idea how to convey the intensity of Mr. Khadem's feelings. Suddenly, amidst his voluminous papers, letters, historic documents, notes, extracts, and files, I discovered his own words concerning the passing of the beloved Guardian. The following extract from Mr. Khadem's papers, though brief, conveys the tender, intimate feelings he experienced as his heart burned with love for his departed beloved, and it explains how he was finally able to get through this, the greatest crisis of his life:

The passing of the beloved Guardian, Shoghi Effendi, grieved the hearts of the Bahá'ís in a manner that defies explanation. How many nights his faithful ones did not sleep because of their separation from their beloved. How many days they did not have any desire to continue to live in this world.

The first gathering of the Hands of the Cause after the passing of the beloved Shoghi Effendi was held in the Mansion of Bahá'u'lláh at Bahjí. All were seated around a table at the head of which a chair was left empty in respect for the beloved departed one. Tears poured over their faces at intervals, causing one of the Hands of the Cause to observe that they "would blind our eyes." We supplicated to the Blessed Beauty [Bahá'u'-lláh] that He would help us to find our way and that we would arise to show our loyalty and devotion and to serve the Cause befittingly, according to our capacities.

For an entire year I was in a state of extreme agony and many times repeated to myself a poem of Nabíl-i-Zarandí alluding to a passage in the Qur'án: "Those Egyptians, they saw a youth (Joseph) and cut their palms. Thou who had seen such a king hath not sacrificed thyself for him."[1]

After a year a breeze of consolation wafted over me in a dream. In the dream, while dressed in mourning clothes, including a thick topcoat, I arrived, perspiring, in the presence of the beloved Guardian. He ordered me to be seated. When I prepared to sit down, he motioned to me to take

The resting-place of Shoghi Effendi,
the Guardian of the Cause of God,
in London's Great Northern Cemetery.
Mr. Khadem is paying homage to the one
whose passing in 1957 left him devastated.

off the topcoat. In order to follow his commandment and out of reverence to him I took my arms out of the sleeves, as was the custom of the early believers, but left the coat over my shoulders. The beloved Shoghi Effendi with a penetrating glance and a heavenly smile and in the utmost kindness said, "You will be hot and uncomfortable; take off the coat."

The next day my mood changed, and a little serenity came to my heart. Nevertheless, the burning fire of separation was still alive. How appropriately Na'ím has written:

The fire of love in my heart for my beloved,
Lacking control, frequently bursts into flame.

Once it is there, it returns with sighs,
Year after year moaning, month after month sobbing,

Laughing aloud in the morning like the Caucasian partridge
Sobbing at night like the dawn bird,

In agony and separation from my beloved.
So great and noble is his face, so eloquent his speech.

Penetrating, uplifting are his words,
So delicate his features, so powerful his arms.

His station is exalted; his threshold is lofty.[2]

8 Later Service

*O Bahá'u'lláh! What hast Thou done? O Bahá'u'lláh! May my life be
sacrificed for Thee! O Bahá'u'lláh! May my soul be offered up for
Thy sake! How full were Thy days with trials and tribulations! How
severe the ordeals Thou didst endure! How solid the foundation Thou
hast finally laid, and how glorious the banner Thou didst hoist!*

—'ABDU'L-BAHÁ

A NEW BEGINNING

After the passing of the beloved Guardian in 1957, the Hands of
the Cause of God assembled and consulted on the consolidation of
the Bahá'í communities around the world. Though grief stricken
and leaderless, weathering grave difficulties, they maintained the
unity of the Faith by strict adherence to Shoghi Effendi's divinely
conceived plan—the Ten Year International Bahá'í Teaching and
Consolidation Plan. Through that document they received the
Guardian's infallible spiritual guidance.[1] Later, after the completion
of the Ten Year Crusade and the election of the Universal House of
Justice in 1963, they would continue their functions under the
guidance of this new institution. But in the intervening five years,
the Hands of the Cause all worked feverishly to fulfill the Guardian's
visionary goals. They were his "standard-bearers" of the planetary
"Spiritual Crusade."[2]

THE LIGHT THAT CANNOT BE CONCEALED

Returning to Iran after a tour of Europe in 1958, Mr. Khadem
and I stopped in Zagreb, Yugoslavia. On our arrival we discovered
there were no hotel accommodations available. In order to find
lodging, we had to refer to the police, as did every visitor upon arrival

The Hands of the Cause of God and the Universal House of Justice assembled in front of the Mansion at Bahjí, near the Shrine of Bahá'u'lláh. After the completion of the Ten Year World Crusade (1953–1963) and the election of the Universal House of Justice in 1963, the Hands of the Cause of God continued their functions under the guidance of this new institution.

in Yugoslavia. The police sent us to room in one of the homes of the city. The owner, a refined and charming woman, was a professor at the university. She was very kind and did her best to make us comfortable. As she had no shower or bathtub, she would warm water for our baths in a big barrel with great apology about the inconvenience.

In Zagreb we visited many churches and discovered that the people were quite religious and had a great spiritual yearning. However, the government discouraged religious pursuits. There was almost no organized activity in the churches, but the people were there, sitting silently, praying in their hearts. Their faces were solemn and dignified. They would light candles, murmur prayers, and drop coins into a collection box as they filed out of the church. Despite the silence and lack of ceremony, nobody could dissuade them from remembering their God. I was very moved by such scenes. It demonstrated that people, no matter where they are or what their condition in life, hunger for spirituality.

The woman from whom we rented our room demonstrated the same spiritual receptivity. On our day of departure I went into her kitchen to thank her for her many acts of kindness, as she had truly done her very best to accommodate us in every way during the two days we were her guests. She was very gracious and expressed pleasure in having us stay with her.

"Where are you heading?" she wanted to know.

"We are Persians. We are going back home," I said.

"Are you Muslims?"

"No, we are Bahá'ís."

"What is a Bahá'í?"

Our conversation was very cumbersome because of a language barrier. Since she spoke German and a little French in addition to her native language, and I spoke French, we conversed in French, though with great difficulty. She was able to understand that the Bahá'í Faith is a new revelation that fulfills the prophecies of all the past religions. She was very interested.

"Is it possible for you to show me these prophecies in the Bible?" she asked in a hushed and secretive manner, wary of being discovered. She quickly closed the windows and drew the curtains so that no one could see the exchange or eavesdrop on the conversation. She then brought into the kitchen a ladder that she climbed in order to reach the top shelf of a small closet. From the back of this closet she produced her Bible.

"I have been expecting this," she said excitedly. "I have always prayed that I may know the fulfillment of Jesus' promise."

I ran to get Mr. Khadem, who was preparing the car for our journey. I called out in Persian, "Hurry, this lady wants to see the prophecies about Bahá'u'lláh in the Bible!" I had never seen a seeker so anxious to know about the Faith. She had many questions and was thirsting for knowledge. She spoke in French with my husband for several hours. When we left, we had established a very precious bond.

Later we received from her a letter in German telling us in veiled language that her colleague at the university was very interested in the subject about which we had talked and asking if we could send her a book in German. She also invited us to visit her and her colleague and to be her guests again in Zagreb. Mr. Khadem forwarded the letter to the Holy Land. The Hand of the Cause of God Adelbert Mühlschlegel, who spoke German, was given the assignment of following up on her interest in the Faith.

Mr. Khadem remarked, "What testimony to the fact that nothing, no law, no prohibition, is capable of extinguishing this innate and burning desire in the heart of man to be reunited with his Creator and to know the truth. There are receptive souls everywhere."

Hand of the Cause of God for the Western Hemisphere

On 25 November 1957 the twenty-six Hands assembled in the Holy Land* and unanimously adopted a resolution "constituting a body of nine Hands to serve the interests of the Faith at its World Center, to prosecute from the Holy Land the provisions of the Guardian's World Crusade, and to discharge the primary responsibilities of the Hands in protecting and propagating the Faith of

---

*Corinne True was absent because of health problems and old age.

Bahá'u'lláh."[3] Thus nine Hands were to reside in the Holy Land while the others agreed to reside in different parts of the world in order to protect the interests of the Faith and stimulate its propagation worldwide.

At the 1959 Conclave of the Hands of the Cause of God the need for another Hand to reside in the Western Hemisphere was evident.* Mr. Khadem volunteered to move to the United States. He was to be responsible for the protection and propagation of the Bahá'í Faith in North, Central, and South America, as well as for the guidance and administration of the Auxiliary Board members.

To facilitate the move, he requested that the Hands find a way of acquiring immigration papers for him, our two youngest children, and Riaz, who was already in the United States on a student visa (the older two—Mozhan and Jena—were already studying in the United States), and me. Through voluminous correspondence between the National Spiritual Assembly of the Bahá'ís of the United States (on behalf of the Hands in the Holy Land) and the American authorities, green cards signifying permanent resident status were eventually granted to all of us. This was an important victory, because the American authorities accepted the Hands, collectively, as the "Chief Stewards," able to request such immigration concessions for their representative.[5] Furthermore, they recognized the special status of Hands as completely different from any other leadership in religious organizations.

We arrived in the United States in the summer of 1960, fulfilling the prediction the Guardian had made to Mr. Khadem in 1937 that

---

*Of the living Hands of the Cause of God appointed to serve in the Americas, only Corinne True still resided there. Leroy Ioas had moved to Haifa in 1952. Paul Haney and Horace Holley had moved to Haifa, in 1958 and 1959 respectively, to serve on the Body of the Hands of the Cause of God Residing in the Holy Land.

[5]Shoghi Effendi referred to the Hands of the Cause of God as "the Chief Stewards of Bahá'u'lláh's embryonic World Commonwealth, who have been invested by the unerring Pen of the Center of His Covenant ['Abdu'l-Bahá] with the dual function of guarding over the security, and of insuring the propagation, of His Father's Faith" (letter dated October 1957, *Messages to the Bahá'í World: 1950–1957,* rev. ed. [Wilmette, Ill.: Bahá'í Publishing Trust, 1971], 127).

he would send him to the West to witness the glorious victories of our beloved Faith.*

Mr. Khadem willingly accepted the difficulties of resolving our affairs in Iran, settling in a foreign culture, becoming more fluent in English, and beginning a new life in order to promote the work assigned to him. He served the friends and the National Spiritual Assemblies of the United States, Canada, Central America, and South America and the surrounding islands by himself for some time. Later the Hand of the Cause of God Ugo Giachery served in Central America, and the Hand of the Cause of God Jalál Kházeh moved to South America.

ELECTION OF THE UNIVERSAL HOUSE OF JUSTICE

In 1963 Royal Albert Hall in London witnessed the gathering of seven thousand Bahá'ís from all over the world, from every conceivable background, race, class, creed, and nation, celebrating not only the victorious completion of the Ten Year Crusade but also the centenary of Bahá'u'lláh's declaration of His mission and the first election of the Universal House of Justice.[5] What a victory! Our beloved Hands of the Cause of God, the Chief Stewards of this unique embryonic world order, were in the front row. They had had a weighty responsibility suddenly thrust upon them in 1957 after the passing of the beloved Guardian. They had discharged that responsibility with exemplary devotion, steadfastness, and zeal and had asked that the friends not elect them to that august body, thus allowing them to continue their labors under the direction of the Universal House of Justice. Their hearts were brimming with joy and gratitude as they hailed the first Universal House of Justice, which would lead the Bahá'í world.

The hearts of those thousands of participants were turned in

---

*See p. 55 and Mr. Khadem's last letter to the National Spiritual Assembly of the Bahá'ís of the United States on p. 150.

[5]The Centenary of the Declaration of Bahá'u'lláh, 28 April–2 May 1963, commemorated the declaration of His prophetic mission to His companions in the Garden of Riḍván in Baghdad, 22 April 1863.

thanksgiving to the beloved Shoghi Effendi who had led them to this victory. Mr. Khadem used to say that the dearest wish of the Guardian was the establishment of the Universal House of Justice. This crown of the Administrative Order was finally won; this fruit of his years of tireless labors was now ripe for the picking. The spirit of thanksgiving was palpable; tears, laughter, and uproarious cheers greeted that institution as the members were introduced on the platform. All seven thousand Bahá'ís rose in unison. It was a memorable scene when the nine members stood before us with great humility and selflessness, with audacity, determination, dignity, and joy. They communicated to the audience their love and supplicated for its prayers.

The first message of the Universal House of Justice to the Bahá'í world was vibrant, penetrating, and majestic.[4] It was so moving and carried so much authority that it seemed as if the Guardian himself were still directing us. For me this was a confirmation of its station. The only befitting response was to resolve to serve this mighty institution with heart and soul.

In the same manner in which he had served the Guardian, Mr. Khadem was ready at every moment to respond to the wishes of the Universal House of Justice, which he served with great love and devotion, often marveling at this unique institution. In addition to expressing passionate devotion to the Guardian, Mr. Khadem would also emphasize anywhere he went the importance of obedience to and reverence for the Universal House of Justice, often quoting from the Will and Testament of 'Abdu'l-Bahá:

> The sacred and youthful branch, the Guardian of the Cause of God, as well as the Universal House of Justice to be universally elected and established, are both under the care and protection of the Abhá Beauty, under the shelter and unerring guidance of the Exalted One (may my life be offered up for them both). Whatsoever they decide is of God.[5]

In speaking of the Guardian and the House of Justice, Mr. Khadem always employed reverent adjectives: the *beloved* Guardian or the *beloved of all hearts,* Shoghi Effendi, and the *infallible* body or the *supreme* body, the Universal House of Justice. In this way Mr. Khadem instilled into the hearts of the friends obedience and love not only for the Guardian but also for the Universal House of Justice.

Mr. Khadem often remarked that the institution of the Universal House of Justice was the crown of the Administrative Order erected by the beloved Guardian. He participated in many conferences as the representative of this august institution.

BAHÁ'Í SCHOOLS

Mr. Khadem always encouraged the friends to participate in Bahá'í schools and institutes. He reminded us that these schools are very important Bahá'í educational institutions. They are places of learning, growth, self-education, and consolidation. Socially, they are environments in which one can witness Bahá'í society in action. Mr. Khadem always encouraged parents to take their children to Bahá'í schools, beginning in early childhood. In this manner, the

Mr. Khadem celebrating Ayyám-i-Há (Intercalary Days) with the Broward County, Florida, Bahá'í children's class, 1968.

children would be educated in the concept of the unity of mankind, and they would learn about loving people of all classes, all religions, all colors, and all nationalities. He believed such schools to be one of the best instruments for the elimination of prejudice.

Mr. Khadem talking to children at a Bahá'í school. He always encouraged parents to take their children to Bahá'í schools, for he believed such institutions to be one of the best instruments for eliminating prejudice.

Mr. Khadem supported his views on Bahá'í schools by quoting from Shoghi Effendi's statements on the subject.[6] He also felt it was a good idea for Bahá'í communities to offer scholarships for those who could not afford to go and to subsidize seekers who wished to participate in such an environment but needed encouragement and support. Everyone can benefit from the spiritual environment, he said. By supporting Bahá'í schools, the communities automatically would strengthen themselves.

Over many years of attending Bahá'í schools, I observed that the seekers who participated in such experiences would invariably become Bahá'ís. Who can resist love? Our souls yearn for it. Our beings thrive on it, if we only give it a chance. Whenever a seeker declared

Bahá'í friends gathered around the Hand
of the Cause of God Zikrullah Khadem at a Potosi, Missouri,
spring institute. Often when Mr. Khadem attended
Bahá'í events he would stay up late at night to
answer questions and talk to the Bahá'ís.

his or her belief and became a new Bahá'í, Mr. Khadem would congratulate that person in a most touching way. He would embrace the new believer and share the ineffable joy of that unique moment of the recognition of the Lord of the Age. He was deeply moved by the transforming power of the Faith.

Mr. Khadem enjoyed Green Acre Bahá'í School very much. Almost every year, while he was in good health, Mr. Khadem would ask me to telephone Green Acre and inform the staff that we would be attending a session. Whenever we were there, he said he could feel the spirit of the Master.* This special bounty is unique among all the summer schools in the Bahá'í world. Mr. Khadem would spend most of his free time in the library, delighting in the precious old books that he found there. He studied them intensely and became inspired to write articles. He kept notes from those books in his own library, notes that will be valuable for future generations of scholars.

At Green Acre he usually spoke in the evenings, when the friends at the school and those from the surrounding areas gathered to hear him. The lecture hall was always filled to capacity and often over-flowed outside. Sometimes there was a fire in the fireplace, as Green Acre can be chilly even in summer. I can still see the way he used to stand in front of the fireplace with the glow of the fire reflecting the glow of the love in his heart for his beloved.

Mr. Khadem loved to talk about the beloved Guardian, and the friends loved to hear him talk on this subject, because it touched their hearts. The Bahá'ís were awed as he informed them about the sacrifices and strenuous labors and wondrous accomplishments of the Guardian in erecting the Administrative Order. When Mr. Khadem talked on these occasions, he became a changed man. The audience would come to life. He shared light stories and laughter; he shared deep insights and tears. Often there was total silence in the hall, but the atmosphere was electrified by his expressions of love and adoration for the Guardian, of whose spirit and assistance he was always acutely aware. Many times he remarked, "If I felt for one brief moment that the Guardian was not with us, I would perish."

Often in his talks Mr. Khadem would take the friends on a spiritual journey back to the time of 'Abdu'l-Bahá, when He had walked and taught at Green Acre. He would thrill them with the recognition of their rich spiritual heritage. When he thought the audience might be tired, he stopped and answered questions.

---

*Green Acre Bahá'í School is the only Bahá'í school in the United States visited by 'Abdu'l-Bahá. For an account of His stay there, see H. M. Balyuzi, *'Abdu'l-Bahá: The Centre of the Covenant of Bahá'u'lláh* (London: George Ronald, 1971), 240–51; for a collection of 'Abdu'l-Bahá's talks at Green Acre, see 'Abdu'l-Bahá, *The Promulgation of Universal Peace: Talks Delivered by 'Abdu'l-Bahá during His Visit to the United States and Canada in 1912,* comp. Howard MacNutt, 2d ed. (Wilmette, Ill.: Bahá'í Publishing Trust, 1982), 253–75.

Mr. Khadem and participants at a Bahá'í summer school
in Frogmore, South Carolina. Called upon frequently to address Bahá'ís at
conferences, conventions, Bahá'í schools, and study classes, Mr. Khadem
enthusiastically agreed to do so whenever he could.

On one occasion a very loving Bahá'í and his non-Bahá'í father
were in the audience. This young man had brought his father to the
school with the hope that his heart would be touched and he would
become a Bahá'í. During the question-and-answer period, the father
asked, "Is it true that parents of Bahá'ís are under the grace of
Bahá'u'lláh?" Mr. Khadem replied, "Yes, it is true," and gave the
reference in the Bahá'í writings.[7]

When the talk was over that evening, we went to the dining room
to socialize. As usual, many of the friends followed, gathering around
and asking questions on many subjects. The non-Bahá'í who had
come with his son was also present. Smiling, he said, "Now my son is

assured that I am under the compassion and protection of Bahá'u'-
lláh, just like him."

Mr. Khadem, also smiling, replied, "Your son wanted to help you
and provide you with the pleasure and comfort of the Faith." He
then continued half-jokingly, "Now, you, in your turn, have to do
your utmost to provide this for *your* parents. This is why you should
continue your search for the truth, not only for yourself, but to make
your father happy. Your son wishes blessings and protection for his
grandparents as well."

Green Lake

Almost every year, if he was available, Mr. Khadem participated in
the annual autumn conference in Green Lake, Wisconsin. He was
very touched when, at the conference's twenty-fifth anniversary, the
planning committee presented him with a framed memento in appreciation of his participation there for so many years. He treasured
that gift and hung it in his office.

In 1984 he gave a talk on sacrifice. In that session his heart was
touched by the spirit of the recent martyrs of Iran. He was enraged
by the fanatic cruelty of those martyrdoms but also deeply touched
by the love and devotion of those who went to the field of sacrifice so
joyously. He shared that special spirit of the martyrs with the audience. Finally, in a dramatic moment, Mr. Khadem recounted the
story of a recent Persian martyr, Ḥabíbu'lláh Awjí, one of those
blessed and heroic souls.* In a moving voice, he called to Awjí in the
Abhá Kingdom to join while he read the poem that Awjí had
composed and recited at the time of his martyrdom. Mr. Khadem
translated the poem thus:

> O Messenger of the Monarch of Love,
> Waft these words o'er the wind to that Nightcrawler:
> "Pity, pity thine eyes have never had sight;
> Mine eyes blaze with brilliant light:
> The Sun of Reality dazzles, dazzles this night!"

---

*Mr. Awjí was executed on 16 November 1982 in Shiraz, one of some thirty
Iranian Bahá'ís who were martyred in 1982.

Mr. Khadem lovingly embracing a young Bahá'í at the Green Lake
Conference, Green Lake, Wisconsin, 1973. Mr. Khadem was especially fond
of the Green Lake conference and made a point of attending it
almost every year for over twenty-five years.

Mr. Khadem then called upon the Messenger of the Monarch of
Love to waft the news to that same Nightcrawler that the doors of
the House of Worship in the heart of the Pacific—Western Samoa—
had been flung wide open before all humanity, that the Cause would
continue to win still mightier victories!* The conference participants

---

*The Bahá'í House of Worship in Western Samoa was dedicated on 1 September
1984.

were spellbound by the courage of the martyrs. One could see in every face the traces of love and passionate admiration for the purity and integrity of their sacrifice.

This feeling was reinforced the next morning when Dr. Jane Faily, in her eloquent, poetic style, recalled Mr. Khadem's message:

Last night . . . in front of us, holding aloft a banner, the Hand of the Cause of God took us by the hand, lifted us up to the heights of enkindlement and rapture as he shared with us the moments when his *own* heart surrendered itself to the spiritual ecstasy, an ecstasy gained by one of Iran's martyrs in the last moments of his life. Mr. Khadem brought us with him to the inner courts of holiness, close enough to hear the silken

The Hand of the Cause of God Zikrullah Khadem talking with Jamaican Bahá'ís at the Caribbean Conference in Kingston, Jamaica, 1971

rustle of the robes of holiness, to sense the very presence of the Blessed
Perfection. . . .[8]

THE LOVERS OF THE CAUSE

Mr. Khadem was particularly enamored of all lovers of Bahá'u'lláh
because they were ready to sacrifice so much in the path of love. They
were his closest and dearest friends. He received spiritual sustenance
from them, and they from him. He longed to serve them, whether in
the north or the south, the east or the west. In a letter to me,
Counselor Ruth Pringle described the May 1971 Carribean Conference in Kingston, Jamaica, which Mr. Khadem addressed as a representative of the Universal House of Justice:

> We can never forget Mr. Khadem at the Jamaica Conference, and how
> he set everyone at ease. Nor can we forget the closing session of the
> Conference when he spoke of the glorious Saturday evening performance
> in the coliseum. Then he asked the friends if they knew the song "Would
> You Give Your Life For Baha'u'llah", and invited them to sing. When
> they had finished singing the song, eyes were filled with tears, emotions
> were running high. He said very simply words to the effect, "Now you
> have made your promise to Baha'u'llah." It was a moment to be remem-
> bered and cherished, one that we will share with our children and
> grandchildren.[9]

One summer he participated in a Bahá'í summer school in Ireland. He was deeply touched by the experience and, afterward, often
spoke of the Irish Bahá'ís, their sacrificial efforts, their spirit, and
their devotion. He became young-hearted and joyful when he saw
the friends serving with such devotion and dedication. He had a
special attachment to the Irish Bahá'ís because of the love he felt
among them.

He was especially moved by the lovers of Bahá'u'lláh who sacrificed their lives in the path of serving His Cause. His tender heart
was deeply affected by their suffering. He suffered with them, feeling
their pain. When he heard news of martyrdoms in Iran, he became
greatly saddened and silent. He sought refuge in prayer, tearfully
beseeching Bahá'u'lláh for their relief. How many sleepless nights he

spent agonizing over their trials. Because he was so sensitive to the suffering that befalls lovers of Bahá'u'lláh, I dreaded the times he would receive news of martyrdoms. I worried about his health and feared that such news might cause a heart attack. I requested that the National Spiritual Assembly of the Bahá'ís of the United States give him such news very gently or else permit me to prepare him for it beforehand, as the effect was overwhelming to him. I recall his mentioning many times that he wished he were in Iran to share the sufferings of the Persian friends. Many times he contemplated going back to be with them in their time of need. He was deeply grateful for and marveled at the great majesty of the Universal House of Justice in dealing with the situation with such wisdom and divine guidance.

THE MARTYRS AND THE LORDS

One day in 1982, as Mr. Khadem was reviewing his daily mail, he became very joyful and energetic. Since that was a time, after the Islamic Revolution, during which the news was often filled with depressing stories of new attacks against the Iranian Bahá'ís, I could not imagine what news could elicit such excitement. Then he called me. "Come quickly! See what Bahá'u'lláh has done! See the amazing result of the sacrifices of the Bahá'ís of Iran! They sacrificed their lives, not knowing that their noble actions would produce such victories. This document," he said excitedly, holding aloft a thick envelope, "is the *House of Lords Official Report!*" He eagerly began to read aloud: "Lord McNair rose to ask Her Majesty's Government whether they are aware of the persecution being suffered by the Bahá'is in Iran and, if so, whether they will use their influence to help these unfortunate people."

"See what Lord McNair says later," Mr. Khadem exclaimed before reading on:

> I would only say that, to my, I hope, unbiased mind, the religion of the Bahá'is, asserting, as it does, the oneness of the human family and the oneness of God, revealing his will from time to time through his prophets, of whom Bahá'ulláh [sic] is not necessarily the last, seems to me the most comprehensive and the least dogmatically exclusive religion of

which I have heard. The moral precepts by which Bahá'ís conduct their daily lives should also commend them to us all. It was extraordinarily enlightened, in the middle of the 19th century and in the Middle East, for a religious writer to attach the importance which Bahá'u'lláh attached to education, and in particular, because of their influence on children, to the education of women. In short, of all the peoples of this earth, I can think of none less deserving of persecution than the believers of the Bahá'i faith.[10]

"Imagine!" Mr. Khadem said, barely able to contain his joy and gratitude. "They are teaching the principles and history of the Bahá'í Faith in the Parliamentary debates! They are defending the Faith against the attack of its enemies! See what Lord Whaddon says":

> Those of us who have religious faith should certainly remember them in our prayers and make it known to the Bahá'is that we are doing so.
> . . . From the blood of every martyr there will undoubtedly spring 1,000 new adherents to the Bahá'i beliefs. If they realise this, they may not be so keen to produce new martyrs.[11]

Mr. Khadem could not wait to share this exciting development with other Bahá'ís. From then on, he carried a copy of this document with him wherever he went and quoted from it in his talks. He was especially eager to thank the Lords who so courageously spoke as advocates for the Bahá'ís. This desire was fulfilled a few months later when he went to visit the Bahá'ís of the United Kingdom.

During a talk at the Bahá'í Center in London, he publicly expressed his heartfelt appreciation for the efforts that had led to such an historic step—a debate, in the House of Lords, in defense of the Bahá'ís of Iran—and his desire to thank Lords Whaddon and McNair personally for the vital role they had played in it. A few days later, Mr. Khadem received unexpected news from the secretary of the National Spiritual Assembly of the United Kingdom, Mrs. Mary Hardy, that he was invited to a reception and would have a chance to meet Lords Whaddon and McNair. Mr. Khadem eagerly attended the reception so that he could meet and personally express his gratitude and admiration for the efforts of these two notables on behalf of the Bahá'ís.

When he returned to the United States, Mr. Khadem wrote to both Lord and Lady Whaddon and Lord and Lady McNair, thanking them for their actions. Lord Whaddon responded with a promise to keep in touch with the National Spiritual Assembly of the Bahá'ís of the United Kingdom and to seek other opportunities to aid the Bahá'ís in Iran.

Mr. Khadem immediately shared all of his correspondence with the two Lords with the Universal House of Justice so that it could be kept for posterity. The handwritten copies of these documents are in Haifa. This episode was characteristic of how Mr. Khadem, like the other Hands of the Cause of God, became ablaze whenever the Cause achieved a signal victory. His being became galvanized and radiant and resulted in a powerful charm that affected everyone, including leaders such as Lords Whaddon and McNair.

KINDLING "THE FIRE OF THE LOVE OF GOD"[12]

After the Hands of the Cause of God in the Holy Land decided that Mr. Khadem should serve in the Western Hemisphere, he continued to travel extensively; however, he spent most of his time visiting the Bahá'ís in various parts of the West—North America, South America, Central America, the islands of the Caribbean, and Europe. The Universal House of Justice frequently asked him to be its representative at the formation of new National Spiritual Assemblies in the Western Hemisphere. Thus Mr. Khadem was called upon again and again to address the Bahá'ís at conventions as well as conferences, Bahá'í schools, and study classes.

Even though Mr. Khadem spoke often, very few of his talks were taped, for he did not wish his words to be recorded. He wanted to preclude the possibility of being the source of any controversy or disunity in the Faith and thought that great care should be taken in recording the words of people such as himself. He reminded the Bahá'ís repeatedly that the Bahá'í writings are our touchstone.

But whenever the institutions of the Faith suggested any way in which he could serve the Bahá'ís, he immediately and enthusiastically agreed. Thus when the National Spiritual Assembly of the Bahá'ís of the United States asked him to prepare a speech for an audio tape to be sent to spiritual assemblies for playing at the Feast of

'Alá', 2 March 1985, he readily complied with its wishes. The following is a transcript of the tape:

Friends,

The National Spiritual Assembly has asked me to address you at this Feast. I am so excited to speak to the "apostles of Bahá'u'lláh." In your praise the beloved Master, 'Abdu'l-Bahá, said, "May my life be sacrificed for you!" "Consider how exalted and lofty is the station you are destined to attain." 'Abdu'l-Bahá promised that "in the near future the whole earth may be stirred and shaken by the results of your achievements."[13]

When I was in the presence of the beloved Guardian, so many times I heard him quote passages from the exalted Báb, Bahá'u'lláh, and the Master, extolling this country as "the land" where the splendor of the light of Bahá'u'lláh "shall be revealed, where the mysteries of" the Faith "shall be unveiled."[14] I wish you were present when "the sign of God" on earth shared these passages and showered his bounties upon this community.[15] How I wish you were there to see his luminous face. He glowed with joy when mentioning your services and your achievements.

As you can imagine, this created within me a burning desire to see your shining faces. Well, the beloved Shoghi Effendi, he read my heart and promised to send me to the West to witness all these glories, mysteries, and lights. This has been such a great—very great—bounty that I shall never be able to thank Bahá'u'lláh for its fulfillment. Friends, I am now with you. I am a witness that these promises have been fulfilled. I have traveled to all parts of the world. During the lifetime of the beloved Shoghi Effendi, I saw how the American pioneers brought the message of Bahá'u'lláh to the ten goal countries in Europe. Now, all over the world, there are pioneers, torchbearers of the light, carrying the torch from one country to another, sacrificing their lives, and, even as a candle, burning to the last drop until they pass to the Abhá Kingdom in battle dresses.

Now we are in the final phase of the Seven Year Plan given to us by the supreme body of the Faith, the Universal House of Justice.* Thank God,

---

*The Seven Year Plan referred to is the Seven Year International Teaching Plan launched by the Universal House of Justice in April 1979; it concluded in April 1986.

we are receiving constantly their guidance and are beholding the astounding victories. This is our destiny. This is the fruit of the blood of the martyrs and the result of the triumph of the pioneers all over the world. It is the outcome of your achievements.

There are many important subjects to discuss, such as pioneering, which is the prince of all deeds and has been emphasized greatly by the Universal House of Justice; the Funds, which are the lifeblood of the Cause; homefront goals; and so on. You may study carefully in the messages of the [Universal] House [of Justice]. We need earnestly to turn our faces and our hearts to Bahá'u'lláh and, ardently and with great devotion, beseech His help and assistance to accomplish these goals.

Now is the time of the Fast. This is the best time to seek assistance for our efforts. We have the promise of 'Abdu'l-Bahá: "Behold the portals which Bahá'u'lláh hath opened before you!"[16] If we arise at dawn during the Fasting month for prayers, while we are detached from worldly things, the portals of Bahá'u'lláh's grace will open wide before us. All throughout the history of the Faith, fasting and prayers have been the key of success and have done miracles. The early believers of the Faith relied so much on prayers and fasting. Mullá Ḥusayn spent days and nights, rapt in fasting and prayers, beseeching God to show him the way. This is how all the Letters of the Living and so many others found the path to their Beloved. Their prayers were answered. They were led by the Almighty to the very home of their hearts' desire, where they found and recognized the Promised One. Then, with a firm resolution, they arose to serve Him until they changed the course of history.

We are their spiritual descendants. We can follow their footsteps by observing [the] Fast, by turning to Bahá'u'lláh, clinging to the Hem of His robe, and beseeching Him to help us to arise to serve Him with all our energies, our resources, and even our lives, until we make sure that He is pleased with us.

Did you know this month of Fasting and the next one—Loftiness and Splendor—are named after the names of the Báb and Bahá'u'lláh ('Alá' and Bahá)? These two months belong to Them. They are very significant.

In the beautiful, inspiring words of the Universal House of Justice, "It is a time for rejoicing. The Sun of Bahá'u'lláh is mounting the heavens. . . . Lift up your hearts. The Day of God is here."[17] With all these promises and bounties, we *can* surely win all the goals. Please God, we may achieve it.

Edifying "the Souls of Men"[18]

On 22 June 1972, while Mr. Khadem was in the Holy Land, the Universal House of Justice asked him to undertake the task of researching all of the places associated with the lives of the three Central Figures of the Faith—Bahá'u'lláh, the Báb, and 'Abdu'l-Bahá. When he returned from that trip he was brimming with joy. He immediately secured a modest office in downtown Evanston, every inch of which was needed and put to use. With the help of a part-time secretary, he began working on the project right away. Since the World Center was funding this project, he was extremely thrifty with expenditures. He chose the most economical supplies and even used the backs of envelopes as scrap paper in order to conserve resources.

He thought a great deal about a name for the project and finally called it "Registry of Bahá'í Holy Places." He worked very hard on the project, reading all available sources about the Faith's beginnings and the early believers, including all the old manuscripts and out-of-print books he could find. He studied Persian, Arabic, English, and French accounts, often late into the night, and obtained translations of materials in other languages. He corresponded with individuals who he thought could help to identify locations because they lived or had lived in areas under study. In addition, he wrote to any national spiritual assembly or local spiritual assembly that might be able to help him in the project. He also corresponded with early believers, asking for their recollections. Green Acre Bahá'í School library, where he had gone almost every year to read all the old manuscripts, was a rich resource. He worked on this project so intensely and with such fervor that I worried about his health. I remember pleading with him often not to work so hard.

"I cannot!" he would insist. "I have to finish this project while I still have time."

He copied all the references from sources verifying the places the Central Figures had visited. In his meticulous and orderly fashion, he compiled the extracts, with accompanying photographs, into large notebooks.

The book that aided him most was *God Passes By;* he was able many times to verify places and details by following up on the information supplied in it.[19] He loved this masterpiece of history and prose by the Guardian. He often marveled, "Everything, *everything* is in this book!" He called it his "Bible."

The work would normally have required ten years, but he completed it in five because he sensed its urgency and felt there was a shortage of time. He sent all 134 volumes to the Holy Land. He was thrilled when he received a letter from the Universal House of Justice dated 17 March 1977 commending his services and conveying "on behalf of Bahá'í historians of the future, as well as the entire Bahá'í community, deepest gratitude for the meticulous research and thorough investigation you have made of historic sites hallowed by the sacred associations of the past."

"My mind is now at rest" was his response.

THE BOUNTY OF HUQÚQU'LLÁH

Once the great undertaking of documenting Bahá'í holy places was behind Mr. Khadem, he was free to attend to other matters. One such matter that was of great concern to him was the financial sustenance of the Faith. He often spoke of the enormous costs of restoring, maintaining, and acquiring holy sites—not to mention the costs of building the administrative centers on the Arc of which the Guardian so often spoke.

As a Hand of the Cause of God, and as a former treasurer during the 1950s of the National Spiritual Assembly of the Bahá'ís of Iran, Mr. Khadem was well aware of the Faith's financial needs. The expenses of the Cause and the responsibilities of the Bahá'ís were always on his mind. He thought that nourishing ourselves spiritually and immersing ourselves in the ocean of the holy writings would ensure the material success of the Cause. He felt very strongly that the spiritual and the material are intimately connected.

The Persian Bahá'ís, whether living in the East or the West, have been blessed both spiritually and materially by observing the law of Huqúqu'lláh.* Mr. Khadem had experienced the blessing of this law

---

*Huqúqu'lláh (meaning "Right of God") is a payment instituted in the Kitáb-i-Aqdas that Bahá'ís make to the head of the Faith on a portion of their earnings after meeting their expenses. It is 19 percent of one's savings greater than the value of 2.22

in his own life. Whenever he received a profit in his business, he immediately calculated and submitted the 19 percent "Right of God." Thus he was able to use the remaining income as he wished. He was recompensed to such a degree that he was able to serve as a Hand of the Cause of God from 1952 until the end of his life without drawing upon the resources of the Faith. He was also recompensed in many other ways, for he was given countless opportunities to use all his talents to serve the Faith, and he received constant encouragement from the beloved Guardian. He hoped that the time would soon come when the Universal House of Justice, through its infallible guidance, would see fit to bestow the blessing of this law upon the Western Bahá'ís. Mr. Khadem believed that, if the Universal House of Justice would bestow this honor upon the Bahá'ís of the United States, all of the Faith's financial needs would be met. I knew of this firm conviction, but I never knew what he intended to do about it.

In 1984 the National Spiritual Assembly of the Bahá'ís of the United States called upon Mr. Khadem to address the historic Seventy-Fifth U.S. National Bahá'í Convention. On this occasion delegates and guests from all over the country had assembled at Chicago's McCormick Inn. Just before the convention closed, a remarkable thing occurred. Mr. Khadem became very excited. He turned to me and said, "I must say something. I have an assignment; I must do it!" Often he reviewed with me the contents of the talks he planned to give, but this time his presentation was a surprise to me. I do not know whether he had prepared what he would say, or if it had suddenly come to him.

Very often when Mr. Khadem addressed the believers, he became radiant and joyous. It was as if years of age disappeared. He became young and energetic, his face beaming. On the occasion of the Seventy-Fifth U.S. National Bahá'í Convention, however, he was

---

troy ounces of gold, after expenses have been met. Ḥuqúqu'lláh is to be paid only once on a given amount. The payment the following year is whatever new profits a person may have gained above and beyond the amount already taken into account.

Mr. Khadem's business was an ongoing side interest in land development, which he maintained from before we were married until 1960, when we moved to the United States.

*The Hand of the Cause of God Zikrullah Khadem delivering his moving
address on the bounty of Ḥuqúqu'lláh to the Seventy-Fifth
U.S. National Baháʼí Convention, 1984*

completely transformed; he became like a new person. He was exhilarated!

He addressed the believers about the importance of Ḥuqúqu'lláh
and about its blessings. He reminded the Baháʼís of the scroll of
names sent to ʻAbduʼl-Bahá in 1907 by the American believers
petitioning for permission to build the Mother Temple of the West.*
He inspired the Baháʼís to feel the same zeal toward Ḥuqúqu'lláh. He
was utterly convinced that the Baháʼís' obedience to this law would
purify their financial affairs and ensure a recompense by God and
that it would resolve all the material needs of the Cause.

He so inspired the audience that, when he suggested they sign a
scroll asking the Universal House of Justice to consider permitting

---

*The petition asking ʻAbduʼl-Bahá for permission to build the House of Worship
was sent in 1903. The scroll of names asking ʻAbduʼl-Bahá to bless the united effort
to build the Temple was hand carried to Haifa in 1907. See Bruce W. Whitmore, *The
Dawning Place: The Building of a Temple, the Forging of the North American Baháʼí
Community* (Wilmette, Ill.: Baháʼí Publishing Trust, 1984), 4–5, 26.

the Western believers to have the blessing of the law of Ḥuqúqu'lláh, a scroll was hastily assembled, and many rushed forward to sign their names. Long lines formed. The friends seemed anxious not to miss this opportunity to add their names; it was as if they feared the paper would run out or the scroll would be removed before they could write on it. I felt that, if asked, those who were present would empty all their wealth onto the platform.

The scroll was submitted to the Universal House of Justice, beseeching it to confer upon the American Bahá'í community the blessing of the law of Ḥuqúqu'lláh. In a letter dated 3 January 1985 to the followers of Bahá'u'lláh in every land, the Universal House of Justice referred to that scroll:

> Last April we were deeply touched by receiving a petition from the delegates gathered at the National Convention of the Bahá'ís of the United States, requesting that the Law of Ḥuqúqu'lláh be made binding on all the believers in that country. Although it is not yet the time to take this far-reaching step, we were moved to decide that, as a preliminary measure, the text relating to the Law of Ḥuqúqu'lláh will be translated into English for general information against the time when this law will be applied more widely.

With deep gratitude Mr. Khadem read this message from the Universal House of Justice. I noticed a great calmness and deep satisfaction in his face as he studied the message. He was certain that the necessary financial assistance was within reach. Thereafter, even as his health began to fail, he expressed great confidence in the ability of the believers to meet the challenges ahead. I have no doubt that Mr. Khadem's spirit is exhilarated in the Abhá Kingdom by all of the progress and development that has occurred in preparation for the realization of the great milestone of Ḥuqúqu'lláh in the maturation of the Cause in the West.

9 Mr. Khadem's Passing

O Breakwell, O my dear one!*

Where now is thy fair face? Where is thy fluent tongue? Where thy clear brow? Where thy bright comeliness? . . .

Where is thy fire, blazing with God's love? Where is thy rapture at His holy breaths? Where are thy praises, lifted unto Him? Where is thy rising up to serve His Cause?

. . . .

I ask of God to draw thee ever closer, hold thee ever faster; to rejoice thy heart with nearness to His presence, to fill thee with light and still more light, to grant thee still more beauty, and to bestow upon thee power and great glory.

—'ABDU'L-BAHÁ

During the last decade of his life, Mr. Khadem was very active, giving talks, participating in conferences, attending to correspondence, and even traveling, though at a greatly reduced pace. He maintained such activities through the spring of 1986, when he first noticed a nagging backache.

In July, after Mr. Khadem had complained for months of gradually increasing back pain, we were devastated to learn that he had metastatic cancer. Between July and November his health gradually deteriorated. He was confined to bed most of the time and spent

---

*Thomas Breakwell, whom Shoghi Effendi referred to as "the first English Bahá'í" (Shoghi Effendi, *God Passes By*, rev. ed. [Wilmette, Ill.: Bahá'í Publishing Trust, 1974], 259), was highly esteemed by 'Abdu'l-Bahá. He died circa 1902, within a few months after making a pilgrimage to Akka to visit 'Abdu'l-Bahá.

most of his days in the hospital. Yet, during much of this period, he remained active. He attended to unfinished business, communicated his love and support to the institutions of the Bahá'í Faith, which he so greatly admired, and shared with us his wealth of knowledge, reminiscences, and love.

He was especially anxious to dictate letters about matters he considered urgent. Several heartfelt letters were dispatched to the Universal House of Justice, that institution he loved so deeply, served so devotedly, and honored with all his heart. He also wished, once again, to pay homage at the holy shrines. Words fail me in my expression of profound gratitude to our Supreme Body, the Universal House of Justice, which, when informed of Mr. Khadem's grave illness, granted permission to Mr. Khadem and me to visit the Holy Land with our five children. When I gave Mr. Khadem this news, it made him very happy. He agreed that we should thank the Universal House of Justice and avail ourselves of this great bounty. However, God had planned otherwise. Mr. Khadem's illness was progressing very fast, and soon traveling became impossible. Though we could not make the physical journey, we turned our hearts to the holy shrines to implore God's assistance and consolation.

In his talks Mr. Khadem had often spoken of the grandeur and significance of the institutions of the World Order of Bahá'u'lláh, their divine origin, and the perfection of this awesome system erected and nurtured by the beloved Guardian. Especially during the final four months of his life, he expressed profound love for the institutions of the Faith and prayed fervently for their success in the service of our beloved Cause. At night the children and I would often gather around him and share the latest news of the progress of the Faith. This always brought him joy. One night we were reading from the Canadian *Bahá'í News.* When he heard about the Canadians' teaching projects and their successes in promoting the Faith, he was ecstatic. He asked me to write a letter on his behalf, telling the National Spiritual Assembly of the Bahá'ís of Canada how much he appreciated their efforts and their victories. He wanted me to convey his love and encouragement and to exhort the Bahá'ís to be " 'encouraged, enthusiastic, united, and self-sacrificing' in service to the Cause, that, as 'Abdu'l-Bahá admonished, 'like candles they must weep their lives away drop by drop in order to give forth their flame of light.'" He also wanted me to tell the Canadian National Assembly, "'Thanks to Bahá'u'lláh, the Cause is in good hands.'"[1] Unfortunately, time did not permit me to complete the letter for his review. I carried out his request after his passing.

In October 1986 Mr. Khadem also sent a letter conveying his high regard for the beloved National Spiritual Assembly of the Bahá'ís of the United States:

> My Beloved friends,
>
> I wish to thank you from the bottom of my heart for all your kindnesses, as representatives of the American Bahá'í Community, that you've shown to me over the past 26 years. I am deeply indebted to our Beloved Guardian for having sent me to the West to witness the glorious victories of our Beloved Faith. As I look back over the years, I can only humbly supplicate: "O Lord, increase my astonishment at Thee!"[2]
>
> Please be assured of my deepest gratitude and love for each one of you and for the entire American Baha'i Community. I have been thinking of you and your heavy task in the years to come, especially these next crucial years of the Six Year Plan. I wish for you Baha'u'llah's blessings and assistance in continually promoting the unity of the friends and rising to your high destiny. . . .
>
> May He continue to guide you to fulfill the glorious destiny of this wonderful community as foreseen by the Beloved Master. May He protect you and surround you with His bounties and blessings.[3]

To this letter he received a most loving reply, full of tenderness and appreciation:

> Your letter of love and gratitude brought tears to our eyes. The National Spiritual Assembly can never repay its debt to you for all you have given the institutions and the American Bahá'í Community.
>
> Your tireless efforts for the sake of the community, your love and your wise guidance have long since set a standard for service to the Cause.
>
> There are no words which can convey our gratitude and appreciation of your services. However, you must know that your example has served as an inspiration to the National Assembly and to the friends throughout the American Bahá'í Community.[4]

During the earlier days of his illness, Mr. Khadem spent long and eager hours preparing a talk for the Bahá'í International Peace Conference to be held in San Francisco in August 1986.* He revised and amended the talk numerous times. Though he longed to be present for that historic occasion, his health made the trip impossible. Therefore, he asked me to deliver the talk on his behalf. He also began preparing an address to be given at the dedication of the House of Worship in India on 23 through 27 December 1986 but was unable to finish writing the speech before his passing. Again, he asked me to go in his stead. He was especially eager to participate in the dedication, as he had been present in Bahapur in 1954 when the site for the temple was purchased,§ and he had followed the progress of the construction with great interest.

The late summer and fall of 1986, though heartrending for the family, was filled with many precious moments in which we could drink our fill of Mr. Khadem's stories, reminiscences, and advice. He generally felt better and was more energetic and talkative in the evenings. At such times we clustered around him, listening to recollections of his earlier years, of his family, and of great Bahá'í figures. He constantly thanked Bahá'u'lláh for all the blessings he felt he had been given in his life. Fortunately, he permitted us to record some of these treasured moments on tape.

As he became weaker, and speaking required effort, we would gather around him and play tapes of prayers and tablets that he particularly enjoyed. One of his favorite selections at this time was a passage found in *Gleanings from the Writings of Bahá'u'lláh* that begins, "Release yourselves, O nightingales of God, from the thorns and brambles of wretchedness and misery, and wing your flight to the rose-garden of unfading splendor."§ Out of respect for the word of God, he always insisted on being in an upright position. As so many people have recorded, he was always in a state of communion with his Lord. This was increasingly apparent as his illness progressed.

During the early morning of 13 November 1986, while our daughter Jena was with him, Mr. Khadem passed away from this life into the arms of his Lord. What devastation for us, but what peace for him. At 4:00 A.M. I received a call from his doctor, who said that I should go to the hospital. I cannot begin to describe the turbulent

---

*For a transcript of the talk, see *Bahá'í News,* no. 669 (Dec. 1986): 4–7.
§See pp. 103–05.

emotions that surged within me. I was in a state of shock. I stayed
with him until daylight, when I could communicate the heartbreaking news to the secretary of the National Spiritual Assembly of the
Bahá'ís of the United States.

Later that morning I received a call saying that the secretary of the
National Spiritual Assembly, Dr. Robert Henderson, and one of the
Continental Counselors, Mrs. Loretta King, wished to meet with
me. How tender, how loving, how very supportive that meeting was.
The Board of Counselors for the Americas, the Auxiliary Board for
the United States, and the National Spiritual Assembly of the United
States had gathered in Wilmette that weekend for meetings. The
support and the love of these institutions enfolded our family and
consoled us during this very difficult time.

I cannot adequately render my thanks to the National Spiritual
Assembly. They acted immediately. They informed the Universal
House of Justice of Mr. Khadem's passing. They informed the Counselors and the Auxiliary Board members at their morning session.
Grateful to be of help in any way, they took on the responsibility for
preparing the programs for the funeral and memorial services, which
were carried out in the most beautiful and moving manner possible.
They prepared memorable presentations and set aside an entire day
to participate in the services.

The Counselors and Auxiliary Board members, likewise, immediately set aside their business in order to assist with and participate in
the memorial services for Mr. Khadem. Since one of the duties of the
Hands of the Cause of God is to be available to consult with the
institution of the Continental Boards of Counselors as necessary,
Mr. Khadem's passing from this earthly life removed a resource and
left a greater burden of responsibility for the protection and propagation of the Bahá'í Faith on their shoulders. It seems that a new spirit
of dedication within this institution resulted from his passing. The
following message, sent to the Universal House of Justice from the
Continental Board of Counselors, the National Spiritual Assembly,
and the Auxiliary Board members on 16 November, communicates
their loving sentiments:

Joy and sorrow embrace in the passing of our treasured Hand of the
Cause of God Zikru'lláh Khadem to the welcome of the Concourse on
High. Words are inadequate to express the transforming power and the

unifying effect of this event and its commemoration. The Hand of the Cause William Sears, six Counselors, the National Spiritual Assembly, 27 newly appointed members of the Auxiliary Board, and national committees gathered for Six Year Plan consultation in Wilmette have achieved an intimacy and an astonishing sense of connectedness. The flame of love engendered here will soon enkindle the American Bahá'í community to an unprecedented depth of commitment to achieve the goals of the Plan.[6]

The Universal House of Justice replied the next day:

Deeply touched, greatly heartened contents your message reporting extraordinary circumstances, occasioned by passing Hand Cause Zikru'lláh Khadem, which attended your meeting on Six Year Plan. Grateful presence Hand Cause William Sears. May unifying, invigorating effects you experienced be manifested throughout American Bahá'í community in unprecedented achievements, rendering during new Plan enduring memorial to dearly loved departed Hand Cause.[7]

After news of Mr. Khadem's passing was shared with the Bahá'í World Center, we received many letters, notes, and cables from the Bahá'ís living there. The same love and concern they had expressed during his illness were conveyed again and again in these communications, and we took comfort in hearing that so many prayers were being offered on his behalf at the holy shrines. My profound gratitude is offered to the Universal House of Justice for its loving support, communicated in the following cablegram, which was sent to all National Spiritual Assemblies and institutions:

With sorrowful hearts announce passing indefatigable fearless defender Faith deeply loved Hand Cause Zikrullah Khadem. His sterling services to the Cause, his total consecration to tasks assigned to him by beloved Guardian, his outstanding efforts as member National Spiritual Assembly Cradle Faith, his valuable soul-uplifting stimulation imparted body believers North America, particularly United States Bahá'í community, his untiring endeavors through his talks and writings in safeguarding Covenant and in instilling appreciation love for Shoghi Effendi shed undying luster over period his admirable stewardship Cause God.

Offering prayers holy shrines progress his radiant soul Abhá Kingdom. Urge hold befitting memorial gatherings his name at all Houses of Worship as well as in all local Bahá'í communities.[8]

The Hand of the Cause of God
Zikrullah Khadem
c. 1 January 1904–13 November 1986
"Indefatigable fearless defender Faith"
—The Universal House of Justice

10 Memorials

We all, verily, worship God.
We all, verily, bow down before God.
We all, verily, are devoted unto God.
We all, verily, give praise unto God.
We all, verily, yield thanks unto God.
We all, verily, are patient in God.   —BAHÁ'U'LLÁH

MEMORIAL GATHERING IN THE HOLY LAND*

On 14 November 1986, the day after his passing, the pilgrims and the resident Bahá'ís in the Holy Land were called to assemble in the Shrine of the Báb for prayers to commemorate the life of the Hand of the Cause of God Zikrullah Khadem. Each was given a copy of the Universal House of Justice's beautiful cablegram about him.§ My gratitude goes to the Universal House of Justice for this memorial service. My family and I were profoundly touched by such loving acts.

The two antechamber rooms of the Shrine of the Báb were filled to capacity. Many had to remain outside. Among those present were the two Hands of the Cause of God residing in the Holy Land, Amatu'l-Bahá Rúḥíyyih Khánum and 'Alí-Akbar Furútan, and the members of the Universal House of Justice. Amatu'l-Bahá Rúḥíyyih

---

*This account is drawn from the many communications received from those present in Haifa at the memorial gathering for Mr. Khadem.

§See p. 153.

<u>Kh</u>ánum read in English the prayer for the departed that begins "He is God, exalted is He, the Lord of loving-kindness and bounty!" Dr. David Ruhe, a member of the Universal House of Justice, read the prayer for protection that begins "O God, my God! Shield Thy trusted servants. . . ." Mr. Furútan chanted the Tablet of Visitation of Bahá'u'lláh in Arabic.[1]

After saying prayers in the Shrine of the Báb, the friends gathered in the Pilgrim House, where Mr. 'Alí Na<u>kh</u>javání, another member of the Universal House of Justice, gave a eulogy. He later wrote to me about the salient points upon which he had touched. Some of his comments are recorded here:

> The ties of friendship which bind me to Jináb-i-<u>Kh</u>ádem stretch as far back as nearly half a century. . . . He showered upon me his love and consideration and very soon his home became a haven of hope and comfort. I could sense in him his deep love for the Guardian, his utter consecration to the Cause, his vigilance regarding its welfare, and his indomitable desire to promote and protect its interests.
>
> . . . In any matter which involved the protection of the Covenant, he was a fearless defender. In his dealings with the friends, however, he was the essence of gentleness, of tenderness, and of compassion. . . .
>
> His recurrent pilgrimages to the Holy Land to visit the Shrines and seek the presence of the Guardian had inspired and reinforced him, and had renewed an undying loyalty to the Covenant. Shoghi Effendi's magic influence not only galvanized him, but also through him, all those who came in contact with his soul when he was communicating to them Shoghi Effendi's comments or instructions, or describing for them some aspects of his pilgrimage involving the "Beloved of all Hearts," as he was wont to refer to the Guardian of the Cause.
>
> . . . He was trusted by the Guardian for his conscientiousness, his constancy, and his utter devotion. For many years, prior to his becoming a Hand of the Cause, he was a member of the National Spiritual Assembly of Iran, and in my associations with him as a member of that body, I could easily witness the total dedication he always evinced, the purity and selflessness of his motives and the irrepressible passion with which he wished to ensure that the guidance received from the Guardian was unreservedly carried out.
>
> When, in the early forties, the Guardian called on the friends in Persia to pioneer to 'Iráq, Jináb-i-<u>Kh</u>ádem spearheaded this effort and it was, to

a large extent, due to his perseverance and self-sacrifice that 95 families were able to settle in nearby 'Iráq.

The message of the Guardian to the 1944 Convention held in Shiraz was received through him, and it was thanks to Jináb-i-Khádem's indefatigable resolve and surveillance that the message was delivered in time to the friends assembled in the House of the Báb on the 100th anniversary of His declaration.*

. . . Shoghi Effendi referred to him in one of his messages as the "itinerant Hand of the Cause," as Jináb-i-Khádem travelled quite often at his instruction to different lands.

. . . He has been a lion protecting the stronghold of His Cause in North America during all these years, acting as a champion of the Covenant, and an example of steadfastness and stability, rallying the friends around the banner of the Faith. He has inspired many souls, and his example will be before us so that we may follow the path he trod with humility, single-mindedness and fearless vigour.[2]

Amatu'l-Bahá Rúhíyyih Khánum also consoled my heart with two cablegrams and a lengthy letter. I particularly treasure her very precious gift of rose petals collected from the holy shrines on the day of the memorial service. Likewise, the many pilgrims and others who were present on that day sent poignant condolences and love.

MEMORIAL SERVICES IN WILMETTE

The funeral service in Skokie, Illinois, and the memorial gathering at the Bahá'í House of Worship in Wilmette were held on Saturday, 15 November, two days after Mr. Khadem's passing. Bahá'ís, hundreds of them, were drawn from all over the nation. Some traveled thousands of miles from foreign countries on forty-eight hours' notice or less. All came to pay respects to their beloved Hand of the Cause. The funeral services began in the morning. The hall was filled to overflowing with friends, but the flowers outnumbered the people. Roses, hyacinths, orchids, carnations, chrysanthemums, and exotic plants of many varieties perfumed the air with their love-scents.

---

*For the account of Mr. Khadem's part in the centenary observances, see pp. 40–44.

At nine o'clock a funeral observance was held in Persian, beginning with the Arabic Prayer for the Departed, which was followed by Persian chanting and prayers from Mr. Khadem's grandchildren.

At ten o'clock the English service began with Judge James Nelson, member of the National Spiritual Assembly of the Bahá'ís of the United States, welcoming the guests to this gathering where "joy and sorrow embrace." The Hand of the Cause of God William Sears offered tender words in memory of his close friend and colleague in the service of the beloved Guardian. In his usual lighthearted and charming style, he remarked that he now had more friends in the Abhá Kingdom than in this world.* He continued with words of love and appreciation and said that only future generations could begin to appreciate Mr. Khadem's spiritual qualities and scholarship. Selections of harp music were played between the various prayers, which ended with the Prayer for the Departed in English.[5]

Pallbearers obscured the sight of Mr. Khadem's precious casket, for many wished to participate in that last act of love and homage. The funeral cavalcade was impressive; a line of headlit cars stretched as far as the eye could see. At the graveside more prayers were said. As each mourner bid a tearful good-bye, the chill in the weather matched the chill in the hearts of those who grieved, while the brilliant sunshine suggested the brilliant and glorious world to which this treasure among us had repaired.

The memorial gathering, held at two o'clock in the House of Worship, was a ceremony of love and appreciation for one who loved greatly. The program, which began in the auditorium upstairs, included choir music, Persian chanting, and readings from *Gleanings from the Writings of Bahá'u'lláh* and the Tablet of Carmel, which Mr. Khadem loved so much. The service continued downstairs in Foundation Hall, the dais of which was filled with flowers with loving sentiments attached. The friends entered to the strains of piano music until the hall was full; many had to remain outside for lack of

---

*The Abhá Kingdom is the world beyond this world, or, literally, the Most Glorious Kingdom.

[5]See Bahá'u'lláh, in Bahá'u'lláh, the Báb, and 'Abdu'l-Bahá, *Bahá'í Prayers: A Selection of Prayers Revealed by Bahá'u'lláh, the Báb, and 'Abdu'l-Bahá*, new ed. (Wilmette, Ill.: Bahá'í Publishing Trust, 1985), 40–41.

*The graveside service held for the Hand of the Cause of God
Zikrullah Khadem at Memorial Park, Skokie, Illinois,
15 November 1986. Many Bahá'ís traveled thousands
of miles to pay their respects.*

room. The program began with Beethoven's haunting "Moonlight
Sonata," which conveyed that sense of joy and sorrow embracing, a
concept of the beloved Guardian's to which Mr. Khadem often
referred in his talks.

Mr. Khadem's daughter-in-law, Mrs. Linda Khadem, read a
prayer for the departed.* The secretary of the National Spiritual
Assembly of the Bahá'ís of the United States, Dr. Robert Henderson,
who chaired the memorial program, opened by saying:

> We gather here today to have a memorial service for a man who was one
> of the true champions of the Bahá'í Faith . . . a life that represents a
> shining star that has illuminated this continent for the past twenty-six
> years and for which we all feel so enriched and so blessed.

---

*The remainder of this chapter consists of extracts that were transcribed by Dr.
Richard Czerniejewski from an unedited videotape of the memorial service.

Dr. Jena Khodadad, Mr. Khadem's eldest daughter, was asked to explain the Bahá'í beliefs about life after death. She consented because "My father would have wished that I do it." She began by saying:

> My father was the personification of all that was beautiful and gentle. He was the personification of high ideals. . . . With him gone, there will be a perceptible void, for how can you not miss a mountain when it is removed. He was a mountain, a giant of a man. . . . Even the time of his death was significant, that it should take place when the members of his beloved Auxiliary Board and Counselors were in town and the members of the National Spiritual Assembly.
>
> I have learned so much from him. . . . Those moments when we were playing tapes, recordings of prayers to him, he could hardly talk, and he could hardly breathe, but he would point to his bed, asking me to raise it, so that he could be in a position of reverence. . . .
>
> I feel that he left with me great lessons and great memories and great heritage. So, I cannot really mourn his death, but I do miss his physical presence. I cannot even glorify him adequately because he has that glory already. My only pride is that I am his daughter. I hope and pray that I will be able to fulfill that which he expected of me.

Jena then explained the Bahá'í teachings about life after death, comparing death to the process of birth into this world.

After Jena's comments, Dr. Henderson outlined the history of Mr. Khadem's services in the United States, saying, "During that twenty-six years, he taught us the posture of reverence and demonstrated spiritual constancy and steadfastness such as we had never seen."

When Dr. Henderson finished his tribute, the Hand of the Cause of God William Sears was introduced. All stood in a moving silent tribute to him and to the institution of the Hands of the Cause. He remarked about the magnificence, abundance, and fragrance of the flowers in the room, recalling the historic scene in the Garden of Riḍván when flowers were piled high as the Blessed Beauty walked and revealed the Word of God late at night while the nightingales warbled:*

---

*"Blessed Beauty" refers to Bahá'u'lláh. The historic scene recalled is that of Bahá'u'lláh's stay, from 22 April through 3 May 1863, in the Garden of Riḍván (Paradise) in Baghdad, where He declared His prophetic mission to His compan-

We have the wonderful assurance that my colleague and fellow Hand and dear brother Zikrullah Khadem was never asleep. He was one of those nightingales that sang from dusk 'til daylight and daylight 'til dusk, all the hours of his life. . . .

I know that Zikrullah is here in spirit; I've been feeling it very strongly all day. And the friends who've been at the conference have said it's given an entirely different atmosphere to their consultations. . . . I've prayed over at the Cornerstone,* . . . and I've put in a few "beseeches" for the conference . . . that we would have a whole flood, a Mississippi flood of victories. . . .

I was learning; he was teaching me about the Covenant and all these things. I'd just recently been appointed. . . . He was a great and wonderful help to me and very tender. . . . And he was chanting in the car. . . . It was so exciting going back from a wonderful gathering. You looked off, and you could see the silvery city of Akka and the Mediterranean Sea, how Bahá'u'lláh came "from sea to sea" and on the left was the Garden of Riḍván, when He went "from the fortress to the river," as Micah said in his prophecies. . . .[3]

I said, "Zikrullah, why don't you teach me a chant? . . ."

"How about the Remover of Difficulties?"

Next Mr. Sears recounted how, as he learned the prayer, the Hand of the Cause of God Abu'l-Qásim Faizí and Mr. Khadem praised his chanting but agreed that he chanted with an Irish accent:

I still chant that prayer, and I can still see Mr. Khadem beside me, with the moonlight coming through the window and that shining, radiant face nodding with that beautiful smile as I'm chanting along with him. . . .

---

ions. The historian Nabíl has recorded that before dawn, the gardeners would pick the roses lining the avenues of the garden and pile them in the center of the floor of Bahá'u'lláh's tent. There were so many blossoms that Bahá'u'lláh and His companions could not see each other over the flowers as they drank their morning tea. Nabíl has also recorded that, while His companions slept, Bahá'u'lláh would pace the moonlit garden and that the singing of the nightingales was so loud that only those who were near Bahá'u'lláh could distinguish His voice.

*The cornerstone laid by 'Abdu'l-Bahá in 1912 for the House of Worship in Wilmette is preserved in a room near Foundation Hall. Bahá'ís often use the room for prayer and meditation.

Following Mr. Sears' recollections, Dr. Firuz Kazemzadeh, vice-chairman of the National Spiritual Assembly of the United States, shared remembrances of Mr. Khadem. "It is impossible," he began, "to think of Mr. Khadem without thinking of his association with the Guardian, and so his death brings back the memory of Shoghi Effendi and revives the pain. . . ." Dr. Kazemzadeh described two memorable characteristics of Mr. Khadem:

> One characteristic was his boundless, unlimited love and devotion for Shoghi Effendi. I suppose that the closest thing that many of you that have not had the bounty of meeting the Guardian, the closest thing that you could experience to that event, would be to listen to Mr. Khadem, because in his eyes, in the inflections of his voice when he talked about Shoghi Effendi, you caught reflections of those marvelous events.
>
> The other element that impressed me very deeply, and I hope that . . . it will live with all of us, was the personal humility of a man who bore the highest rank attainable by a Bahá'í. Mr. Khadem greeted everyone as if everyone were a Hand of the Cause, and he were just a simple individual. He put people at ease. He talked to them, if not as an equal, then as an older brother, with concern for their well-being, with genuine love and without any condescension. Therefore, it was very comfortable to be with him, because one could make mistakes and not have one's nose rubbed in them, because you could expound your understanding of the Faith and be corrected ever so gently so that you didn't even know you were being corrected.

Mr. Khadem's son-in-law, Dr. Richard Czerniejewski, requested that all present join in expressing the sentiment of joy and sorrow embracing by singing together nine times the Blessed Báb's invocation, "O God, my God, my Beloved, my heart's Desire."[4]

A collection of slides of Mr. Khadem at various occasions accompanied by the harp selection, "Dance of the Blessed Spirits" from Gluck's *Orfeo ed Euridice,* brought him very close.

Then Dr. Wilma Brady, a member of the Continental Board of Counselors, addressed the gathering:

> Who was he? The answers are so many. He was a gentle and kind and devoted husband and father. He was a fierce defender of our Faith. He showed so many, by his life, how to balance these roles. He showed through the dynamic force of example how to be a leader and how to be

humble. He was the counselor to the Counselors. He left us a legacy. . . .
I don't know how to do this [be a Counselor], but if I think about Mr.
Khadem and the life he led and the balance in his roles, I know a little
better how to do it. . . . The way he did it was to put the Faith in the
middle of his life. It *was* his life. . . . This giant of a man . . . , so significant to so many and so approachable to everyone. . . .

Mrs. Lauretta King, a Native American member of the Continental Board of Counselors, spoke next, representing the Bahá'ís of Alaska:

It is indeed a privilege to convey to . . . the Khadem family the greetings
of . . . the Bahá'ís of Alaska, because, as in many parts of the world, their
hearts were deeply touched by the love of Mr. Khadem. . . . He made
three visits to Alaska throughout the years, and two of them were in the
early sixties after the passing of the Guardian. He's remembered very
dearly for helping them to understand that passing and the role of the
institution of the Hands in that interim time that was so worrisome to
us, while we felt the loss of the Guardian. . . . They spoke about the time
when they were preparing to have a picture taken with Mr. Khadem. The
National Spiritual Assembly members were all in a line and Mr. Khadem
with them. They had been in such awe over the station of the Hand and
in such awe of this beautiful, beautiful man that they were reflecting that
to him. He was aware of how they felt. . . . As he stood in the line with
them, he took one step forward, and he said, "Am I really any closer to
the sun?" . . . I'd like to speak on behalf of the native peoples, especially
of North America. . . . Every one of us whose lives were allowed to be in
his presence were touched and encouraged by his devotion . . . to allow
us to come out of that period of timidity and the feeling of no worth, to
come forward in the path of service to Bahá'u'lláh.

She recounted his exemplary visits to Indian reservations in the
United States and Canada and his participation at the Native-
American gathering in August 1980 at the House of Worship and
the Ḥaẓíratu'l-Quds* in Wilmette for the Continental Indigenous
Council:

---

*Literally, the Sacred Fold, the official title designating the headquarters of Bahá'í
administrative activity in a particular country or region, in this case referring to the
Bahá'í National Center of the United States.

The vision that I have . . . is when he was around an Indian drum with about six other drummers. . . . His face was just beaming, and you could just see the power flow through as he beat that drum. . . . And that blending, that absolute assurance that he accepted us as we were, just permeated each of our souls. . . .

ZIKRULLAH KHADEM (seated at right) at the
Native American gathering at the Ḥaẓíratu'l-Quds in Wilmette, Illinois,
August 1980. Mr. Khadem's visits to Indian reservations in the
United States and Canada and his attitude of acceptance
created a special relationship with the Native American Baháʼís.

Dr. Jane Faily, representing the National Spiritual Assembly of the Baháʼís of Canada and the Canadian believers, spoke after Mrs. King:

It is a high honor for me to speak, on this occasion, of Mr. Khadem with the voice of his thousands of lovers in Canada. And first, we would like to

say "Light and glory, greeting and praise be upon" . . . "The indefatigable, fearless defender Faith deeply loved Hand Cause Zikrullah
Khadem."*

The Supreme Body tells us that he was totally consecrated to his tasks,
and we in Canada have seen that. One of his tasks is that "the declaration
of authority shall be proven of God."⁵ Mr. Khadem saw Canada through
the eyes of the Center of the Covenant 'Abdu'l-Bahá and His Tablets of
the Divine Plan. He first came in 1960 and with those Tablets as his map,
he was the first Hand of the Cause of God to visit the Indian people in
the Yukon Territory. And when I went there some twenty years after, they
told me stories of him. They remembered his love. They cherished his
courage. Canada is a large country, and he crossed it. . . .

The other tasks for the Hands of the Cause of God include the "light
of long-suffering."# And how can I speak of that sacred privacy that
everyone has mentioned, the depth of love and the depth of grief which
Mr. Khadem felt for our Guardian. That light he brought to Canada. He
spoke of Shoghi Effendi with such an attraction that our hearts were
stimulated. We followed his longing to fulfill the Ten Year Crusade.

One of the Counselors in North America at an Auxiliary Board and
Counselors' conference told us that he first understood the depth of the
meaning of the word *love* by observing Mr. Khadem at the funeral of
Shoghi Effendi in London. He saw the traces of grief so deep that he
reflected to discover the secret of love. This is the outer shore of the "light
of long-suffering."

---

*"Light and glory" is quoted from Bahá'u'lláh's Tablet to the World. In this para-
graph and the next four paragraphs, Dr. Faily uses the translation appearing in
Bahá'u'lláh and 'Abdu'l-Bahá, *Bahá'í Prayers: For Special Occasions*, rev. ed. (London:
Bahá'í Publishing Trust, 1975), 58. A new translation can be found in Bahá'u'lláh,
Tablets of Bahá'u'lláh Revealed after the Kitáb-i-Aqdas, comp. Research Department
of the Universal House of Justice, trans. Habib Taherzadeh et al. (Wilmette, Ill.:
Bahá'í Publishing Trust), 83. "The indefatigable, fearless defender" is from the 14
November 1986 telex from the Universal House of Justice regarding the passing of
Mr. Khadem.

⁵In Bahá'u'lláh, *Tablets of Bahá'u'lláh*, 83, the phrase is translated as "the truth
hath been established that the authority to choose rests with God."

#In Bahá'u'lláh, *Tablets of Bahá'u'lláh*, 83, the phrase is translated as "light of for-
titude."

Participants at a Bahá'í summer school in Montreal, Quebec, listening to Mr. Khadem. He frequently visited the Bahá'ís in Canada, where he is remembered for his love and courage.

Another task is that "the breeze of the favor of God, the Lord of mankind shall be wafted."* Many favors of God reached us through Mr. Khadem: light and love and joy—the light of knowledge. His last trip to Canada was for the Association for Bahá'í Studies. This scholar, this man whom I remember speaking at Green Acre about *The Book of Certitude,* the *Kitáb-i-Íqán,* and in *one* paragraph of that book, astounding his students, losing us in awe. So he came to the Association for Bahá'í Studies, the professional scholars of the Faith, and he shared a quality of knowledge which is unforgettable. It is the knowledge of the enraptured mind, the attracted mind, the love-illumined mind. . . .

He communicated love through his patience, through his tenderness, through his gentleness, and through his strength. And he communicated joy. The fragrance of laughter followed his footsteps. In one Auxiliary Board conference, one of the first Auxiliary Board members named for

---

*In Bahá'u'lláh, *Tablets of Bahá'u'lláh,* 83, the phrase is translated as "the fragrance of the gracious favours of God, the Lord of Mankind, hath been diffused."

North America was Peggy Ross. She's less than five feet tall, . . . and she was showing us slides of her trip to Greenland. . . . The glaciers are like mountains and the lakes she crossed and the villages she went to and the boats she got in and out of. And as she told these stories, Mr. Khadem's face just was transfigured in a radiant happiness and delight. He was proud of his champion. And I recall that he was fond of audacious women. . . .

Shoghi Effendi has called the Hands "standard-bearers". . . .* So what is this standard of flesh and blood and word and deed? For a spiritual army, it is a standard of the Spirit. And if we wish to carry that Spirit, we can carry it in our hearts and give it expression in *our* words and *our* deeds. Please God, we may achieve it!

Then followed Judge Dorothy Nelson, member of the National Spiritual Assembly of the Bahá'ís of the United States:

"Bibínid! Bibínid! [Behold! Behold!]" . . . What Mr. Khadem used to say when he was very pleased with a victory was *"Bibínid!* O God, increase my astonishment!"⁵ He would have been very happy today . . . as he looked at this audience, its diversity. How proud he would have been of his family, the audaciousness of his beautiful daughter, and how pleased he would have been . . . because he would see this gathering as a chance to advance the Cause of God.

Bahá'u'lláh . . . has said, "Let deeds, not words, be your adorning."⁵ It was his deeds and his humility in performing those deeds. . . . In South Dakota . . . we [the National Spiritual Assembly of the Bahá'ís of the United States] received word that many Native Americans had become Bahá'ís. . . . We called his home, and we found that he was ill. . . . Then the phone rang, and he said, "I understand that you called me. What may I do for you?" And we said, "Oh, Mr. Khadem, we had wanted to send you to meet with the friends in . . . South Dakota, but we know you are ill. . . ."

He said, "You are my National Spiritual Assembly; I will go." . . .

---

*See Shoghi Effendi, letter dated 4 May 1953, *Messages to the Bahá'í World: 1950–1957*, rev. ed. (Wilmette, Ill.: Bahá'í Publishing Trust, 1971), 153.

⁵One of Mr. Khadem's favorite exclamations was "O Lord, increase my astonishment at Thee!" (Bahá'u'lláh, *The Seven Valleys and The Four Valleys*, trans. Ali-Kuli Khan and Marzieh Gail, 3d ed. [Wilmette, Ill.: Bahá'í Publishing Trust, 1978], 34.

Mr. Khadem and a group of Native American Bahá'ís.
Mr. Khadem was very fond of the Native American Bahá'ís
and visited them as often as possible.

Indeed, he had a very special relationship to the Native-American believers. . . .

I said that he spoke by deeds and not by words. It was his relationship to his wife that caught my attention from the very beginning. . . . I think that he understood and internalized the teaching of the Bahá'í Faith about the equality of men and women as well as anyone I have ever known. . . .

. . . Most notable was his tolerance, nay patience for diversity. . . . To also see this proper Persian gentleman sit during a youth party and listen to modern rock and roll and *smile!* . . . You realize that his sole consideration was, "Were these youth going to carry foward an ever-advancing civilization? Were these youth devoted to the Word of God?" And if they were, let them dance; let them sing; let them express their feelings in their own way.

. . . Only if we turn our grief into action will we vindicate those who have died. . . .

Donna Kime sang from *The Hidden Words* with piano accompa-

Mr. Khadem greeting Bahá'ís in Dallas, Texas. His love, tenderness, gentleness, and joy touched the hearts of Bahá'ís around the world.

niment. Dr. Robert Henderson then quoted from Mr. Khadem's letter to the National Spiritual Assembly.* He asked, "Is it any wonder we loved him so dearly and respected him so much? Even in his passing he gave us inspiration, courage, direction, and, unbelievably, . . . expressed his high gratitude for the privilege of being able to serve. . . ."

ENCOMPASSING LOVE

The atmosphere of love that pervaded that meeting and the fragrance of the Abhá Paradise that perfumed all who gathered gave me a deep sense of gratitude to the National Spiritual Assembly of the Bahá'ís of the United States, who had planned the program so beautifully, and to the one who had departed from our midst. I felt a mixture of deep pain and great awe that I had had Mr. Khadem with me nearly all my adult life. Encompassed by the limitless love of

---

*See p. 150.

those who were gathered there in Foundation Hall, I spontaneously felt compelled to go to the dais to thank them and to share my feelings with these, my loving friends. I knew that our children felt the same. Our three sons had flown from Boston, Atlanta, and Bangkok, Thailand, and our two daughters had come from Winnetka, Illinois, and Grenada. There on the platform in Foundation Hall of the Mother Temple of the West, our five precious children and I were able to share what was in our hearts. My children's intimate feelings about their treasured father's influence upon them are recorded in part 2.*

For myself, I found that in those moments of pain and deep sorrow a sense of calmness and succor surrounded me, convincing me that I was neither abandoned nor alone; I had thousands and thousands of friends as well as my family. We were all together in grieving Mr. Khadem's passing, and we shared the realization that serving the Cause of God provides the greatest relief from this sorrow. I felt just as I always had whenever my husband was with me at a Bahá'í gathering, smiling with encouragement and approval; I recognized that I had not only to console myself and my family but also to console, on his behalf, all those gathered there. I conveyed to the friends the pledge our family had made. Although our hearts were grieved by the passing of such an outstanding servant of Bahá'u'lláh, we were dedicating our lives to carrying on the devotion and love that distinguished him and that he cultivated in each of our hearts through the bounty of Bahá'u'lláh. The only compensation for our loss would be the love and service we could offer at the Threshold of Bahá'u'lláh. Our only enduring tie to the man we cherished so dearly would be the quality of our love and actions. In those moments I felt Mr. Khadem's closeness, as if he were kindly, gently, still urging me, "Please, love God and the Guardian as I do."

---

*See pp. 175–240.

*The resting-place of the Hand of the Cause of God Zikrullah Khadem
in Memorial Park, Skokie, Illinois*

Part 2/ OUR FATHER
Reminiscences by
Zikrullah Khadem's Children

1 "All Is the Beloved, The Lover Is a Veil"*

by Mozhan Khadem

Sometimes I wonder, sweetest love, if you
Were a mere dream in a long winter night,
A dream of spring-days, and of golden light
Which sheds its rays upon a frozen heart;
A dream of wine that fills the drunken eye.
And so I wonder, sweetest love, if I
Should drink this ruby wine, or rather weep:
Each tear a bezel with your face engraved,
A rosary to memorize your name . . .
There are so many ways to call you back—
Yes, even if you only were a dream.

—ANNEMARIE SCHIMMEL
"MAULANA'S LAST LETTER TO SHAMS"[1]

My dear father, I remember during July 1986 all of our family came to Chicago to attend my niece's wedding ceremony. You were complaining of a backache; otherwise, you appeared quite healthy. You told us that months ago you had had a dream of the beloved Guardian. In that dream he asked you to arrange for the pilgrims to attend his presence, as you used to do during his lifetime. You looked around but could find no one. Since there was no one, you asked permission to make the pilgrimage yourself. The Guardian granted your request. You interpreted your dream to mean that you were going to leave us. You were thankful to Bahá'u'lláh for having

---

*"All is the Beloved, the lover is a veil" is a famous line of Rúmí's poetry from his *Mathnaví*. He likens the reality beyond the world of phenomena to the beloved, and the world of phenomena to the lover. He suggests that our relationship to the Divine is like that of a lover to the beloved and likens our egos to a veil. To realize the Divine, we must lift the veil by transcending our egos.

JAVIDUKHT and ZIKRULLAH KHADEM with MOZHAN,
their firstborn child. The birth of each of the Khadems'
five children brought them great joy and was marked
with a special celebration of thanks.

permitted you to serve His Cause and to leave the world having witnessed the physical and spiritual ascendancy and triumph of His Faith, a Faith that you loved with your entire being. You prayed that all of your children and grandchildren would serve this Faith and place it at the center of their lives. We tried in vain to convince you that your dream could have other interpretations and that it did not necessarily mean that you were going to leave this world. But you, in your characteristic, uncompromising manner, were convinced that the remaining days of your life were, indeed, numbered.

In early August we learned that your backache was the result of a malignant tumor, and you were hospitalized. I made frequent trips to Chicago to be with you as much as I could. My dear father, I cannot tell you what a great privilege it was to spend so much time with you during the last months of your life. Your happiness was all I desired, and every smile I received from you consoled my aching

JAVIDUKHT and ZIKRULLAH KHADEM
Their storybook marriage of over fifty years was based on
mutual love, respect, and devotion to God.

heart. During those visits, I tried to be a source of strength to my mother, but how could I? She was suffering so much. She told us in the hospital sitting room one day that she fell in love with you the first time she set eyes on you and that after more than fifty years of marriage she loved you with an even greater intensity. The two of you were like one soul in two bodies. Yours was a storybook marriage. You were, indeed, a lucky man to have a life partner whose support, wisdom, loyalty, and love contributed so much to your achievements in the service of Bahá'u'lláh. Do you remember how the beloved Guardian, addressing my mother, said, "You are the assistant and aid of Jináb-i-Khadem"? She performed her duties well.

During my stay with you, you usually talked about your desire for all of us to be steadfast and to serve the Faith. Rest assured, my dear father, that we will, to the last days of our lives, remain loyal and dedicated to this magnificent spiritual legacy you have left us.

In your lifetime you committed to memory many lengthy and glorious passages from the Bahá'í writings. To cheer you during one of my visits, I told you I was going to recite from memory a passage from the Bahá'í writings. I said I wanted to test you to see if you could identify the source. It was an unexpected pleasure for you, and you gave me a benevolent, fatherly smile because none of the other family members teased you that way. The passage I chose was a magnificent selection from *The Book of Certitude,* in which Bahá'u'-lláh Himself seems to be overwhelmed by the beauty and the majesty of His revelation. The passage begins with Bahá'u'lláh's exclaiming over the "sweet savours of God" that "rejoiced anew the heart, and imparted immeasurable gladness to the soul." It continues with many other exclamations over the splendor of His revelation and makes reference to "the art of love's ways." The passage ends with Bahá'u'lláh's explaining that He has "illuminated the heavens of utterance with the splendours of . . . divine wisdom and understanding" so that we may find peace and certitude and "be of those who . . . have soared unto the heaven of the love of their Lord, the All-Merciful."[2]

You thoroughly enjoyed my recitation and on other visits asked me to recite the same passage for you, even to the last days of your life. You were sometimes overwhelmed by the beauty of the words and interrupted me, saying, *"Bah! Bah!"* (How beautiful! How beautiful!). Of course, due to the circumstances, I was always overtaken by emotion when I recited this passage for you. Even now, when I read it in the privacy of my room, your heavenly face, your fatherly smile, your expression of approval, and your frequent exclamations appear before me through a veil of my tears.

During such visits you told us many remembrances concerning the Faith, the early believers, relatives, your childhood, and the condition of the Faith or the persecution of the Bahá'ís during your childhood. You told us how ignorant and fanatical Muslims and their children harassed you in the winding streets of Tehran and its bazaars. My sister Jena recorded these stories, as they are undoubtedly of historical importance. When I think of the changes you witnessed during the span of your lifetime—from your childhood, in one of the most traditional and fanatical cities in the world (Tehran) during the opening decade of the century, to the time of your passing, in one of the most modern, high-tech metropolitan centers (Chicago)—I marvel at your indomitable spirit. You adjusted to such radical change, always resolute and unwavering in your focus on serving the Cause of Bahá'u'lláh.

My dear father, during the last months of your life, when we were together, sometimes you talked to me, sometimes you asked me to read and chant to you from the Bahá'í writings, and sometimes with your heavenly voice you chanted for me. Your constant invocation was "*Yá Bahá!*"* To the end, you recalled the name of Bahá'u'lláh, the Abhá Beauty, and the beloved Shoghi Effendi. Do you remember telling us one day that your heart was full of love for everyone? During the last days of your life you also said, "I have never cheated anyone." How wonderful it must be to leave this world with that knowledge. I have often wondered how many people at the hour of their death can attest to such a clear conscience.

I have so many precious memories of the times that you were with us. I remember your energy and youthful enthusiasm whenever the Guardian called upon you to perform a service. I recall your uncompromising firmness. When you were convinced that a matter of principle was at risk of being violated, you were unshakable in your position, whether the opponent was a friend or a foe. I remember your sternness and your love, your hopes and concerns for the future. I remember how heartbroken you were after the Beloved Guardian's passing, how you suffered and mourned for him. Yet, being a true lover, you remained faithful to the letter of his instructions. I remember the state of utter bewilderment in which you received the news of your elevation to the rank of Hand of the Cause of God. I remember your strengths and your weaknesses. I remember how you mesmerized your audiences with tales of love. Your recitations of classical Persian poetry and the Bahá'í writings, especially those of the Guardian, always inspired me. And I remember how majestically you used to recite the opening address of the Persian tablet of the Guardian for the occasion of Ridván 113 B.E. I often recite this in your memory because it fills me with strength and joy.

During November of 1984, when I came to Chicago for medical treatment, you were alone in your apartment. My mother was out of town on a Bahá'í assignment. You received me so lovingly. You were full of enthusiasm and joy. You had come upon a rare book contain-

---

* *Yá Bahá!* (O Bahá!) is an invocation of the name of Bahá'u'lláh. It is a short version of *Yá Bahá'u'l-Abhá!* (O Thou the Glory of the Most Glorious!).

ing the poetry of Ṣuḥbat-i-Lárí.* You showed me a long passage of
this Persian poet's *mathnaví*,⁵ where, in the most beautiful verses, he
seems to have anticipated the details of the encounter of Mullá
Ḥusayn and the Báb on that auspicious, holy night of 22 May 1844,
when Mullá Ḥusayn gained admission to the privacy of the inner
chamber of his Beloved. How excited you were! You pointed out for
me different passages, different lines of the poem that seemed to
cover the details of that blessed visit. Every movement of your hand,
the expression in your eyes, the ecstatic tone of your voice, conveyed
joy and wonder. You had an almost childlike enthusiasm when you
so melodiously recited that beautiful poem to me. I loved it, every
minute of it. You especially admired the following passage, in which
Lárí makes a demand upon the enchanted lover who is completely
overwhelmed by the beauty of his beloved:

> After you have promptly obeyed His commandments, be calm,
> For you will gently fall in the inner circle of His engulfing charm.
> The fold of His gracious robe when you succeed to grasp,
> Pray, unto the hem of your robe, help me then, hold fast.
> Should you deprive me of this grace, I weep, I weep,
> And woe! In the day of judgment satisfaction I seek.
>
> When parting with the company of my Beloved and His blessed place,
> Should you desire to bring me a souvenir as a token of His grace,
> Verily, I seek naught save one or two strands of
> His magnificent tress.
> Or a trace of the fragrance of His beatific face,
> Or a handful of dust from the threshold of that holy place.³

You later showed me the article you had written about the blessed
house of the Báb and how you honored Lárí by including his poetry
in your essay.⁴

My dear father, you know you were a master of the Persian

---

*Ṣuḥbat-i-Lárí (d. 1835–36), also known as Mullá Muḥammad-Báqir, was a
nineteenth-century Iranian poet and scholar. Several of his poems are associated with
the Bahá'í poet Ṭáhirih and were once thought to have been by her.

⁵*Mathnaví* refers to the meter and rhyme scheme of a type of Persian poem
written in couplets. The form is commonly used for epic, mystical poems. "His
Beloved" refers to the Báb, the Prophet-Herald of the Bahá'í Faith.

language, but this article of yours was truly a masterpiece: the style, the choice of words, the subtleties, and, above all, the love that permeated this beautiful piece of writing left a profound impression on me. We must have read and recited poetry together long past midnight. Oh, how I enjoyed that evening! I only wish we had had more visits like that while you were alive. I always appreciated and admired your style and your mystical insight.

You had a fantastic memory and could recite the Bahá'í writings and classical Persian verses for hours. Since childhood I have loved the verses you read and have committed them to memory. Since childhood I have loved your literary taste, and I still do. You would not admit it, but I think you were quite proud to have been blessed with such a memory. The following summer you visited Boston. I drove you and my mother to a Bahá'í meeting in a neighboring community. Remember my teasing you in the car about your memory and challenging you to recite the entire poem of Lárí's that you loved so much? You asked me to do it, and, like a little boy, I obeyed. You enjoyed it very much. You must have known that I had memorized this poem because you loved it. I recited it during the memorial service held immediately after your funeral, for I felt it described how you were gaining admittance to the privacy of the inner chamber of *your* Abhá Beloved.

During my childhood you made one thing the focus of your life, and that was the good pleasure of your beloved. Your beloved Shoghi Effendi became the beloved of our family. You took me several times at a tender age to behold his beauty.

I was a youth of seventeen when you and my mother received permission to visit the Guardian for the last time. You initially did not plan to take me with you, and my heart was broken. You could not bear it because you knew your beloved had become my beloved too. I was very eager to see him. That night I opened *The Hidden Words* and, by chance, turned to the following passage:

O SON OF DESIRE!
The learned and the wise have for long years striven and failed to attain the presence of the All-Glorious; they have spent their lives in search of Him, yet did not behold the beauty of His countenance. Thou without the least effort didst attain thy goal, and without search hast obtained the object of thy quest. Yet, notwithstanding, thou didst remain so wrapt in

the veil of self, that thine eyes beheld not the beauty of the Beloved, nor did thy hand touch the hem of His robe. Ye that have eyes, behold and wonder.[5]

I was moved to tears. I showed the passage to you. You were touched, and a few days later you and my mother surprised me with a box of chocolates on top of which I found a telegram from the beloved Guardian. He had granted me permission to accompany you on pilgrimage. How wonderful! I was overwhelmed with joy.

Do you remember that morning of 11 March 1952, when we left for the airport to take the BOAC flight leaving Tehran for Tel Aviv? It was during the Nineteen Day Fast.* We had started the morning with your melodious chanting, which filled the house and, like a magnet, attracted the hearts and minds of our family. I am still overwhelmed when I recall your erect posture facing the Qiblih,[§] your palms raised in supplication, your voice filling the air with a beautiful chant of the long obligatory prayer: "O Thou Who art the Lord of all names and the Maker of the heavens! . . ."[6]

On the plane we had breakfast, for it is permissible not to observe the Fast while traveling. You, however, refused to eat or drink. I became very curious. You would not explain why you were observing the Fast, lest we would feel as if we had done something wrong. I insisted on knowing the reason, and you told me that you would observe the Fast and that you would break it with the spiritual nourishment that you would soon receive when you finally gazed upon the beauty of your beloved.

This was the first lesson I learned about the manners of pilgrimage. It appealed profoundly to my youthful spirit. What a beautiful thought, to start a fast with physical nourishment and end it with spiritual sustenance! Later on, as we approached Haifa by car, and the slope of Mount Carmel and the Shrine of the Báb and its beautiful gardens gradually appeared in the distance, and we came closer to

---

*The annual nineteen-day period (2–21 March, the Bahá'í month of 'Alá', or Loftiness) of spiritual renewal and development during which Bahá'ís abstain from food and drink from sunrise to sunset. A symbol of self-restraint, the Fast is a time of meditation, prayer, and spiritual recuperation and readjustment.

§The Qiblih is the point of adoration toward which the faithful turn in prayer. The tomb of Bahá'u'lláh at Bahjí is the Qiblih of the Bahá'í world.

the abode of the beloved, your eagerness, rapture, and intoxication became so overwhelming and contagious that I cannot describe the experience. You, my dear father, transformed that trip from Tehran to Haifa into a spiritual journey from the self to the Self.

When the car stopped in front of the house of the beloved Guardian, and you saw the metal gate, the inner garden, and the sign of 'Abdu'l-Bahá 'Abbás on the garden wall, I remember distinctly how you prostrated yourself, tears flowing from your beautiful eyes. In that position you proceeded, kissing the ground and hugging the pebbles of the walkway. All this time the bewildered cab driver stood on the sidewalk, utterly amazed and confused. You removed your shoes as you approached the flight of stairs leading to the entrance of the house. To the left was the room where the beloved was to receive us. In that prostrate position, you went up the stairs, kissing each as you moved forward. I followed you and emulated you. I did everything that you instinctively did, for you knew in your heart of hearts how to perform this pilgrimage. A pilgrimage to the presence of the beloved of all hearts, the Sign of God on Earth, the Priceless Pearl that had emerged from the twin surging seas, the Guardian of the Cause of Bahá'u'lláh.

Oh how vividly I remember when, in the privacy of his chamber, we first fixed our gaze upon the beauty of our beloved. He rose and, with a most beautiful smile and in the most magnificent Persian, welcomed us: *"Khush Ámadíd! Khush Ámadíd!"* (Welcome! Welcome!). My mother the and Hand of the Cause of God Jalál Kházeh were with us. The spiritual atmosphere was intense, and you were utterly overwhelmed. I feared you would be unable to en-dure his majesty and beauty. Remember, my dear father, how we held to the hem of his robe, prostrate. Gently and lovingly he helped us arise. At that moment I knew he was, indeed, peerless and that you would love him and serve him with all your being to the very end.

During our pilgrimage, his car appeared every afternoon on the driveway to the Eastern Pilgrim House.* He would leave the car and

---

*The Eastern Pilgrim House is a stone building in the vicinity of the Bahá'í holy shrines in Haifa, Israel, which was originally used to house the Eastern pilgrims. It is now used as a center for pilgrim activities as well as special celebrations and social gatherings.

walk toward the Shrine of the Báb and, with a gentle gesture of his right hand, signal for us to join him. You would run to him so swiftly, like a falcon eagerly seeking the arm of his king. We emulated you, but it was hard to keep up. The gardens and Mount Carmel rang with his beautiful and majestic voice, addressing us in eloquent Persian, the likes of which the great masters Sa'dí and Háfiz would have envied and yearned to hear.*

> How shall I ever describe that voice and the verses it intoned, and His gait, as He strode before me! Methinks, with every step He took and every word He uttered thousands of oceans of light surged before my face, and thousands of worlds of incomparable splendor were unveiled to my eyes, and thousands of suns blazed their light upon me![7]

How lucky I was, my dear father, to have made this pilgrimage in your company and to have learned from the master lover himself the subtleties of the art of love's ways.

Last year you told me the beloved Guardian had appeared in your dream and granted you another pilgrimage.[§] You knew you were going, and you tried to prepare us. Six months ago you left us.[#] This time you left alone. I am sure you repeated the same rites of love in performing your last pilgrimage as you did some thirty-four years ago when I followed you and emulated you. Nay, I imagine that, being the ardent lover you are, you have thought of additional subtleties to render these rites more beautiful and to attain the presence of your beloved with more befitting ceremony. The lover and the beloved are at last united. Felicitations, my dear father, for having attained the privacy of His inner chamber forever. And now I remind you of these lines from Lárí's poem: "The fold of His gracious robe when you succeed to grasp, / Pray, unto the hem of your robe, help me then, hold fast."

---

*Sa'dí (also known as Mosleh od-Dín Sa'dí, or Mosharref od-Dín, 1213–1292) and Háfiz (Muhammad Shams od-Dín Háfiz, 1325/26–1389/90) are Persia's two greatest classical lyric poets.

§My father told me of this dream in July 1986.

#This account was written on 13 May 1987. My father passed away on 13 November 1986.

2 In Memory of My Precious Father
by Jena Khadem Khodadad

How do I remember my father? I remember him for the intense love he had for this magnificent Bahá'í Faith and for its Guardian, the beloved Shoghi Effendi. I remember him for his unwavering devotion to the Central Figures of the Faith and to its administration. I remember him for his dedication to furthering the establishment of a new world order. I remember him for his staunchness in the Covenant. I remember him for the love and gentleness that he showered on everyone. I remember him for his wealth of knowledge about the Faith. I remember him for his humility and reverence, and I remember him for much more.

The love my father harbored for the beloved Shoghi Effendi seemed to permeate his entire being, but he also had enormous love for the Exalted Báb; for the Blessed Beauty, Bahá'u'lláh; and for the Master, 'Abdu'l-Bahá. The depth and magnitude of his love for Shoghi Effendi, in my view, emanated from the fortuitous coincidence of his being a contemporary of the Guardian. He was in Shoghi Effendi's presence on numerous occasions. For him the Guardian was the closest link to the divine Source of the Faith, Bahá'u'lláh. Coming face to face physically and spiritually with that Reality through Shoghi Effendi revolutionized my father's entire being. This tangible love expanded into the love of Bahá'u'lláh and God, loves that were interrelated and inseparable. These loves set his soul ablaze with such ardor that it was impossible to be in his presence and remain unaffected by its radiance and heat. This love had a mystical dimension. Often, while driving through the Iranian countryside, and also in our home, my father recited in a melodious tone verses from certain poets and mystics that were written to express their love of and quest for God, the Absolute, the Divine, the Beloved. The poem he most frequently intoned is by Shaykh Muḥammad 'Ámilí, who assumed the name Shaykh Bahá'í over three centuries before the advent of Bahá'u'lláh. This poem speaks with immense longing of the quest for "the Unique One, my Beloved."*

It is the depth and quality of such mystical love that enriched and animated our family life and imparted to it ecstasy. It electrified the atmosphere of our home. I was frequently in a state of euphoria. The beloved Guardian was in command, and all seemed well with the world; we felt assured of ultimate victory. Love for the Faith was the hearth of our home. A magical sense of wonderment prevailed. Indeed, the quotation my father most frequently repeated was "O Lord, increase my astonishment at Thee!"[1] He instilled in our family a sense of wonder before divinity, a sense of awe before the immensity of this Faith, and a sense of astonishment at the incredible significance of our times in the annals of spiritual history. He often said that the Bahá'í Faith is like an ocean, enormous, magnificent, and beyond the ken of men. If we had but a thousand lives in which to demonstrate our gratitude, we still could not render adequate thanksgiving for being born in such a day, the day of the advent of Bahá'u'lláh. My father often referred to the writings of Bahá'u'lláh, in which we are told that this is the day in which "mankind can behold the Face, and hear the Voice, of the Promised One," the day for which "The soul of every Prophet of God, of every Divine Messenger, hath thirsted," and "the Day when the Speaker on Sinai hath mounted the throne of Revelation and the people have stood before the Lord of the worlds."[2]

I was raised in a remarkable home environment. As a child I considered it to be the norm, but as an adult I came to appreciate its uniqueness. It was close to the ideal Bahá'í home, that "home of peace" to which 'Abdu'l-Bahá refers.[3] It was my parents, my father and, to an equal extent, my mother—that most remarkable woman,

---

*Shaykh Bahá'í (1547–1621) was the renowned late sixteenth-century Muslim scholar who first claimed that the Greatest Name of God is "Bahá" (from which the name Bahá'u'lláh and the word Bahá'í are derived). He was born in Lebanon and traveled to Persia, where he achieved eminence in the court of Sháh 'Abbás for his accomplishments in the arts, sciences, and theology. For more information about his discovery of the Greatest Name and for a translation of the poem, see my father's essay entitled "Bahá'u'lláh and His Most Holy Shrine," pp. 304–06.

Members of the Khadem family, visiting the cabin in Teaneck, New Jersey, 1957. The Khadem children were raised in a remarkable home environment, for Mr. and Mrs. Khadem created a "fortress for well-being" that was peaceful, loving, and harmonious. Left to right: May, Jena Khadem Khodadad, Zikrullah, Mozhan, Ramin, Jena's husband Manucher Khodadad, and Javidukht (Riaz was not present).

Javidukht Khadem—who established and fortified this environment, this nucleus of peace, love, and harmony. It was an environment that excited, nourished, fortified, and spiritualized me. It provided shelter and refuge from the surrounding ills, uncertainties, and strife. I remember clearly that, when I started to attend school, I would leave that shelter every morning with the sense of assurance that I could go out and conquer the world and overcome the prejudices and fanaticism of those around me, and that every afternoon I could return to it to become reassured, cleansed, and purged. It was, indeed, a "fortress for well-being" that my parents established.[4]

My father's life with my mother was idyllic. Not a harsh word nor any other manifestation of discord passed between them. He was a secure man who did not need to establish his identity by dominating his wife. It should be said, at the same time, that he had married a unique woman who genuinely loved him and was, herself, determined to fashion a Bahá'í life for her family. She was always by his side, always encouraging him, and always devoted to the Faith. In those early days when my father was very busy and immersed in Bahá'í administration, she was always with us. There was never any question about which was more important, the Bahá'í Faith or her family. The dilemma did not exist, as the two were integral. The Faith was important and so were the children, because the Bahá'í teachings place great importance on their education. Their upbringing could not be neglected. It was only after we grew up and left home that my mother traveled extensively, first as a member of the Auxiliary Board of the Hands of the Cause of God and later of the Continental Board of Counselors. My father always encouraged her in her many activities for the Faith.

In our home, Bahá'í events and issues were common subjects of discussion. The Bahá'í writings and the progress of the Faith in Iran and in the world community were considered significant matters. My father spoke often of the heroes and heroines of the Faith, of the beloved Bahá'í poets Nayyir and Síná, of Martha Root, of Thomas Breakwell, of Dorothy Baker, and of many others whose dedicated services have embellished the pages of Bahá'í history.* These were the role models my father held up to us. My father also spoke of his own father, Mírzá Nasru'lláh, who served 'Abdu'l-Bahá for four years and thus was granted the distinguished title of "Khadem," which means "servant." This title he admonished us to cherish and keep in our family as a constant reminder that the greatest distinction to be attained comes through servitude to Bahá'u'lláh.

---

*Nayyir and Síná—twenty-first descendants of the Seventh Imam, Músá Kázim—were Bahá'í brothers born in Isfahán in the late 1840s. My father met them in Tehran, where they held well-known and well-attended meetings to discuss the Bahá'í Faith. He often referred to their exemplary unity and ardor for the Faith and recounted that their oneness was such that, when one brother composed part of a line of verse, the other would complete it. Martha Root (1872–1939), posthumously appointed by Shoghi Effendi as the "foremost Hand [of the Cause of God]," devoted many years to traveling around the world to spread the Bahá'í teachings (Shoghi Effendi, quoted in M. R. Garis, *Martha Root: Lioness at the Threshold* [Wilmette, Ill.: Bahá'í Publishing Trust, 1983], 493). Thomas Breakwell, whom Shoghi Effendi referred to as "illumined," and as "the first English believer," was the first English

My father frequently spoke of his childhood and early youth. He described to us the extreme fanaticism of the orthodox Muslims and the trials and tribulations the Bahá'ís suffered as a result of the prejudices and injustices inflicted upon them. The Bahá'í community at that time was forced to meet in secret. Many dedicated and distinguished Iranian Bahá'ís met in my father's childhood home and in other adjoining Bahá'í homes in the fanatical region of Tehran, Ḥayát-i-Bágh. At these sessions they read the Bahá'í tablets (letters) and writings and shared and discussed the latest news of the progress of the Faith in Tehran, in other regions of Iran, and in the Bahá'í world community. Through my father's narrations one could visualize scenes of early Bahá'ís walking through narrow and labyrinthine alleys and passageways guarded by street urchins. Whenever these urchins suspected or detected that a passerby was a Bahá'í, they would follow him as far as the home that was to be the site of that evening's gathering, hurling curses, abuse, and sometimes stones. One can only imagine the sense of relief those early Bahá'ís must have felt upon arriving at their destination, having escaped some of the stone missiles. They found peace and love within the blessed walls of such a refuge and within the welcome embraces of its occupants. The Bahá'ís gathered one by one, thirsting for any news from 'Abdu'l-Bahá or the Bahá'í World Center, eager to discuss the Faith, the sacred writings, prayers, or any new letters from 'Abdu'l-Bahá.* Only after ablutions were performed were these writings shared by the dim light of a single candle. Excitement prevailed.

The small groups of devoted believers, heroes and heroines of this

---

person to make a pilgrimage to the Bahá'í Holy Land (Shoghi Effendi, *God Passes By*, new ed. [Wilmette, Ill.: Bahá'í Publishing Trust, 1974], 259; O. Z. Whitehead, *Some Early Bahá'ís of the West* [Oxford: George Ronald, 1976], 68). Dorothy Baker (1898–1954), a distinguished Bahá'í administrator, was posthumously appointed as a Hand of the Cause of God (*The Bahá'í World: A Biennial International Record, Volume XII, 1950–1954*, comp. National Spiritual Assembly of the Bahá'ís of the United States [Wilmette, Ill.: Bahá'í Publishing Trust, 1956], 670).

*The Bahá'í World Center, in Haifa, Israel, is the international administrative center for the Bahá'í Faith. From 1892 until 1921 'Abdu'l-Bahá was the head of the Bahá'í Faith; Bahá'u'lláh, in His will and testament, appointed 'Abdu'l-Bahá His successor and the sole interpreter of His writings.

Faith, in secrecy, contemplated world peace and the unity of human-kind. How incongruous such ideals must have seemed amidst the ignorance and narrowness that surrounded them. One can only imagine the impact this electrifying atmosphere must have had on the souls of the participants. Those must have been delicious moments. One can only attempt to comprehend the depth of love and unity that existed among them. From such gatherings the early believers would emerge, leaving behind that refuge, that open embrace of the friends, going out into the hostile alleys, and becoming vulnerable again to physical assault. Now, however, they were in a state of ecstasy, ready to inform others about the Faith, and to revitalize the Bahá'í community.

During my own childhood I became aware, from time to time, of the resurgence of the same type of fanaticism, although the Bahá'ís had gained considerably more freedom. The frequency and rigor of such episodes depended on the whims of those in power, the exigencies of the times, and the desirability of once again using the Bahá'ís as scapegoats to divert the attention of the populace from the actual problems and the subversive activities of those in command. I remember vividly that during those recurring periods of persecution our home was filled with many Bahá'ís who came to be consoled, strengthened, and comforted. In that haven they were revitalized, informed of the progress and victories of the Faith, and given news about the World Center. It seemed to me that the atmosphere of these gatherings must have been similar to the earlier meetings of Bahá'ís during my father's childhood. My father was a pillar of strength and a source of encouragement for the members of the community. He prayed with them, spoke to them, and discussed spiritual matters in an enraptured tone.

My parents entertained a great deal. My mother was a charming hostess, beautiful, exquisitely dressed, radiant, sociable, intelligent, and hospitable. My father was handsome, debonair, well educated, and prosperous. They were a couple whose company was considered desirable, a couple who could shine in any circle, the sort one invites to add charm and excitement to social events. They could have excelled in any setting, but it was the Faith, and gatherings that related to the Faith, that mattered most. Our home was open to all the friends of the Faith, who constituted our family's social world. It was rare to have a period of several nights in sequence when our house was not the gathering place for small or large groups, for intimate or formal meetings and dinners. Those who came to such gatherings were from all strata of society, rich and poor, educated and illiterate, powerful and humble, dressed modestly or elegantly. It did not matter. All were showered with respect, hospitality, acceptance, love, and encouragement.

Such a level of excitement prevailed in our home that I did not associate the atmosphere and activity with the notion of religion. In the later years of my childhood, I was exposed to the "typical" religious person in Iran, both Muslim and Christian. I became puzzled, wondering how the Bahá'í Faith could be a religion when it was contemporary, exciting, and fun—how my parents, who were neither austere, judgmental, nor narrow, could be "religious." As I grew older I realized that, indeed, within the Bahá'í Faith, the concept of religion has acquired a new meaning. Religion is not a system of doctrines; it is vibrant; it is all of life.

The very atmosphere of our home reverberated with the sweet and powerful intonations of Bahá'í tablets and prayers in my father's strong and melodious voice. I remember often waking up in the morning to hear the voices of my father and my mother in an adjoining room, chanting the long obligatory prayer in tones of absolute rapture.* To this day I can hear my father uttering with meaning and strength each word of that magnificent and powerful prayer, supplicating God and the divine threshold of Bahá'u'lláh, beseeching and imploring divine grace and assistance. I can still hear his voice ringing: "O Thou the Desire of the world and the Beloved of the nations! . . . Make my prayer, O my Lord, a fountain of living waters whereby I may live as long as Thy sovereignty endureth, and may make mention of Thee in every world of Thy worlds."[5]

During the period of the Fast my father's chanting was especially powerful. Before dawn on these days that are "endowed with a special virtue," my father seemed to be tapping directly into the

---

*The long obligatory prayer is one of three prayers revealed by Bahá'u'lláh from which all Bahá'ís must daily choose one to recite. See Bahá'u'lláh, the Báb, and 'Abdu'l-Bahá, *Bahá'í Prayers,* 7–16.

Source of transcendence.[6] The observance of the Fast, in fact, the entire duration of the Fast in our household, remains as one of the most memorable recollections of my childhood and adolescence. We woke before dawn, surrounded with the sound of prayer. We gathered together and listened to my father chant in Arabic his favorite prayer of the Fast, "I beseech Thee, O my God. . . ." In unison we all chanted the refrain, "Thou seest me, O my God, holding to Thy Name, the Most Holy, the Most Luminous, the Most Mighty, the Most Great, the Most Exalted, the Most Glorious, and clinging to the hem of the robe to which have clung all in this world and in the world to come."[7] After partaking of this delicious spiritual feast, we ate the plentiful and delectable food whose aroma had permeated the entire house. The samovar in the background provided fragrant and delicious tea.

At dusk we broke the fast in a similar fashion, always beginning with prayers, often in the company of invited guests. I remember that, after I left Iran to attend college in the United States, I would awaken during the Fast in the solitude of my dormitory room, the only Bahá'í at Wooster College in Wooster, Ohio, starting the day with a leftover sandwich from the night before. At such times it was the memories of the Fasts with my father, mother, and family that fortified, nourished, and sustained me. Those cherished and profound memories remain to this day a precious legacy.

We always observed Bahá'í holy days in our home.[8] We requested permission from our teachers and principals to absent ourselves from school and commemorated the days as a family in an appropriate and befitting manner. For the days of celebration—that is, the days commemorating the Birth of Bahá'u'lláh and the Birth and the Declaration of the Báb, the three days of Riḍván, and Naw Rúz—a happy and festive mood prevailed. The days marking the Ascensions of 'Abdu'l-Bahá and Bahá'u'lláh and the Martyrdom of the Báb were somber, reflective, and quiet. We focused our attention on the significance of these days. In particular, I have vivid memories of the commemorations of the Ascensions of Bahá'u'lláh and 'Abdu'l-Bahá. On those nights we observed the practice of keeping vigil with the rest of the Bahá'í community. We gathered together with the other Bahá'ís and listened to prayers, tablets, and narrative accounts of the Ascension, which were followed by the chanting of the Tablets of

Visitation with all participants standing and facing the Qiblih.* The whole atmosphere of those late hours was charged with spirituality. They were laden with a special quality and power. The night marking the Ascension of 'Abdu'l-Bahá was always cold in Tehran. On such nights in the crisp weather and in the still of predawn hours, the sidewalks of Tehran echoed with the sounds of footsteps signifying that Bahá'ís were returning from their vigils.

The night of the anniversary of Bahá'u'lláh's Ascension has left an unforgettable mark in my life. It was on this night in 1953 that, as a young girl and a pilgrim, I accompanied my grandmother, Mrs. Radyyih Khádem, to the Holy Land. I had the blessed opportunity, together with other pilgrims, of spending the night of the Ascension in the presence of the beloved Shoghi Effendi at the Shrine of Bahá'u'lláh and of listening to him chant the Tablet of Visitation of Bahá'u'lláh. The impact of this most profound experience jarred my entire being. Later that night, still in the predawn hours, I had the unique bounty of praying and meditating in the solitude of the very room in which Bahá'u'lláh ascended to the realms above.⁵ I was close to the bed that had held His blessed frame, close to the slippers that had touched His holy feet, close to the headdress that had covered His magnificent crown, and close to the mirror that had reflected His beautiful countenance. The impact of the spiritual atmosphere in that room, more potent than an earthquake, revolutionized my entire being. Reminded of the phrase, "Thus far and no farther," I was unable to withstand that ineffable power and was forced to leave that holy environment, carrying with me a sense of the enormous grandeur of Bahá'u'lláh.⁹ To this day the blessed anniversary of the Ascension of Bahá'u'lláh remains for me sublime; it offers the opportunity, each time, to recall that night and to attempt to tap into that divine source of spirituality, opened wide and accessible. All of this I

---

*The Qiblih (literally that which faces one; prayer-direction; point of adoration: the focus to which the faithful turn in prayer) for Bahá'ís is the Shrine of Bahá'u'lláh near Haifa, Israel.

⁵"Realms above" refers to the spiritual world. See Bahá'u'lláh, *Gleanings from the Writings of Bahá'u'lláh*, trans. Shoghi Effendi, 2d ed. (Wilmette, Ill.: Bahá'í Publishing Trust, 1976), 26.

owe to my father and mother; it was their resolve to send each of their children to the holy shrines and the presence of the beloved Guardian.

My father was a scholar, continually in pursuit of knowledge. For every scriptural question he had many answers that included intricacies unraveled and derived from the writings of the Faith and from biblical and Qur'anic sources. He was constantly discovering new meanings and nuances in such passages. He was a scholar in the Persian and Arabic languages and literature. In the original texts of the Bahá'í writings these languages are intertwined and inseparable. Hence, in order to read and to comprehend the holy writings accurately, one must know them both. Not all Iranians are educated in Arabic; therefore, it is not unusual for them to commit errors in reading the Bahá'í texts. Many erudite Iranian Bahá'ís criticized and objected vehemently if they noticed that an error was committed in such readings, particularly by the youth. Not my father; he never corrected these errors, nor did he show annoyance. I remember I often apologized for mispronouncing the Arabic words in the writings. I was especially aware that an incorrect vowel sound could easily impart a different meaning to a word. My father always responded compassionately, saying it is the sincerity with which holy words are uttered that is significant, for God always hears correctly.

Among the Western Bahá'ís, my father was known for his "sin-covering eye."[10] He never corrected, never reprimanded, never exposed the ignorance of the individual, never caused embarrassment.

My father had committed to memory a large volume of the holy texts, including *The Hidden Words, The Seven Valleys and The Four Valleys, The Book of Certitude,* the Tablet of Carmel, and numerous other texts.[11] During the course of his terminal illness, it was these sacred writings that flowed incessantly from his tongue in the hospital, in the still of the night. His room was transformed into a "court of holiness and nearness and beauty," for he seemed to be swimming "in the sea of the spirit" and soaring "in the holy air of light."[12] What a treasure-house was his. I could not help but think that of the many possessions he had acquired in his lifetime only those gems he had committed to memory had been welded into his soul and had become an integral part of him. All else he had to leave behind, but these priceless pearls he took with him.

My father was kind, compassionate, and tender. I believe that he never knowingly offended anyone. He was tactful and guarded in his speech, always weighing the impact his words might have on the listener. If he did not have a pleasant and kind comment to make, he remained quiet. He was modest and very much aware of the responsibilities and implications the distinguished position of Hand of the Cause of God might have for this and future generations. Therefore, in general, he did not agree to the tape recording of his talks. He consented only on a few rare occasions on the condition that he could later review and edit the recordings. He reasoned that we must exercise extreme caution in recording the words of individuals such as himself in order to avoid future controversy and disunity. He often reiterated that the answers to all questions are available in the Bahá'í holy writings. These are the standard.

My father's reverence was exemplary. It was evident in the manner in which he spoke of the Central Figures of the Faith, of the holy texts, and of all that pertains to this glorious Faith. Whenever he approached the holy writings, the holy relics, and the holy shrines, he totally forgot himself and assumed a posture of reverence. He performed ablutions before touching Bahá'í relics. He held Bahá'í writings, portraits of 'Abdu'l-Bahá and Shoghi Effendi, and messages and cablegrams from the Guardian, with both hands, and bowed before examining them. Whenever prayers were being said, his posture bespoke his total absorption. In the holy shrines and in places associated with the Central Figures of the Faith, both in the East and the West, he would take off his shoes and humble himself at the threshold, for it is said that God told Moses, "Take your sandals off your feet, for the place you stand is holy ground."[13] He actually became oblivious of his surroundings at such times. It did not matter to him that in the Western world he sometimes received stares for such unusual behavior. All that mattered to him was that he was standing on holy ground and that he was approaching that which was associated with his Lord. While he was ill in the hospital, he frequently requested that his head and torso be elevated so that he could assume a posture of reverence at times of prayer or whenever he heard the names of Bahá'u'lláh, the Báb, 'Abdu'l-Bahá, and Shoghi Effendi.

He aged very gracefully, remaining vital, mentally astute, and physically energetic and active. The passing of the beloved Guardian was, for him, the greatest tragedy in his life, and yet he showed unusual stamina and fortitude. His love for the Guardian remained ever so strong, enduring and surmounting incredible loss and suffering. This love emanated from him whenever he was with the American Bahá'ís. He felt that, once this love was imparted to and adopted by the American Bahá'í community, it would ignite the entire American continent.

My father was transplanted to North America in the early 1960s as a Hand of the Cause of God for the Western Hemisphere. Because he was progressive, he was very flexible and accommodating in his attitude toward Western thinking. Being a devoted Bahá'í meant, to him, steadfastly adhering to the Covenant of Bahá'u'lláh, following the injunctions of the Bahá'í writings, and furthering the cause of unity. He did not carry narrow views or conceptions of the Bahá'í mode of behavior. He believed Bahá'ís could enjoy whatever was not forbidden, for Bahá'u'lláh has left us free to dance, eat, be merry, adorn ourselves, and partake of and enjoy the blessings of life as long as we do not become attached to them. My father was one of the most balanced and progressive Eastern Bahá'ís I have ever known, yet he was unshakable in his firmness in the Covenant and stern about anything that disrupted the unity of the Bahá'í community. Every remark he made was weighed and assessed according to the impact it might have on the Bahá'í world. Could it in any fashion become the cause of disunity? It is significant that among his last words were "Guard the unity of the Faith."

My father was approachable and accessible to all. At Bahá'í conferences, summer schools, conventions, and institutes, despite exhaustion, and despite often having been kept awake beyond reasonable hours by those who needed to talk to him and who needed his understanding and encouragement, he remained accessible. He never retired to his room early to avoid meeting the friends. He loved them and treated them all with love, deference, and respect, regardless of rank or position or level of knowledge. He often rejected the place of distinction and the seat of prominence reserved for him at meetings and remained in the back, unobtrusively listening and observing—following the example of 'Abdu'l-Bahá, who considered Himself "as dust in the pathway of Thy [God's] loved ones."[14] He attended many public appearances at gatherings of a few or of thousands. At such gatherings the Bahá'ís would invariably stand to honor him, an action he never expected but could not prevent.

Whenever he spoke in public, he began with the praise of God and the Central Figures of the Faith and ended with expressions of wonderment and astonishment at the grandeur of this Cause. He stimulated and inspired his audiences, helping them to draw closer to the Faith by sharing with them his immense love, understanding, and reverence for the Faith.

My parents' home—in Champaign (Illinois) and later in Staten Island (New York) and Evanston and Skokie (Illinois)—was always the center of activity. Evenings in their home were unforgettable. There were firesides, meetings, dinners, and study classes. Some of the Bahá'ís in these communities sought out my father, as did many others from around the world. He loved all of the Bahá'ís, especially the selfless, devoted pioneers from various regions of the world. He loved these Bahá'ís deeply, for they had a special quality of dedication and depth in the Faith. These lovers of Bahá'u'lláh gathered around him like moths attracted to the light, partaking of and imparting love, ecstasy, and devotion to the Faith. They recited poems they had composed for Bahá'u'lláh, related messages that bespoke the steadfastness and love of the martyrs for Bahá'u'lláh, and discussed their perceptions and mystical understandings of the holy writings.

My father was often in states of ecstasy or agony. He was elated whenever his readings of the holy writings produced a new insight, whenever there were reports of the Faith's progress throughout the world, and whenever an individual was attracted to the Faith. He was overjoyed when the Faith was mentioned in the House of Lords in England, when the Universal House of Justice's peace statement, *The Promise of World Peace,* was issued,[15] when that statement was presented to local and national leaders, when a head of state visited the Bahá'í World Center in search of guidance, and when tribes and indigenous people of the world accepted the Faith. But he was in a state of agony whenever he heard of disunity within the Faith or whenever he witnessed expressions of ego and love of power. He was terribly saddened and grieved over the persecutions, the martyrdoms, and injustices imposed upon Iranian Bahá'ís. He was among the first in the Bahá'í community to receive such news, and in his later years these reports became particularly burdensome, for he was unable to participate by being present at the site of the martyrdoms. For my father, true sympathy required that he join those at the battlefront. But that was not his destiny; hence he suffered and agonized. He prayed frequently; and, finally, during his hospital days he prayed for the delivery of the beloved, persecuted Bahá'ís of Iran from hardship, expressing the wish that his life be accepted as a sacrifice on behalf of the oppressed Bahá'ís of that land.

In the last year of his life (1986) my father made numerous allusions to his imminent passing. In April of that year he had a dream of being reunited with his beloved Guardian. He had a strong feeling that the end of his earthly life was at hand. I was in my office the day I heard of the diagnosis of his fatal malady. I reached for *Gleanings from the Writings of Bahá'u'lláh* and spontaneously opened the book to the following passage:

> Be ye guided by wisdom in all your doings, and cleave ye tenaciously unto it. Please God ye may all be strengthened to carry out that which is the Will of God, and may be graciously assisted to appreciate the rank conferred upon such of His loved ones as have arisen to serve Him and magnify His name. Upon them be the glory of God, the glory of all that is in the heavens and all that is on the earth, and the glory of the inmates of the most exalted Paradise, the heaven of heavens.[16]

It is my deep conviction that, within the crucible of physical suffering, my father was transformed and elevated to a higher spiritual state, that of the traveler in the seventh and last valley of spiritual progress, the Valley of True Poverty and Absolute Nothingness.[17] That process profoundly affected those who were with him during his last days. To me, a daughter who was privileged to witness those final scenes that were at once poignant and mystical, he left a far-reaching spiritual heritage incalculable in its magnitude. He taught me the ultimate lesson in fortitude, steadfastness, detachment, reverence, and love. This experience forged our father-daughter relationship into a bond stronger than ever before.

O, my beloved father, I remember you in so many ways. I remember you every day of my life. You are ever present before my eyes. I remember you as that gentle, kind, loving, and spiritual father. I remember you as that unshakable mountain, that steadfast and immovable rock, that lion of the Faith. I remember you intensely whenever anything of beauty, such as the music of Bach or Mozart, touches my soul. It seems that you have become related to the essence of that which is sublime and can be reached and tapped through that which is noble and beautiful. I remember you for the hopes and aspirations you harbored and expressed for your children and grandchildren. You wished us success in this earthly world, but, foremost, you wished us success in serving Bahá'u'lláh. This, indeed, was your desire for us. Since your passing, this Faith has become even more glorious before my eyes, more glorious than I could have imagined. I find myself repeating more frequently than ever before that beloved phrase of yours: "This Faith is an ocean, vast, and far, far beyond the comprehension and ken of men."

The eternal resting-place of your body, that physical garment, is in Memorial Park in Skokie, Illinois, in close proximity to the National Bahá'í Center of the Bahá'ís of the United States, but the eternal resting-place of your glorious soul is in the company of the Exalted Báb; the Blessed Beauty, Bahá'u'lláh; the Master, 'Abdu'l-Bahá; the beloved Guardian, Shoghi Effendi; and the Concourse on High.*

---

*The "Concourse on High" refers to the company of holy souls of the spiritual world.

3 The Power of Example
by Riaz Khadem

EARLY YEARS—1955

It is a cold November day in 1955. I have just turned sixteen, full of youthful enthusiasm and pride. Today I walked from school to our home on Arfa' Street in Tehran to have lunch with my parents and my brother and sister. It is noon, and we are awaiting my father's arrival.

I hear his car stop by the gate of our house, and I rush to open the gate. My father drives in. He has his usual pleasant disposition and smile. He is full of energy. Today he is especially happy. He is in such a good mood that I know he has good news to share with us. At the lunch table he makes an announcement.

"Riaz's permission has arrived."

"Permission!" I exclaim. "When?"

I know exactly what he means. He is referring to permission to go on pilgrimage to the Holy Land. He has applied on my behalf, and today he has received the beloved Guardian's answer. Although I am thrilled with the news, I feel unworthy of going on pilgrimage. I know I have done no worthy service for the Cause, nor has my life reflected the spiritual attributes that are the essential prerequisites of being a Bahá'í. Surely the Guardian knows my heart. In his presence I will be so embarrassed. What am I going to say? How am I going to act?

Noticing my anxiety, my father smiles. "One is recreated on pilgrimage," he says. "It is a breath of life. It will be a new beginning in your life."

He looks at me with great love and continues. "Do you know what a bounty the beloved Guardian has bestowed upon you?"

I remain speechless.

"The beloved Guardian knows what is in our hearts."

These words trigger for my father memories of his own pilgrimage, causing his face to become luminous as he begins to recount his own experiences in Haifa. We listen attentively as he speaks of the Guardian's love, knowledge, majesty, and humility. My father's frame of reference is Shoghi Effendi. He lives for Shoghi Effendi and breathes for Shoghi Effendi. One can see this love reflected in his eyes.

After a pause he looks at us, and with his usual sincerity begins to share with us the guiding principle of his life.

"The sweetness of life is the good pleasure of the beloved," he says. "All of our actions and humble efforts for this Cause are subject to his acceptance. If the beloved Guardian is pleased with us, then our lives have meaning. Otherwise, we have lived in vain. *Khasira addunyá wal ákhira* [a loss in both this world and the world to come]."

There is a pause. He is moved by his own statement. In a melodious voice he begins to chant his favorite poem of Shapúr Rássekh, *"Ján-i jahán fidá-yi tu bád iy jahán-i ján."* I have heard him recite this verse at least a thousand times in praise of the beloved Guardian. It means "May the spirit of the universe be a sacrifice to thee, O Universe of a Spirit." He continues with other verses from the same poem. *"Rúh-i Hayát lutf-u ridáy-i tu dilbar ast* [the spirit of life is in the bounty and good pleasure of thee, my beloved]."

Tears flow down his cheeks. He continues to recite the entire poem and, afterward, chants a prayer from 'Abdu'l-Bahá. I cannot understand why he is weeping. Yet I can feel the love he has in his heart for Shoghi Effendi. I am touched by the sentiments he has expressed. His words and counsels are a helpful guide to my own pilgrimage.

I am now truly excited about my pilgrimage and about the opportunity of being in the presence of Shoghi Effendi. My father's words keep ringing in my ears all the time, at home and at school, as I anxiously await my departure for Haifa. His love for Shoghi Effendi has been planted in my heart.

PILGRIMAGE

It is midmorning on 10 February 1956. Dr. Lutfu'lláh Hakím, a devoted Bahá'í whose life is dedicated to the service of the beloved

Guardian in Haifa, has escorted me and my fellow pilgrims to the house of 'Abdu'l-Bahá.* Dr. Ḥakím is our guide, our mentor, and the intermediary between us and the Guardian while we are in the Holy Land. We have arrived at a gate on Abbas Street and are ushered into a waiting room by the gate, where we sit with expectation. My fellow pilgrims are conversing. I am sitting quietly, remembering my father's praises of Shoghi Effendi and his burning desire to attain the Guardian's good pleasure. In the midst of these thoughts, I hear Dr. Ḥakím announcing that the Guardian is expecting us.

I follow the group. We walk down the staircase of the waiting area, through the front yard, and up the stairs leading to the inside entrance of the house of 'Abdu'l-Bahá. At the top of the stairs we turn into the reception room to the left.

The beloved Guardian is standing to receive us. He is wearing a dark robe and a Turkish hat. He looks happy. This is the moment I have been waiting for.

I walk in and am overwhelmed at being in the Guardian's presence. The Guardian embraces me. "_Khush ámadíd, bifarmá'íd bálátar binishtníd_ [Welcome, please be seated farther up the room]."

The beloved Guardian seats himself. We sit too. I am in a chair opposite him but do not feel worthy of sitting in his presence. I feel a force pulling me toward the floor. Yet I control myself to conform to what the older pilgrims are doing.

"In the past the pilgrims used to spend six months on the road, walking on foot all the way from Iran to the Holy Land to see Bahá'u'lláh. They encountered many difficulties on the way. After arriving, they were content to view the Blessed Beauty from a distance and walked all the way back.⁵ Now the means of transportation are improved. It has taken you days to come here, and you have come with the full support of the Israeli authorities."

I feel numb as I listen to these words, wondering why I have the good fortune of being here. I cannot believe where I am and what I am witnessing. Just as I am becoming fully conscious of my sur-

---

*Dr. Lutfu'lláh Ḥakím, who died 12 August 1968, was a member of the International Bahá'í Council (the precursor of the Universal House of Justice) and of the Universal House of Justice.

§"Blessed Beauty" refers to Bahá'u'lláh.

roundings, the audience with the beloved Guardian is over, and he bids us farewell.

My first meeting with Shoghi Effendi has shaken me beyond my expectations. I do not know what has happened or what I have heard, but I feel that my life has taken on a new course. I cannot express how I feel, except that I cannot wait until the next time I will be in the Guardian's presence.

Later, after lunch, it is again my privilege to share a visit with the beloved Guardian. Standing by the door of the Eastern Pilgrim House, next to the Shrine of the Báb, we see the Guardian walk through the gate and turn onto a path above the Shrine.*

"Run," Dr. Ḥakím says. We all run up the hill toward the Guardian. As we approach him, he greets us with a smile.

As the youngest of the pilgrims, I prefer to walk behind everyone, thinking that in this way I will hide in the crowd, get a better perspective of everything that is happening, and be better able to cherish these precious moments.

Suddenly the beloved Guardian turns to me and smiles. I feel a chill as I encounter this unexpected attention.

"Has your father returned from his trip?"

I manage to reply in the affirmative as respectfully as possible.

"Jináb-i-Khadem," the Guardian explains to the other pilgrims, "has recently traveled to Japan, Hong Kong, India, and Burma, visiting and encouraging the friends. He has rendered significant services to the Cause. In the future the account of his services will be recorded in the pages of history."

I listen to the beloved Guardian's encouraging words. I ponder their significance. I recall the day my father gave me the news of my pilgrimage and his own longing to attain the good pleasure of Shoghi Effendi. How I wish he were here to see that the Guardian is pleased with him.

---

*The Eastern Pilgrim House is a stone building located near the Shrine of the Báb in Haifa. For many years it was used to house Bahá'í pilgrims from Eastern countries. As the flow of pilgrims increased, other housing accomodations were found, and the building now serves as a center of pilgrim activities. See David S. Ruhe, *Door of Hope: A Century of the Bahá'í Faith in the Holy Land* (Oxford: George Ronald, 1983), 177–78.

Shoghi Effendi continues to talk to us about the progress of the Cause throughout the world—in Asia, Europe, and Africa. We walk to the cyprus trees by which Bahá'u'lláh pitched His tent, and the Guardian tells us the story of how the Shrine of the Báb came into being in fulfillment of Bahá'u'lláh's instructions.

We continue walking along the pathway above the Shrine. When we have walked a half circle around the Shrine of the Báb, the beloved Guardian invites us to sit on chairs arranged on the terrace at the left boundary of the Bahá'í property. We are facing the Shrine of the Báb. At the Guardian's request, Dr. Ḥakím serves us tea. The Guardian explains the history of how the properties were acquired for the Shrines. After tea we walk toward the Shrine. We take off our shoes and follow the Guardian into the Shrine. The Guardian prostrates himself on the threshold of the holy Shrine. He then stands, facing the shrine, to chant the Tablet of Visitation.* I have heard my father describe the beauty of the Guardian's voice, the majesty of his bearing, and the prophecies fulfilled through his chant. These I can now witness with my own eyes and ears.

The Guardian walks backward to exit the Shrine. We follow suit. After reclaiming our shoes, we silently follow the beloved Guardian along the path leading to the Eastern Pilgrim House, where the Guardian's car is waiting to drive him to the house of 'Abdu'l-Bahá.

This second visit leaves me equally numb. I have been absorbing these unique experiences and receiving spiritual nourishment. I pray that these events will produce in me a worthy fruit.

Today I am visiting Bahjí, the Shrine of Bahá'u'lláh. We are sitting in the Pilgrim House, waiting to go to the Shrine. Dr. Ḥakím has briefed us on the significance of this spot and on the attitude it deserves. I am sitting on the sofa, thinking about my experiences in the presence of the Guardian. I think of my father and his descriptions of the days of Bahá'u'lláh in Akka. I pick up an English prayer book and begin reading a prayer in English for the first time. "O my God!

---

*The Tablet of Visitation read at the Shrine of the Báb is found in Bahá'u'lláh, the Báb, and 'Abdu'l-Bahá, *Bahá'í Prayers: A Selection of Prayers Revealed by Bahá'u'lláh, the Báb, and 'Abdu'l-Bahá*, new ed. (Wilmette, Ill.: Bahá'í Publishing Trust, 1985), 230–33.

O my God! Unite the hearts of Thy servants, and reveal to them Thy
great purpose. May they follow Thy commandments and abide in
Thy Law."[1] Suddenly my tears begin to flow. I had always watched
my father chant prayers and wondered why tears flowed from his
eyes. I had never understood the connection. I do now. I cannot
stop. My fellow pilgrims are concerned. We circumambulate the
Shrine, enter it, say prayers in the Shrine, come back out, and return
to Haifa, and still I cannot stop the tears. I know my father would
understand.

EARLY YEARS—1957

It is seven o'clock in the morning on a spring day in 1957. My
brother, sister, and I are getting ready for school. My father is about
to go to work. It is time for breakfast.

There is a knock at the door. My younger brother answers. "It is
the cable man!" he announces. We know this means that a cable has
come from the beloved Guardian. We all know what to do when
such a cable arrives.

My brother receives the cable with respect, signs for it, and gives
the messenger a generous tip. He carries the cable to my father and
hands it over, using both hands, the Persian sign of respect.

My father is already in another world. He has performed his
ablutions and has been praying since the knock at the door to
prepare himself for receiving the message. He seems to be in the
presence of the beloved Guardian.

My father kisses the cable and raises it to his forehead, indicating
the utmost respect for the sacred communication. Then he opens the
envelope, takes out the paper, and reads the message silently. We
watch him with admiration and wait to see if there is something in
the cable he feels he can share with us.

My father's agenda for the day has just changed. He will attend to
the cable received from the Guardian before doing anything else. He
has just canceled all of the important meetings he had scheduled for
the morning. We know what he is going to do when we go to school.
He will be on his way downtown to the central post office, the only
place from which one could send a telegram. The city is crowded.
The traffic is heavy. It takes about an hour to get to the post office.
He will stand in the post office queue. When his turn comes, he will

submit a cable to the Holy Land indicating receipt of the Guardian's cable.

He will then be relieved that he has performed part of his duty. Leaving the post office, he will then deliver the message to the person addressed by the Guardian. Having delivered the message, he will resume his other activities.

What has happened today is not a rare occurrence. It happens several times a week, and often several times a day. I am fascinated by his consistency of approach every time. I marvel at his devotion to his job of serving as the messenger for the beloved Guardian. I wonder what it would be like to have this supreme bounty.

Today is a summer noon of 1957. My father is about to take a trip with my mother to visit the friends outside Iran on behalf of the Guardian. My father has asked me if I would fulfill the sacred function of delivering the Guardian's cables during his absence. I am touched by the trust he is putting in me.

My older brother and sister are studying in America. By giving me the opportunity to serve the beloved Guardian, he is telling me, "You are old enough to step forth and serve. The time has come to arise. You can do it." For a young boy in his teens who is aware of the significance of such a sacred task, this degree of confidence is overwhelming. I am thrilled by the opportunity but filled with a great sense of unworthiness. I accept the reponsibility with great joy.

During my father's absence, I review again and again the steps I am to go through. I want very much to do the job right. Memories of my recent pilgrimage flood my mind and give me added enthusiasm for this unique opportunity to serve the Guardian. When I receive the first cable from the beloved Guardian, I am terribly excited. I carefully perform each step I have been taught.

I keep wondering during these days what the Guardian thinks about the job I am doing. Surely he is aware that I am filling in for my father, for it is he who has sent my father on a mission. The Guardian, in his infinite love, knows the longing in my heart and addresses me personally in the next cable.

When my father returns from his trip, I give him a full report of the cables I have received and the replies I have sent. He examines them carefully. I am sure there are things that I have not done correctly. Yet he praises me, and his acceptance of my work reinforces my identity as a Bahá'í youth.

Mid-Years—1967

Today is a typically cold, foggy, and wet morning in London. It is 1967, and my father is arriving at Heathrow Airport en route to the United States. I have driven from Oxford this morning, excited to see him. I am anxious to drive him to my university and show him Balliol College, where Shoghi Effendi studied in 1920–21, and the Manchester College library, where 'Abdu'l-Bahá spoke in 1911.

My father is thrilled, yet he has a different agenda. Before he does anything else, he wants to pay his respects to the resting-place of his beloved Guardian. Despite his tiredness and the cold, wet weather, we proceed to Arnos Grove for our pilgrimage. On the way there I can tell that he is thinking about the Guardian. When I ask him questions, I realize that he is in a different world; spiritually, he is with Shoghi Effendi.

We stop at a flower shop near the cemetery. He gets out of the car himself to buy flowers. He returns to the car with a beautiful plant with dozens of buds. We proceed to the Great Northern Cemetery. He asks me to park the car outside of the gate. He wants to walk.

My father gets out of the car, and we walk together. His posture is one of humility and lowliness. He walks with absolute respect. I can hear the murmur of humming I have heard from him so many times, *"Ján-i jahán fidá-yi tu bád iy jahán-i ján."*

As we get closer, and he has his first glimpse of the column and the eagle, he hums, *"Yá Bahá'u'l-Abhá"* (O Thou the Glory of the Most Glorious). He stops and chants a prayer. Then he moves a little closer. Upon reaching the Guardian's resting-place, he removes the wrapping from the plant and pours water on the flowers, using the faucet close to the gate, and performs his ablutions in the freezing cold weather.

He prostrates himself on the threshold of the gate leading to the monument, then gets up and walks inside the gate leading to his beloved's resting-place.

He places the plant with utmost love by the marble, and, with his forehead on the stone and the praise of Shoghi Effendi on his lips, he communes with his beloved for a long time.

I wonder what thoughts are passing through his mind. Could it be that the special memories he has often shared with me are now flooding his mind? These are memories of his pilgrimages to the presence of Shoghi Effendi when the Guardian told him that he would be with him always, the memory of the day he received the Guardian's cable appointing him as a Hand of the Cause of God, or the other numerous loving messages he has received.

My father stands up to say several more prayers. He circumambulates that sacred spot, then walks backward with his face full of tears, and exits the gate. We get into the car and drive toward Oxford. On the way there I realize that he is still thinking about the Guardian. Spiritually, he is still with Shoghi Effendi. He chants passages of Shoghi Effendi's writings from memory, following them with poetry in praise of Bahá'u'lláh from both Bahá'í and Sufi poets. This goes on for almost an hour. Then he turns to me, and with a smile he says, "Tell me about your experiences at Oxford."

I am happy to tell him about my work, but I know that he is mostly interested in my Bahá'í work. I respond.

"I have recently begun a research project to unearth documents

Riaz Khadem (in the center, smiling) participating in commencement ceremonies at Balliol College, Oxford University, where Shoghi Effendi, the Guardian of the Bahá'í Faith, had studied several decades earlier. When Mr. Khadem visited Riaz at Oxford in 1967, Riaz was able to show his father many of the places that Shoghi Effendi had frequented and took him to visit the beloved Guardian's resting-place.

THE POWER OF EXAMPLE

about the period of time when the beloved Guardian was a student at Oxford."

My father listens with great interest.

"I have convinced one of the dons at Balliol College—Russell Meiggs, a professor of ancient history—to join me in writing a biography about this subject."

My father is curious. I continue.

"I have written to the Universal House of Justice and have received their encouragement and support."

"How is the project going?" he asks.

"I don't know if we have enough material to write a biography, but we have found several important documents."

"What have you found?"

"The class picture of Balliol College that includes the beloved Guardian. I found it one day while I was having tea in the Junior Common Room. The college had just brought down old albums, and as I was browsing through them I came across this picture. Fearing that it would be lost, I got the school's permission to have a negative made for the Universal House of Justice. I have already sent this picture to the Holy Land to be included in Rúḥíyyih Khánum's book, *The Priceless Pearl.*"[2]

"What else have you found?"

"I have found several original letters from tutors of the Guardian along with his transcripts from the American University of Beirut."

My father is pleased and full of smiles. The happiness I see in his eyes is the greatest encouragement for me. I continue.

"I have found about two hundred names and addresses corresponding to all living Balliol contemporaries of the beloved Guardian. I intend to write to each of these people to ask for their recollections of Shoghi Effendi. They are now advanced in years, and when they are gone, their remembrances will be lost."

My father is pleased. He is anxious to read these precious documents. He wants me to send him copies of the letters I receive from the Guardian's contemporaries.

We arrive at Oxford. Despite his tiredness, he wants to visit Balliol and Manchester colleges. We park the car and walk to the entrance of Balliol College, the same entrance through which the beloved Guardian must have walked hundreds of times. As soon as we arrive at the gate, my father's entire posture changes. He is again with

Shoghi Effendi. He feels a respect for the spot where his beloved once lived. He shows me a humility beyond description, walking with absolute respect as I guide him across the outer quadrangle, through a narrow archway, and up a narrow staircase to the library of Balliol College. There, several students are busy studying.

My father stands for a long time. He is communing with his beloved.

We walk down the staircase and turn right, entering the main quadrangle. Here the beloved Guardian used to pace back and forth, reading the Holy Bible and Gibbon's *The Decline and Fall of the Roman Empire*. I point out to him that at his far right is the dining hall where the young Shoghi Effendi ate his meals. We walk toward the hall, up the stairs, and enter. We spend a long time in this hall.

We walk back to the quadrangle. On our right is Balliol's other gate. I point out that the Guardian's room was off one of the staircases next to this gate. He wants to go in that room and pray.

"I have not been able to verify the exact location."

"Why not?"

"Because I have not been able to get two independent sources to identify the same room."

He is not too disappointed. He believes that whenever and wherever he turns his heart to the Guardian, the Guardian is with him. He closes his eyes and chants a prayer in the quadrangle. I, too, feel the beloved Guardian's presence more than I have ever felt it before in this college.

LAST YEARS—1985

It is seven o'clock on a winter morning in 1985. My wife, Linda, our three children, Nasr, Tina, Gregory, and I wake up, in my father's condominium in Skokie, Illinois, to the sound of his chanting. In his melodious voice, he is reciting the long obligatory prayer.* I sit up and listen to each word. This is a prayer I have heard him chant at least a thousand times all through my childhood and adolescence, a

---

*The long obligatory prayer is one of three prayers revealed by Bahá'u'lláh from which all Bahá'ís must daily choose one to recite. See Bahá'u'lláh, in Bahá'u'lláh, the Báb, and 'Abdu'l-Bahá, *Bahá'í Prayers*, 7–16.

voice that has given me strength during the darkest moments of my life. Even now, his chant is a source of power. There is a new feeling in his voice, and new meanings are opened to me.

When the chant is over, we gather around him at the breakfast table in his small kitchen. He is full of life and energy, happy to see me there with my own family.

He calls my son Nasr and gives him a generous kiss. He asks Nasr about his life and his interests. He is very pleased that Nasr is named after his own father, Naṣru'lláh. He tells Nasr about his great-grandfather Naṣru'lláh's life—about the days he spent serving the beloved Master and about the tablets he received from the Master. My son Nasr is listening to every word. He cannot but feel a sense of history and see his life as a link between the past and the future. I can see his identity as a Bahá'í child taking form.

He then calls Tina and Gregory and puts them each on one of his knees. He gives them hearty kisses on both cheeks. He smiles at Tina and says, "Do you know that your name is mentioned in the Qur'án? God swore by two mountains, Tina and Olive."* She smiles back. Both children love every minute of this attention, yet they seem anxious to go and play. He says, "If you didn't like those kisses, then I'll take them back," and he kisses them again. They know he is joking. He makes them feel special. *"Ján, ján, ján* [Darling, darling, darling]" are the words he repeats.

He calls my mother. "Mommy, where are the presents for these children?" He wants to give them gifts while they are still on his lap. The presents are generous, and the children love them. They are full of smiles; they feel loved and secure.

He peels grapefruit, using a sharp knife to take the skin off each piece. He looks around, and, with a smile and great love, he offers it to Linda, saying, *"Bifarmá'íd* [Please]."* When she replies in polite Persian, he is pleased. He converses with her in polite Persian, with a

---

*The verse referred to is "I swear by the Fig and by the olive, by Mount Sinai, and by this inviolate soil!" (Qur'án 95:1). The Arabic words for "fig" and "olive" are *tín* and *zaytún,* respectively. 'Abdu'l-Bahá says that this verse is an allusion to the mountains Tíná and Zaitá, two hills in Jerusalem, which symbolize the reality of Christ and the reality of Muḥammad. See 'Abdu'l-Bahá, quoted in 'Alí-Akbar Furútan, *The Story of My Heart: Memoirs of 'Alí-Akbar Furútan (Hikáyat-i-Dil),* trans. Mahnaz Aflatooni Javid (Oxford: George Ronald, 1984), 208.

laughter that shows he is enjoying the conversation immensely. He praises her.

My mother is busy preparing our breakfast. Despite our offers to help, she insists that we sit down and relax while she serves us. While she is preparing the tea, my father calls her with a special love. "Why don't you come and sit down with us?" he says. He calls the children to join us at the table and encourages them to eat. He loves seeing them eat at his table.

"Show them your indexing of the writings!" my mother suggests. He consents, gets up, walks into his office with his back slightly bent. My mother tells us his back is hurting. My father returns with a collection of Bahá'í writings for which he has devised his own indexing system in the margins and on the front page. His writing is beautiful and so small that it is difficult to read. In a small space he has written so much, and it is written with extreme care.

I ask him to explain some of the passages, and he tells us fascinating stories that give the background for the text. These stories are about the early believers, and each story leads to another. We marvel at his knowledge, his memory, and his devotion to the Cause. We are moved and transformed.

My wife asks him why he does not write down these marvelous stories. She says she has rarely heard such novel and uplifting accounts. He smiles silently. He says that there is so much that is already written.

My mother asks him if he would chant a few tablets for us. He never refuses such requests, never says, "I don't feel like it right now." He is always ready to engage in the "remembrance of God," which is the literal meaning of his name, Zikrullah. He sits in a posture of extreme reverence. The words he is chanting are most sacred. He feels their sanctity in his heart and soul and begins chanting as we listen. He chants with the most beautiful melody and feeling. Even the words we do not understand are meaningful.

He chants a tablet from the Master in which He states that a Bahá'í is known through deeds, not words, and through good character, not physical appearance. He chants the entire moving tablet from memory. He repeats a verse several times and wipes the tears from his eyes. "Look at 'Abdu'l-Bahá's humility," he says, "and His longing to serve Bahá'u'lláh." My father tells me 'Abdu'l-Bahá said that, when He looked at Himself, He was filled with shame, for He

*Zikrullah (left) and Riaz Khadem in the gardens of
the Bahá'í House of Worship in Wilmette, Illinois, during
the 1986 Bahá'í National Convention.*

had not accomplished what He felt was worthy of this Cause. The Master hoped we would achieve it.

My father asks each of the children to say a prayer. When they do, he praises them and embraces them. Nasr chants two new prayers by heart, one in Arabic. This makes my father so happy that he gets up, goes to his office, and brings Nasr a box containing a small radio/recorder, which he knows Nasr will like. He kisses Nasr and tells him how well he chanted the prayer.

He asks me and my wife about our work. While we explain, he listens attentively. Any part of our account that reflects service to the Faith and to humanity makes him visibly happy. He encourages us and shows how pleased and proud he is.

It is, by now, midmorning, and our souls are refreshed. We are reminded of the sacredness of the writings of our Faith and the richness of our Bahá'í heritage. The inspiring stories of early believers have lifted our spirits and renewed our dedication. We have been loved, nurtured, and deepened. These precious few hours have given us memories to cherish long after we are deprived of my father's physical presence.

4 Glimpses of an Endearing Father

by Ramin Khadem

As I bring pen to paper, I am overcome by a profound feeling of inadequacy. I have written and rewritten the following pages again and again, searching in vain for a befitting account of this magnificent personage, Zikrullah Khadem, seen through the eyes of his youngest son, the fourth of his five children.

Many thoughts and sweet memories rush to my mind as I begin to canvass my years with one whom I was privileged to call my dear father, *"Daddyjún."** Little did I realize in those early days that my *"Daddyjún"* would be the beloved of so many the world over. Oh, how I wish I could relive those years and treasure every second, cherish every moment, observe every example, and watch his every movement.

In the next several pages I will attempt to recount some of my memories and impressions, however inadequate these may be.

My early childhood memories are of happy occasions. While my parents created an environment that allowed us to indulge in the many small pleasures of life, we were also raised with a serious regard for our beliefs and our role in life. The Bahá'í education that most children in Iran received through the weekly Friday schools§ was supplemented with my father's and mother's emphasis on 'Abdu'l-Bahá's exhortation and wish for distinction for Bahá'ís.[1] My father often reminded us that Shoghi Effendi advised young Bahá'ís to ask,

---

**Jún is a Persian suffix indicating endearment.

§The Friday Schools originated during the time of 'Abdu'l-Bahá and later were formalized during the ministry of Shoghi Effendi. The curriculum primarily covered the history and principles of the Bahá'í Faith and matched the twelve grades of the educational system in Iran.

before taking any action (even something as simple as crossing a certain street) whether it would be in the interest of the Faith. This aspiration for high ideals tended to distinguish Bahá'í children from others. Bahá'í children could usually be spotted in public schools by their manners, their serious pursuit of education, and their avoidance of loose talk and other trivial matters. As a result, we often had to endure ridicule for our standards and beliefs. However, our parents and teachers emphasized the sufferings of the early martyrs of our Faith so much that these slight distractions were of no real consequence. Indeed, they helped consolidate our beliefs and helped build our sense of Bahá'í identity.

The treatment Bahá'í children received at school was predictable; sometimes we were beaten for no reason other than being a Bahá'í. After one such incident my father approached my school principal and demanded that the offending student (who happened to be bigger than I and a number of years older) be put on notice. The principal complied, and the individual was brought before my father and me. To my amazement the boy denied any wrongdoing, but I sensed that more trouble was in store for me. My father, recognizing the boy's double-talk, assured him that if I should have any further harassment from him or his friends, my father would personally see to it that justice was rendered. Clearly, he was not going to stand by and watch his family being abused even though he knew the ridicule and persecution that our forebears had suffered and that we might also have to undergo. In doing so, he taught a young boy that, despite the hostility of the world outside, there was a haven and refuge within our home where we could always seek protection and comfort.

A dominant memory from those childhood years was the general uprising against the Bahá'ís, which, fomented by religious fanatics, reached a climax in 1955.* Bahá'ís throughout the country were

---

*The persecutions began in earnest during the month of Ramadán—the Muslim month of fasting—in the year 1955. After the noon prayer in the mosques, religious leaders unjustly accused the Bahá'í Faith of being the enemy of Islam and encouraged the faithful to arise against "false" religions. One such cleric, named Falsafí, had his speeches broadcast throughout the country over government radio. He stirred up hatred that led to pillage, destruction, rape, and murder. The Bahá'í Center in Tehran was seized, and its famous dome was demolished. Shoghi Effendi swiftly

being persecuted, and in Tehran the National Spiritual Assembly of the Bahá'ís of Iran (of which my father was a member) was singled out for retribution. I recall having to leave our home quietly one night to stay at a friend's house after we learned that certain homes were targeted for attack. As I look back at the circumstances, I recall the adventure and the joy of joining fellow believers in the sanctuary of their home and the unity and oneness that permeated the atmosphere as we huddled together in fellowship, chanting prayers.

Ever since my early childhood the month of the Fast* has held a special significance for our family. Hours before dawn we would wake up to the sound of my father's chanting. How vividly I recall rushing to the warm dining room whence the chanting came. The month of March is cold in Tehran, particularly in the early hours, and a fire would already be in full splendor. My father's chant seemed to come from the depths of his heart, and the supplication in his voice was very moving. He would motion for us to join him in the refrain of the prayer.[5] We would take turns chanting our own prayers. Our mother, meanwhile, was adding the final touches at the breakfast table and pouring tea for everyone. This was the sign to move to the table and begin eating. Even though we children were too young to fast, joining in the morning meal was the next best thing to fasting. Each breaking of the Fast in the evening was like a feast—rich in physical and spiritual nourishment.

During my first year away from home, I found the loneliness during the Fast more difficult to cope with than anything else, and I remember calling my parents to tell them how much I missed their

---

rallied the Bahá'í world community into sending cables of protest to the Shah and his prime minister. Simultaneously, he appealed to the United Nations on behalf of the Bahá'í International Community. The combined forces of numerous telegrams from around the world and the increasing pressure of world public opinion and the United Nations helped relieve the wave of persecutions.

*The annual nineteen-day period (2–21 March, the Bahá'í month of 'Alá', or Loftiness) of spiritual renewal and development during which Bahá'ís abstain from food and drink from sunrise to sunset. A symbol of self-restraint, the Fast is a time of meditation, prayer, and spiritual recuperation and readjustment.

[5]The prayer referred to can be found in Bahá'u'lláh, the Báb, and 'Abdu'l-Bahá, *Bahá'í Prayers: A Selection of Prayers Revealed by Bahá'u'lláh, the Báb, and 'Abdu'l-Bahá*, new ed. (Wilmette, Ill.: Bahá'í Publishing Trust, 1985), 238–45.

presence and the unforgettable atmosphere of our home. Fortunately, I had a recording of my father's melodious chanting on tape, which helped me to recreate somewhat the spirit of those early morning sessions. I still listen to this tape during the Fast and find refreshing the melody of my father's voice and the words revealed by Bahá'u'lláh.

Another special memory is of the day we received news of my father's appointment as a Hand of the Cause of God.* It was a sunny Friday morning, and, as Fridays were public holidays in Iran, we were at home having a late breakfast when the doorbell rang. It was the man from the telegraph office. It was normal to receive such calls on a daily basis. Indeed, according to my father, he received up to five cablegrams daily from the beloved Shoghi Effendi. My father, being the Guardian's postman in Iran, would, with a ceremony replete with humility and self-effacement, promptly respond to each and every one after taking whatever action was appropriate. On this occasion, as my father respectfully opened and quietly read the cable, I noticed that tears were streaming down his cheeks. My mother became alarmed and asked him what was the matter. He remained quiet, but my mother persisted until he showed her the cablegram. Now both of them were crying, and the rest of us were alarmed. We were not informed, but we guessed that something terrible must have happened. Later we learned that Shoghi Effendi had appointed my father as one of the second contingent of Hands of the Cause of God. For days he felt undeserving of his new station and withheld the information from everybody except his wife and his mother. His appointment surely constituted a turning point in his life and in his recognition of a mission and purpose that only a few individuals, the Chief Stewards of our Faith,§ are destined to enjoy. The year was 1952, the month, February. Zikrullah Khadem was about forty-seven years old. That sense of mission and purpose was to be his guiding

---

*See pp. 46–48 in chapter 3. For Shoghi Effendi's 29 February 1952 cablegram announcing to the Bahá'í world Mr. Khadem's appointment as a Hand of the Cause of God, see Shoghi Effendi, *Messages to the Bahá'í World: 1950–57*, rev. ed. (Wilmette, Ill.: Bahá'í Publishing Trust, 1971), 21–22.

§Shoghi Effendi, in his last message to the Bahá'í world, dated October 1957, referred to the Hands of the Cause of God as "the Chief Stewards of Bahá'u'lláh's embryonic World Commonwealth" (*Messages to the Bahá'í World*, 127).

light for the next thirty-four years of his earthly life until his passing to the Abhá Kingdom* on 13 November 1986 in Chicago, Illinois.

During the summers of 1958 and 1959, my sister May and I traveled with our parents from Europe to Iran by car. The trip took almost two weeks each time, partly because we stopped en route to see friends and partly because of the treacherous roads in Turkey and Iran.

One episode that combined adventure and daring and that illustrates my parents' sense of faith and trust occurred in Turkey in 1958. We had traveled quite a distance along some fairly primitive roads and had arrived at a village in the early afternoon. It was a hot and sunny day, and as we stopped for some refreshments, we were told that the bridge we needed to cross had been washed away the day before. This posed a serious dilemma for us, as the crossing was the only route forward. Few roads existed in Turkey in those days (particularly east-west, cross-country routes), and it would have meant two extra days and retracing hundreds of kilometers to take a different, more roundabout path. My parents consulted about what course of action to take while my sister and I listened intently. There was great trepidation at the thought of getting stuck in the middle of the shallow river. Because cars were still a novelty in small villages, the inhabitants had gathered around ours and were staring at us as we talked. We asked about the depth of the river and were told it was "only a few feet deep." We said prayers for guidance and meditated silently. Suddenly, my father said, "With the grace of Bahá'u'lláh, let us go!"

The starting of the car's engine dispersed the crowd, but as we set off toward the river, a young boy chased us, motioning and yelling. It was not unusual for local children in the villages to do so, and we often took these expressions of enthusiasm with good humor. In this case, though, we stopped to see what he wished to say. He pointed to the back tire, which was almost flat. We thanked him for his warning and his concern, for the car would undoubtedly have gotten stuck in the river bed. After repairing the tire, we chanted the Remover of Difficulties, a prayer revealed by the Báb,[2] and my father stepped on

---

*Literally, the most glorious kingdom: the spiritual world beyond this world.

Ramin Khadem and his sister May standing at the gate of the resting-place of Shoghi Effendi in the Great Northern Cemetery, London, during one of the Khadems' summer trips to Europe. Years later, in 1986, when Mr. Khadem was ill, Ramin made a pilgrimage to Shoghi Effendi's grave on behalf of his father.

the gas. We sped off while the onlookers on both sides of the car waved good-bye. The banks of the narrow river were shallow, but as we approached the middle, the water rose, and the car was suddenly slowed. I could see from the window that the water had reached the lower part of the doors and was rising toward the middle. Had I rolled down the window, I could have touched it. Fortunately, the current was not strong, and the car never came to a stop. With the grace of God we passed through the worst part of the river and approached the opposite side. As we pulled out, I could see from the rear window the cheering villagers' amazement. We all cried tears of joy and gratitude. My father praised the Lord for His assistance with the invocation *"Yá Bahá'u'l-Abhá! Yá 'Alíyu'l-A'lá!* [O Thou the Glory of the Most Glorious! O Thou the Exalted of the Most Exalted!]" and continued to chant fervently, as he so often did during car trips.

My father's firm resolve to pursue a course of action once he had made a decision set an important example for us children. My mother also played a significant role by debating the pros and cons of alternatives and expressing her views forthrightly. Once a decision was reached, she fully and unreservedly supported my father and encouraged him to reach his goal. Her strength of character and perseverance in seeing matters through was often the factor that made their life together so eventful and meaningful. The unity of thought and action we children saw in our parents was a lesson; rarely did we witness a major disagreement between them. Nor did we see them argue with each other over how we should be reared. My father respected my mother's views and would not allow us to put either of our parents in the position of taking sides and creating family disunity.

Another episode during our trip to Iran in the summer of 1959 taught me the value of courage. Late at night in a remote part of Turkey, some hours from Ankara, our car broke down. Since we were in the middle of nowhere, we took turns sleeping in the car while one of us stayed up to guard our luggage, most of which was on the roof rack. In the morning my father walked to a nearby hamlet and had the car towed to the local mechanic, who doubled as the owner and main waiter of the coffeehouse. The mechanic let us know that he would fix the car right away and proceeded to pull apart the gear box. During a full day's work he extracted more parts from the car's underside. Since he was working in a long trench under the car, there was no way to inspect his work. By nightfall it was clear that he was nowhere near completing the job and that we would need to stay overnight. This we did in the room above the coffeehouse, in circumstances only slightly more comfortable than those of the night before.

Our initial optimism was destroyed the next day by what we saw: a gunnysack full of parts lying by the side of the car. The car would have to be hauled to Ankara on the back of a truck. My parents agreed that I should accompany my mother and sister while my father accompanied the car. A passerby offered to drive my mother and sister and me to Ankara. I still vividly recall the anxiety I felt when we said good-bye and I saw my father sandwiched between two burly looking chaps in the truck's cabin. Our car, held only by rope, was protruding from the back of the truck. The sight was disconcerting; the vintage of the truck, its broken windshield, and its tilted frame, made one wonder which of the two vehicles needed more attention. I was equally worried about my father's safety as he bade us good-bye and proposed we rendezvous with the Bahá'ís of Ankara. Even though both of my parents must have been apprehensive about the whole arrangement, the courage they showed was reassuring.

In Ankara my mother contacted the local Bahá'ís and found a hotel. Given the state of the truck, we expected my father to be late, but we hoped he would not be more than a few hours behind us. It was difficult to hide our anguish. My mother, who needed comforting herself, did not want us to become alarmed; she asked us to say some prayers for our father's safety. To keep us occupied, she coached us in memorizing some prayers, which we recited repeatedly. My father finally arrived a day and a half later.

My mother displayed this same inner strength at the memorial service held for our beloved father in Foundation Hall of the Bahá'í House of Worship in Wilmette. Even we, her own children, were astounded as she addressed the assemblage. Setting the example herself during the memorial service, she asked us not to cry but to rejoice that his spirit had ascended to the Abhá Kingdom. However, we know the anguish and sorrow she still carries for the loss of her lifelong companion and dearest friend.

After I married, my family visited my parents often, and they frequently came to see us, first in Canada and later in Great Britain. Sometimes my work or a vacation would bring me to the United States, or my parents would plan a trip to the Holy Land, to Europe, or to visit the pioneers* in parts of Asia. I am grateful that I had the bounty of being with my father and mother on at least three or four occasions a year over the last several years of my father's life.

On two occasions my father and my wife, our two children, and I drove from England to the continent, crossing the English Channel by ferry, to visit, in the first instance, Bahá'í communities in Europe and, in the second, to attend Landegg, a summer school in Switzerland. For a man in his late seventies my father's stamina, fortitude, and *joie de vivre* were exceptional; we spent days traveling by car,

---

*Bahá'ís who change residence in order to teach the Faith.

stopping en route to visit friends. My father was very fond of car trips, though he did not particularly care for air travel.

On both trips my father suggested detours that allowed us to see special places. On the first trip, during the summer of 1982, my father especially wanted to visit the grave of the late Hand of the Cause of God Valíyu'lláh Varqá, the son and brother of the two Varqá martyrs.* My father was very fond of Mr. Varqá and recounted many stories about him and his family. He told us that during his pilgrimage in 1952 the beloved Guardian had told him that, in the company of the Hands of the Cause of God, Valíyu'lláh Varqá was "outstanding." He had passed away while he was in Germany receiving medical treatment and was buried in Stuttgart. In the company of my beloved father, my wife, and our older children, we laid flowers on his tombstone and said prayers in his memory.

During our trip, my father often recounted stories from the early days of the Faith and from his numerous pilgrimages to the Holy Land during Shoghi Effendi's ministry. He also shared with us poems and letters written by the recent martyrs in Iran. He chanted some of the poetry and interjected every so often, saying, *"Bah! Bah!"* meaning, "Wonderful! Lovely!" One of his favorites was the poem by the martyr Habíbu'lláh Awjí. Often the stories, poems, and letters were followed by music. We listened to tapes of Bahá'í songs and classical music as we sped down the scenic roads of Europe. Those were wonderful and unforgettable days, full of spiritual nourishment and the material delights of life. We would often find scenic locations, particularly in Switzerland, at which we stopped to eat and rest. My father loved such scenic places and was often in awe of the rolling hills and pastures. With good weather and fine food, such interludes were heavenly indeed, and our excitement over these small, earthly delights was almost childlike. While waiting to be served, my father played with the children and exchanged jokes and

---

*Valíyu'lláh Varqá, appointed on 24 December 1951 by Shoghi Effendi as one of the first contingent of Hands of the Cause of God, passed away in 1955. He was the son of the eminent Bahá'í Mírzá 'Alí Muhammad—surnamed "Varqá" (Dove) by Bahá'u'lláh—and the brother of Ruhu'lláh, who, together with his father, was brutally murdered during a violent anti-Bahá'í uprising in May 1896.

Zikrulláh (left) and Ramin Khadem shortly before Ramin,
his wife, and his family departed with Mr. Khadem from London to attend
Landegg, a Bahá'í summer school in Switzerland, where
Mr. Khadem was going to teach a course on the
ministry of Shoghi Effendi.

pleasantries. We also remembered the rest of the family, particularly my mother, who had stayed in the United States to pursue her tasks as an Auxiliary Board member. Her presence would certainly have made the trip more complete.

Often when seeing verdant fields, my father recounted 'Abdu'l-Bahá's reflections on how Bahá'u'lláh loved such greenery but was deprived of seeing it the many years he spent in captivity in the prison city of Akka.[3]

His course at Landegg that summer was about Shoghi Effendi's ministry, a topic that he would have gladly traversed the universe to deliver. He gave his talks in English, and they were translated to German. Although he delivered two lectures each day, he also participated in the entire program and was often one of the last to retire for the evening. He so thoroughly enjoyed visiting with the friends and discussing Bahá'í topics that he seemed to have boundless energy. Indeed, I believe he actually derived this energy from such get-togethers.

Before some of my many trips to the United States, I tried to compile questions on which I needed guidance or on passages in the Bahá'í writings that I could not understand. I remember one occasion when I brought questions about Bahá'u'lláh's *Kitáb-i-Íqán,* or *Book of Certitude.*[4] The very mention of my wish to ask questions brought a twinkle to my father's eyes. He listened carefully. But instead of rushing to give me an explanation, he simply said, "Let us study the passages together. You read." It was not his style to lecture or indoctrinate. He preferred that we come to our own understanding after independent study and questioning. In asking me to read out loud he was encouraging me to think and reason independently. As I read on, the passages that earlier had confused me seemed now to make perfect sense, and the explanations seemed self-evident.

Even so, when I stopped to raise a question, his responses were gentle. He had a wonderful way of giving his entire attention to whomever he was conversing with, and he treated even the most trivial questions as though they were important and deserved his reverent attention. I had seen this quality surface many times in both public meetings and private encounters. His attentiveness, his total concentration on the individual with whom he was talking, his erect yet reverent posture with his hands clasped together, all combined to show the truly noble person he was.

When his serious illness first became apparent in late July of 1986, the entire family flocked to him from different parts of the world. Before leaving England for the United States, I paid a visit to the resting-place of the beloved Shoghi Effendi,* a location that for my beloved father perhaps represented the most holy spot outside the Holy Land and the Cradle of the Faith.[5] It was here, in North London, that he had seen his beloved laid to rest some twenty-nine years earlier, amidst a grieving Bahá'í world and the personal grief of his fellow Chief Stewards of the Faith.

I thought of how much he loved this place and how he would

---

*The Great Northern Cemetery in London.
[5]Iran.

have paid his respects, in his own special way, if he had been there. At the distant sight of the classical Corinthian column, he would have bowed down and kissed the ground. Prayerfully he would have approached the shrine; at the entrance he would have washed his hands and face, using the water tap at the side of the gate. Then, once again, he would have prostrated himself at the foot of the gate and entered the pebbled pathway leading to the monument. Once there, with an indescribable humility he would have kissed the headstone and rested his head on the marble, tears streaming from his cheeks, his entire body in turmoil as though that fateful day in November 1957 were just yesterday.* One could only guess, but surely my father would have relived memories of the beloved, and his many kindnesses, sufferings, and self-sacrifices, and the poignant and moving example he left behind as a legacy.

While I visited Shoghi Effendi's resting-place on my father's behalf, I chanted one of his favorite prayers that he would chant whenever there. It was revealed by the Master and recounts how Abraham was tested by the angel Gabriel, who offered Abraham a wish. In it Abraham declares that he does not want a wish granted by Gabriel, for the Almighty knows his needs and wishes. 'Abdu'l-Bahá ends the prayer with a reminder that we, too, should direct our attention to God, the All-Knowing. During this visit I felt I was on pilgrimage in my father's stead, and I could not help feeling his emotions, however inadequately. I realized he might never have a chance to come here again, and I wanted him to know that this visit was particularly devoted to him as a supplication for his recovery.

A week later I arrived in the United States with my family, including our youngest child, my father's youngest grandson, whom he had not seen but whose name he had helped select only a few months earlier. What a joy it was to see him, even in a hospital setting. In private I recounted my London pilgrimage and gave him the receipt for a contribution I had made on his behalf toward the upkeep of the beloved Guardian's resting place. A heavenly smile appeared across his face, followed by tears of joy and sorrow, as I recounted the episode. I hugged him, and he whispered to me, "You have made me so happy." He asked me to bring him his personal

---

*4 November 1957, the date of Shoghi Effendi's passing.

diary, which was on the dresser. He said he wished to put the receipt next to the prayers revealed by the Guardian, which my father had transcribed in his own handwriting. Housed in a leather carrying case with side pockets and extra attachments, that diary contained a wealth of information as well as some of my father's most cherished items tucked into the pockets. Indeed, when it was photocopied for members of the family after his passing, it exceeded one hundred pages, excluding the calendar section. He was exceedingly happy when I left him, and as I kissed him goodnight, tears were still streaming from his eyes and mine. It was an occasion I shall never forget.

My father was brought home a few days later for recovery. Early one morning while my mother was at the 1986 Bahá'í International Peace Conference in San Francisco to deliver a talk on my father's behalf,* I heard him call from the adjoining room. I rushed in to find him awake and wishing to be moved onto his side. His face betrayed his agony, but as he began to feel more comfortable, a radiant smile appeared on his face. He asked me how I was, and as I held his hand, he asked me to sit next to him in the adjoining bed. He wanted to talk, and I felt thrilled and honored to listen to him.

He recounted the circumstances of the Faith after the Guardian's passing and the challenges and responsibilities that faced the Hands of the Cause of God. He spoke of the Hands' annual conclave and of the significant accomplishments achieved during these historic meetings. As he shared with me intimate recollections interspersed with references to and quotations from the Bahá'í writings, I became aware of the stature of this great man whom I was privileged to call *Daddyjún*. While his body was aged and listless, his mind was as sharp and clear as ever. I could not help but marvel at the breadth of his knowledge. I tried to absorb everything he was saying, and I toyed with the idea of taking notes. But, on reflection, I thought it best not to interrupt his train of thought. I knew how modest he was and that he would feel embarrassed at the thought of having his words recorded. Indeed, on a number of occasions, the family had wished to record his discourses, and invariably he would decline. He

---

*For the text of the speech, see *Bahá'í News* no. 669 (Dec. 1986): 4–7.

maintained that these recordings could, in the future, become the source of difficulty, should what he said be misinterpreted or should it deviate from the authentic text of the Bahá'í writings. On the few occasions that he did yield to our insistence, he made it clear that, particularly when referring to the writings, what he said should be judged in light of the Bahá'í writings for confirmation.

As he proceeded now, he stopped suddenly and said, "I am telling you these things for your spiritual understanding." I acknowledged his remark and had a peculiar feeling that this might be the last time I would have the privilege of hearing him speak so openly and intimately. His advice and biddings, which he said were the result of "a lifetime's experience," I shall always cherish and remember. His admonitions to serve the Faith and humankind are still with me, acting as a constant reminder of his own example. I asked him every question I could think of. I wanted to partake of his every utterance and extend the precious moments forever. Alas, it had to come to an end. Nearly three hours had passed, and it was time to have breakfast and review the daily mail.

That was the last time I was to hear my father talk with such ease and communicate his inner feelings, although I was able to spend a few more good days with him before departing for Europe in early September.

One of his best days during the period of late August 1986 was when my mother had just returned from the Bahá'í International Peace Conference in San Francisco, where she had delivered his message to those gathered there. My mother recounted the events of the conference, which truly delighted him. We discussed the monumental tasks before the Bahá'í world and the many efforts needed to promulgate the peace message of the Universal House of Justice.* We also spoke of his contributions to the Faith, and my mother encouraged him to hurry up and get well, as there was a lot to do.

The next morning, one could see the vitality in him. He was, once again, positive about his recovery and spoke of feeling better. He looked forward to being out of bed soon and continuing his work

---

*The message referred to is *The Promise of World Peace: To the Peoples of the World* (Wilmette, Ill.: Bahá'í Publishing Trust, 1985).

and writing. He was particularly keen to follow up on some of his work that had been published in Persian but not yet in English. These accounts of his many pilgrimages to the Holy Land during the ministry of the Guardian contain many episodes that express his pure love and devotion for Shoghi Effendi. My father's sudden improvement was a source of great joy to the family, and those of us who were around him almost began to feel that this was the start of a turnaround in his health. But a genuine turnabout was not to be: while his spiritual outlook was positive, and he was increasingly resigned to the will of the Almighty, his physical state was deteriorating.

The day of my departure was particularly difficult. A taxi was to pick me up at nine o'clock in the morning; now every second was precious. I was so choked up I could not talk, as was my dear father, who was very quiet. At one point my mother asked why he was not having his breakfast—was it because of my departure? He nodded. I went to him and hugged him, trying my best to control my emotions. In a faltering voice I assured him I would be back as soon as possible. But I could not help feeling this might be the last time. As I hugged my mother, the doorbell rang, and I knew I had to leave. Seized with emotion, I turned, took a long look, and said good-bye. As my mother saw me to the door I sensed the same turmoil in her and yet marveled at her fortitude in the face of such heavy responsibility.

My next visit was in late October. My father was in the hospital again, for his condition had deteriorated considerably. During this period, whenever he was strong enough to talk, he would dictate letters to be sent in response to correspondence received. Among these letters were his cablegrams to the World Center to thank the Universal House of Justice for its prayers, and his last letter to the National Spiritual Assembly of the Bahá'ís of the United States.* Even when he was so gravely ill, he did not lose his sense of responsibility and duty. His self-discipline was a lesson to all who were close to him.

Mr. Hádí Rahmání Shírází, a longtime friend and associate of my

---

*For the text of the letter to the National Spiritual Assembly of the United States and the National Spiritual Assembly's reply, see p. 150.

father's during the days when they both served as members of the National Spiritual Assembly of the Bahá'ís of Iran, recalls that whenever a message from Shoghi Effendi was received, my father responded immediately. One such cablegram had to do with the Guardian's wish that his message be taken to a fellow Bahá'í. Very late that night, Mr. Raḥmání recounts, my father set off by car looking for the person. When Mr. Raḥmání suggested waiting at least until the next morning, my father responded, "Suppose I should not be living tomorrow? How will I then explain to my beloved that I failed to carry out his commandment?"

While he was extremely disciplined in his private and public life, he was also a most loving human being. One of the first occasions on which I recognized his abundant love for the public occurred during the first year after our family emigrated to the United States. It was the summer of 1960, and we were attending Green Acre Bahá'í School. I was sixteen and was seeing my father among Western Bahá'ís for the first time. During one of his informal talks the spirit of love and fellowship that I saw showed me how much more he was than just a loving father. The experience of listening to this Hand of the Cause of God talk with such love and humility to a cross section of Bahá'ís both old and young, black and white, from East and West, was confirmation to my youthful mind that this is the Faith of God.

He was also a refreshingly practical person, and his interest in the world around him allowed us to see him in a different light. The richness of his manifold experiences served as a storehouse of knowledge and insight into worldly affairs. He was immensely concerned about social and political issues. Being an avid observer of world events, he enjoyed discussing their various implications and ramifications. He saw and interpreted many developments in the world scene within the context of Bahá'u'lláh's unfolding world order. I recall that as he watched the news on television, he occasionally related specific news stories to the promises of Bahá'u'lláh, often as expressed by the Guardian during those priceless moments when my father was in his presence. But, as knowledgeable as he was, my father still sought out and listened to others' views, even those of his youngest children. Knowing my interest in world affairs, he would, for example, ask with genuine interest for my opinion on certain issues.

At such times I felt as if I were conversing with my dearest friend and peer. I was surrounded by the boundless love and attention he gave to all who approached him. Deep inside I knew that this figure was not only my dearest friend, but my guide and example, a Hand of the Cause of God, my very own father. What an undeserved bounty this was! And yet this remarkable person who was a combination of spirituality, practicality, wisdom, common sense, and humility, demanded neither special attention nor special status from his family. On the contrary, he sometimes withdrew from discussions to allow us to develop our own thoughts and ideas and to pursue our own interests without feeling any obligation toward him.

His example is, perhaps, the greatest heritage that he has left for his immediate family. I do not recall ever hearing him talk about himself. He never said "I" accomplished this or that, or "I" was or will be responsible for this achievement. Perhaps he learned this humble attitude from the beloved Guardian, whom he often cited as his example. The Guardian always gave credit to the Bahá'ís of the world for the achievements of the various teaching plans. Indeed, my father's modesty was such that we had to learn from others about his many accomplishments during the Guardian's ministry and thereafter. 'Abdu'l-Bahá's tablets, addressed to my grandfather Mírzá Naṣru'lláh, and numerous letters from the beloved Guardian that extol my father's services, are only now coming to our attention. Modesty and simplicity were the virtues to which he aspired. Although he achieved success through his hard work, he never bragged and never let his achievements become obstacles to his social interactions. He led a simple and moderate life, both when he was a young man and when he was older, married, and considerably better off. His admonition to us was not to aspire to be rich and famous, but rather to aspire to be of service through whatever means with which God has blessed us.

My father was a man of rich contrasts: He was concerned about our well-being, yet he had a deep and abiding faith that whatever was best for us would surely come to pass. He relied on prayer for guidance in pursuing God's will; yet he admonished us to act decisively once we have searched our hearts and reached a decision. He never compromised on matters concerning the Bahá'í Faith; yet he was flexible in other matters of life. He loved his wife and family immensely; yet his life was totally dedicated to the work of the Cause of God.

He had a deep conviction that his mission in life was to serve the "beloved of all Hearts," as he so often referred to Shoghi Effendi, and that anything else he did was overshadowed by this purpose. Yet he maintained a truly remarkable balance in his life. He was neither an ascetic nor a hermit, nor was he a religious fanatic. He was a loving husband and father, genuinely concerned about the welfare of his family, fully involved in their pursuits of education, career, and family. Yet his life also had another purpose that did not negate his role as husband and father, but complemented it. This sense of purpose must have been with him from early youth, when his most ardent desire was to go on pilgrimage to the holy shrines and to serve the beloved Shoghi Effendi.

It is our responsibility, as his children, to follow his example, heed his admonitions, keep alive his memory, and pass on his life's story to our children and grandchildren. For his example belongs not to us alone but to generations to come, and such an eventful life forms an integral part of that history, that rich mosaic, that the Bahá'í world proudly inherits.

5 *With Gratitude*

by May Khadem Czerniejewski

It has been one year since my father passed away.* I have rewritten these pages several times since. The first draft was overwhelmed by the piercing, agonizing, crushing pain of loss, for he was so much more than just a father. He was a role model, a comforter, a guide, a mentor. With each draft, as the acute pain subsided, I discovered, in wonderment, that a new entity was being born and taking root—a gradually unfolding and growing sense of gratitude. This gratitude, at times overwhelming, is an unexpected refuge from the oppressive despair that enveloped our whole family. It stems from an increasing appreciation for what he gave to us, his children. Those intangible gifts cannot find expression in words, for it was not through words that he taught us the meaning of love, devotion, and service. Rather, he imprinted these lessons into our beings by his life.

Throughout that life, and even in his illness, my father taught us by his example. His only desire for us was that we, too, would anchor our lives to the love animating him. Yet he never told us what to think, how to behave, or what choices to make. He created a yearning in our souls by the sterling example he set, by the contagious love he radiated, by the tone of his voice, and the humble dignity of his bearing when he shared this love. He had seen, experienced, and been immersed in a ray of divine love in his relationship with the beloved Guardian. That ineffable blessing sustained him, motivated him, inspired and guided him his entire life. So charismatic and awesome was his love that it was impossible for those around him not to be touched by it, moved by it, inspired and attracted by it.

---

*This account was written in November 1987.

*Mr. Khadem—role model, comforter, guide,
and mentor—with his daughter May*

My father never told us to pray, yet our house echoed with his prayers daily. He did not tell us to study the Bahá'í writings, yet I cannot recall a day when he was not studying some Bahá'í book. He did not require of us ritual acts of reverence. However, his whole demeanor, attitude, and posture when praying, or when handling relics of the Faith, or when visiting holy sites, bore testimony to his profound inner love and devotion. I will never forget those very special and precious occasions when he would take out 'Abdu'l-Bahá's wallet* and other precious gifts he had received from the Guardian, so that we could view them in the spirit of "making pilgrimage." After he prayed, he would remove each item with great reverence. With tears streaming down his face, he would kiss the silk

---

*My father received this most precious gift from Shoghi Effendi on 15 February 1940. In his notebook he recorded the words of the Guardian: "This is the blessed billfold of 'Abdu'l-Bahá. . . . I'm giving this to you. It was found amongst the personal belongings of the beloved Master. It will remain with you."

wrapping and press the priceless treasure to his forehead. Why would
he ever need to tell us about reverence, or love, or devotion, when his
every gesture ingrained those concepts into our consciousness?

My earliest memories of our life in Iran are rather vague. Most of
my recollections of those years with my father have to do with a
world that centered around me and only me. I remember his lavish
praises, his convincing exaggerations of my beauty, my sweetness,
the silkiness of my hair, my absolute preciousness in his eyes. It was
inevitable that as I grew up I would discover I was not so beautiful or
so special. But for each of his children he provided a stronghold of
security during those most vulnerable years. I can remember all the
nursery rhymes we would say together and the way he would tenderly caress me with his eyes. I recall how he loved to play with my
hair and would hold it high, releasing it a few strands at a time to the
melody of his endearments. I reveled in the web of security that his
love wove around me. He used to tell me that he would not trade one
strand of my hair for all the treasures in the world. I believed him.
We were initiated into the world from this fortress of love and
security. Drawing strength from that haven, no task seemed impossible and no barrier insurmountable.

When I was seven, I went with my parents and my brother Ramin
on an extended trip through the United States and Europe. So many
wonders and adventures flash through my mind as I recall those
days. My father would give talks to large audiences while I sat with
my mother and played with my doll, Susie, or colored pictures.
Every once in a while he would mention Ramin's or my name in a
story or would smile at us from the platform. His affection was
always evident. Yet the most outstanding and memorable event of
that prolonged trip was when my father's ever-present love (which I
expected and took for granted) was magnified by the unexpected
love and attention of the Hand of the Cause of God Abu'l-Qásim
Faizí. We met him in Geneva. I adored him from that moment on.
He used to hold me on his lap and read stories to my doll, Susie. His
tender heart was so attuned to the special needs of children and his
love was so bountiful that he intuitively provided what each child
most desired. One time I was especially captivated when he made a
point of running after us to say good-bye to my Susie. There was no
child who was not charmed by him.

The Hand of the Cause of God ABU'L-QÁSIM FAIZÍ (far right) with May Khadem and her doll, Susie, on his lap while visiting with the Khadems in Geneva, Switzerland. May's brother Ramin is standing behind her; Mr. Khadem is at the far left; Mrs. Khadem, in the center.

My father, likewise, appreciated my attachment to Susie. I took her everywhere I went. When my brother teased me about her, my father would come to her defense and boast that Susie was a very special doll. Being dragged around for years took its toll on Susie; one day her leg ripped off. I was devastated. My mother cried in sympathy. I think even my father was affected by it. He very gently calmed me, saying, "Things like that happen even to people. They simply have to go to a doctor to get it fixed." He assured me he could fix it. Meticulously, he sewed my doll back together. I was so relieved and so grateful.

A few years later, in August 1960, we moved permanently to the United States. My grade school and early high school years were spent in Champaign-Urbana, where my brother Riaz was studying at the University of Illinois. I remember each of our homes as the center of numerous activities. My mother, perpetually gracious and charming, always entertained all kinds of people from every walk of life.

When we were looking for a house in Champaign, I remember that the requirement it had to meet was having a room large enough to accommodate big gatherings. Indeed, the house we chose, in spite of its many weaknesses, lived up to that promise. It was a red brick corner house on the edge of town. Tall hedges obscured the view and enclosed a garden of fruit trees and a small Concord grape arbor. It was a nice but ordinary house, not unlike the others in the neighborhood. What attracted my parents, however, was its extraordinary, spacious, and well-appointed basement, complete with a kitchen and its own separate entrance to the large, private backyard. That lovely yard boasted a string of lights that could illuminate the darkest night. "This is exactly what we need—a house where we can entertain fifty, maybe even one hundred people at once!" was my father's immediate reaction. I know the garden also attracted him. He loved the outdoors and appreciated the beauty of nature. The house was reminiscent of our homes in Iran, with their large gardens and acres of fruit trees.

The former owner was a very boisterous, portly Greek gentleman. He obviously loved to entertain, too, and theatrically exaggerated the virtues of the house. He even offered to leave all the furniture, including an upright piano in that most important basement room. We were very grateful, overcome by his apparent generosity, until we moved in and tried to relocate the furniture. It could not be done. Each item was artfully placed to hide a major flaw. The piano, for example, if moved even an inch, uncovered a cavernous hole in the wall. We left the furniture where it was.

Little did we realize at the time that the yard would be virtually unusable in the summer because of mosquitoes. It seemed as if all the mosquitoes of the neighborhood held their nightly conclave in that yard. Also overlooked was the inordinate amount of maintenance those six-foot hedges demanded in order to keep the abode of the mosquitoes private.

The basement, however, true to promise, served us well. Every week we had parties and gatherings there. My mother would cook for sixty people each time. The whole Bahá'í community of Champaign supported these efforts. My father, with great warmth and enthusiasm, welcomed all who flocked there—the Bahá'ís, their friends, friends of friends, university students—everyone was welcome. It became a gathering place and haven for the university students, many of whom perhaps came to enjoy a sumptuous Persian feast in the warm embrace of my parents' hospitality. But they stayed for other reasons, sometimes late into the night and the early morning hours. They enjoyed fellowship with a cross section of races, classes, and ethnic backgrounds—the environment Bahá'ís work so hard to incorporate into their lives and the lives of their communities. What captivated them and brought them back week after week was the spirit of love and unity demonstrated in those gatherings. They heard about the Bahá'í Faith, Bahá'í ideals, the quest for peace and unity in the world and also witnessed the teachings of Bahá'u'lláh being put into practice. In spite of the foreign-sounding names, the reality of Bahá'u'lláh's message touched the souls of many seekers who were moved to join the Bahá'ís' pursuit of peace and brotherhood.

The Bahá'ís of Champaign, Illinois, 1965. The Khadems moved to Champaign shortly after Mr. Khadem was allocated to serve as a Hand of the Cause of God for the Western Hemisphere, thereby fulfilling Shoghi Effendi's promise that he would send Mr. Khadem to the West to witness with his own eyes "the secret, the mystery, the light of the Cause in those lands."

During those years in Champaign, my father continued his extensive travels. From his tiny study he managed the activities of the Auxiliary Board members in the United States, Canada, and South and Central America. He carried on voluminous correspondence with all of the National Spiritual Assemblies and individuals who wrote to him. The study, barely able to accommodate a desk and chair, belied the massive paperwork that streamed in and out of its door. He was ably assisted in his work by Dr. Garreta Busey,* of whom he was very fond. He had great respect for her command of English and often consulted with her in writing articles for Bahá'í publications.

My mother also worked hard in the local community. She was a member of the Spiritual Assembly of the Bahá'ís of Champaign. It was a remarkable Assembly. The members were so active, united, and enamored of each other that the entire community was ignited by that spirit. Even now, many years later, when we talk about those years in Champaign, we are moved by the unified spirit the community demonstrated.

The environment of activity and hospitality was typical of my parents' life wherever they were. They were completely united; their priorities were the same.

As I reflect on those years, two remarkable elements stand out. First, I never witnessed a quarrel between my parents. When they had disagreements, one of them was invariably silent. They did not succumb to verbal battles requiring a winner. Second, and equally remarkable, something I fully appreciated once I had children of my own, was that my father rarely punished us. Of course, he never punished us physically. The times when he became angry or raised his voice were so rare that I can count them. I remember each of those episodes even now. They were terrible. The knowledge that we had disappointed our father was devastating. No punishment could have been greater.

During my father's illness the entire family, with spouses and children, gathered at his side. He greeted each of us with profuse tears. He rarely cried, except when moved by the memory of the

---

*Later assistants included Mrs. Florence Avis and Mrs. Lois Goebel, both of whom he praised for their dedication and excellence.

beloved Guardian. We asked him, "Why the tears?" He said he was overwhelmed with happiness at all the blessings that God had showered on him. He said that the gifts he had received had greatly surpassed his expectations. Bahá'u'lláh had been so good to him, so kind to him, so very generous!

My beloved father passed away from this world at 4:00 A.M. on 13 November 1986. How can I describe my anguish when I arrived at his hospital room on that day? There was a "do not enter" sign on the door. The nurse stopped me and said, "I am sorry." Sorry? How hopelessly inadequate the word! I felt as though I were suffocating with the agonizing weight of those crushing words.

I entered the room, his home for the last six weeks of his life. It was empty—empty of reverence and gentleness, empty of dignity and devotion—so empty! Such a vacuum! What love and tenderness had inhabited that room for a month and a half. Flowers from all over the world had left their love-scents there. Messages of love as well as prayers for healing had been received and read there. They still echoed—yearning!

A few days later, when the pain of separation was still acute, I composed the following letter to him. I wished to put into words my unspoken thoughts, hoping thereby to alleviate some of the pain. Those feelings still apply. Those thoughts are still relevant. The pain is still present—and bittersweet—for such is the steed of the Valley of Love.[1]

> My beloved *Daddyjún!** How numerous were those precious, unfor-
> gettable, never-to-be-retrieved moments we had with you that we so
> casually accepted and took for granted. We were not worthy of you, yet
> you were so patient with us. How often you sat in your silence while we
> chatted about trivialities. You were unmindful, yet never scornful, of
> material pursuits and the usual distractions that occupied us. You were
> alone amongst us, set apart by the nobility and purity of your love. You
> never participated in the frivolous, yet you never berated us. You tried to
> inspire us to service through the lustrous example of your love-chiseled
> character. What a standard of love, devotion, reverence, and steadfastness
> you still are to us! What scholarship you embodied, what a brilliant, love-
> trained mind!

**Jún* is a Persian suffix indicating endearment.

Though we failed to appreciate you fully when we had you amongst us, you must now be aware of how precious you are to us, of how deeply we love you, of how profoundly you have enriched our lives, of the outstanding example of uncompromising steadfastness and devotion that you have left us, of the sweet and inspiring echo we will hear, for the rest of our lives, of your mentioning the name of the Beloved. What a rich inheritance you have left us, this legacy of love. The anguish of your separation from the beloved Guardian, which I still remember vividly though I was only a child, was redeemed by your never-faltering devotion. You strove for perfection in the meticulous manner with which you attended to all your affairs. However, the matchless victory you achieved in the pursuit of excellence was the excellence you achieved in love.

I am grateful that you have had your lifelong and most cherished yearning granted: reunion with the source of that all-consuming love, the beloved Guardian. But I miss you so desperately! You left an unfillable chasm in my heart. This icy pain of separation has numbed my senses. This flood of anguished tears has blurred my way. However, through the veil, I can still see the tenderness of your beloved face. I can still hear your warm endearments and the inspiring, uplifting resonance of your voice in prayer. I can still feel the firm, protective grip of your hand in mine. I can still smell the divine fragrance of the attar of roses from the holy shrines, which you saved and with which we anointed your precious body. I will forever cherish the sweet, enveloping intensity of your love when, as I leaned over your hospital bed, you tenderly caressed my cheek and poignantly whispered, *Júnam!**

My precious father, pray for us that we may honor this priceless legacy in our actions, that we may become attracted to divine pursuits with this lodestone of love that you placed in our hearts, that we may arise to that love-intoxicated quality of service that you exemplified.

---

*A Persian endearment meaning "my dear, my beloved."

Part 3 / *A SAMPLING OF ARTICLES*
/ *by Zikrullah Khadem*

Introduction

During the 1930s the beloved Guardian wrote several letters to Mr. Khadem, encouraging him to translate Bahá'í literature from English into Persian. In a letter dated 15 March 1932, Shoghi Effendi directed him to establish regular communications with the publishing committee of the National Spiritual Assembly of the Bahá'ís of the United States in order to receive copies of materials that were being published in the United States. These items, Shoghi Effendi wrote, he should translate into Persian for distribution to the Iranian Bahá'ís by the East-West Committee. Shoghi Effendi continued by wishing him success and saying he hoped Mr. Khadem would undertake the project with enthusiasm and joy.

Thus began Mr. Khadem's literary efforts. His early translations were articles from volumes 5 and 6 of *The Bahá'í World*. For example, from volume 6 he translated comments about the Faith from various dignitaries, scholars, and other eminent figures.* This project took a long time and resulted in a very attractive book. I asked him why his name did not appear anywhere in the book as the translator (which seemed odd for a project of such size). He replied simply, "A name is not important; actions are important."

In a letter dated 6 July 1939, the Guardian praised Mr. Khadem's efforts and his perseverence in translation. Shoghi Effendi said that the translation and dissemination of Bahá'í literature are among the most important services to the Cause; he encouraged Mr. Khadem to

---

*See *The Bahá'í World: A Biennial International Record, Volume VI, 1934–1936* (comp. National Spiritual Assembly of the Bahá'ís of the United States and Canada [New York: Bahá'í Publishing Committee, 1937]), 449–82, for the English text that Mr. Khadem translated.

continue his efforts and to translate articles, important reports, historic announcements, and official testimonies from volume 7 of *The Bahá'í World,* a copy of which he sent to Mr. Khadem through Daoud Toeg in Baghdad. This undertaking and the visiting of all Bahá'í centers in Iran, the Guardian assured him, were important, meritorious services. Shoghi Effendi concluded his letter by saying that Mr. Khadem should continue with absolute joy and that he should be assured that the Guardian was truly grateful and pleased with him.

A letter of 26 November 1939 from Shoghi Effendi asked Mr. Khadem to translate part of *The Advent of Divine Justice* for the Bahá'ís in Persia.* The beloved Guardian praised Mr. Khadem's travels throughout Iran and informed him that the detailed report Mr. Khadem had submitted about the wonderful Bahá'ís of Sang-i-Sar, Iran, had been placed in the Mansion of Bahjí for pilgrims to view.

In addition to translating parts of *The Advent of Divine Justice,* Mr. Khadem was chosen to translate portions of *The Promised Day Is Come.*⁵ He treasured the original English copies of these works, which the Guardian had sent. He later began to translate from Persian to English and eventually, after moving to the United States in 1960, began writing in English.

Part 3 is a sampling of Mr. Khadem's articles written in English as well as an early article written in Persian and translated into English, upon the Guardian's instruction, by Mrs. Marzieh Gail. The latter was published in volume 12 of *The Bahá'í World.*⁴

The common thread woven throughout Mr. Khadem's literary work was his passionate love for the Faith and his perpetual longing

---

* *The Advent of Divine Justice* (new ed. [Wilmette, Ill.: Bahá'í Publishing Trust, 1984]) is a letter from Shoghi Effendi to the American Bahá'í community setting forth the spiritual prerequisites for success in every activity of the Faith and explaining America's spiritual destiny and the purpose of the Faith.

⁵ *The Promised Day Is Come* (3d ed. [Wilmette, Ill.: Bahá'í Publishing Trust, 1980]) is a letter written in 1941 from Shoghi Effendi to the Western Bahá'ís. In it, Shoghi Effendi explains the reason for the world's present moral and social chaos, recapitulating the sufferings and persecutions of the Central Figures of the Bahá'í Faith.

⁴ The essay is reprinted on pages 246–65.

to please the beloved Guardian, the source of his inspiration. Mr. Khadem undertook his writing and translating assignments from Shoghi Effendi with the same passionate zeal that characterized his other services to the Faith. Whatever the assignment, he immersed himself in it, working so diligently and earnestly, and infusing such love and care into the work that he felt himself to be the beneficiary. He worked so hard at collating, compiling, and organizing materials into volumes that such tasks became a lifelong art and avocation. To expedite the work, he taught himself how to bind books and put pockets in all his volumes to hold extra materials.

A number of recurrent themes characterize Mr. Khadem's articles and his many talks and addresses that could not be included in this volume. Among such themes are the sufferings of the Central Figures of the Faith, the significance of their holy shrines and of Mount Carmel, the import of key events in Bahá'í history, and his love for and devotion to Bahá'u'lláh, the Báb, 'Abdu'l-Bahá, and Shoghi Effendi. Again and again, the fragrance of that love and devotion was wafted through his own words in his communications with the Bahá'ís. The articles that follow provide a glimpse of the wealth of information and love Mr. Khadem so generously shared with the Bahá'ís after his first pilgrimage to Haifa and his first meeting with Shoghi Effendi in 1925.

1 Pilgrimage to the Scenes of the Báb's Captivity and Martyrdom

by Zikrullah Khadem

An essay written in 1950 on the occasion of the centenary of the martyrdom of the Báb, the Prophet-Forerunner of the Bahá'í Faith, and translated by Marzieh Gail for publication in The Bahá'í World: A Biennial International Record, Volume XII, 1950–1954, *comp. National Spiritual Assembly of the Bahá'ís of the United States (Wilmette, Ill.: Bahá'í Publishing Trust, 1956), 217–26. Copyright © 1956 by the National Spiritual Assembly of the Bahá'ís of the United States. It is reprinted here with minor corrections.*

A hundred years have now gone by since the meek and holy Báb, the Gate of God, was put to death at noon on 9 July 1850, and even to the present day the world and its peoples ("except for those into whose eyes God hath shed the radiance of His Face") are fast in a deathlike sleep, unconscious of a mighty Faith, a transcendent Dispensation, which made prophets and seers of past ages cry out and weep with longing for it.

At this time the Bahá'ís of the world, from the northernmost point of the globe to the southernmost, and from Far East to Far West, following the example of Shoghi Effendi, turned their hearts toward the country of sorrows to commemorate at the Guardian's bidding the first centenary of the Báb's martyrdom. In recognition of this event the National Spiritual Assembly of the Bahá'ís of Persia went on a nine-day pilgrimage into Ádhirbáyján. This is an account of their journey and what it meant to one of them.

JOURNEY TO TABRÍZ

It is Thursday, the sixth of July 1950. It is the day of Istijlál, the day of Qudrat, the month of Rahmat, of the year Javáb, of the sixth

Váhid of the first Kull-i-Shay'. The group of travelers has set out as
pilgrims, in a spirit of humility and penitence and great love, going
to the place of the Báb's last agony. They are traveling to that spot
whose very name, some thousand years ago, set fire to the heart of
Muhammad's descendant the Imám Muhammad-Báqir, so that he
spoke these words of it: "Inevitable for us is Ádhirbáyján. Nothing
can equal it. . . ."

They are traveling to see the place with their physical eyes, but
also to weep over the anguish of that Lord of men in the Country of
Sorrows itself, where earth and air, mountains and lakes, streams,
trees, and stones bear witness to the wrong that was done Him. They
will pour out for Him as a libation something of the sorrow of their
hearts.

The bus goes fast. Again it slows. It fulfills the promise about the
Day of the Lord and the coming of the Kingdom when, as the
scripture says, the earth will be rolled up. All along, our talk is of the
passion of the Báb. We pass through Zanján and remember how
lightly Hujjat and his companions tossed away their lives there.
Wherever the new road replaces the old, we turn like compass
needles to the abandoned thoroughfare, because it was there that the
Báb passed by. At Míyánaj we see Him again—in that house with
the upper room. One of the friends calls our attention to the fact that
the Báb loved high places, that even when they were leading Him
away to prison, wherever they would stop, in whatever town or
village, and even if there were only one upper room in the place, it
was there He chose to stay. His prisons, too, whether in Tabríz or
Máh-Kú or Chihríq, were always in high places. In His Tablet to
Muhammad Sháh, revealed at Máh-Kú, He speaks, however, of His
abode as being still higher than the prison, for He says, "It is as if I
were dwelling in the loftiest Paradise, delighting Myself with the remembrance of God the Most Great."

As we talk of all this, mountains and deserts and pasture lands
pass by us, and about midnight we come to Tabríz. Waiting for us
here are the believers. They welcome us, and, carrying out the
efficient arrangements of the Tabríz Assembly, they guide us away
singly or by twos to the different houses where we are to stay. Here
are people who have never laid eyes on us before, approaching us
with such pleasure. And afterward, when we went away, although we
had been with them only a few days, they wept, and so did we. It is

this that is stirring all over the Bahá'í world today, because the love of God has transfigured human nature.

It is two days before the commemoration. Early on the day itself, all are to gather at the Ḥaẓíratu'l-Quds, where a general meeting will be held; communes will be chanted, the Guardian's letter will be read, and then, one by one or two by two, the visitors, guided by local believers, are to circle around the barracks square where the Báb was offered up as a sacrifice, the holy place of which it is written: "The souls of the Prophets and Messengers do pace about it."

The meetings arranged throughout Tabríz are brilliant. Absent friends are remembered and missed. We feel that the hearts of all believers throughout East and West are focused on this city, and this gives rise to emotions that are best communicated not in words but from heart to heart.

THE COMMEMORATION

Now it is the eve of the Martyrdom. The Bahá'ís are in their houses; they are gathered in small groups, or quite alone. They are communing with their Lord. I cannot tell how it is. We recall the aspect of that other night one hundred years ago: How Mírzá Muḥammad-'Alí, surnamed Anís, and Siyyid Ḥusayn, the amanuensis, remained in the presence of the Báb; the conversation that took place that night between disciple and Beloved; all this came to mind again. To emulate the kind of obedience that Anís offered his Lord that night—this is the ultimate wish of every Bahá'í.

In a commentary, the Báb had referred to the circumstances of His approaching martyrdom in this wise: "Had I not been gazing upon this secret fact, I swear by Him in Whose hand is My soul, should all the kings of the earth be banded together they could not take from Me so much as a single letter of a word."

And again, in the Tablet to Muḥammad Sháh: "All the keys of heaven God hath chosen to place on My right hand, and all the keys of hell on My left. . . ."[1] It was His own unconditioned will to cast down His holy life in the pathway of the "Remnant of God"[2]—He Whom the Splendor of God has named "My previous Manifestation,[3] the Precursor of My Beauty." Of Whom, again, He has said, "I am He, He is I; I am His Beloved; He is My Beloved."

Could we sleep on a night like this? Day finally breaks. The appointed time approaches. It is as if from all the streets and passageways of Tabríz souls are gathering for Judgment. Yes, it is the Resurrection Day, the rise of the Qá'im and the Qayyúm. The squares of Tabríz are black with crowds. Deliver us, most exalted Beloved, "forgive us then our sin, and hide away from us our evil deeds" (Qur'án 3:193).

Some are hurrying, reverently, prayerfully, up to the "Ark," the Citadel where the Báb was imprisoned, to that high place which even today dominates the whole city and which, once seen, is impressed on the heart forever. They go here, that they may, prior to commemorating the hour of the Martyrdom, witness yet another stage in the long passion of the Báb. Some wait till a later hour to make this pilgrimage. These stay in the vicinity of the Báb's upper chamber and, bowing their foreheads to the earth in that exalted place, are repeating excerpts from His writings, such as the Commentary on the Súrih of Joseph. Not one has a thought except for the Beloved; they are in another world now, and they cannot easily return from it.

At the base of the terrifying "Ark," at the entrance to the courtyard, the Báb has once again demonstrated His power; for on a structure they have raised here in memory of the dead, we find inscribed this verse from the Qur'án: "repute not those slain on God's path as dead. Nay, alive with their Lord, are they richly sustained" (Súrih 3:163). It stands as a secret allusion to the Báb's agony and death. The pilgrims, reading this holy verse, seek leave to enter here, and thus they pass into the prison with their hearts free from everything except God.

The time has come to attend the meeting in Tabríz. The program goes forward; it is well arranged and deeply moving. Although the friends in other areas have been advised not to attend in large numbers, nevertheless some are here from other parts of Ádhirbáyján for this historic day, and the great auditorium of the Hazíratu'l-Quds is jammed; those who cannot find seats stand in the doorways and in the embrasures of the windows. Prayers are chanted. Then we listen to the Báb's Tablet to Muḥammad Sháh. Today the holy blood of the Báb is coursing through the world; it is flowering everywhere, and where is Muḥammad Sháh? We search, but find no trace of him. That foolish Minister of his has also sunk into his tomb, and that other Prime Minister, Taqí the Bloodshedder, the Brazen, who condemned the Lord of the world to death, has vanished in eternal night.

In the Turkish language, the Assembly secretary then speaks. He tells impressively of the spread of the Faith across the world, and of the building of the Báb's shrine on Mount Carmel.* The account of the martyrdom is read. A strange spiritual atmosphere prevails; you would say a glimmer from the world beyond is hovering here. With complete humility, the Visitation Tablet of the Báb is chanted.

It is almost noon. The pilgrims, led by some of the local friends, have come in utter lowliness, imploring the help of God, to circumambulate that place which is worshiped by the people of Paradise. Unobtrusively they pass around the barracks square. They see the very spot where the Martyrdom took place. They visualize the barracks as they were that day, and the rooftops black with people. They see the Báb there, bound to Anís and suspended from the ropes. They hear again the words that passed between the Báb and the farrásh-báshí; between the Báb and Sám Khán. Then Anís, making himself a living shield for the Báb. Then the first volley, by the will of the Báb, setting forth His proof to the stupefied people, taking no effect. Anís stands there before them in his immaculate white robe; not even the smoke from the seven hundred and fifty rifles has settled on it. The Báb concludes His interrupted conversation with His amanuensis. Other soldiers are drawn up. The Báb utters His last words, and His blessed voice still seems to ring across the barracks square:

> O wayward generation! Had you believed in Me every one of you would have followed the example of this youth, who stood in rank above most of you, and would have willingly sacrificed himself in My path. The day will come when you will have recognized Me; that day I shall have ceased to be with you.[4]

In the words of 'Abdu'l-Bahá, "The groaning of the Supreme

---

*Construction of the Shrine of the Báb was completed in October 1953 during the closing weeks of the Holy Year (October 1952–October 1953) commemorating the centenary of the termination of the Bábí Dispensation and of the birth of Bahá'u'lláh's revelation.—ED.

Concourse is lifted up. . . . The people of Paradise wail and cry out, their eyes shedding tears, their hearts afire." At this moment we are conscious of the loving attention of the Guardian, the beloved Shoghi Effendi, who labors at all times to exalt the Báb, who spreads His utterances abroad, who is now devoting his nights and days to constructing the Shrine of the Martyr-Prophet on Mount Carmel.

The circumambulation is complete. A feast is ready. But it is as if our bodies had sustained a death wound, and the pain does not lessen. . . .

During the remainder of our stay a great number of gatherings are held, each one generating a vivid, never-to-be-forgotten quality of the spirit.

Visit to Urúmíyyih

The following day we leave for Saysán. Some of the friends have come out along the way to welcome us while others have repaired and leveled the road ahead. What is this joy, this feeling of exhilaration? In the spacious auditorium—I think it measures nine by nineteen meters—of the new Ḥazíra, a morning and an afternoon meeting are held. The auditorium is packed; there is no room even to walk through. Many are crowding the embrasures of the windows and the doorways, and others stand outside the building. Prayers are being chanted. As the Assembly welcomes us in the accents of Ádhirbáyján, we recall the well-known verse, "When they speak Persian, Turks are life-bestowers." Two of us, Varqá and Furútan, reply with addresses in Turkish, telling of victories already won by the Faith, and victories to come. Labíb, famed Bahá'í photographer, takes pictures. He has made photographs of all these places that relate to the Báb in Ádhirbáyján, the way-stations on His journey, the historic sites. . . . Food is prepared for us.

The next day we visit the holy sites at Urúmíyyih. We are to meet the friends of this area on our return. The lake of Urúmíyyih rises before us, and we recall the Báb's arrival at the city here, Ridá'íyyih. As one of the friends has said, it is not saddening to visit these holy places, because outwardly at least the Báb suffered no afflictions here. He was the guest of Malik Qásim Mírzá, who received Him with ceremony and forbade that any disrespect be shown Him. The room of the Báb, in the upper story of the prince's house, is like His upper chamber in Shiraz; it lifts the spirit.

The entrance door and wall of the public bath attended by the Báb have been preserved; they are just as they were then. Dumbly they address the pilgrim. The pool of the bath is empty now. The people had carried away, to the last drop, the water used by the Báb for His ablutions, to bless themselves with it and keep it as medicine for their ills. . . .

We know that even an animal had a care for Him here. The prince's unmanageable horse became quiet under His hand and let Him mount—a strange thing to witness, and the memory of it will endure forever.[5] At the same time, a warning to mankind; for how is it that man in his unawareness has sunk even below the animal and has shut himself away from grace?

We cannot forget the meeting with our friends of Ridá'íyyih, in a house blessed by the Báb with His presence. Here, too, the invisible hand of the Báb has been at work—across from the Bath we read the inscription: "God is the LIGHT of the Heavens and of the Earth" (Qur'án 24:35). This verse appears in delicate calligraphy on sky-blue tile and serves as a guidepost to *the Countenance of God Whose splendor can never be obscured, the Light of God Whose radiance can never fade*—words uttered by the Primal Point Himself concerning His own Essence.[6]

THE MOUNTAIN OF SUFFERING

It is morning. Our bus leaves for Tabríz. The driver has agreed to stop all along the way so that we can meet with local friends, and some of these have been alerted ahead of time. The first place where we stop is Sháhpúr (Salmás), and a meeting is held. The pioneers here are solidly established; like their spiritual brothers and sisters across Persia, they have left their homes, and it is their great joy to have taken part in the extensive teaching campaign; to have earned the approval of the beloved Guardian, who wrote of the Plan: "It is a vital undertaking of the followers of the All-Merciful, conceived and established in the opening years of the second century of the Bahá'í Dispensation, and without peer or precedent throughout all the brilliant history of the first century of this wondrous Cause in that holy land"; and to have assisted in the Plan's successful completion by the Centenary of the Martyrdom.*

They are rendering enviable services, and their faces are nothing but light. Unforgettably now, a woman believer chants; her voice rises, all lowliness and supplication, so that our hearts are drawn toward God. And out of that place, Salmás, which lies near Chihríq —and which the poet Háfiz has named "the abode of Salmá," greeting it six hundred years ago and calling down blessing upon it, saying, "Hail, a thousand times hail, to thee, O abode of Salmá! How dear is the voice of thy camel-drivers, how sweet the jingling of thy bells!"—out of Salmás, which lies between the "Open Mountain" (Máh-Kú) and the "Grievous Mountain" (Chihríq), our unspoken prayers ring out from one mountain to the other. Surely they are heard as well in the holy worlds of the Beloved.

Suddenly we decide to follow the road taken by Mullá Husayn when, in Mashhad, he vowed to walk the whole distance that separated him from the Báb, and come to Him on the mountain of Máh-Kú. We long to visit the spot on the mountain where the Lord shone forth, as promised by God in the Qur'anic verse: "when God manifested Himself to the mountain" (Súrih 7:139).

It so happened that the Guardian's message, sent by telegraph in commemoration of the Martyrdom and addressed to the long-afflicted Bahá'ís of Persia, was dated at this very day and hour.

The words of the Imám who said, "I have known God by His disposal of man's resolves," were now demonstrated. Everyone felt a longing to go on pilgrimage to "the Open Mountain." The plan to turn back to Tabríz was changed; we determined to remain in Khuy and prepare for the pilgrimage to Máh-Kú.

Some feel that although they are unable to walk the entire distance that separated Mullá Husayn from the Báb,⁵ they will at least go on foot from Khuy to Máh-Kú, following in the footsteps of Mullá Husayn's faithful attendant, Qambar-'Alí. Unfortunately this

---

*The Plan referred to is the Forty Five Month Plan formulated by the National Spiritual Assembly of the Bahá'ís of Iran.—ED.

⁵Mashhad is in the northeast corner of Persia; Máh-Kú, in the extreme northwest corner.

cannot be done. It is now almost half past three in the afternoon, and
the bus is leaving for Máh-Kú. Some of the friends of Khuy are with
us. We find ourselves looking up and down the road, searching for
Mullá Husayn and Qambar-'Alí, and we think of those two holy
souls; we consider their humility, their spiritual quality, their evanes-
cence. Mountains and valleys pass by. The goal nears.

Over a wide area around Máh-Kú the plains are black; the world
mourns at Máh-Kú; for mile on mile the land is studded with
outcroppings of glistening black rock. Like ebony planets, these
rocks rise out of the land; they flood it like waves of an ebony sea.
Posted haphazardly at the mountain pass are other, monstrous
shapes, terrifying rock formations that guard the entry. All nature is a
prison here, on guard over the Beloved of mankind, over that
Captive of Whom Bahá'u'lláh has written: "The purpose in creating
the world and making it to flourish was His Manifestation."

We come to a river that boils and clamors through the rocks; it has
cut its way through solid rock and is maybe fifteen feet deep. We
remember how Nabíl tells us that the night before Mullá Husayn
and his servitor arrived—it was on the eve of the Feast of the New
Year—'Alí Khán, the frontier officer in charge of the castle of Máh-
Kú, had a dream. He saw the Prophet Muhammad, followed by a
companion, advancing to meet him from beside the bridge. In the
dream, Muhammad was on His way to visit the castle, to greet the
Báb on the occasion of the New Year. 'Alí Khán awoke with a sense of
exhilaration. He performed his ablutions and prayed, dressed himself in his best garments, sprinkled rose water on his hands, and went
out on foot to receive the Visitor. He further instructed a servant to
saddle and bridle his three best horses and hold them in readiness at
the bridge. But when he met Mullá Husayn there, 'Alí Khán was told,
"I have vowed to accomplish the whole of my journey on foot, to
visit an illustrious Personage who is being held prisoner on top of the
mountain. For this reason I will not ride."[7]

We strain our eyes, but we cannot see 'Alí Khán now, and his
honored visitors. But the memory of this event has, even till our day,
made the hearts of hundreds of thousands of Bahá'ís all across the
world beat faster; and God alone in His wisdom knows how many
billions of other hearts, throughout the length of the Bahá'í Cycle,
which in the words of 'Abdu'l-Bahá is to last "at least five hundred

thousand years," will turn their attention toward this place.

We are still in the defile. We cannot see Máh-Kú. And then suddenly, around the bend, there is "the Open Mountain" and the town of Máh-Kú on its slopes.[8]

You who may read this, believe me: I would swear by Him Who is the Lord of the mountain that in all the world there is no such terrifying sight as this. Those who have traveled to the ends of the earth will bear me out: There is no other mountain like this. It has no like, just as the anguish of the Báb had no like, so that the Blessed Beauty wrote in the Visitation Tablet: "I bear witness that the eye of creation hath never gazed upon one wronged like Thee."[9]

If, as scientists believe, our globe of dust detached itself one way or another from the sun, and down through the endless ages came at last to be as we know it, it is certain that wind and cloud, sun, moon, and sky worked from the beginning that had no beginning to bring about this mountain of Máh-Kú, in just this wise, to serve as the prison of the Báb. It is not a place that writers and painters can describe, this spot that was the destined setting against which the meekness of the Báb shone out. The reader must see the mountain for himself, and the prison house and the place where the Lord made Himself manifest, and he must then observe what the sight has done to his own heart, and meditate on these things through long, wakeful nights and at many a dawn, and then, if he can, let him write of it.

We are speaking of this when, after a brief detour from the road in the frightening pass that leads through the mountain, we see on our right a view of "the Open Mountain" and on its slopes the town of Máh-Kú. At this point the pass, lying between Máh-Kú and another high mountain that pushes into the sky across from it, widens out. And again we come face to face with the heights of Máh-Kú. Then the pass narrows again as if it were the mouth of the Fathomless Pit.

The mountain stretches like a bow, between the entrance and exit of the pass. It rises, awesome, overpowering, into the sky. It rivals the moon's heights, and shuts the moon away. At either end of the bow, nature has piled two massive towers, lifting out of the mountain, up and up into the Milky Way. From a distance you would say these two are jailers, adding to the cruelty of the Báb's imprisonment. Or again, that they are minarets from which was raised the cry, "Hasten ye to salvation! Hasten ye to salvation! I bear witness that He Who is

'Alí before Nabíl ('Alí-Muḥammad, the Báb) is the Gate of the Remnant of God!"*

The city of Máh-Kú lies within the curve of the bow, the opening of which is several hundred meters across; it clings to the steep slopes. An almost perpendicular street rises jaggedly from house to house, leading finally up to the mountain top. Panting and sweating we climb toward the summit. Not all of us, however. One or two of the band who set out from Khuy to make this pilgrimage cannot keep on; the road is too rough, too steep. They cannot reach that last point of all, the prison of the Báb. They complete their pilgrimage by the roadside, and who knows, perhaps they show a special reverence in this.

As the Báb writes in the Tablet to Muḥammad Sháh, the castle lies in the center of the mountain, and there is no higher point. The slope ends abruptly at the castle, and above it there is not a span of earth where anything could be built or find a foothold. Not jutting straight up in fortress-like walls, but inverted here in a wide arc, the mountain becomes a great parasol or cupola sheltering the prison place. Rain and snow cannot fall here; stars and moon cannot cast down their light; only the cruel cold, the scorching heat can enter here. For all day long in the heat of summer, the fortress and the mountain, like a concave mirror, gather in the heat, and all night long, while in other places people are restfully asleep, they radiate it back. And wintertimes the cold is so intense that the water which the Báb used for His ablutions froze on His face.

It is here that the Monarch of love was beset by the legions of tyranny, and the Dove of holiness prisoned by owls.

The two towers which nature has planted on the slopes of the mountain seem from here more vigilant than ever, holding their Captive in full view.

A deep cleft runs crookedly from the summit all the way down the mountain and across from the prison, like a knotted black cord hanging; thousands of feet it swings down, a symbol of the anger of God. Perhaps it means that God desires to pull down the mountain,

---

*According to the abjad reckoning, "Nabíl" and "Muḥammad" are numerical equivalents, the letters of each word totaling ninety-two.

to crush out nature and man as well. Yet again, we believe that Máh-Kú, the prison of His Holiness, should exist forever, that, as the ages unroll, the peoples of the earth may come at last to understand some hint of the Báb's agony. So it is that the pull of the earth has not been able to draw down this curving, roof-like peak, raised up "without pillars that can be seen" (Qur'án 31:9) and that castle and mountain stand in their place.

This is Máh-Kú. . . .

The pilgrims, with two of the Bahá'ís who are pioneers at Máh-Kú, reach only the base of the mountain at sunset. They must climb the mountain before night shuts down, for at the summit is their long-desired goal.

At this time we bring to mind what Shaykh Ḥasan-i-Zunúzí said to the historian Nabíl: That as the Báb dictated His Teachings at Máh-Kú, the rhythmic flow of His chant could be heard by those who lived at the foot of the mountain, and mountain and valley reechoed His voice. What a melody that must have been; how it must have shaken the spirit! Our ears strain now in the effort to hear it again, or to catch the song of the Kingdom that reverberates from slope to slope.

After long twisting and turning up the mountain, we draw near to the abode of the Well Beloved. Here is another "oratory"* at the base of the walls; from the heart of the mountain, gushing beneath the castle, a stream of pity and anguish jets out with a noise like sighs and sobs and plunges down the mountain, scattering over the surface of a massive rock. Here is clear, delicate water, well suited to this holy place, for our ablutions. The friends are very careful not to muddy it.

We come to the castle steps. Step after step, our yearning mounts. Here, then, is the prison of the Lord of the Age. Here is the place where they brought as a captive the Sovereign and Possessor of the earth, of Whom it is written: "My Lord hath ordained that all which is and all which is not should belong to the Adored One that liveth forever."

Now we can make out His cell and that of His guards. The

---

*Muṣallá, "The Oratory," a favorite resort of the poet Ḥáfiẓ near Shiraz, watered by the stream of Ruknábád.

sorrowing voice of the Báb, which could move a heart to its depths, seems to be ringing against the mountainside, and the sacred verses He addressed to Muhammad Sháh from this very place speak to our souls: "I swear by the Most Great Lord! Wert thou to be told in what place I dwell, the first person to have mercy on Me would be thyself. In the heart of a mountain is a fortress . . . the inmates of which are confined to two guards and four dogs. Picture, then, My plight. . . ."10

All of us, in complete humility, praying and supplicating God, visit the cells and rooms. We take up the dust of the holy place for a blessing. We chant verses of the Báb: "O Thou the Consolation of Mine eyes! Verily Thou art the Great Announcement!" "O Thou Remnant of God! I have sacrificed myself wholly for Thee; I have accepted curses for Thy sake; and have yearned for naught but martyrdom in the path of Thy love."11 We call to mind His Manifestation and His longing to offer Himself up in death. The Visitation Tablet is chanted. As we stand there in the dark of the night, we remember that the Holy Being spent His nights on the mountain in total darkness; there was not even a candle for Him here.

Our hearts are heavy; grief bows us down. But suddenly we are comforted by the words of the Primal Point to His own Essence: "Be patient, O Consolation of Mine eyes, for verily God hath vowed to establish Thy glory in every land, amongst all that dwell on earth." Our minds are now flooded with joy. It is as if from one end of the sky to the other a blinding light shines down. We see that the Báb—Who in this place, out of the very depths of His captivity and His anguish, revealed unnumbered utterances—completely disregarded the prison, and continued to exercise that all-powerful, all-pervasive Will, against which no worldly might prevails. In His Book, the Persian Bayán, written on this mountaintop, from this dark and narrow cell, He alludes to His own glory, and with His promise of World Order bestows new life on all mankind, and relates the exaltation of His own eternal rank and station to the spreading awareness of this Order.

In the heart of this mountain the wrongs inflicted on Him Whom the world has wronged stand before us. But in the heart of another mountain, which seems now to rise face to face with this one and in sharp contrast with this, the sovereignty, dominion, and might of the

Lord are made manifest. The Guardian of Bahá'u'lláh's followers, the "primal branch" that hath grown out "from the Twin Holy Trees," watches us here, watches the two mountains.[12] Here is Máh-Kú; and there is the holy mountain where the Báb's body is laid to rest—named by Prophets thousands of years back in time the Mountain of God (Mount Carmel). The King of Glory has related that mountain to His own Self. The Heavenly Father has chosen that spot to hold the dust of the Báb and has set it apart as the center of His new World Order.*

THE MOUNTAIN OF VICTORY

Now that we speak of these things here at Máh-Kú in the Báb's prison, and Mount Carmel rises suddenly before us, it is not inappropriate to turn our thoughts toward His everlasting resting-place so that we may note how the long cruelties, the prison, and at last the bullets—intended, in the words of the Almighty, to free mankind from the chains of self and passion—were changed into abiding glory. How Bahá'u'lláh, in the pathway of Whose love the Báb sought and found death, fulfilled the promises voiced by the Prophets of God back through the endless ages, when He named Mount Carmel as the Shrine of the Báb. How at His command the blessed hands of 'Abdu'l-Bahá reared the divine edifice; how redemption of the promises set down in the Tablet of Carmel[13] was entrusted to the mighty arm of Shoghi Effendi, the wondrous, unique, and priceless Guardian.

What is the best way to go on pilgrimage to the City that has come down from heaven, as the Shrine of the Báb is called in the Tablet of Carmel—the Shrine which, Bahá'u'lláh tells us, Mount Zion circumambulates? Shall we take the path that leads from the Pilgrims' House all the way to the Tomb—the house that, after its

---

*The Báb's body is entombed in the Shrine of the Báb on Mount Carmel in Haifa, Israel. Bahá'u'lláh, the Prophet-Founder of the Bahá'í Faith—who was exiled from Tehran to Baghdad, to Constantinople, to Adrianople, and finally to Akka in Palestine—designated the spot on Mount Carmel where the building was to be erected and designated it as the world spiritual and administrative center of the Bahá'í Faith.—Ed.

builder, is named Ja'far-Ábád?* 'Abdu'l-Bahá said that Ḥáfiẓ referred to this house when he wrote:

> Between Ja'far-Ábád and Muṣallá
> Laden with ambergris the north wind blows.

Or, as in the case of Máh-Kú, when we looked first at the mountain itself, shall we contemplate the Shrine from a distance and set these two mountains against each other and compare them each to each? I think this last is best. . . .

We follow the Guardian over the flowering slopes of Haifa. They seem to glitter with colored gems and pearls, like a bride at her wedding, and we repeat to ourselves the lines, "From every branch within the blossoming grove, a thousand petals are cast before the king." We observe the Guardian's gait, and we think that if men's eyes were seeing eyes, this in itself would be proof enough.

We have watched the sea in the sunset, and now we are returning. We look upon Carmel, heart of the world, and at its center the Báb's Shrine, heart of Carmel. We see its terraces from far away, burning like lighted torches before the eyes of its builder. The Guardian smilingly contemplates all this. His voice, strong and clear, rings down the mountain; he is saying, "Terraces of light; light upon light."

His words echo back from the slopes and the sea. We think of the contrast between those long nights on Máh-Kú, when the Báb was denied even a candle, and now, when the terraces of His Shrine are light upon light, the face of the building is a solid sheet of light, the whole mountain is to blaze with light. We remember two lines that were chanted by 'Abdu'l-Bahá: "Glad tidings, glad tidings! Zion is dancing! Glad tidings! The Kingdom of God whirls in delight!"

Instead of panting and struggling up the narrow twisted road at Máh-Kú, stopping at times because we can climb no more, here we can rest on every terrace in the midst of gardens and trees, in lovely settings of mountainside and sea. Pools and fountains are to be built here that will reflect the sky and heaven. Each terrace is dedicated to one of the Letters of the Living, and we are received, as it were, by

---

*The Eastern Pilgrim House was built by Mírzá Ja'far Raḥmání.—ED.

him. We forget our sorrows as we take deep breaths of the delicate air.

No longer is the Báb a captive on Máh-Kú. He rests in the divine gardens on the Mountain of God. He lies across the Bay of Haifa from His Well-Beloved, Bahá'u'lláh, the Point of Adoration, Him Whom God made manifest.*

'Abdu'l-Bahá, Who had cast aside His turban and wept and sobbed aloud as, with His own hands, He laid the Báb's body in the heart of Carmel, Himself rests now beside the Báb. The companion who died with the Báb has never been separated from Him. Near them are built the tombs of the Most Exalted Leaf,⁵ and of the brother, the mother, and consort of 'Abdu'l-Bahá.

From the foot of the mountain all the way to the Shrine, the nine terraces rise in memory of nine Letters of the Living, and, in accord with the Guardian's design, from the Shrine to the summit of Mt. Carmel nine more shall complete the number.*

The beloved Guardian, called by the Master "My Shoghi," was from his early childhood enamored of the Báb.¹⁴ He dreamed of the Báb, and he was named Rabbaní in memory of the Báb's title Rabb-i-A'lá. It is he who, standing on the heights of the Shrine, drew the geometric designs of the terraces. He laid out the gardens and established the International Bahá'í Endowments about the Shrine. He has placed here the International Archives, of whose treasures Bahá'u'lláh had promised, "Ere long souls will be raised up who will preserve every holy relic in the most perfect manner." The portrait of the Báb, drawn in Urúmíyyih and gazed upon by Bahá'u'lláh Himself, is here. Here, too, are His outer garments and His shirt, soaked in His blood. A copy of the portrait and locks of the Báb's hair have been sent as a historic gift to the Bahá'í House of Worship in the

---

*Bahá'u'lláh is buried at Bahjí, where he spent the last years of His life. It is near Akka, where He was exiled by the Turkish authorities in 1868.—ED.

⁵The Greatest Holy Leaf, Bahíyyih Khánum, the daughter of Bahá'u'lláh and the outstanding heroine of the Bahá'í Dispensation.—ED.

*In a letter dated 31 August 1987 to the followers of Bahá'u'lláh throughout the world, the Universal House of Justice announced its intention to implement plans to complete the nineteen terraces from the foot of Mount Carmel to its crest.—ED.

United States, which has been completed under the Guardianship of Shoghi Effendi,* and the Guardian has promised a copy to Persia, cradle of the Faith, as soon as the first Persian Ma<u>sh</u>riqu'l-A<u>dh</u>kár is built.

The Guardian has added to the Shrine on Mount Carmel three rooms built according to the same plan as those already constructed by the Master. He has extended the length, width, and height of the Shrine, and is now protecting the Edifice like a pearl of great price within the shell of an arcade and crowning it with a balustrade set with panels, the central one to the north bearing a great green and gold mosaic of the Greatest Name.

It is the Guardian who has widely spread the works of the Báb. In "The Dispensation of Bahá'u'lláh" he has set forth the exalted station of the Báb.[15] By translating the narrative of Nabíl he has published the days of the Báb across the earth.[16] He has seen to it that in every area the Centenaries of the Báb's Declaration and of His Martyrdom were befittingly celebrated. Across over a hundred countries he has added thousands upon thousands of souls to the company of those who love the Báb, and he is looking for yet more countries to come.

At this time the Guardian is concentrating his labors on completion of the Edifice, importing marbles and granite and other priceless rock materials that had lain in the earth down endless ages until at last they should serve for the building of just such a Shrine—rock materials in jade and rose, that are symbols of the Báb's lineage and the way He died. Following the architect's design (you can see it in color, in the pages of that mirror of Bahá'í activities around the globe, *The Bahá'í World*),[17] the arcade and balustrade have been completed, and the Guardian is now working day and night to direct completion of the superstructure and rear the great golden dome. Then the light will pour out of this source of light and envelop all mankind, and the "people of Bahá" referred to in the Tablet of Carmel will be made manifest,[18] and God will sail His ark upon His holy mountain, and the laws of God will be make known to all men,

---

*The superstructure of the dome of the House of Worship in Wilmette, Illinois, was completed in 1931. The exterior ornamentation was completed in 1943; the interior ornamentation and surrounding gardens, in 1953. The dedication of the Wilmette House of Worship was held in May 1953.—Ed.

and the Tabernacle of the Lord of Hosts will be pitched on the heights of Carmel, and the divine World Order be unveiled; and there near the resting place of the Most Exalted Leaf (the sister of 'Abdu'l-Bahá) and the other blessed ones, and in the neighborhood of the Holy Shrine, the Universal House of Justice will be established, and the promise "Then shalt thou see the Abhá paradise on earth" will be redeemed.*

Let us go into the gardens around the Shrine-Tomb. Let us walk there on the Mountain of God and "unravel the mysteries of love from its wind-flowers," for "Solaced are the eyes of them that enter and abide therein!"[19] Let us see with our own eyes how "the rose-gardens that grow around His Holy Tomb have become the pleasure-spot of all kinds and conditions of men," how the flower beds and fruit-bearing trees cluster so thick around the Shrine. Visitors, not Bahá'ís, will tell you these fresh and green and delicate gardens have no equal anywhere else.

When the famed Orientalist A. L. M. Nicolas, who had longed to see the Báb's shrine exalted, received as a gift from Shoghi Effendi a copy of its design, together with a copy of *The Dawn-Breakers* of Nabíl, he was so moved that he kissed the bearer's hand. Strangers love this place; how much more do the friends.

Within the holy precincts we put on slippers and anoint ourselves with rose water poured out by the Guardian himself, this wonderful personage who has arisen, "with the most perfect form, most great gift, most complete perfection." His handsome face is so phenomenally bright that the Master wrote, "His face shineth with a brightness whereby the horizons are illumined."

Within the Shrine his voice, resonant, haunting, lifts in the Visitation prayer: "The praise which hath dawned from Thy most august Self, and the glory which hath shone forth from Thy most effulgent Beauty, rest upon Thee. . . ."[20]

---

*God's sailing his ark on Mount Carmel (see the Tablet of Carmel in Bahá'u'lláh, *Tablets of Bahá'u'lláh revealed after the Kitáb-i-Aqdas,* comp. Research Department of the Universal House of Justice, trans. Habib Taherzadeh et al. (Wilmette, Ill.: Bahá'í Publishing Trust, 1988), 3–5) is a reference to the establishment of the Universal House of Justice, which was first elected in 1963. The Seat of the Universal House of Justice was completed in 1983.—ED.

I wonder if I am awake or in a dream. "Bless Thou, O Lord my God, the Divine Lote-Tree and its leaves, and its boughs, and its branches . . . as long Thy most excellent titles will endure and Thy most august attributes will last."[21] If we observe the Guardian when he places flower petals on the threshold of the Báb's sepulcher, we shall see as he strews the roses and violets there how intense are the stirrings of His love.

Today from the mountain of Máh-Kú the anguished cry of the Báb is raised no more: "In this mountain I have remained alone, and have come to such a pass that none of those gone before Me have suffered what I have suffered, nor any transgressor endured what I have endured!" With these great victories, these new and mighty institutions, surely the sorrow of His heart is stilled at last, and out of the verses of the Bayán He is calling: "Well is it with him who fixeth his gaze upon the Order of Bahá'u'lláh, and rendereth thanks unto his Lord."[22]

Today the Báb is not alone on the mountain anymore: "The people of the Supreme Horizon and the presences who dwell in the eternal paradise circle around His Shrine." The love of the Bahá'ís around the globe, from Anchorage to Magallanes, from farthest East to farthest West, gathered within the shelter of the Branch of the Sinaitic Tree, centers on this place and is offered up continuously to Him, while the Guardian labors by day and by night to bring to pass the prophecy of the Master when He said: "I see the ships of all the kings of the world berthed at the docks of Haifa. I see the sovereigns disembark. Bareheaded and barefooted, and carrying on their shoulders vases studded with jewels, they advance toward the Shrine." And to fulfill these written words set down by the Pen of Glory:

> After that which is inevitable shall have come to pass, these very kings and presidents will follow in the footsteps of the champions of the Cause of God. They will enter the field of service. They will fling in the dust the crowns of their perishable sovereignty and place on their heads the diadems of utter servitude, and in the front ranks of the pioneers they will labor with all their heart, with all their possessions, with all that God in His bounty hath bestowed upon them, to spread this Faith. And when their labors are completed they will hasten to this sacred place, and in complete humility, supplicating God, bowing down before Him, in utter

lowliness, they will circle round the Holy Shrines, and lifting their voices will cry out to heaven, extolling and magnifying and glorifying the Lord, and they will unveil and establish before all the peoples of the earth the incalculable greatness of this almighty Faith.

In this unfaithful world, this house of grief, where all things die except the Face of the Beloved, where in a little while there will be no sign of us left, let us bequeath to those who will come after us an enduring proof of what we feel—so that they will remember us, who lived in the days of the first Guardian,* so that they will tell one another, for five thousand centuries to come, how we loved the Primal Point.

---

*Shoghi Effendi left no heirs and thus was the first and only Guardian of the Bahá'í Faith—ED.

2 From Badasht to Saint Louis:
An Evaluation of the First Bahá'í Conference and the Largest

by Zikrullah Khadem

An examination of the first Bahá'í Conference—the Conference of Badasht, held in Iran in 1848, publicly signaling the end of the Islamic Dispensation and the beginning of the Báb's revelation—and the largest Bahá'í Conference, held in Saint Louis, Missouri, 29 August through 1 September 1974, marking the beginning of the Five Year International Teaching Plan inaugurated by the Universal House of Justice.* Reprinted with minor revisions from Bahá'í News, *no. 522 (Sept. 1974): 8–14. Copyright © 1974 by the National Spiritual Assembly of the Bahá'ís of the United States.*

The beloved of all hearts, Shoghi Effendi, emphasized that the Conference of Badasht should be the source of inspiration for all Bahá'í conferences and that the spirit of that Conference should be reflected in all of them. In Badasht, the site of that historic gathering organized by Bahá'u'lláh, the clarion call of the new Order was sounded. Recently in Saint Louis more than ten thousand people from every region of America and from many countries in the Bahá'í world arrived to participate in the final step of the phased launching of the Five Year Plan in the United States. At the end of four days the believers streamed from that arena, ready to strive to establish still farther afield outposts of Bahá'u'lláh's new order. The Conference at Badasht was the first in Bahá'í history; Saint Louis was the largest. But these two milestone events are related in other interesting and significant ways, some of which will be explored in this article. It begins with an account of the Conference at Badasht and will follow

---

*The Five Year International Teaching Plan began in April 1974 and concluded in April 1979. It was part of an unfolding series of plans to spread the Bahá'í Faith around the world.—Ed.

with a discussion of the conference in Saint Louis, held August 29 through September 1.

THE CONFERENCE OF BADASHT

The Blessed Beauty made elaborate arrangements for Táhirih's journey to Badasht and sent her off with an equipage and retinue. His own party left for that region some days afterward.[1]

When the Conference of Badasht was held at the beginning of the summer 126 years ago, the Báb was a captive in the fortress of Chihríq in the mountains of Ádhirbáyján. As He Himself had predicted, He was confined for nine months in the fortress at Máh-Kú, whereupon He was transferred to Chihríq.[2] On His way to captivity the friends had begged Him to flee, but He replied, " 'The mountains of Ádhirbáyján too have their claims, . . .' "[3] In a tablet of the Báb as yet unpublished,* He asked how the wayward people could have been tested had He not consented to be confined in those mountains, and how the truth of the saying of the Imám Báqir, the fifth Imám, (" ' "The things which will happen in Ádhirbáyján are necessary for us, nothing can prevent their occurrence." ' "[4]) could have been fulfilled.

From His captivity the Báb urged His followers to " 'hasten to the Land of Khá,' " "the province of Khurásán,"[5] where Quddús and Mullá Husayn had kindled amazing devotion in the hearts of the people of Mashhad (the capital).[5] Many were still on their way there

---

*The original of this tablet was sent to Shoghi Effendi by Mr. Khadem.

[5]It was in Mashhad that Mullá Husayn received the most glorious honor and gift from the Báb (His green turban) together with the command to unfurl the Black Standard and hasten to Jazíriy-i-Khadrá'. It was in Mashhad that Mullá Husayn, in obedience to the Báb's command, later hoisted the Standard and, waving it before him, led two hundred and two of his companions out of that city (they were gradually joined by others). It was this Standard which "was carried aloft all the way from the city of Mashhad to the shrine of Shaykh Tabarsí," "the same standard of which Muhammad, the Prophet of God, had thus spoken: 'Should your eyes behold the Black Standards proceeding from Khurásán, hasten ye towards them, even though ye should have to crawl over the snow, inasmuch as they proclaim the advent of the promised Mihdí, the Vicegerent of God' " (Nabíl, *Dawn-Breakers*, 324–25, 351).

when the historic events of K̲h̲urásán ended. On his way back from K̲h̲urásán, Quddús, the eighteenth Letter of the Living, whose station was second only to that of the Báb, arrived in the hamlet of Bada<u>sh</u>t at the hour of dawn. There he encountered a great number of his fellow believers. He resumed his journey to S̲h̲áh-Rúd, however, but was informed en route ". . . that Bahá'u'lláh and Ṭáhirih had, a few days before, left S̲h̲áh-Rúd for that hamlet; that a large number of believers had already arrived from Iṣfahán, Qazvín, and other towns of Persia and were waiting to accompany Bahá'u'lláh on His intended journey. . . ." "No sooner had Bahá'u'lláh been informed . . . of the arrival of Quddús at S̲h̲áh-Rúd than He decided to join him. Attended by Mullá Muḥammad-i-Mu'allim-i-Núrí, He set out on horseback that same evening for that village, and . . . returned with Quddús to Bada<u>sh</u>t the next morning at the hour of sunrise."[6]

Upon His arrival in Bada<u>sh</u>t, "Bahá'u'lláh rented three gardens, one of which He assigned exclusively to the use of Quddús, another He set apart for Ṭáhirih . . . and reserved the third for Himself."[7] "The eighty-one disciples who had gathered from various provinces were His guests from the day of their arrival to the day they dispersed."[8] 'Abdu'l-Bahá shares with us the beauty of the scene and the details of these gardens:

> In Bada<u>sh</u>t there was a great open field. Through its center a stream flowed, and to its right, left, and rear there were three gardens, the envy of Paradise. One of those gardens was assigned to Quddús, but this was kept a secret. Another was set apart for Ṭáhirih, and in a third was raised the pavilion of Bahá'u'lláh. On the field amidst the three gardens, the believers pitched their tents.[9]

"In those days the fact that the Báb was the Qá'im had not yet been proclaimed. . . ."[10] Even though the traditions of Islam stated that the promised Qá'im would come with a new Book and new Laws, the believers were not fully aware of the fact that the revelation of the Báb represented the Dawn of a New Day and that His teachings would abrogate and repudiate the ancient laws. It was Bahá'u'lláh, with the assistance of Quddús, Who arranged through the memorable gathering at Bada<u>sh</u>t to make the friends fully aware of these grave realities.

"Evenings, Bahá'u'lláh, Quddús and Táhirih would come together."[11] "According to the 'Kashfu'l-Ghitá',' a decision had been previously arrived at between Quddús and Táhirih, in accordance with which the latter was to proclaim publicly the independent character of the Revelation of the Báb, and to emphasise the abrogation of the laws and ordinances of the previous Dispensation. Quddús, on the other hand, was expected to oppose her contention and strenuously to reject her views. This arrangement was made for the purpose of mitigating the effects of such a challenging and far-reaching proclamation, and of averting the dangers and perils which such a startling innovation was sure to produce (p. 211). Bahá'u'lláh appears to have taken a neutral attitude in this controversy, though actually He was the prime mover and the controlling and directing influence throughout the different stages of that memorable episode."[12]

Although Bahá'u'lláh "was the possessor of countless and boundless perfections,"[13] was praised in the Qur'án as the Lord of the Day of Judgment, the Remnant of God, was referred to by Isaiah as "Wonderful, Counsellor, The mighty God, The everlasting Father, The Prince of Peace,"[14] through the Divine Wisdom, and because of the immaturity of man, He remained "still behind the veil of glory."[15] It is not inappropriate to note certain references to the Báb and Bahá'u'lláh in the Islamic traditions. In the year 59 (1843, a year before the declaration of the Báb), the Qá'im and the Qayyúm (the Báb and Bahá'u'lláh), it was prophesied, would both be manifest with all the virtues and powers of revelation, and that together their fame would become known. However, the year 59 belonged to them as the year prior to their declarations. The Qayyúm (Bahá'u'lláh) would also not declare until after the Qá'im (the Báb) was martyred, the traditions said, and He would remain silent for a total of eleven years.[16]

This Hidden Treasure (Bahá'u'lláh), Who loved to be known, decided in Badasht to appear with His Most Great Name (Bahá), the Name which had been a concealed mystery and which adorns each of the 114 súrihs of the Qur'án. The inscription *"El-Bá, Bahá'u'lláh* [*B* means "Bahá'u'lláh"],*"* in Arabic, adorns the margins of some of the Latin editions of the Qur'án published in Turkey.

The following reference to the name of Bahá'u'lláh and to Akka was made over one thousand three hundred years ago: "Ere long God will shine from the face of Bahíyu'l-Abhá [the Glory, the Most Glorious] with the name of Bahá, on the Day of Absolute, in the plain of 'Akká."[17]

The writer, when quoting these and similar references to the prime minister of one country, was told, "It seems you Bahá'ís have gone to great lengths to add those passages to the Holy Books." And the reaction of a dignitary in another country was that Bahá'u'lláh must have given Himself that name because He knew of these references. He didn't stop to think that, if Bahá'u'lláh was the only one to have that knowledge, then He must have been the Promised One Who was exiled to Akka, and that He had not proceeded there by His own Will.

"On each of the twenty-two days of His [Bahá'u'lláh's] sojourn in that hamlet He revealed a Tablet, which was chanted [by Mírzá Sulaymán-i-Núrí] in the presence of the assembled believers. On every believer He conferred a new name, without, however, disclosing the identity of the one who had bestowed it. He Himself was henceforth designated by the name Bahá. Upon the Last Letter of the Living was conferred the appellation of Quddús, while Qurratu'l-'Ayn ["Solace of the Eyes"] was given the title of Ṭáhirih. By these names they were all subsequently addressed by the Báb in the Tablets He revealed for each one of them."[18] The tablets read at Badasht may in fact be considered the first tablets revealed by the pen of Bahá'u'lláh.

ALL THINGS MADE NEW

Quddús and Ṭáhirih had a passionate love for Bahá'u'lláh. They could not have failed to recognize Him and know His station. Quddús, in responding to the Qur'anic hymn of glorification and praise, "Holy, holy, the Lord our God [Subbúhun Quddús], the Lord of the angels and the spirit!"[19] intoned for him by a band of enthusiastic admirers, directed their attention instead to Baqíyyatu'-lláh, the Remnant of God, Bahá'u'lláh.* "The Baqíyyatu'lláh will be

---

*Baqíyyatu'lláh, meaning "Remnant of God," is a title applied both to the Báb and Bahá'u'lláh.—ED.

best for you if ye are of those who believe,"[20] he said. Ṭáhirih, the pure, "the noblest of her sex in that Dispensation,"[21] praised Bahá'u'- lláh in one of her glorious poems:

The effulgence of thy face flashed forth and the rays of thy visage arose on high;

Why lags the word "Am I not your Lord?" and "Yea that thou art," let us make reply.[22]

She also extolled Bahá'u'lláh in the Conference of Bada<u>sh</u>t with the title of the "potent King" mentioned in the Qur'án.[23]

"Each day of that memorable gathering witnessed the abrogation of a new law and the repudiation of a long-established tradition."[24] The spirit heightened constantly until "the clarion-call of the new Order had been sounded."[25]

The fixed hour reached, the Great Resurrection made manifest the rise of the Qá'im and the Qayyúm.

"Then one day, and there was a wisdom in it, Bahá'u'lláh fell ill; that is, the indisposition was to serve a vital purpose. On a sudden, in the sight of all, Quddús came out of his garden, and entered the pavilion of Bahá'u'lláh."[26] "He seated himself, when ushered into His presence, on the right hand of Bahá'u'lláh. The rest of the companions were gradually admitted to His presence, and grouped themselves around Him."[27] "But Ṭáhirih sent him a message, to say that their Host being ill, Quddús should visit her garden instead. His answer was: 'This garden is preferable. Come, then, to this one.' Ṭáhirih, with her face unveiled, stepped from her garden, advancing to the pavilion of Bahá'u'lláh. . . ."[28] With utmost dignity, "Ṭáhirih stepped forward and, advancing towards Quddús, seated herself on his right-hand side."[29] "And as she came, she shouted aloud these words: 'The Trumpet is sounding! The great Trump is blown! The universal Advent is now proclaimed!' The believers gathered in that tent were panic struck, and each one asked himself, 'How can the Law be abrogated? How is it that this woman stands here without her veil?' "[30]

" 'She concluded her address with this verse of the Qur'án: "Verily, amid gardens and rivers shall the pious dwell in the seat of truth, in the presence of the potent King." As she uttered these words, she cast a furtive glance towards both Bahá'u'lláh and Quddús in such a manner that those who were watching her were unable to tell to which of the two she was alluding. Immediately after, she declared: "I am the Word which the Qá'im is to utter, the Word which shall put to flight the chiefs and nobles of the earth!" ' "[31]

" 'Read the Súrih of the Inevitable,' said Bahá'u'lláh; and the reader began: 'When the Day that must come shall have come suddenly . . . Day that shall abase! Day that shall exalt! . . .' and thus was the new Dispensation announced and the great Resurrection made manifest. At the start, those who were present fled away, and some forsook their Faith, while some fell a prey to suspicion and doubt, and a number, after wavering, returned to the presence of Bahá'u'lláh. The Conference of Bada<u>sh</u>t broke up, but the universal Advent had been proclaimed."[32]

Súrih 56—The Inevitable

When the day that must come shall have come suddenly, . . .
Day that shall abase! Day that shall exalt!
When the earth shall be shaken with a shock, . . .
And they who were foremost on earth—the foremost still [Quddús and Ṭáhirih].
These are they who shall be brought nigh to God,
In the gardens of delight; . . .
No vain discourse shall they hear therein, nor charge of sin,
But only the cry, "Peace! Peace!"
And the people of the right hand—oh! how happy shall be the people of the right hand! [believers gathered]
Amid thornless sidrahs . . .
And in extended shade,
And by flowing waters,
And with abundant fruits, . . .

. . . .
Praise therefore the name of thy Lord, the Great.

Súrih 75—The Resurrection

It needeth not that I swear by the day of the RESURRECTION, . . .
He asketh, "When this day of Resurrection?"
But when the eye shall be dazzled, . . .
And the sun and the moon shall be together,
[the sun, Muḥammad; the moon, 'Alí: 'Alí Muḥammad, the name of the Báb]

[This verse confirms a well-known tradition addressed to 'Alí by the Prophet Muḥammad in the book of Váfí: "There will be one advent for me and two for you, once before Muḥammad ('Alí-Muḥammad, the name of the Báb) and once after Ḥusayn (Ḥusayn-'Alí, the name of Bahá'u'lláh)."]
On that day man shall cry, "Where is there a place to flee to?" . . .
On that day shall faces beam with light,
Outlooking towards their Lord; . . .

THE SAINT LOUIS CONFERENCE

The first national Bahá'í conference of the Five Year Plan, which manifested the spirit of the historic Conference of Badasht, opened in Saint Louis with an exciting devotional program in praise and thanksgiving to the Author of our glorious Cause, and with a message from the Supreme Body of the Faith, the Universal House of Justice. This conference was the largest ever held in the history of the Faith. Attending were more than ten thousand followers of the Greatest Name, recruited from many nations, tribes, races, and colors of the globe.

The purpose of the conference was to proclaim the Faith to the world and to discuss the fulfillment of the goals of the Five Year Plan of the Universal House of Justice, launched by that Body through its representatives, the Hands of the Cause of God, as standard-bearers, at national Bahá'í conventions around the world.

The convener of the conference was the National Spiritual Assembly of the Bahá'ís of the United States, a divinely ordained institution, its members the generals of the Army of Light in this country.

The participants at the Conference of Badasht in the cradle of the Faith were the eighty-one Dawn-Breakers who went to offer up their lives in the path of their Beloved at a time when the call of God had reached only two countries, Persia and Iraq. The participants at Saint Louis were thousands of the spiritual descendants of the Dawn-Breakers, an envious title conferred upon the Bahá'ís of America by the beloved Shoghi Effendi himself. They came to the conference in the cradle of the Administrative Order to follow the example of their spiritual ancestors in offering their time, their resources, their very lives—to serve and sacrifice for Bahá'u'lláh. They responded to the call of His House of Justice at a time when the love of Bahá'u'lláh is filling the whole world, as the waters cover the sea, and His Message is penetrating all the corners of the planet, to cities and villages whose very names—according to the beloved Guardian—are difficult to pronounce.

During the Conference of Badasht, the Báb, the Prophet-Martyr and Herald of Bahá'u'lláh, was a captive in the mountains of Ádhirbáyján. He is no longer in captivity. The light of His might and dignity has dazzled His admirers, and His promise addressed to His Blessed Self *("Be patient, O Apple of My eyes. Verily, God has pledged with Him Thy might in all the lands")*[33] has been fulfilled. He, exalted be His Name, now sits upon His throne of dignity. And as a consequence of the astounding labors of the beloved Shoghi Effendi, the Sign of God on earth, the Queen of Carmel (the Shrine of the Báb), in all its glory, with all of its embellishments, has become a Supreme Paradise, one of the wonders of the planet, and the spiritual world center of the Cause of God. The Ark of God (the Universal House of Justice), long prophesied by the Tongue of Power and Glory (Bahá'u'lláh), has sailed on the mountain of Carmel; its guidance is apparent everywhere. It was apparent, for example, at the Saint Louis conference, where the friends prepared to exert themselves to teach the Faith and to vie with one another in winning the goals of the Five Year Plan.

The World Order of Bahá'u'lláh was heralded in the Bayán, the Mother Book of the Báb, written while He was a Prisoner at Máh-Kú: " 'Well is it with him who fixeth his gaze upon the Order of Bahá'u'lláh, . . .' "[34] A year later the clarion call of that new Order was sounded at Badasht.

Today that new Order is firmly established. We have seen the Constitution of the [Universal] House of Justice published, and the Seat of Legislation, one of the goals of the Five Year Plan assigned to the World Center, is on the verge of construction.* According to the beloved Shoghi Effendi, "The Ark of God will be built around the Arc." No wonder that "Mankind's ordered life hath been revolution-

---

*The inauguration of the use of the Seat of the Universal House of Justice occurred on 17 July 1982; it was occupied by the Universal House of Justice in January 1983.—Ed.

ized through the agency of this unique, this wondrous System [the
World Order of Bahá'u'lláh],"[35] and the eyes of every dweller of the
earth are each day witnessing the collapse of the present order. Lord,
increase my astonishment at Thee!

How earnestly we wish that the beloved Shoghi Effendi, who so
often quoted from memory the verse from the Tablet of Carmel,
"Ere long will God sail His Ark upon thee,"[36] who urged the believers to pray and to await the fulfillment of the prophecies of that
glorious Tablet, and who did not leave us before he brought it into its
embryonic form, were present amongst us to witness all these glories,
the choice fruits of his strenuous labors.

How ardently we wish that he were with us and that we could hear
him melodiously exclaim with joy and excitement, *"Bi-bíníd
fuyúḍát-i-Jamál-i-Mubárak-rá!* [Behold the bounties of the Blessed
Beauty (Bahá'u'lláh)!]"; or to hear his sweet voice echoing along
Mount Carmel, reciting one of the poems of Bahá'u'lláh that refers
to the growth of the Faith in the West, "O beauty of God, unveil
Thyself so that the sun may rise from the West";[37] or to hear him
confidently exclaim, "The Cause will become a flame in America."
O beloved Shoghi Effendi: "For how long should these torrents of
tears stream from my every eyelash! Multitudes are praising Thee
with a passionate love, whilst Thou art absent from amongst
them."[38]

At the Conference of Bada<u>sh</u>t Bahá'u'lláh Himself was present. At
the Saint Louis Conference His blessings and bounties were apparent. At some of the sessions many cried for joy continually, as if in
those sessions they saw reflected the kingdom from on high. The
participants were surrounded by the showers of the abundant bounties of Bahá'u'lláh. They felt in spirit the presence of their Belov-
eds—Bahá'u'lláh, the Báb, 'Abdu'l-Bahá, and Shoghi Effendi—as
well as the heroes and heroines of the Faith. What a joy! What a
bounty!

At the Conference of Bada<u>sh</u>t a new name was bestowed upon
each of the participants. In Saint Louis all felt they were numbered
among the "chosen" rather than the "called" (Jesus said that many are
called but few are chosen) and that the names of all of the believers,
as Bahá'u'lláh said, are more known to God than to themselves.

At Bada<u>sh</u>t "the veils that guarded the sanctity of the ordinances

Islám were sternly rent asunder, . . ."[39] In Saint Louis, the call of peace, goodwill, love, and the oneness of mankind was raised and proclaimed; the signs of the Kingdom of the Father were apparent; discussions were held on strengthening the foundations of Bahá'u'-lláh's Commonwealth, Bahá'í life, etc.; and the call of *Yá Bahá'u'l-Abhá! Yá 'Alíyu'l-A'lá!* [O Thou the Glory of the Most Glorious! O Thou the Exalted of the Most Exalted!] was raised to the heavens from the hearts and lips of more than ten thousand believers.

Bahá'u'lláh has shared with us the exalted words He heard in the Síyáh-Chál, the Black Pit in the slums of Tehran where He was imprisoned: "*'One night in a dream, these exalted words were heard on every side: "Verily, We shall render Thee victorious by Thyself and by Thy pen. Grieve Thou not for that which hath befallen Thee, neither be Thou afraid, for thou art in safety. Ere long will God raise up the treasures of the earth—men who will aid Thee through Thyself and through Thy Name, wherewith God hath revived the hearts of such as have recognized Him.*" ' "[40]

Let Násiri'd-Dín Sháh arise from his grave, as 'Abdu'l-Bahá said, and see how "the treasures of the earth" have been raised up to aid the Wronged One of the world. And it is only the beginning. Imagine the Síyáh-Chál, and now this glorious Saint Louis gathering! There were those calamities, and now there are all these dignities!

For the sake of brevity I refrain from presenting all the details of the exciting talks of the speakers at Saint Louis. These have been recorded with the best modern devices, with cameras, television, and radio. Some details were published with astounding rapidity in *The American Bahá'í*, and the rest will surely be shared with the believers.*

My pen is again out of my control! Think of the Síyáh-Chál and the chains of Qará-Guhar, "chains of such galling weight that their mark remained imprinted upon His [Bahá'u'lláh's] body all the days of His life";[41] then think of the contrast in Saint Louis where almost three thousand Bahá'ís hastened to the Gateway Arch at dawn to raise their voices in prayer and praise Bahá'u'lláh, the Wronged One;

---

*See the special edition of *The American Bahá'í* (Sept. 1974) produced in Saint Louis while the conference was in session; see also the October 1974 issue, pp. 5–12.—ED.

where from a building high overhead, unbeknownst to those below, a film was made which was later broadcast over local television stations; where the mayor of Saint Louis paid a glorious tribute to the Faith of Bahá'u'lláh; and where the Cause of God was boldly and publicly proclaimed with astonishing success.

This great gathering, the largest in Bahá'í history, was held in Saint Louis to discuss the role of the American believers in the Five Year Plan and to inspire them to arise wholeheartedly and unitedly to promote the Cause of Bahá'u'lláh. The friends gave thanks for the bounties 'Abdu'l-Bahá showered upon the American believers and determined to expend lavishly all their God-given resources in winning the goals of the Universal House of Justice.

" 'O ye apostles of Bahá'u'lláh! May my life be sacrificed for you! . . . Behold the portals which Bahá'u'lláh hath opened before you! consider how exalted and lofty is the station you are destined to attain; how unique the favors with which you have been endowed. . . . Ere long ye will, with your own eyes, witness how brilliantly every one of you, even as a shining star, will radiate in the firmament of your country the light of Divine Guidance and will bestow upon its people the glory of an everlasting life. . . . The range of your future achievements still remains undisclosed. I fervently hope that in the near future the whole earth may be stirred and shaken by the results of your achievements. . . . Be not concerned with the smallness of your numbers, neither be oppressed by the multitude of an unbelieving world. . . . Exert yourselves; your mission is unspeakably glorious.' "42

Finally, as at the Conference of Bada<u>sh</u>t, where the believers invited to celebrate befittingly that great occasion—"the day of festivity and universal rejoicing"43—arose and embraced each other and with unparalleled enthusiasm left the Conference, while "mountain and valley re-echoed the shouts with which that enthusiastic band," journeying to the arena of martyrdom, "hailed the extinction of the old, and the birth of the new Day,"44 the participants in the gathering at Saint Louis similarly determined, with unprecedented joy and excitement, and with the saying *"Yá Bahá'u'l-Abhá, Yá 'Alíyu'l-A'lá!"* raised aloud, to follow the way of their great Exemplar, 'Abdu'l-Bahá.

They closed the conference by singing the hymn "Look at Me, follow Me, be as I am, 'Abdu'l-Bahá, 'Abdu'l-Bahá. . . ." The floor and ceiling seemed to vibrate as their voices strained to reach the heavens and penetrate to the Abhá Kingdom. That beautiful hymn brought tears to the eyes. The friends left the conference for the arena of action and sacrifice, many embracing each other as they left. The spirit of that conference prompted many to hold a vigil all night in ardent prayer with no aim of sleep, beseeching their Lord to make them worthy for service to Bahá'u'lláh and His glorious Faith.

"*'O that I could travel,'* 'Abdu'l-Bahá, crying out from the depths of His soul, gives utterance to His longing, in a memorable passage, in the Tablets of the Divine Plan, addressed to the North American believers, *'even though on foot and in the utmost poverty, to these regions, and raising the call of "Yá Bahá'u'l-Abhá" in cities, villages, mountains, deserts and oceans, promote the Divine teachings! This, alas, I cannot do. How intensely I deplore it! Please God, ye may achieve it!'*"[45]

Please God, we may achieve it!

3 Carmel: The Mountain of God and the Tablet of Carmel

by Zikrullah Khadem

*An article on Mount Carmel in Haifa, Israel, and on Bahá'u'lláh's
Tablet of Carmel, the charter for the world spiritual and administrative centers of the Bahá'í Faith. The Tablet of Carmel was one of Mr.
Khadem's favorites and one that he memorized at Shoghi Effendi's
bidding. The essay, published here with some passages newly
translated by the Universal House of Justice, revisions by the author,
and other minor corrections, first appeared in* Bahá'í News 52, *no.
8 (August 1975): 1–12. Copyright © 1975 by the National
Spiritual Assembly of the Bahá'ís of the United States.*

THE MOUNTAIN OF GOD

The beloved Shoghi Effendi, in referring to the Tablet of Carmel,
designated it as the "Charter of the World Spiritual and Administrative Centers of the Faith on that mountain."[1] Many prophecies had
been made by the prophets about Mount Carmel. The mountain
was called after the name of God: *Carm* (the Vineyard) and *el*
(God).*

Bahá'u'lláh Himself, in *Epistle to the Son of the Wolf,* testified that
"Carmel, in the Book of God, hath been designated as the Hill of
God, and His Vineyard."[2]

'Abdu'l-Bahá, in His prayer during the war, wrote:

> Thou seest me, O my God, in this lofty Mountain, this high and
> exalted place . . . , the abode of the prophets, the haven of Elijah, the
> sanctuary of Isaiah, the heights which the Spirit of God, Jesus Christ—
> upon Him rest salutation and praise—hath traversed, this most exalted
> Spot blessed by the footsteps of the Lord of Hosts. O Lord! This is the

---

*In fact, all words ending with the *el* suffix have their significances, such as *Israel*
(hasten to God), *Ishma'el* (listen to God), etc.

Mountain that Thou hast named Carmel in the Torah, and hast related unto Thyself within the treasury of the holy Scriptures and Tablets. In the midst of the darksome nights, O Lord, I earnestly pray unto Thee in this most exalted Spot.[3]

The Master also told pilgrims around the end of 1907:

This mountain [Carmel] is where Israel's prophets passed their nights in prayers. Every step of it has been blessed by the footsteps of the prophets. . . . This land will be the envy of the world, the center of arts and sciences. 'Akká and Haifa will be connected and all the vacant lands will be cultivated. All these caves that you see have been the abode of the prophets, step by step.* Every atom of this soil is holy. All the prophets, while praying, longed to reach this day and give the glad tidings of the coming of the Lord. They prophesied that the Lord of Hosts would come and the tent of the Lord would be pitched on Mount Carmel. . . . in all these mountains and caves the prophets of God prayed at night, shed tears, and longed to be with us in these days of the Blessed Beauty. Since I am a prisoner and cannot move, you make a pilgrimage on My behalf. My utmost desire is to go and visit in freedom, but I cannot. You go on behalf of 'Abdu'l-Bahá and make a pilgrimage to all of the Holy Places . . . and beseech God's bounty. I cannot go. I am a prisoner. I am reincarcerated, and I have no permission to go out. The government prohibits me.[4]

He also said in 1914:

Many Israelitish prophets either lived here or passed a portion of their lives or sojourned for a while or spent the last days of their existence on this mountain. . . . Abraham, Isaac, Joseph, David, Solomon, Moses, Isaiah, Zechariah and, last of all, Christ. Elijah lived on Mount Carmel. . . . His Holiness Christ came to this holy mountain many times.[5]

Shoghi Effendi adds that "Even Zoroaster came to this land (Holy

---

*Including the Lower Cave of Elijah, known also as Maqám-i-Khidr, blessed by the footsteps of Bahá'u'lláh for three days (according to Memoirs of Dr. Mu'ayyad, 2:258) and of 'Abdu'l-Bahá for about two months (according to an unpublished manuscript). See also David S. Ruhe, *Door of Hope: A Century of the Bahá'í Faith in the Holy Land* (Oxford: George Ronald, 1983), 186–88.

Land). That lofty figure also made a trip to this region and met some of the Israeli prophets. . . ."[6]

For thousands of years man read prophecies and ardently prayed for their realization:

> And it shall come to pass in the last days, that the mountain of the Lord's house shall be established in the top of the mountains, and shall be exalted above the hills; and all nations shall flow unto it.
>
> And many people shall go and say, Come ye, and let us go up to the mountain of the Lord, to the house of the God of Jacob; and he will teach us of his ways, and we will walk in his paths. . . .
>
> And he shall judge among the nations, and shall rebuke many people: and they shall beat their swords into plowshares, and their spears into pruninghooks: nation shall not lift up sword against nation, neither shall they learn war any more.
>
> O house of Jacob, come ye, and let us walk in the light of the Lord.[7]

With great sorrow Carmel was being consumed in separation from her Lord, impatiently awaiting the fulfillment of these prophecies.

The Templars had already emigrated from Stuttgart, Germany, in anticipation of the coming of the Father and Son and had built their houses at the foot of Mount Carmel. The inscription over the window of a Templar house, *"Der Herr ist nahe"* (the Lord is nigh) on Hagefen Street (known as a German street) is still in existence.

When the promised hour did strike in 1890, Bahá'u'lláh, accompanied by 'Abdu'l-Bahá, came to the mountain and sat under a circle of planted cypress trees. His blessed eyes gazed upon the German street and upon the view of the sea. He pointed with His blessed finger to the site where the Shrine of the Báb is now located and uttered that, indeed, that spot was best and proper for the resting place of the Throne of the Exalted Báb. He instructed 'Abdu'l-Bahá that it should be purchased for that purpose. After two or three days, the Tablet of Carmel was also revealed.[8] An eyewitness had mentioned to the beloved Guardian the details of that historic day and was ordered by him to record it for posterity.[9] His account said that Bahá'u'lláh sat on a chair in the middle of the round of trees with but little shade (it consisted of fifteen trees, each as thick as a finger), facing east, and 'Abdu'l-Bahá was seated on another chair one meter away, facing west. The cypress trees still exist above the Shrine of the Báb.

The beloved Guardian also told the writer on 7 April 1937 that 'Abdu'l-Bahá Himself said that the Blessed Beauty, with His own blessed hand, pointed out the location for the Shrine of the Báb and directed Him that the pure remains of the Báb should be entombed there, in a structure with nine rooms, additional stories, and a dome.

The entombment of the remains of the Báb was, indeed, in accordance with the will of Bahá'u'lláh.

The beloved Guardian told the pilgrims that the Blessed Beauty had said that Palestine, now called Israel, is the Qiblih of the nations and the heart of the world. Geographically, it is in Asia, adjacent to Europe and Africa. The enemies of the Faith, the Persian and Turkish governments, had united for the banishment of Bahá'u'lláh and were the cause of His emigration. It was called the Holy Land and now has become the Most Holy Land. In the heart of this Most Holy Land is situated the Mountain of the Lord and, in its heart, the Shrine of the Báb.

He has also noted the great significance of that holy place, now the Queen of Carmel, in these words:

> This magnificent Edifice [the Shrine of the Báb] stands facing Bahá'u'lláh's Most Great Prison, extolled by the Pen of Glory as the "Heaven of heavens," and looks toward the Qiblih of the people of Bahá, that Spot within the Vale of Security and Peace, the Plain of 'Akká, round which circle in adoration the Concourse on high. To her right are the hills of Galilee in which nestles the childhood home of the beautiful Christ, and the locality by the banks of the Jordan River where He who is the Spirit [Jesus] was called to prophethood; and on her left, on the crest of Carmel, are to be found the Cave of Elijah and the exalted Spot which was blessed by the footsteps of the Most Holy Abhá Beauty and was ennobled through the revelation of the Tablet of Carmel from the treasury of the Pen of Glory. Behind her stand the twin Mounts of Zion and Olivet and the holy and ancient city of Jerusalem, within whose walls lie the site of the martyrdom and the burial place of Jesus Christ, the seat of the Throne of David, the glorious Temple of Solomon and the Aqṣá Mosque, which ranks third among the shrines of the Islamic world. Beyond these there rises Mount Sinai, the cradle of the Jewish Faith, that Sacred Mount, the Párán of light, that holy land where He Who con-

versed with God heard the Voice from the Blessed Tree. And further beyond lies the Arabian Peninsula, the land of Ḥijáz, the cradle of the Muḥammadan Dispensation, with the two cities of Baṭhá and Yathrib, the noble Mecca and the bright Medina, one enshrining the Qiblih of Islám and the other the resting-place of Him Who is the Lord of mankind [Muḥammad]—upon Him be countless salutations and praise.

High, immeasurably high is this Shrine, the lofty, the most great, the most wondrous. Exalted, immeasurably exalted is this Resting-place, the fragrant, the pure, the luminous, the transcendent. Glorified, immeasurably glorified is this Spot, the most august, the most holy, the most blessed, the most sublime.[10]

The beloved Guardian told the pilgrims that, upon hearing of Bahá'u'lláh's instructions to 'Abdu'l-Bahá to acquire the site on Mount Carmel for the resting-place of the Báb, the Covenant-breakers attempted to win the glory. Mírzá Badí'u'lláh started negotiations and worked hard to buy that land. He had intended to acquire the land and report the good news to Bahá'u'lláh. But he did not succeed. Bahá'u'lláh told him, "This is none of your business, it is for Áqá (the Master) to accomplish."

After the ascension of Bahá'u'lláh, the first thing 'Abdu'l-Bahá did, in spite of the mountains of difficulties constantly created by the Covenant-breakers, was to purchase the site of the Shrine of the Báb. This was followed by construction of a water reservoir, preparation of the land for building the road, and, finally, commencement of the construction of the Shrine itself. In the meantime, He issued instructions for the transfer of the remains of the Báb from Persia, which arrived in the Holy Land on 31 January 1899. Shortly thereafter He was reincarcerated. He was in Akka while construction of the Shrine was in progress on Mount Carmel according to His instructions.

The Covenant-breakers started great intrigues and machinations that led to the arrival of the Sulṭán's Commission of Investigators. They approached the Commission and offered their cooperation. The Commission also started its own investigation and made trips from Akka to Haifa for this purpose. One of the members of the Commission touched the wall of the Shrine and said in Turkish, "_Chukh matín dur_ [It is very strong]." They thought that the building was going to be used to fight the Ottoman government. 'Abdu'l-Ḥamíd, the Sulṭán, became worried and fearful. The Commission was busy with its investigation when suddenly a bomb exploded in Istanbul. The Sultán changed his mind. 'Abdu'l-Bahá said, "God's bomb exploded." 'Abdu'l-Ḥamíd was imprisoned while 'Abdu'l-Bahá gained His freedom.

In the following year, 1908, a constitutional government was announced. A year later, 'Abdu'l-Ḥamíd was dethroned. The same year, 'Abdu'l-Bahá transferred His residence from Akka to Haifa, where He ceremoniously deposited, on Naw-Rúz 1909, the holy, the luminous remains of the Báb (which had been transferred from one place to another for sixty years) in the sacred sarcophagus ordered from Burma, within the exalted Shrine on Mount Carmel.

The remains of the Báb, which had been hidden for ten years in Akka in the room of 'Abdu'l-Bahá, were then transferred to Mount Carmel in Haifa before construction of the Shrine, and were finally deposited on that day of Naw-Rúz in the sarcophagus.*

'Abdu'l-Bahá gave the glad tidings to the friends in America. The same day, the American convention met and decided to initiate the Mashriqu'l-Adhkár project. The beloved Guardian said that Naw-Rúz 1909 was an historical date.

Although 'Abdu'l-Bahá started construction of the Shrine and even completed six of its rooms, He still did not consider it built. The Guardian relates that as 'Abdu'l-Bahá was "sitting, facing the holy Shrine and gazing upon that holy structure, a phrase issued from His pure tongue: 'It did not come to pass that the Shrine of the Báb be completed. God willing, it will be done. We have brought it thus far.' "[11] It is apparent that this was left for the Sign of God, the beloved Guardian, to perform.

With an unfading zeal and resolution, the beloved Shoghi Effendi took it upon himself to comply with the wishes of Bahá'u'lláh and 'Abdu'l-Bahá and complete this important assignment. He enlarged the property by acquiring vast areas of land for the gardens, added three more rooms in the same architectural style as the original six built by 'Abdu'l-Bahá, and commenced the construction of the Shrine on Naw-Rúz 1949. The arcade and the parapet (the first

---

*The remains of the Báb were actually hidden in the room of 'Abdu'l-Bahá's sister, Bahíyyih Khánum (the Greatest Holy Leaf), during the ten years before they were interred (see Ruhe, *Door of Hope*, 66).—ED.

crown of that great Edifice) were completed for the commemoration of the centenary of the Martyrdom of the Báb on 9 July 1950. The beloved Guardian placed a fragment of plaster from the Báb's prison cell in Máh-Kú in the golden dome of the Shrine on 29 April 1953 (to contrast the Báb's suffering, when He had not even a candle at night, to the glories and victories won for the Faith when the exalted name of the Báb and His fame reached to approximately 128 countries and territories of the globe). Finally, in October 1953, the beloved Shoghi Effendi completed that glorious Shrine, the spiritual world center of the Faith, as designated by Bahá'u'lláh in the Tablet of Carmel. He had not only gladdened the heart of the Prophet-Martyr of the Faith and performed the desire of the Author of the Cause and the Center of the Covenant, but he had also fulfilled the promises of God from ancient scriptures as well as from the Qur'án.

The Guardian created a new style—new in the heavens and the earth. Prophecies regarding the terraces of light, "light upon light" (Qur'án 24:35), which refer to the terraces of the Shrine, have been fulfilled. That "eight shall bear the throne of thy Lord above them, on that day" (Qur'án 69:17) is evident in the arcades, the octagon, the eight-cornered stars in the gardens, and so on. The small minarets over the eight corners of the octagon not only carry the temple of the Lord already referred to in the Qur'án, but also guard it. In fact, the beloved Guardian, while preparing the plan, advised Mr. Sutherland Maxwell, the dear Hand of the Cause of God and the architect of that glorious Edifice, to consider the significance of eight in the Qur'án and quadruple it by placing eight columns for each of the four arcades. He also advised him to plan eighteen lancet windows around the clerestory (representing the eighteen Letters of the Living).

The beloved Guardian must have been so pleased and thrilled with his marvelous and majestic work, as he was moved to send these greetings and record them for posterity:

Upon thee, O Queen of Carmel, be the purest, the most tender salutations, the fairest, the most gracious blessings! Glorified is He Whose footsteps have ennobled the spot whereon thou standest, Who ordained thy Seat, and Who extolled thee in His Tablet and Book. How great is the potency of thy might, a might which has bewildered the souls of the favored ones of God and His Messengers.

Methinks I behold thee in my dreams established upon thy glorious throne, attired in thy white raiment, crowned with thy golden crown, resplendent with the lights shining within thee and around thee, calling aloud in ringing tones and raising thy voice between earth and heaven.

Methinks I perceive the souls of the holy ones and of the dwellers of the realms above hastening toward thee with utmost joy, eagerness and ecstasy, pointing to thee, circling round thee, inhaling the perfume of thy flowers and roses, seeking blessing from the earth of thy precincts, bowing their foreheads to the ground before thee in recognition of the majesty and glory which surround the Holy Dust reposing within thee, the Pearl which is enshrined in thy bosom.

Blessed, immeasurably blessed is the person who visits thee and circles around thee, who serves at thy threshold, waters thy flowers, inhales the fragrance of holiness from thy roses, celebrates thy praise and glorifies thy station for the love of God, thy Creator, in this hallowed and radiant, this great, august and wondrous age.[12]

Thanks, a thousand thanks to Bahá'u'lláh, who constantly assisted His beloved Guardian from on high in accomplishing all these victories. We are so inadequate to express our humble gratitude to the beloved Shoghi Effendi for his miraculous achievements. We are extremely grateful to observe that he, in this mortal world, witnessed, with his own blessed eyes, the beauty and glory of his work and undoubtedly, in the Abhá Kingdom, enjoys the eternal expressions of tender love from Bahá'ís of all countries, cities, mountains, caves, valleys, lands, seas and islands, repeating the greeting addressed by him to the Queen of Carmel.

THE TABLET OF CARMEL

Earlier in these pages reference was made to the Tablet of Carmel as the "Charter of the World Spiritual and Administrative Centers of the Faith on that mountain."[13] With completion of the Shrine of the Báb, the establishment of the Queen of Carmel on Her glorious throne, the glad tidings of Bahá'u'lláh concerning the world spiritual center of the Faith were realized.

'Abdu'l-Bahá recounts the circumstances surrounding the occasion when Bahá'u'lláh pitched His tent on Mount Carmel:

"He [Bahá'u'lláh] proclaimed His Cause in prison and hoisted His standard under the menace of the sword. He was a person against whom two reigning monarchs arose in enmity and were bent upon His extermination. These two sovereigns gave orders that the Blessed Beauty should be imprisoned in one room and be excluded from all outside intercourse. They prevented me from attaining His presence. Notwithstanding this strict prohibition, His pavilion was raised here on this lofty spot of Carmel."[14]

He tells us in *Memorials of the Faithful:*

Although the policy of Sultán 'Abdu'l-Ḥamíd was harsher than ever; although he constantly insisted on his Captive's strict confinement—still, the Blessed Beauty now lived, as everyone knows, with all power and glory. Some of the time Bahá'u'lláh would spend at the Mansion, and again, at the farm village of Mazra'ih; for a while He would sojourn in Haifa, and occasionally His tent would be pitched on the heights of Mount Carmel. Friends from everywhere presented themselves and gained an audience. The people and the government authorities witnessed it all, yet no one so much as breathed a word. And this is one of Bahá'u'lláh's greatest miracles: that He, a captive, surrounded Himself with a panoply and He wielded power. The prison changed into a palace, the jail itself became a Garden of Eden. Such a thing has not occurred in history before; no former age has seen its like: that a man confined to a prison should move about with authority and might; that one in chains should carry the fame of the Cause of God to the high heavens, should win splendid victories in both East and West, and should, by His almighty pen, subdue the world. Such is the distinguishing feature of this supreme Theophany.[15]

The beloved Guardian shares with us in *God Passes By:*

Bahá'u'lláh's tent, the "Tabernacle of Glory," was raised on Mt. Carmel, "the Hill of God and His Vineyard," the home of Elijah, extolled by Isaiah as the "mountain of the Lord," to which "all nations shall flow." Four times He visited Haifa. . . . In the course of one of these visits, when His tent was pitched in the vicinity of the Carmelite Monastery, He, the "Lord of the Vineyard," revealed the Tablet of Carmel, remarkable for its allusions and prophecies.[16]

Nearing the evening of His life, Bahá'u'lláh, noting that "the fragrances of mercy have been wafted over all created things," addressed Carmel:

"Render thanks unto Thy Lord, O Carmel. The fire of thy separation from Me was fast consuming thee, when the ocean of My presence surged before thy face. . . . Rejoice, for God hath in this Day established upon thee His throne, hath made thee the dawning-place of His signs. . . . He, verily, loveth the spot which hath been made the seat of His throne. . . .

"Call out to Zion, O Carmel, and announce the joyful tidings: He that was hidden from mortal eyes is come! His all-conquering sovereignty is manifest; His all-encompassing splendor is revealed. Beware lest thou hesitate or halt. Hasten forth and circumambulate the City of God that hath descended from heaven, the celestial Kaaba round which have circled in adoration the favored of God, the pure in heart, and the company of the most exalted angels. . . . Ere long will God sail His Ark upon thee, and will manifest the people of Bahá who have been mentioned in the Book of Names."

Sanctified be the Lord of all mankind, at the mention of Whose name all the atoms of the earth have been made to vibrate, and the Tongue of Grandeur hath been moved to disclose that which had been wrapt in His knowledge and lay concealed within the treasury of His might. He, verily, through the potency of His name, the Mighty, the All-Powerful, the Most High, is the ruler of all that is in the heavens and all that is on earth.[17]

No wonder He had not disclosed the hidden glad tidings earlier, waiting until the evening of His life to do so. Man was not ready, nor did he deserve it.

GLAD TIDINGS FORETOLD BY THE PROPHETS

When "by the grace of the Lord of Revelation, the Tabernacle of Glory hath been raised" on Mount Carmel, all the promises Bahá'u'lláh deemed advisable were revealed.[18] The Kingdom of the Father on earth long prophesied by Jesus Christ was initiated, and the Truth of the revelation of Saint John became manifest: *Malakút-i-Pidar mubárak bád* (Blessed be the kingdom of the Father)![19]

And I saw a new heaven and a new earth: for the first heaven and the first earth were passed away; and there was no more sea. . . .

And I heard a great voice out of heaven saying, Behold, the tabernacle of God is with men, and he will dwell with them, and they shall be his people, and God himself shall be with them, and be their God. . . .

And he that sat upon the throne said, Behold, I make all things new.[20]

The Pársís were long awaiting the fulfillment of their prophecies that, "After the victory of the Arabs and the decline of the Zoroastrians I [God] will raise a great man in Iran from the dynasty of the Kíyáns, who will gather the people of the world from the east and the west to the worship of God."[21] "He [the Promised One], then [at that time] will make the whole universe anew."[22]

Isaiah, the greatest prophet of Israel, again referred to Bahá'u'lláh and His Kingdom:

For unto us a child is born, unto us a son is given: and the government shall be upon his shoulder: and his name shall be called Wonderful, Counsellor, The mighty God, The everlasting Father, The Prince of Peace.

Of the increase of his government and peace there shall be no end, upon the throne of David, and upon his kingdom, to order it, and to establish it with judgment and with justice from henceforth even for ever. The zeal of the Lord of hosts will perform this.[23]

And righteousness shall be the girdle of his loins, and faithfulness the girdle of his reins.[24]

In further reference to the revelation of Bahá'u'lláh and to the Universal House of Justice, the beloved Guardian said that Muslims have recited the first chapter of the Qur'án in their daily obligatory prayers (five times), praying for the coming of the "king of the day of judgment."[25] Referring to the "king," the exalted Báb said the king of the day of judgment would appear in the year 80* (1280 A.H., the year of Bahá'u'lláh's revelation in the Riḍván Garden, Baghdad). The Báb, in His Mother Book, the Bayán, revealed in explicit language: "Well is it with him who fixeth his gaze upon the Order of Bahá'u'lláh. . . ."[26]

All these predictions were, in a sense, realized with the revelation

---

*One vaḥíd (nineteen years) after the revelation of the Báb. The year 1280 A.H. corresponds roughly to the year 1863 A.D.

of Bahá'u'lláh, with His proclamation to the kings and leaders of the world, with His Messages and Tablets to the whole of mankind, and with the revelation of the Book of His Laws, the Most Holy Book, the [Kitáb-i-]Aqdas. The earth was indeed filled with "the knowledge of the Lord, as the waters cover the sea."[27] However, because of the inadequacy of man, Bahá'u'lláh did not reveal the mysteries which were still hidden in the Tablet of Carmel.

FORMATIVE AGE

With the passing of 'Abdu'l-Bahá the Formative Age started. The beloved Guardian nurtured and consolidated the Administrative Order, the foundation of which was laid by 'Abdu'l-Bahá. He strengthened the Local Spiritual Assemblies, the bedrock of the World Order of Bahá'u'lláh. He trained the Bahá'ís, constantly urged them to promote the Cause, guided them in electing National Spiritual Assemblies, and encouraged them to collaborate with him until the final crown, the Universal House of Justice, was won.

His deeply inspiring messages, as bountiful rains of divine blessings, showered upon all communities without interruption, causing them to arise and respond befittingly to his heavenly calls.

In his moving message of August 1927 addressed to the long-suffering Bahá'ís in the East, he announced the glad tiding that "The divine springtime hath come to an end, and the summer season with its abundant fruit is now at hand."[28]

Later, in November 1927, he shared the great triumph of the members of the Central Assembly of the American Bahá'ís and highly praised them for enacting their constitution and by-laws, and for presenting this document to the official authorities of their government—an act which led to the recognition of the Cause in that continent. In that same message the beloved Shoghi Effendi was moved to offer his thanks to Bahá'u'lláh and to quote some of the preceding passages from the Tablet of Carmel. He ended his thirty-two-page message with a very moving and heartrending prayer. He continued to quote some of the passages of the Tablet of Carmel in his further messages, such as one in a twenty-four-page message of 27 November 1929:

O Carmel.... Well is it with him that circleth around thee, that proclaimeth the revelation of thy glory, and recounteth that which the bounty of the Lord thy God hath showered upon thee.

I had the great privilege and honor to listen with gratitude to the revelation of the glory of Carmel proclaimed by the beloved Shoghi Effendi on 3 April 1937 in the vicinity of the Master's house. Oh, that I could have been able to grasp and recall all the gems and inter- pretations recounted by him on that great day! How sweet, how very sweet, was the melody of his voice!

"Have you read the Tablet of Carmel?" was his query. "The Tablet is there in the Pilgrim House.* The Blessed Beauty revealed this Tablet when His tent was first raised on Mount Carmel near the Deyr (Carmel- ite Monastery).§ The Tablet was not completed. It contains the divine mysteries of God. Bahá'u'lláh said, 'Call out to Zion, O Carmel,' which means, O Carmel, address Jerusalem, 'and announce the joyful tidings: He that was hidden from mortal eyes is come! . . . Hasten forth and circumambulate the City of God. . . .' The City of God refers to the es- tablishment of the Shrine of the Báb on Mount Carmel. The City of God in this Tablet is Bahá'u'lláh's promise to entomb the sacred body of the Báb. A 'celestial Kaaba' is a mystery [which he did not disclose, nor did I dare to ask]. These are mysteries. Bahá'u'lláh proceeds in this Tablet, 'Ere long will God sail His Ark upon thee,' a further mystery which means the Universal House of Justice will be established here on Mount Carmel under the shadow of the Shrine of the Báb. The Ark, in this Tablet, is the Ark of God's civilization. And 'the people of Bahá,' the occupants of the Ark, are members of the House."

These were some of the explanations (already confirmed in his messages) which I heard on that historic day in my life from the blessed lips of the beloved Guardian. As I took my leave from him, I

---

*The Tablet of Carmel was written with excellent penmanship. It is now enclosed in a big frame and hangs in the middle of the wall in the upper hall of the Pilgrim House. The beloved Guardian used to sit facing the Tablet of Carmel in a wicker chair two chairs from the window (the first chair naturally remained unoccupied).

§This spot is very close to the obelisk marking the site that the beloved Guardian designated for the future Mashriqu'l-Adhkár.

found myself incapable of recalling any of his further statements, so powerful were his words, words of the Sign of God on earth.

Later the beloved Guardian explained that the Tablet of Carmel was revealed from the holy lips of Bahá'u'lláh in a loud voice and recorded by His amanuensis, whom Bahá'u'lláh called to take dictation. The power and melody of His voice deeply impressed the monks of the monastery who were standing in reverence and listening.

A year later, the beloved Guardian bade me to memorize the Tablet of Carmel, visit Shiraz and Yazd, and chant it for the Afnán (kindred of the Báb).

MONUMENT GARDENS

Bahá'u'lláh offered up His dear son, the Purest Branch, *"'created of the light of Bahá,'* the *'Trust of God'* and His *'Treasure'* in the Holy Land . . . as a *'ransom'* for the regeneration of the world and the unification of its peoples."[29]

In a highly significant prayer in memory of the Purest Branch, Bahá'u'lláh revealed: " *'I have, O my Lord, offered up that which Thou hast given Me, that Thy servants may be quickened, and all that dwell on earth be united.'* "[30] This was a "death" exalted "to the rank of those great acts of atonement associated with Abraham's intended sacrifice of His son, with the crucifixion of Jesus Christ and the martyrdom of the Imám Husayn."[31]

The beloved Shoghi Effendi, on Christmas Eve 1939, transferred the remains of the brother and mother of 'Abdu'l-Bahá to Mount Carmel and announced the glad tidings:

> Blessed remains Purest Branch and Master's Mother safely transferred hallowed precincts Shrines Mount Carmel. . . . Cherished wish Greatest Holy Leaf fulfilled. Sister, Brother, Mother[,] Wife 'Abdu'l-Bahá reunited one spot designed constitute focal center Bahá'í Administrative Institutions at Faith's World Center. . . . *Shoghi Rabbani.*[32]

He had already erected the monument of the Greatest Holy Leaf and designated it as symbolic of the World Order of Bahá'u'lláh. He had explained, both in his messages and his talks to the pilgrims, that the three steps of the monument of the Greatest Holy Leaf are symbolic of the three steps of the election of the Universal House:

first, the election of the delegates of the believers to the National Conventions; second, the election of the members of the National Spiritual Assemblies by the delegates; and third, the election of the Universal House of Justice by the members of the National Assemblies. The nine pillars of the monument symbolize the National Assemblies, and the dome, the Universal House of Justice.

He also explained that when the nine pillars on the monument were being constructed, he called the engineer and directed him to place the head pillar so that it precisely faces the Shrine of Bahá'u'lláh, and not Akka.

The beloved Guardian emphasized in his writings as well as in his talks to pilgrims that in the Tablet of Carmel Bahá'u'lláh established and gave the glad tidings for two institutions: the world spiritual and the world administrative centers of His Faith on Mount Carmel. The world spiritual center is the Shrine of the Báb; the world administrative center is the Universal House of Justice. These two, according to his message on the occasion of the transfer of the remains of these two blessed souls, are inseparable—a fact that is significant and unique.

The spiritual and administrative centers of the Muslim faith which, in the beginning of Islam, were together in the Arabian Peninsula, became separated from each other. Mecca and Medina remained as the spiritual centers, but the administrative center moved to Damascus, Iraq, and eventually to Turkey, where it collapsed (the Caliphate). The same thing happened in Christianity. After the crucifixion of Jesus Christ, Jerusalem, where Jesus Christ was crucified and buried, was considered the spiritual center of Christianity. The first Christian church under the leadership of one of Christ's brothers was also located in Jerusalem. However, because of the teaching activities and the dispersal of His disciples, the administrative center moved to Rome, where the Pope resides.

DEDICATION OF THE TWIN MONUMENTS

The writer had the bounty to be present at the dedication of the monuments of the brother and mother of 'Abdu'l-Bahá, which took place on 9 February 1940 (first Muḥarram 1359, birthday anniversary of the Báb, according to the lunar calendar).

After a large meeting in the Pilgrim House and en route to visiting the Shrines of the Báb and 'Abdu'l-Bahá, the Guardian bade me to chant two prayers, one in each Shrine. At the time, I was unaware of the purpose of these prayers, but upon leaving the Shrines, I learned from the beloved Guardian that one was for reducing the persecution of Bahá'ís in Iran and the other for opening the door of pilgrimage. He stated further that, as a result of these prayers, the door of pilgrimage would indeed open, and all the Bahá'ís who had been permitted to go on pilgrimage but were deprived because of the strict passport restrictions would come, openly proclaiming their purpose. It is interesting to note that seventy years earlier the Purest Branch, on his deathbed, entreated Bahá'u'lláh to accept him as a ransom that the door of pilgrimage be opened for those of His loved ones who yearned, but were unable, to come; again on this day of the dedication of the twin monuments, the beloved Shoghi Effendi gave the joyous tiding of the opening of the door of pilgrimage. Indeed, the Guardian's prediction came to pass. Over 120 pilgrims attained their hearts' desire, openly proclaiming that they were proceeding on pilgrimage to the Bahá'í holy Shrines in Akka and Haifa. So many came that the Guardian finally temporarily discontinued the pilgrimages.

On that historic day of the dedication, the beloved Guardian gathered all the petals from the Shrines of the Báb and 'Abdu'l-Bahá and spread them in two big white sheets. These were then taken to the monuments, where an entire sheet with the rose petals was spread over each monument, following which the beloved Guardian added a rose to each with such care that it seemed as if he were searching for the exact spot to adorn their holy and blessed hearts, an act, the tenderness of which deeply moved all who were present at the dedication. He then chanted their Tablets of Visitation:

Upon thee, O Branch of God! be the remembrance of God and His praise, and the praise of all that dwell in the Realm of Immortality, and of all the denizens of the Kingdom of Names. Happy art thou in that thou hast been faithful to the Covenant of God and His Testament, until Thou didst sacrifice thyself before the face of thy Lord, the Almighty, the Unconstrained. Thou, in truth, hast been wronged, and to this testifieth the Beauty of Him, the Self-Subsisting. Thou didst, in the first days of thy life, bear that which hath caused all things to groan, and made every pillar to tremble. Happy is the one that remembereth thee, and draweth nigh, through thee, unto God, the Creator of the Morn. . . .

Blessed art thou, and blessed he that turneth unto thee, and visiteth thy grave, and draweth nigh, through thee, unto God, the Lord of all that was and shall be. . . . I testify that thou didst return in meekness unto thine abode. Great is thy blessedness and the blessedness of them that hold fast unto the hem of thy outspread robe. . . .[33]

O Navváb! O Leaf that hath sprung from My Tree, and been My companion! My glory be upon thee, and My loving-kindness, and My mercy that hath surpassed all beings. We announce unto thee that which will gladden thine eye, and assure thy soul, and rejoice thine heart. Verily, thy Lord is the Compassionate, the All-Bountiful. God hath been and will be pleased with thee, and hath singled thee out for His own Self, and to serve Him, and hath made thee the companion of His Person in the day-time and in the night-season.

Hear thou Me once again, God is well-pleased with thee, as a token of His grace and a sign of His mercy. He hath made thee to be His companion in every one of His worlds, and hath nourished thee with His meeting and presence, so long as His Name, and His Remembrance, and His Kingdom, and His Empire shall endure. Happy is the handmaid that hath mentioned thee, and sought thy good-pleasure, and humbled herself before thee, and held fast unto the cord of thy love. Woe betide him that denieth thy exalted station, and the things ordained for thee from God, the Lord of all names, and him that hath turned away from thee, and rejected thy station before God, the Lord of the mighty throne.[34]

Then the beloved Guardian proceeded to the monument of the Greatest Holy Leaf, where he chanted with a melodious and sweet voice a prayer, walked to the two-foot columns* of her monument, and said the Tablet revealed in her honor, engraved with pure gold on the crown of the monument. This, according to him, is the highest tribute to her revealed by Bahá'u'lláh:

He is the Eternal! This is My testimony for her who hath heard My voice and drawn nigh unto Me. Verily, she is a leaf that hath sprung from this preexistent Root. She hath revealed herself in My name and tasted of the sweet savors of My holy, My wondrous pleasure. At one time We gave her to drink from My honeyed Mouth, at another caused her to partake

---

*In diameter.—ED.

of My mighty, My luminous Kaw<u>th</u>ar. Upon her rest the glory of My name and the fragrance of My shining robe.[35]

After reciting this Tablet, the beloved Guardian turned to the right and shared certain verses of the fifty-fourth chapter in Isaiah. He said the Master had explained that the whole chapter was addressed to 'Abdu'l-Bahá's mother.

> Enlarge the place of thy tent, and let them stretch forth the curtains of thine habitations: spare not, lengthen thy cords, and strengthen thy stakes; For thou shalt break forth on the right hand and on the left; and thy seed shall inherit the Gentiles, and make the desolate cities to be inhabited. Fear not; for thou shalt not be ashamed: neither be thou confounded; for thou shalt not be put to shame. . . . For thy Maker is thine husband; the Lord of hosts is His name; and thy Redeemer the Holy One of Israel; The God of the whole earth shall he be called. . . . For a small moment have I forsaken thee; but with great mercies will I gather thee. . . .[36]

Then the beloved Guardian said that God promised to build her monument with most precious stones.

> behold, I will lay thy stones with fair colours, and lay thy foundations with sapphires. And I will make thy windows of agates, and thy gates of carbuncles, and all thy borders of pleasant stones.[37]

The beloved Shoghi Effendi said for thousands of years the people read this chapter, ignorant of its significance. Even the Bahá'í teachers did not know its true meaning. How explicitly it is said that "Thy Maker is thine husband; the Lord of hosts is His name." It could not be said more explicitly than this: "Thy Maker [Bahá'u'lláh] is thine husband."

The beloved Shoghi Effendi then, in a very moving way, expressed his thanks: "Thanks to God, now their holy, blessed remains have been placed in pure, shining marble, and the promises of God have been fulfilled. The result of these prophecies will become manifest in the second Bahá'í century."

THE ARK AROUND THE ARC

During my last pilgrimage on the second fortnight in March 1952, the beloved Shoghi Effendi was busy preparing the dome over the octagon in order that gilded tiles could be placed on the third crown of the Shrine of the Báb and completed for the Riḍván Centenary of the Holy Year Nine (1953). In his presence I watched as he pointed with his right hand to the Shrine of the Báb and thanked Bahá'u'lláh that the spiritual center of the Faith on Mount Carmel was almost complete. Then he waved his left hand, pointing to the lands of the Monument Gardens, and said, "From now on we must exert our efforts to build the Administrative World Center there."

He often remarked that the believers must be waiting anxiously for the realization of the promises of God uttered in the Tablet of Carmel: "Ere long will God sail His Ark upon thee."[38]

While walking in the mountains, waving his hand, he said that it means "The Laws of God will flow from Thee, O Mount Carmel, to the world and its inhabitants."

This reminds us that the phrase, "the Laws flowing from the mountains," has been a common phrase in all religions. Please see prophecies of the Old Testament in the book of Deuteronomy, chapter 33, when Moses, for the last time in His life, blessed the children of Israel. He referred to the mountains of Sinai (Moses), Sair (Jesus) and His (God's) shining forth from Mount Párán (Muḥammad).

Thereafter the beloved Guardian started to build an Arc around the monuments in the Monument Gardens, along which would be erected the international institutions of the Faith. The first of these was, according to him, the Archives, majestically built and prepared for the sacred relics and writings of the Faith. For its furniture, he visited England. It was there that he passed away, but he completed his plan. The beloved Shoghi Effendi predicted that the Ark of God (the Universal House of Justice) will be built around the Arc.

The beloved Guardian referred to these institutions in two beautifully different ways. In the first way, he used the original Arabic word *Daru'l* (House of, Center) for all the institutions: *Daru'l-Aṯhár* (Archives), *Daru'l-Tablíg̲h̲* or *Daru'l-Tarwíj* (Teaching or Propagation Center, for the Hands), *Daru'l-Tas̲h̲rí'* (House of Legislation, Universal House of Justice). He also referred to these by using the prefix letter *M,* which in Arabic means "place of," and in a very joyful manner said the members of the Universal House of Justice will first go to the *Maṭla'-i-Anwár* (the Dawning Place of Light, the Shrine of the Báb), to seek blessings, then to the Mashriqu'l-Adhkár (the House of Worship, which is to be built near the obelisk at the top of Mount Carmel), then they will come to *Markaz-i-Athár* (the center of relics, the Archives) for reference to the Holy Texts, and will gather in the *Majma'-i-Abrár* (the gathering place of the righteous, the House of Justice) for deliberation.

Thanks to Bahá'u'lláh, the beloved Shoghi Effendi, through his self-sacrifice and his untiring thirty-six years of work, days and nights of work with no rest, brought that body, the Universal House of Justice—"the source of all good and freed from all error"[39]—into its embryonic form as he promised in his first message to the Bahá'ís of the East. He did not leave us before he completed his ministry.

Again, thanks to the Blessed Beauty, the Supreme Body, the Universal House of Justice, the last refuge for mankind as predicted by all the Prophets, is now formed. The eyes of creation are illumined, the Ark of God is sailing, and His Laws are flowing from Mount Carmel.

The beloved Guardian said the Shrine of the Báb, in spite of all its beauty and marvelous attraction, is under the shadow of the Shrine of Bahá'u'lláh, even as the number eight, symbolic of the octagon and columns in the arcade, is under the shadow of nine (numerical value of *Bahá*). The beloved Guardian had named the Shrines of Bahá'u'lláh and the Báb *Daryáy-i-Núr* (the Ocean of Light) and *Kúh-i-Núr* (the Mountain of Light) (also the titles of the two biggest diamonds in the world), the second one being under the shadow of the first.

Thanks, a thousand thanks, that now, as a result of the abundant bounties of Bahá'u'lláh and the Báb, the miracles of 'Abdu'l-Bahá, and the untiring, strenuous efforts of the beloved Shoghi Effendi, we can go to the Mountain of the Lord, to the House of the God of Jacob, and say, "Come ye, and let us walk in the light of the Lord."[40]

Praise be unto Him (God) that now we can see with our own eyes, in the circuits of Jerusalem (Akka and Haifa), blessed by God, the signs of God shown to Muḥammad, Apostle of God, almost fourteen hundred years ago in His one-night journey.

> Praise be unto him, who transported his servant [Muḥammad] by night, from the sacred temple of Mecca to the farther temple of Jerusa-

lem, the circuit of which we have blessed, that we might show him some of our signs. . . .[41]

Let us examine closely these passages from the recent inspiring and moving message of the House of God, the Universal House of Justice:

> As the Five Year Plan gathers momentum in all parts of the world, with the followers of the Blessed Perfection firmly embarked on the course that will lead to victory, the time has come for us to contemplate, in preparation for its imminent initiation, the project which will rank as the greatest single undertaking of that Plan, the construction of a befitting seat for the Universal House of Justice in the heart of God's Holy Mountain.

> Nearly thirty-six years ago, after overcoming a multitude of difficulties, the beloved Guardian succeeded in transferring to Mount Carmel the sacred remains of the Purest Branch and Navváb, interring them in the immediate neighborhood of the resting-place of the Greatest Holy Leaf, and alluded, in these words, to the "capital institutional significance" that these events constituted in the unfoldment of the World Center of the Faith:

> > For it must be clearly understood, nor can it be sufficiently emphasized, that the conjunction of the resting-place of the Greatest Holy Leaf with those of her brother and mother incalculably reinforces the spiritual potencies of that consecrated Spot which, under the wings of the Báb's overshadowing Sepulcher, and in the vicinity of the future Mashriqu'l-Adhkár, which will be reared on its flank, is destined to evolve into the focal center of those world-shaking, world-embracing, world-directing administrative institutions of the Guardianship and the Universal House of Justice. Then, and then only, will this momentous prophecy which illuminates the concluding passages of the Tablet of Carmel be fulfilled: "Ere long will God sail His Ark upon thee (Carmel), and will manifest the people of Bahá who have been mentioned in the Book of Names."

> The first of the majestic edifices constituting this mighty Center, was the building for the International Archives of the Faith which was completed in the summer of 1957 as one of the last major achievements of Shoghi Effendi's Guardianship. . . . It is now both necessary and possible to initiate construction of a building that will not only serve the

practical needs of a steadily consolidating administrative center but will, for centuries to come, stand as a visible expression of the majesty of the divinely ordained institutions of the Administrative Order of Bahá'u'-lláh.[42]

What a glory for each one of us in this perishing world, where nothing but the Face of God remains,[43] to respond befittingly to the call of the Supreme Body of the Faith by presenting to the altar of the Blessed Beauty our humble means, energies, and resources and to arise unitedly, as never before, to bring into being the Kingdom of the Father, Bahá'u'lláh's Commonwealth.

Please God we may achieve it!

4 Bahá'u'lláh and His Most Holy Shrine
by Zikrullah Khadem

A brief survey of religious literature that anticipated Bahá'u'lláh's coming and an explanation of the significance of the Shrine of Bahá'u'lláh. Reprinted from Bahá'í News, *no. 540 (March 1976): 1–16. Copyright © 1976 by the National Spiritual Assembly of the Bahá'ís of the United States.*

O ye dwellers in the highest paradise!
Proclaim unto the children of assurance that within the realms of holiness, nigh unto the celestial paradise, a new garden hath appeared, round which circle the denizens of the realm on high and the immortal dwellers of the exalted paradise. Strive, then, that ye may attain that station, that ye may unravel the mysteries of love from its wind-flowers and learn the secret of divine and consummate wisdom from its eternal fruits. Solaced are the eyes of them that enter and abide therein![1]

"But for Him [Bahá'u'lláh]* no Divine Messenger would have been invested with the robe of prophethood, nor would any of the sacred scriptures have been revealed. To this bear witness all created things."[2]

"When the friends speak of the Blessed Beauty," the beloved of all hearts, Shoghi Effendi, told the pilgrims, "it is not enough for them

---

*In all the Bahá'í writings it is emphasized: "Let no one meditating . . . on the nature of the Revelation of Bahá'u'lláh, mistake its character or misconstrue the intent of its Author. The divinity attributed to so great a Being and the complete incarnation of the names and attributes of God in so exalted a Person should, under no circumstances, be misconceived or misinterpreted. The human temple that has been made the vehicle of so overpowering a Revelation must, if we be faithful to the tenets of our Faith, ever remain entirely distinguished from that 'innermost Spirit of Spirits' and 'eternal Essence of Essences'—that invisible yet rational God. . . ." (Shoghi Effendi, "The Dispensation of Bahá'u'lláh," in *The World Order of Bahá'u'lláh: Selected Letters,* 2d ed. [Wilmette, Ill.: Bahá'í Publishing Trust, 1974], 112).

to merely say that Bahá'u'lláh is the Great Educator of mankind; let them rather say that He is *'the Most Great Revelation,'*³ the Promised One of all Holy Books and Scriptures, the Dawning-place of Revelation, and the Source of Inspiration. There is a difference between revelation and inspiration. He is also the 'Heavenly Father.'"⁴

Ever since that moment when I heard the beloved Guardian emphasize this, whenever I approach a seeker I quote the following from Isaiah, the greatest prophet of Israel:

> For unto us a child is born, unto us a son is given: and the government shall be upon his shoulder: and his name shall be called Wonderful, Counsellor, The mighty God, The everlasting Father, The Prince of Peace.⁵

In the Kitáb-i-Aqdas, Bahá'u'lláh proclaims His Station and the great Significance of His Day to the kings:

> O kings of the earth! He Who is the sovereign Lord of all is come. The Kingdom is God's, the omnipotent Protector, the Self-Subsisting. . . .
> This is the Day in which He Who held converse with God [Moses] hath attained the light of the Ancient of Days, and quaffed the pure waters of reunion from this Cup that hath caused the seas to swell. Say: By the one true God! Sinai is circling round the Day Spring of Revelation, while from the heights of the Kingdom the Voice of the Spirit of God [Jesus Christ] is heard proclaiming: "Bestir yourselves, ye proud ones of the earth, and hasten ye unto Him." Carmel hath, in this Day, hastened in longing adoration to attain His court, whilst from the heart of Zion there cometh the cry: "The promise is fulfilled. That which had been announced in the holy Writ of God, the most Exalted, the Almighty, the Best-Beloved, is made manifest."⁶

Bahá'u'lláh proclaims: " 'All the Divine Books and Scriptures have predicted and announced unto men the advent of the Most Great Revelation.' "⁷

The Divine Messengers of the past had a mission to prepare the people for this Day and give them glad tidings of the coming of Bahá'u'lláh.

> Of old did we send Moses with our signs: and said to him, "Bring forth thy people from the darkness into the light, and remind them of the days of God."⁸

"Then gave We the Book to Moses—complete for Him who should do right, and a decision for all matters, and a guidance, and a mercy, that they might believe in the Presence of their Lord."⁹

All the Prophets who descended from the seed of Abraham received their mantles in the Holy Land and its vicinity, the Court and Sanctuary of Bahá'u'lláh. Zoroaster also visited the Holy Land and "*held converse with some of the Prophets of Israel.*"¹⁰

THE GREATEST NAME OF BAHÁ'U'LLÁH

The Holy Books start with *B* (the first letter of the name of Bahá'u'lláh). In Genesis, the first word is *Brishit* (Hebrew: beginning or in the beginning).¹¹ The same is true of the beginning of the glorious Qur'án and of each of the 114 súrihs (chapters), all of which begin with *B: B*iSMILLÁH.* The ninth súrih also begins with a *B*, but with a different word, *Bárat*.

The Muslims repeat the first chapter beginning with BiSM-ILLÁH five times a day in their obligatory prayers. They are also urged to repeat the word BiSMILLÁH as many times as they can in their daily lives as a blessing—evidently a reminder of the coming of Bahá'u'lláh.

'Abdu'l-Bahá, in His commentary of BiSMILLÁH, quotes from Imám Ja'far-i-Sádiq (the sixth Imám) that *"El-Bá Bahá'u'lláh"* (*B* means Bahá'u'lláh).¹² Siyyid Kázim-i-Rashtí, in one of his works (Sharh-i-Qasídih), quotes from the same Imám on several occasions, *"El-Bá, Bahá'u'lláh, val-Sín, Saná'u'lláh"* (*B* means Bahá'u'lláh and *S* Saná'u'lláh). In Arabic, the *i* between *B* and *S* is not written; thus *B* is the first letter and *S* the second letter. Saná'u'lláh, again, means Bahá'u'lláh. The inscription *"El-Bá, Bahá'u'lláh"* (the beginning of this analysis in Arabic) adorns the margins of some of the Latin editions of the Qur'án published in Turkey.

The Imám 'Alí explains that the Qur'án is the essence of all Holy Books and the essence of the Qur'án is contained in its first chapter.

---

*BISMILLÁH is the first word of the first verse of every súrih of the Qur'án except the ninth. The verse is composed of nineteen letters; in honor of each letter six chapters were revealed, totaling 114 chapters (the Báb, *The Persian Bayán*, 2d Váhid, 2:2). The translation of the first verse is: "In the name of God, the Compassionate, the Merciful."

Further, the essence of the first chapter is in the first verse, and the essence of the first verse is in the first letter, *B*, to which is added in the commentary of the Khuṭbiy-i-Ṭutunjíyih, *"El-Bá, Bahá'u'lláh, val-Sín, Saná'u'lláh. . . ."*[13]

Hundreds of verses and traditions have been revealed by the Prophets in praise of the name of Bahá'u'lláh. Some of them, together with some of His titles, appear in the majestic work of the beloved Shoghi Effendi, *God Passes By*, chapter 11.

Ezekiel said "the glory of the God of Israel [Bahá'u'lláh] came from the way of the East. . . ."[14]

Isaiah said, "Arise, shine; for thy light is come, and the glory of the Lord is risen upon thee."[15] Not only does "the glory of the Lord" refer to the name of Bahá'u'lláh, but since "Bahá" also means "shining,"* "Arise, shine" may be considered an exhortation to be a Bahá'í![16]

The followers of Krishna also have many references to the name of Bahá'u'lláh. In the prayer, "the Mother of the Vedas," the Hindus stand with great reverence and beseech guidance from the "GLORY OF GOD" (Bahá'u'lláh). Also in Gita XI:30, it is said, ". . . Thine Blazing BHAH, O Vishnu, (the Omnipresent God), doth glow intensely."[17]

AMIT*ABHA* (Infinite Glory), the name of the promised Buddha, is inscribed in the forty-two-foot statue sitting in eternal meditation at Kamakura, Japan, accompanied by the words, "Long ear lobes denote aristocratic birth. Mark on forehead is symbol of spiritual insight."

One of the most explicit references appears in the eleventh chapter of Shams'ul-Ma'ání written by Shaykh-i-Búní[§]: "Ere long God will shine from the face of Bahíyu'l-Abhá [the Glory, the Most Glorious] with the name of Bahá on the Day of Absolute [the Promised Day], in the plain of 'Akká."[18]

The well-known scholar, the illustrious and learned man, Shaykh Muḥammad 'Ámilí, was the first in the Muslim Faith to discover the

---

*"Bahá'u'lláh, . . . signifying at once the glory, the light and the splendor of God" (Shoghi Effendi, *God Passes By*, rev. ed. [Wilmette, Ill.: Bahá'í Publishing Trust, 1974], 94).

§He passed on in the year 622 A.H. (1208 A.D.).

name of Bahá'u'lláh. He was inspired by the guidance of the fifth and sixth Imáms,* who swore that the Greatest Name of God could be found in either of two specific prayers.⁵ In one of these,⁕ recited at dawn during the month of fasting, the name "BAHÁ" is repeated four times in the first verse, a verse that Bahá'u'lláh commanded the "Son of the Wolf" to recite with absolute sincerity while facing the Kaaba of God: " 'O my God! I beseech Thee by Thy *most glorious light,* and all Thy *lights* are verily *glorious.*' "¹⁹

How significant that during the thirty days of Ramadán this prayer echoes melodiously from the minarets at dawn, awakening the populace with the name of Bahá'u'lláh.

In order to attest to his faith in Bahá'u'lláh, he (Shaykh 'Ámilí) assumed the title "Bahá'í" over three centuries ago,** and is now known as Shaykh-i-Bahá'í. He composed a most moving and eloquent poem in praise of his Beloved, some verses of which are as follows:

How long will this torrent of tears flood from each lash in my longing to meet Thee,
O, the Unique One, my Beloved?
Will the night of Thy separation ever end
O, Thou, Whose agony and tribulations have, as an arrow, pierced the hearts of Thy lovers?
Multitudes are occupied in Thy praise whilst Thou art hidden from them.
To the abode of the pious and the religious I went;
Before Thy Countenance, I found all bowing and prostrating. . . .
Of a time I was a hermit of the hermitage,

---

*Imám Muhammad Báqir and Imám Ja'far-i-Sádiq.

⁵Du'áy-i-Sahar and Du'áy-i-Umm-i-Davúd (see commentary of Ash'ár-i-Na'ím by Ishráq Khávarí, 469–70).

⁕Du'áy-i-Sahar. The first verse, transliterated, reads *"Alláhumma inní as'aluka min Bahá ika bi Abháh ya kullu Bahá' ika Bahí."* The illustrious Bahá'í poet Na'ím has pointed out that the Dawn prayer begins with the name of Bahá (Splendor) and ends with the name of 'Alá' (Loftiness), the latter the exalted name of the Báb, the two names of the first and nineteenth months of the Badí' calendar.

**He passed on in the year 1030 A.H., which corresponds to the early part of the sixteenth century A.D. He was seventy-eight. He is buried in Mashhad.

Another, a refugee in the monastery
And again, a resident in the mosque.
Verily, O Beloved, house to house 'tis Thee I have sought.

Upon whichever door I knock, I find the Master of the house is Thee,
    Thee alone.
In Pagan temple, in monastery, Thou art the Beloved, Thee, Thee alone.
My goal in the Kaaba and temple is Thee, Thee alone.
Thou art my purpose; Kaaba and temple are but excuses. . . .

Helpless Bahá'í, whose heart is rent by Thy sorrows,
However sinful he may be, is one among the multitudes of Thy servants,
His hope is Thy perpetual compassion,
His sins anticipate Thy mercifulness.
Surely, no better excuse has one for sins.[20]

In the Qur'án, Moses was addressed by "the Speaker on Sinai" (one of the titles of Bahá'u'lláh) in the following words:

O Moses! Verily, I am thy Lord:. therefore pull off thy shoes: for thou art in the holy valley of Towa. . . .
    Verily, I am God: there is no God but me: therefore worship me, and observe prayer for a remembrance of me.
    Verily the hour is coming:—I all but manifest it—
    That every soul may be recompensed for its labours."[21]

And when Moses came at our set time and his Lord spake with him, he said, "O Lord, shew thyself to me, that I may look upon thee." He said, "Thou shalt not see Me; but look towards the mount, and if it abide firm in its place, then shalt thou see Me." And when God manifested Himself to the mountain he turned it to dust! and Moses fell in a swoon.
    And when he came to himself, he said, "Glory be to thee! To thee do I turn in penitence, and I am the first of them that believe."[22]

Bahá'u'lláh confirms in His *Epistle to the Son of the Wolf* that He is the Speaker on Sinai anticipated by Imám 'Alí:

The Commander of the Faithful (Imám 'Alí)—peace be upon him—moreover, saith in the Khuṭbiy-i-Ṭutunjíyih: "Anticipate ye the Revelation of Him Who conversed with Moses from the Burning Bush on Sinai."[23]

One of the most moving recognitions of the station of Bahá'u'lláh appears in a beautiful poem inscribed by His beloved father in exquisite handwriting on a large wooden plaque. This plaque was given a place of honor over the kingly mansion he built in Tákur, where Bahá'u'lláh spent most of His summers. This gesture, according to 'Abdu'l-Bahá, is proof that he recognized the station of his son as the Manifestation of God. This plaque is still in existence in Tákur. It reads:

When thou attaineth the threshold of thy Beloved
Say yea, for this is not the place to exchange Salám (peace) and 'Alayk (upon thee be peace).
This is the valley of love, mind thy step.
This is the Holy Land, pull off thy shoes.*

Muḥammad, the Apostle of God, received His revelation almost fourteen hundred years ago, in His one-night journey (according to the Muslims, "a journey equal to seventy thousand years") to Jerusalem and there was shown, in "the circuit of" Jerusalem (Akka and Haifa) some of the signs of God:

Praise be unto him, who transported his servant [Muḥammad] by night, from the sacred temple of Mecca to the farther temple of Jerusalem, the circuit of which we have blessed, that we might show him some of our signs. . . .[24]

The Koran is no other than a revelation revealed to him [Muḥammad]:
One terrible in power taught it him,
Endued with wisdom. With even balance stood he. . . .
Then came he nearer and approached. . . .

---

*For a picture of the plaque, see Nabíl-i-A'ẓam [Muḥammad-i-Zarandí], *The Dawn-Breakers: Nabíl's Narrative of the Early Days of the Bahá'í Revelation,* trans. and ed. Shoghi Effendi (Wilmette, Ill.: Bahá'í Publishing Trust, 1932), 112. Translated from the Persian by the author.

Unfortunately, the House of Bahá'u'lláh in Tákur no longer exists. In a telex dated 10 December 1981 the Universal House of Justice announced that this holy place had been totally demolished and offered for sale to the public during a wave of persecutions of the Iranian Bahá'ís.

And he [God] revealed to his servant what he revealed. . . .
He [Muḥammad] had seen him also another time,*
Near the Sidrah-tree, which marks the boundary.[25]

In the Conference of Badasht, Bahá'u'lláh, the Hidden Treasure, Who loved to be known, revealed His " 'Hidden Name' " and appeared with His Most Great Name: BAHÁ—He Who " 'But for Him no Divine Messenger would have been invested with the robe of prophethood, nor would any of the sacred scriptures have been revealed.' "[26]

The Exalted Báb, Who "declared that He had 'sacrificed' Himself 'wholly' for Him [Bahá'u'lláh], that He had 'consented to be cursed' for His sake, and to have 'yearned for naught but martyrdom' in the path of His love," praises Bahá'u'lláh in all His writings (and between the lines) and mentions His name with great exultation.[27] In His formulation of the Badí' calendar, He adorned the first day and first month of the year with the name "Bahá." He "alluded to Him [Bahá'u'lláh] as the 'Abhá Horizon' wherein He Himself lived and dwelt,"[28] called the followers of Bahá'u'lláh in the Qayyúm-i-Asmá, "companions of the Crimson Ark—the Ark which God hath prepared for the people of Bahá."[29] He heralded the Order of Bahá'u'lláh in these words: " 'Well is it with Him who fixeth his gaze upon the Order of Bahá'u'-lláh. . . .' "[30] Prior to His departure from Chihríq, He penned "no less than three hundred and sixty derivatives of the word Bahá" on a scroll and instructed that the scroll, together with His documents, "His pen-case, His seals, and agate rings," be delivered to His Beloved, Bahá'u'lláh.[31] In the ninth Váhid of the Arabic Bayán, the Báb sent His greetings to Bahá'u'lláh in the most touching and delicate way, unprecedented in the annals of all religions, wishing the remembrance and praise of all creation to rest upon Him at all times. He addresses Him in that passage:

> O Bahá'u'lláh! What hast Thou done? O Bahá'u'lláh! May my life be sacrificed for Thee! O Bahá'u'lláh! May my soul be offered up for Thy sake! How full were Thy days with trials and tribulations! How severe the ordeals Thou didst endure! How solid the foundation Thou hast finally laid, and how glorious the banner Thou didst hoist![32]

---

*This refers to the twin Revelations of the Báb and Bahá'u'lláh.

"He ['Abdu'l-Bahá] . . . was heard to exclaim" the above passage [Shoghi Effendi tells us] "one evening as He was being swiftly driven to fulfil His third engagement of the day in Washington." " 'One day, as He ['Abdu'l-Bahá] was strolling,' " the beloved Guardian further recounts:

> "He called to remembrance the days of the Blessed Beauty, referring with sadness to His sojourn in Sulaymáníyyih, to His loneliness and to the wrongs inflicted upon Him. Though He had often recounted that episode, that day He was so overcome with emotion that He sobbed aloud in His grief. . . . All His attendants wept with Him, and were plunged into sorrow as they heard the tale of the woeful trials endured by the Ancient Beauty, and witnessed the tenderness of heart manifested by His Son."[33]

THE SUFFERINGS OF BAHÁ'U'LLÁH

I am moved to share with you, my dear reader, further heartbreaking passages from the writings of Bahá'u'lláh translated by the beloved Guardian; a moving story related by 'Abdu'l-Bahá; and, finally, touching accounts of the Síyáh-Chál by Dr. Yúnis Khán, one of the amanuenses of 'Abdu'l-Bahá.

> . . . They apprehended Us, and from Níyávarán, which was then the residence of His Majesty, conducted Us, on foot and in chains, with bared head and bare feet, to the dungeon of Tihrán. A brutal man, accompanying Us on horseback, snatched off Our hat, whilst We were being hurried along by a troop of executioners and officials. We were consigned for four months to a place foul beyond comparison. As to the dungeon in which this Wronged One and others similarly wronged were confined, a dark and narrow pit were preferable. Upon Our arrival We were first conducted along a pitch-black corridor, from whence We descended three steep flights of stairs to the place of confinement assigned to Us. The dungeon was wrapped in thick darkness, and Our fellow-prisoners numbered nearly a hundred and fifty souls: thieves, assassins and highwaymen. Though crowded, it had no other outlet than the passage by which We entered. . . . Most of these men had neither clothes nor bedding to lie on. God alone knoweth what befell Us in that most foul-smelling and gloomy place![34]

Shouldst thou at sometime happen to visit the dungeon of His Majesty the Sháh, ask the director and chief jailer to show thee those two chains, one of which is known as Qará-Guhar, and the other as Salásil. I swear by the Day-Star of Justice that for four months this Wronged One was tormented and chained by one or the other of them. "My grief exceedeth all the woes to which Jacob gave vent, and all the afflictions of Job are but a part of My sorrows!"[35]

" 'Abdu'l-Bahá tells how one day He was allowed to enter the prison yard to see His beloved father when He came out for His daily exercise. Bahá'u'lláh was terribly altered, so ill He could hardly walk, His hair and beard unkempt, His neck galled and swollen from the pressure of a heavy steel collar, His body bent by the weight of His chains, and the sight made a never-to-be-forgotten impression on the mind of the sensitive boy."[36]

Dr. Yúnis Khán recounts: "All traces of the terrifying dungeon and the chains, the two 'wild dragons,' have now been effaced from the surface of Ṭihrán, just as gigantic wild animals became extinct after Noah's Flood. However, we should preserve their memories in the museum of our minds." He proceeds to give some of the details of the Síyáh-Chál, which will be left unquoted since Bahá'u'lláh testified that "No pen can depict that place, nor any tongue describe its loathsome smell."[37]

"As for Qará-Guhar," Dr. Yúnis Khán writes,

this is the name of a particular chain which belongs to this subterranean dungeon. However it was not an ordinary chain but is referred to by this title because of its thickness and heavy weight. . . . It was over 10 meters in length and had five to seven thick steel collars, each with a heavy lock to which the jailers held keys. The chain took seven prisoners in a row. Each prisoner was given a piece of wood shaped like a "Y" (like a cane with two heads). One end was used to carry part of the weight of the collar, while the other end was held or placed on the damp brick floor of the dungeon should the prisoner prefer to sit. Of course not even a man of great strength could stand or walk with this chain. There was no choice for the prisoner but to sit on his knees, hold fast on to the end of the cane with his two hands, lay his chin on the "Y," rest his eyes on the dark ceiling of this foul, loathsome-smelling prison, and await his fate.

Dr. Yúnis Khán continues:

This is a brief account of the Síyáh-Chál. Why should the believers know the description of the Síyáh-Chál and the chains? Because the "Wronged One of the world," the Abhá Beauty, suffered under their weight for a certain period of time. Years later some of His lovers and followers attained the glory of being imprisoned in the Síyáh-Chál and experienced the same burdens of those heavy chains. You might wonder how I know these details, being unworthy to enter the prison of Bahá'u'lláh, and undeserving to win the glory of bearing the weight of the chain. Fifty-three lunar years ago, when I was a boy, I went to meet my father, Mashhadí Husayn, who was one of the prisoners in the Síyáh-Chál. Then I witnessed this terrifying scene and the unhealthy conditions of the prisoners. This impressed me so much that it has left its agonizing memory on me all these years and will remain with me for the rest of my life. It is a comfort to recall that in spite of all the terrifying scenes, the imprisoned believers, frail and weak, were joyous that their imprisonment was in the path of their Beloved. It was also comforting to see their suffering was somewhat alleviated when His Majesty Násiri'd-Dín Sháh had mercy on them, permitting the prisoners two hours of sunshine in the middle of that cold winter so that they might inhale fresh air after 30 days of deprivation. In addition, their spirits were uplifted to hear from me that their families were safe especially since they had heard from the jailers that the mobs in Tihrán had attacked the Bahá'ís and murdered all the women and children. . . .

On my visit* to the 100-square-meter courtyard, I found the prisoners weak and sickly, sitting before the sun. My father was so weak, thin, and yellow in color that initially I did not recognize him, although he called me by name. The late Mullá 'Alí-Akbar-i-Shahmírzádí, known as Hájí Ákhúnd (Hand of the Cause of God) was chained to my father. . . . Finally, I recognized my father and sat on his trembling knees while the jailers surrounded us and stared. We conversed briefly. I gave the good news of the safety of the Bahá'í families, looked at and touched the collar

---

*The meeting between Dr. Yúnis Khán and the prisoners took place outside the prison, during one of the two-hour periods in which the prisoners enjoyed the outdoor air.

of the Qará-Guhar chain which, due to the dampness of the prison, had rusted.

Fortunately, after six to seven weeks, the prisoners* were transferred to a common prison close to the Síyáh-Chál. In this prison they were allowed to sit on platforms along the corridor at night with every seven prisoners chained together and their legs locked in what is called a Khalílí. The prisoners were permitted light at night. The Bahá'í prisoners among them had secretly taught the Faith to their fellow prisoners (formerly thieves, highwaymen, and assassins) and deepened them in the Cause. After the jailers retired, they chanted prayers and Tablets they had committed to memory and rejoiced in remembrance of their Beloved.

. . .

O, how I envied the nightly celebrations of the prisoners whose sweets consisted of the stories of the chains that bore them down!"[38]

Thus it was in the Síyáh-Chál and under these circumstances that the birth of the revelation of Bahá'u'lláh took place—"a Revelation which [according to the beloved Guardian], flowing out, in that extremely perilous hour, from His travailing soul, pierced the gloom that had settled upon that pestilential pit, and, bursting through its walls, and propagating itself as far as the ends of the earth, infused into the entire body of mankind its boundless potentialities, and is now under our very eyes, shaping the course of human society."[39]

THE ASCENSION OF BAHÁ'U'LLÁH

The Blessed Beauty's "spirit . . . winged its flight to His 'other dominions,' dominions 'whereon the eyes of the people of names have never fallen.' "[40]

"The news of His ascension was instantly communicated to Sultán 'Abdu'l-Hamíd in a telegram which began with the words 'the Sun of Bahá has set' and in which the monarch was advised of the intention of interring the sacred remains within the precincts of the Mansion [of Bahjí], an arrangement to which he readily assented. Bahá'u'lláh was accordingly laid to rest in the northernmost room of the house which served as a dwelling-place for His son-in-law, the most northerly of the three houses lying to the west of, and adjacent

---

*His father and others.

to, the Mansion. His interment took place shortly after sunset on the very day of His ascension" (29 May 1892).[41]

In the eighth Váhid of the Arabic Bayán the Exalted Báb had already anticipated that the Qiblih would be wherever *"He Whom God shall make manifest'* "(Bahá'u'lláh) is.[42] The Blessed Beauty had fixed the Qiblih in the Book of Aqdas.[43]

'Abdu'l-Bahá singled out "the inconsolable Nabíl . . . to select those passages [from the writings of Bahá'u'lláh] which constitute the text of the Tablet of Visitation now recited in the Most Holy Tomb."[44]

'Abdu'l-Bahá also arranged for construction of the Shrine.

"Then the supreme ordeal, the great desolation, came upon us. Qulám-'Alí* took on the carpentry work of the Holy Tomb, exerting all his sure powers. To this day, the glass roof which is over the inner courtyard of the Shrine of Bahá'u'lláh remains as the product of his skill."[45]

THE SHRINE OF BAHÁ'U'LLÁH, THE QIBLIH OF THE BAHÁ'Í WORLD

Let us now prepare to make a pilgrimage to the Shrine of Bahá'u'lláh, which contains the most precious dust that this planet holds in its bosom; let us fulfill our hearts' desire, which is none other than *"the Desire of the Divine Messengers.'* "[46]

'ABDU'L-BAHÁ'S VISITS

'Abdu'l-Bahá's visit to the Holy Shrine was very moving. Evidently He approached the Shrine from the former road,[§] which passes by the Mansion [of Bahjí].

As we reach the bend of the road, the Mansion of Bahjí comes into full view, "a dwelling-place which He [Bahá'u'lláh] characterized as the *'lofty mansion,'* the spot which *'God hath ordained as the*

---

*A resident Bahá'í, "a carpenter and a master craftsman" from Káshán ('Abdu'l-Bahá, *Memorials of the Faithful,* trans. Marzieh Gail [Wilmette, Ill.: Bahá'í Publishing Trust, 1971], 143).

§Before the Universal House of Justice, in their negotiations with the authorities, succeeded in procuring the present access to the main highway.

*most sublime vision of mankind.' "*⁴⁷ We are moved to recall the touching stories told by dearly loved Hand of the Cause of God Taráẓ'u'lláh Samandarí and confirmed by Ḥájí Mírzá Ḥaydar-'Alí* about 'Abdu'l-Bahá's visit to Bahá'u'lláh shortly before His passing.

"On His walk from 'Akká to Bahjí, the moment 'Abdu'l-Bahá approached the bend of the road, He prostrated Himself and laid His forehead on the earth. Bahá'u'lláh turned to those in His presence and told them: 'The Master is coming. Hasten, go to meet and escort Him.'"

Ḥájí Mírzá Ḥaydar-'Alí recounts this story in his marvelous book: "Bahá'u'lláh was sitting in His Mansion. As soon as the light of the beauty of His Branch ['Abdu'l-Bahá] shone from the garden of Jammál [the bend of the road already referred to] Bahá'u'lláh's Face beamed with great joy and fragrance. He bade all to hasten to the garden and its vicinity and welcome the Master."⁴⁸

Dr. Yúnis Khán writes:

Pilgrimages to the Holy Shrine of Bahá'u'lláh started the very first year of His Ascension. . . . Twice on Fridays and Sundays the pilgrims and resident Bahá'ís would go to the Shrine in the presence of 'Abdu'l-Bahá Who chanted the Tablet of Visitation.

On the second and third year after the Ascension there were celebrations during the Bahá'í Holy Days which attracted the attention of the populace, whether friend or foe, particularly of the military and civil authorities, the Judge, and the Muftí. They were all so impressed with the spirit that surrounded visitation of the Shrine that they longed to accompany the friends on these occasions.

Outside the House of the Master there was an open area where the coach house was situated. 'Abdu'l-Bahá had two carriages: a big one called "American cab" that carried nine people and another one that carried four. For weekly visits to the Shrine, Isfandíyár, the cabman of the Master, would prepare the carriage for the pilgrims and resident Bahá'ís, the pilgrims being given priority. Isfandíyár would drive the carriage to Bahjí and come back to take another group. However, the Master would walk alone, sometimes with two believers escorting Him. Upon His

---

*Mr. Samandarí often shared this story with the Hands of the Cause on that spot, as well as with the beloved friends in America.

arrival at Bahjí, He would rest briefly in a room adjacent to the Shrine of Bahá'u'lláh. After summoning the pilgrims and annointing each with rose water in a heavenly manner and with silence, He would chant the Tablet of Visitation with His glorious voice.

During the Feasts, outside the inner court of the House of the Master, beautiful pots of varied colored flowers were ready to be carried to the Holy Shrine. All the pilgrims and residents, dressed in their best attire, would gather in the House of the Master two hours before sunset, or perhaps earlier if the exceeding heat of the mid-day sun had subsided. Each would shoulder a pot and, two by two, they set out for the Holy Shrine. During my pilgrimage the believers would not start from the House of the Master, owing to the tense atmosphere created by the rebellious Covenant-breakers. Rather, they would pick up the pots from outside the Gate of 'Akká, where the pots were ready for them. 'Abdu'l-Bahá, like the Commander of an Army, while Himself carrying a pot, would pace on their flank or ahead of them, monitoring and controlling their march and commanding two or three whose voices were melodious to chant from the *Mathnaví* of Bahá'u'lláh, from "Sáqi az Ghiybi Baqá," or from the poems recited by Bahá'í poets. This band of flower-bearers would walk slowly and majestically to the Shrine. As soon as the Shrine came into full view, 'Abdu'l-Bahá bade them to stop, take the pots from their shoulders and put them on their heads while a moving prayer from Bahá'u'lláh was chanted. . . .

To be brief, the pots were delivered to the Shrine. Another prayer was chanted. All would go for a little rest and after having had tea, some sweets and making ablutions, 'Abdu'l-Bahá would chant the Tablet of Visitation and bid them to sit and chant the appropriate passages for the Feasts with melodious voices. Often times, they would chant some of the exhilarating poems of Bahá'u'lláh, such as "Halih Halih yá Bishárat."*

. . . .

On the night of the (fifth anniversary Ascension) we had a vigil night in the House of the Master, praying and chanting the whole night. At early dawn we were called by 'Abdu'l-Bahá to head to the Holy Shrine. Each was given a bottle of rose water and a lit candle. We left the gate of

---

*In which Bahá'u'lláh in a most glorious, astounding way praises the glad-tidings of His Revelation. The above phrase is repeated in each ode of the poem. See Yúnis Khán, *Memoirs of Dr. Yúnis Khán,* "9 Years in 'Akká," 33–38.

'Akká at dawn heading for the Shrine with the same ceremony already mentioned. Upon our arrival at the Holy Shrine, following 'Abdu'l-Bahá's instructions, the rose water was poured at the base of the flowers inside the inner court of the Shrine and the burning candles planted inside the earth of the inner garden. We all stood in great reverence. 'Abdu'l-Bahá chanted the Tablet of Visitation. It was unbearable for us to see 'Abdu'l-Bahá's agony, especially the noticeable tears in His eyes. . . .

The Feast of Riḍván was at hand and again, with the same ceremony as before, we went on pilgrimage to the Shrine of Bahá'u'lláh. . . . The garden was full of flowers. . . ."[49]

. . . .

In addition to the vases of flowers which had been brought for the commemoration from 'Akká, it was necessary to tend the flower gardens around the Shrine of Bahá'u'lláh. One of the ceremonies which developed consisted of watering this flower garden around the Shrine. About 100 copper pots (called Arabian Jarrih) were secured. During the Feast the pilgrims and residents would fill them from neighboring wells and chant poems and verses from the Writings while watering the flowers. The rapture and devotion with which this task was carried out so deeply impressed Bahá'ís and non-Bahá'ís, especially when 'Abdu'l-Bahá, Himself, would put a copper pot on His shoulder and face the Shrine of Bahá'u'lláh, that everyone would be moved to tears. All the friends would stand with great reverence. Some of the visitors would ask to be given a copper pot so that they too could water the flowers.

After chanting the Tablets of the Feasts and other appropriate passages for Riḍván, we would all return together to 'Akká.[50]

Ḥájí Mírzá Ḥaydar-'Alí recounts:

After 'Abdu'l-Bahá gained His freedom, He resumed visiting the Holy Dust of Bahá'u'lláh and watering the flowers of the garden as was His custom.

In spite of His frailty and illness, every Friday and Sunday, in the presence of the notables of the government, the dignitaries, and some of the inhabitants, He carried on His shoulders 60 to 70 Jarrih of water. While watering, He was attacked by fever several times and became ill. With this illness, His fever was worse than ever. The pilgrims and Bahá'í residents asked His permission to attain His presence. When permission was granted, they all assembled, threw themselves at the knees of 'Abdu'l-Bahá, took the hem of His robe, and in tears beseeched Him, for the sake of His precious health, to stop watering the flowers of the Holy Shrine and leave this job to those devoted believers who longed to be given the bounty of watering the flowers on His behalf. He agreed. However, the grief in His face was so apparent that those who had begged Him to give up this job regretted their act and blamed themselves for having dared to ask 'Abdu'l-Bahá for this. After two weeks, He invited all the Bahá'ís, showered His bounties upon them, served them tea and sweets, and gave them heavenly food. Then in the most loving and affectionate manner He said, "I have agreed to your request and refrained from watering the flowers of the Holy Shrine, but my comfort and the happiness of my heart is in watering these flowers. My physical body and health is not important. The main thing is the happiness of my heart and the healthiness of my spirit. . . . Now please agree with me, from the bottom of your hearts, to water the flowers of the Shrine. All of you may participate in this service to the Abhá Beauty." [Here Ḥájí Mírzá Haydar-'Alí is moved to express his great admiration, praises the exemplary modesty of the Master and offers to give his life for Him.] In response all bowed and joyfully assented. Thus the watering, His permanent custom, was once again resumed."[51]

Dr. Ḥabíb Mu'ayyad writes similar moving accounts of the early years. The following concerns his visits to the Holy Shrine of Bahá'u'lláh on 28 and 30 October 1914:

We went to make our pilgrimage to the Holy Shrine of Bahá'u'lláh. When arriving there our eyes were illumined by gazing on the beautiful countenance of 'Abdu'l-Bahá Who was there in the garden. His beauty surpasses the beauty and fragrance of the flowers. The beloved Master, in His heavenly radiance, was dressed from head to toe in white, and was working in the midst of the white jasmine and white lilies. We bowed, and He answered, "Marḥabá." After a little while 'Abdu'l-Bahá went to the well (a water well with a hand pump) and started to pump for 19 minutes. The water was to be held in reserve for the gardens to water the trees and flowers. Incidentally, one of the friends, Badí' Bushrú'í, counted carefully on his watch. It came to 361 pumps, which came to 19 times 19. Formerly there was no well there and water for irrigation was very scarce. The gardens around the Shrine of Bahá'u'lláh had recently been started and needed continuous watering. . . . 'Abdu'l-Bahá would pump twice a day each time for 19 minutes. . . .[52] 'Abdu'l-Bahá said, "I, with the help of a group of believers, carried the soil (for the gardens of the Shrine) on our shoulders and watered the flowers."[53]

. . . .

'Abdu'l-Bahá anointed us with pure attar on our heads and faces, and said, "I want to anoint your head and face even as in old times when the prophets did so, so that you will succeed in your services and activities."[54]

. . . .

At night, when we are accommodated in the guest house, with a wall between our room and the Master's, we hear the melody of the voice of 'Abdu'l-Bahá in His prayers. The melody of His voice when He chants the Tablet of Visitation, together with the mood of His reverence and rapture, affects everything, even the stones.[55]

. . . .

Many nights when we walked slowly around the room of the Master, we heard the murmur of His voice, but we did not recognize all the words. Those we could recognize were, "O my God, O my Beloved."[56]

Mary L. Lucas shared with us the experience of her pilgrimage to the Shrine of Bahá'u'lláh in the early years:

We got out of the carriage and gathered the flowers, and then proceeded on our way to the Tomb, with the flowers we had plucked.

As we entered this Holy Precinct we took off our shoes.

The silence here was like nothing I have ever experienced. As we advanced toward the door no one spoke, but we all prayed. I remembered the Master's wish, and sang part of Gounod's Sanctus, "Holy, Holy, Holy!" It was the first thing that came to my mind. It seemed as though I was not singing, but the voice of itself was soaring, and had left my body.[57]

And of later years we read in an article written in Haifa in July 1922, by G. L. C. under the heading of "The Plain of Acca":

After we had rested a little while, Fugeta and I went into the Tomb. It was dark by that time, and the lights in the Tomb were lighted. The thing which seemed to me most beautiful about the lighting was that the lights were so placed that they shone out from under a fern in the center of the little inner garden. The light came out soft and green through the fronds of fern. The lights were not all on when we first went in, and I liked it better with the softer light. We stayed there in prayer for perhaps half an hour. . . . Afterward, Hussein turned on all the lights so that I might see them. They turn into a blaze of light, and made me think of Abdul-Baha's comment, when he was in America, that Baha'Ullah always loved light; that they might be economical about everything else, but that he always told them to have much light about him. Fugeta also drew my attention to the vase that the American Bahais had sent in memory of the Master's visit to America. The vase was made by Tiffany, and it is very beautiful. It is of bronze, with insets of jewels and cloisone [sic] work. The latter is of a most exquisite blue, shading off into yellow, as it curves up the slender neck of the vase. It is a very, very lovely thing, as is worthy of such a place.[58]

What a glory for the North American Bahá'ís to be so close to Bahá'u'lláh and to His inner Shrine, "The Holy of Holies"!

Dr. Yúnis Khán, commenting further on his visit to the Holy Shrine in the company of 'Abdu'l-Bahá, shares his impressions with us in a very moving manner. He expresses inadequacy in conveying the heavenly experience he had of hearing the melodious voice of 'Abdu'l-Bahá repeating certain verses in the Tablet of Visitation. He says:

> Dear Reader, if you are touched by reading these lines, if you are moved with a burning desire for such a visit to the Holy Shrine of Bahá'u'lláh, do not feel sad, do not be depressed. In the presence of the beloved Shoghi Effendi, who stands in the place of 'Abdu'l-Bahá chanting the Tablet of Visitation, you will feel the rare heavenly experience. Hasten! Hasten! Grasp the opportunity! Grasp the opportunity![59]

THE BELOVED GUARDIAN'S VISITS

Let us visit the Holy Shrine of Bahá'u'lláh in the presence of the beloved of all hearts, Shoghi Effendi.

Earlier, the beloved Guardian said the first and most important festival of joy is the Feast of Riḍván, the [anniversary of the] declaration of Bahá'u'lláh; the second is the [anniversary of the] declaration of the Báb; the third, the [anniversary of the] birthday of Bahá'u'lláh; the fourth, the [anniversary of the] birthday of the Báb; and the fifth, the Feast of Naw-Rúz and fasting.

Mine was the great bounty to make a pilgrimage on the birthday of Bahá'u'lláh. It was on the morning of 10 February 1940 (2 Muḥarram 1359), the lunar anniversary of the birth of the Blessed Beauty, that the beloved Shoghi Effendi sent all of us pilgrims in two cars to the Mansion of Bahjí after we had visited the monument gardens on Mount Carmel. In the afternoon there was a big gathering of all the Bahá'ís, pilgrims and residents, where prayers were chanted in the open space on the ground floor of the Mansion. Everyone waited impatiently for the arrival of the beloved Shoghi Effendi. When the beloved Guardian arrived, he was accompanied by Ismá'íl Áqá in the car, as was his custom on such occasions.

A message from the beloved Guardian extended an invitation to all to go to the garden facing the Holy Shrine and hold a big gathering in celebration of the anniversary of the birth of Bahá'u'lláh.

Everyone hastened to attain the presence of the beloved Shoghi Effendi, of whom 'Abdu'l-Bahá said:

> Salutation and praise, blessing and glory rest upon that primal branch of the Divine and Sacred Lote-Tree, grown out, blest, tender, verdant and flourishing from the Twin Holy Trees; the most wondrous, unique and priceless pearl that doth gleam from out the Twin surging Seas. . . . Well is it with him that seeketh the shelter of his shade that shadoweth all mankind.[60]

Some, because of the greatness of the gathering, sat on the lawn; others carried wicker chairs. The beloved Shoghi Effendi was seated on a wicker chair in the corner of the garden facing the Most Holy Shrine. His majesty and deportment is beyond us. He bade everyone to be seated as he showed each pilgrim where to sit. All were seated in a *J* shape in the small garden surrounding Bahá'u'lláh's resting-place. (The entire property was 4,000 meters at that time and is now, according to the beloved Guardian's cable dated 12 November 1952, 155,000 square meters.)[61] This *J* shape started from the outer patio of the entrance of the Shrine, leading to the pilgrim house nearby.

The beloved Shoghi Effendi greeted all: "May this Feast be a blessing to you all. 'Abdu'l-Bahá has called these twin Great Feasts (the birth of Bahá'u'lláh and the birth of the Báb) because they follow one another in the lunar calendar." A day earlier, the birth of the Báb had been celebrated on Mount Carmel. "The Blessed Beauty has referred to the Báb as His former Manifestation and Forerunner of His Beauty. He has also referred to Himself as the Báb's Beloved and the Báb as Bahá'u'lláh's Beloved. The twin Feasts are identical, yet the believers must celebrate both." As to the station of the Báb, the beloved Guardian quoted: " *'Point round Whom the realities of the Prophets and Messengers revolve.'* "[62] He continued: "In America the Assemblies exchange greetings by telegram. In Bombay, India, the Bahá'ís invite the government authorities to their celebrations. I have received a greeting from America." The beloved Guardian spoke in detail about the significance of the Mansion of Bahjí and its past history. He also elaborated on the different stages that the Faith has to pass through before the establishment of the Bahá'í Commonwealth. Gems of knowledge and guidance poured from the lips of the Sign of God on Earth [Shoghi Effendi]. He assured us that the promises of Bahá'u'lláh will surely be fulfilled. I was overwhelmed when he bade me to chant a prayer. This was truly a heavenly reunion.

The beloved Guardian requested that the Tablet of the Feast be chanted and urged that on such occasions the specific prayers and Tablets are to be recited. He then quoted a passage from Bahá'u'lláh on the significance of the night journey of Muḥammad and the station of Bahá'u'lláh. The passage explains that Muḥammad, in His flight, took seventy thousand years (as the Muslims believe) until He reached the Threshold of Bahá'u'lláh. After repeating that passage, he waved his hand, pointing to the Shrine, and said, "This is the exalted station of this Holy of Holies, which signifies the glory of this Manifestation." The beloved Guardian then proceeded to the Holy Shrine. When I entered, I found him in the entrance way, now the inner court. From a vial of attar of roses, he anointed each one who entered. While being anointed, he said to me in a low voice: "Chant a prayer." The beloved Shoghi Effendi proceeded directly along the inner garden of the Shrine, walking around it until he reached the door of the Holy Tomb. There he placed his forehead on the holy threshold, bade everyone to sit, and directed me to chant. I chanted a prayer in praise and thanksgiving to God that the light of His Sun of Mercy had illumined the world of creation and His blessings were pouring forth their rain. I also chanted a prayer from the beloved Guardian himself. The beloved Shoghi Effendi then rose on his knees. His voice, resonant and haunting, was lifted in the Tablet of Visitation.

> The praise which hath dawned from Thy most august Self, and the glory which hath shone forth from Thy most effulgent Beauty, rest upon Thee. . . .[63]

He continued chanting the Tablet of Visitation as far as:

> Waft, then, unto me, O my God and my Beloved, from the right hand of Thy mercy and Thy loving-kindness, the holy breaths of Thy favors, that they may draw me away from myself and from the world unto the courts of Thy nearness and Thy presence.[64]

whereupon he paused. He again continued until:

> The remembrance of God and His praise, and the glory of God and His splendor, rest upon Thee, O Thou Who art His Beauty![65]

when he paused again, as if overwhelmed and entranced. After the completion of the Tablet of Visitation, he remained silent for a few moments, proceeded to the holy threshold, bent his blessed knees and placed his forehead on the threshold. Only a few moments passed with the believers standing and witnessing that memorable, precious commemoration.

Then the beloved Shoghi Effendi, without removing his eyes from the holy threshold, walked backwards to the door. This completed a circumambulation around the inner court of the Shrine.

Only Bahá'u'lláh knows what passed between Him and His beloved Guardian on these occasions. However, within the Shrine in the presence of the beloved Shoghi Effendi, one could feel that every prayer would be answered because of his intercession. How sweet, how very sweet the melody of his voice which rings in the ears till the last breath of life! May we attain his good pleasure! May he ever look compassionately upon us with his exhilarating glance and cheer our hearts!

The Ocean of Light

"The Ancient Beauty" Who "hath consented to be bound with chains that mankind may be released from its bondage, and hath accepted to be made a prisoner within this most mighty Stronghold that the whole world may attain unto true liberty"[66] is no longer "*subjected to the abasement of a dungeon.*'"[67] He rests in the Haram-i-Aqdas (the Most Holy Sanctuary) in the midmost of Jannat-i-Abhá (Abhá paradise), as designated by the beloved Guardian. God has already fulfilled His promise, the promise Bahá'u'lláh heard in the Síyáh-Chál:

> "'Verily, We shall render Thee victorious by Thyself and by Thy pen. Grieve Thou not for that which hath befallen Thee. . . . Ere long will God raise up the treasures of the earth—men who will aid Thee through Thyself and through Thy Name. . . .'"[68]

Bahá'u'lláh was from Núr* (i.e., *Light*), and "Bahá" signifies *Light:* thus, "Light upon light"[69] in the Súrih of Núr in the Qur'án fulfilled in Bahá'u'lláh from Núr.[§] His Holy Shrine, the Holy of Holies, is the Ocean of Light (Daryá-yi-Núr), so designated by the beloved Shoghi Effendi, which floods light over the whole creation. "God is the LIGHT of the Heavens and of the Earth."[70] This Ocean of Light has taken the Mountain of Light (Kúh-i-Núr, the Shrine of the Báb) under its shadow.[#] The Queen of Carmel, facing this Ocean, is seated on Her throne of majesty and dignity in the midmost Supreme Paradise (Firdaws-i-A'lá),** the spot blessed and designated by Bahá'u'lláh Himself. Her face is toward the Qiblih that the Báb Himself anticipated. Her breast is ornamented with the Greatest Holy Name.

'Abdu'l-Bahá, the Mystery of God, Whose station is unique and

---

*The native land of Bahá'u'lláh.

[§] *Istidláliyyih Na'ím,* 68. See also Ps. 36:9.

[#] Daryá-yi-Núr and Kúh-i-Núr, the Twin Shrines of Bahá'u'lláh and the Báb as designated by the beloved Guardian (also the titles of the two biggest diamonds in the world).

**So designated by the beloved Guardian.

unparalleled in the annals of all religions, rests by the side of the Báb and faces the Ocean of Light (the Shrine of Bahá'u'lláh).

Missing in that vicinity is the resting-place of the beloved Shoghi Effendi, who, for an unknown wisdom, or perhaps because of his utmost modesty, has rested since his passing in 1957 in London, far, far away from the Holy Land. However, it seems as if Bahá'u'lláh rewarded His beloved Guardian, since the Centenary Jubilee was held there under his shadow in 1963, right after the Universal House of Justice came into existence, as one of the choicest fruits of his labors and of his Ten Year Crusade.

Again, facing the Shrine of Bahá'u'lláh, His beloved daughter, the Greatest Holy Leaf; His martyred Son, the Purest Branch, *"created of the light of Bahá'"*[71]; and His dearly loved Consort, Navváb, who is *"'His companion in every one of His worlds,'"*[72] rest in peace and praise in the Monument Gardens created in their honor by the beloved Shoghi Effendi, thereby fulfilling the promise of God.*

The World Order of Bahá'u'lláh is shaking "the world's equilibrium" before our very eyes.[73] His Ark has set sail on God's Holy Mountain, and His Laws are beginning to flow to the whole world. The Seat of Legislation is in the process of construction around the Arc already prepared by the beloved Shoghi Effendi and the "people of Bahá"[74] ([the Universal] House of Justice); the dwellers of the Ark mentioned in the Tablet of Carmel are calling "the people of Bahá"[§] (we Bahá'ís) to participate in that glorious project.

Beloved friends: We are living in the Most Glorious Day, the Day in which the kingdom of God on earth, long ago prophesied by Jesus Christ, is taking shape. The vibration of the revelation of Bahá'u'lláh has "pierced the gloom" of the walls of "that pestilential pit"[75] and has reached all corners of the world. His love is penetrating deep into

---

*See Isa. 54.

§The dwellers of "the Crimson Ark which God hath ordained in the Qayyúm-i-Asmá for the people of Bahá" (Bahá'u'lláh, *Epistle to the Son of the Wolf,* trans. Shoghi Effendi, new ed. [Wilmette, Ill.: Bahá'í Publishing Trust, 1988], 139). [The inauguration of the use of the seat of the Universal House of Justice occurred on 17 July 1982; its occupation by the Universal House of Justice was announced on 2 February 1983.—ED.]

the hearts of men from amongst all nations, classes, races, colors and religious backgrounds, and " ' "*soon will all that dwell on earth be enlisted under* " ' " His banner.[76] This is the Day about which 'Abdu'l-Bahá writes:

> "*The holy realities of the Concourse on high yearn, in this day, in the Most Exalted Paradise, to return unto this world, so that they may be aided to render some service to the threshold of the Abhá Beauty, and arise to demonstrate their servitude to His sacred Threshold.*"[77]

What a glory to serve Bahá'u'lláh!

Appendix

Remembrances of Colleagues and Friends

Hands of the Cause of God

15 November 1986
DEEPLY GRIEVED PASSING DEAR ZIKRULLAH LOVED ESTEEMED FELLOW HAND. HIS UNWAVERING LOYALTY TO SHOGHI EFFENDI AND DEFENSE COVENANT BOTH DURING GUARDIAN'S LIFETIME AND DURING DIFFICULT YEARS FOLLOWING HIS ASCENSION PENDING ELECTION UNIVERSAL HOUSE OF JUSTICE, HIS TIRELESS SERVICES BELOVED FAITH WELL OVER HALF A CENTURY, EMBRACING BOTH ASIA AND WESTERN HEMISPHERE, UNFORGETTABLE AND CONSTITUTE SHINING EXAMPLE FOR HIS CHILDREN AND GRANDCHILDREN TO FOLLOW. SURELY HIS REWARD ABHÁ KINGDOM VERY GREAT AT HANDS HIS BELOVED, HIS RELEASE FROM PAIN AND TRIALS THIS FLEETING WORLD JOYFUL. DEEPEST LOVING SYMPATHY.

RÚḤÍYYIH

15 November 1986

GRIEVED NEWS PASSING DISTINGUISHED FELLOW HAND ZIKRULLAH KHADEM, HIS SERVICES BOTH ASIA NORTH AMERICA, PARTICULARLY HIS STEADFAST DEVOTION TO SHOGHI EFFENDI BOTH DURING HIS LIFETIME AND DIFFICULT YEARS AFTER DEVASTATING LOSS BELOVED GUARDIAN IRREPLACEABLE AND UNFORGETTABLE. PRAYING JOYFUL GLORIOUS REWARD ABHÁ KINGDOM. DEEPEST LOVING SYMPATHY ENTIRE FAMILY.

HANDS HOLY LAND
RÚḤÍYYIH, FURÚTAN

15 November 1986

GREATLY CHAGRINED DEMISE YOUR GALLANT NOBLE DEVOTED INDEFATIGABLE HUSBAND MUCH LOVED ESTEEMED BY SHOGHI EFFENDI. MONACO BELIEVERS JOIN ME EXPRESS TO YOU AND WHOLE SORROWFUL FAMILY

GREATEST SYMPATHY AFFECTION. TRUSTING BLESSED BEAUTY WILL LESSEN
PUNGENT PAIN YOUR HEARTS. DEVOTEDLY.   UGO GIACHERY

13 November 1986
AT NEWS OF PASSING OF DISTINGUISHED DEAR HAND AND BELOVED OF
THE CAUSE OF GOD JINÁB-I-KHADEM* FROM THE BOTTOM OF MY HEART I
RENDER MY CONDOLENCES AND PRAY THAT HIS EXALTED SPIRIT REJOICES
IN THE PRESENCE OF THE BLESSED BEAUTY, 'ABDU'L-BAHÁ, AND HIS BE-
LOVED GUARDIAN.   JALÁL KHÁZEH**

15 November 1986
WITH UTMOST SADNESS RECEIVED TRAGIC NEWS PASSING AWAY BELOVED
HAND FAITH ZIKRULLAH KHADEM. IN THIS SORROWFUL TIME OUR HEARTS
AND PRAYERS ARE WITH YOU. SUPPLICATING HOLY THRESHOLD ELEVATION
HIS RANK, RADIANT SOUL IN ABHÁ KINGDOM WISHING LONG LIFE ALL THE
BEST FOR HIS DEAR FAMILY.
                        'ALÍ MUHAMMAD AND ROUHANI VARQÁ

[n.d.]
We have just heard the distressing news of the grave illness of dearest
Zikrullah.# We have immediately begun special prayers, and are thinking of
him constantly. He is so dear to us all. . . .

. . . Whenever I think of Zikrullah, I think of our beloved Shoghi
Effendi, and I remembered a letter of his which I have which spoke of those
who were gravely ill, and in some case where it seemed almost hopeless. . . .

. . . The letter says as follows:

"He [Shoghi Effendi] feels that although the physicians have found
the disease too advanced, and pronounced her condition as hopeless,
you should still endeavor, by means of sustained and concentrated
prayer, to bring about her cure. Now that no material effort can be of
any effectiveness you still have one more way open before you, namely
that of prayer, and you should therefore continue to supplicate from all

_____

*"Jináb-i-Khadem" means "His Excellency Khadem" or "His Honor Khadem."
Jináb-i-, placed before a name, is a courtesy title.
**Translated from the original Persian by Javidukht Khadem.
#This letter was received during Mr. Khadem's illness.

your heart that, if it be God's Will, your mother may be restored to full health, and regain all her forces.

"Bahá'u'lláh has revealed special prayers for both spiritual and material healing, and it is therefore your bounden duty to use such prayers on behalf of your mother, and thus put all your trust in the all-sustaining and all-healing power of God. It matters not whether you are endowed with high spirituality or not. The essential is that you pray with sincerity and with full purity of heart, and with the one desire of knowing and accepting His Will." (Shoghi Effendi, 4/22/1938 to Miss Doris Skinner)*

. . . .

I love you both so dearly and tenderly, and Marguerite and I surround you with not only prayers, but with all our deepest love.

Bill and Marguerite [Sears] with warmest love

PS: I also thought as I read the letter, that sometime it might be of help to you in your marvelous work as a member of the Auxiliary Board, that it might be of comfort to some soul you console along the path of your service. With warmest, tenderest love to you both.

(This letter needs no answer. May its love last forever. Tenderly, Bill.)

17 November 1986
GRIEVED LEARN PASSING DEAR ZIKRULLAH KHADEM FELLOW HAND CAUSE AND WITH WHOM AFTER PASSING BELOVED GUARDIAN THERE HAVE BEEN MANY ASSOCIATIONS. MADGE JOINS WITH ME EXPRESSING OUR DEEPEST SYMPATHY AND LOVE TO YOU AND FAMILY AND ASSURE OUR PRAYERS AT THIS TIME OF SORROW.   COLLIS AND MADGE FEATHERSTONE

THE INTERNATIONAL INSTITUTIONS OF THE FAITH

15 November 1986
The heartbreaking news of the passing of the radiant soul, the Hand of the Cause of God, Mr. Zikrullah Khadem to the Kingdom of Eternity immersed the Bahá'í world in the waves of sadness and grief.

---

*Corrections in the letter from Shoghi Effendi were authorized by the Universal House of Justice.

His shining heart full of love for the Faith, his dedicated services to the Threshold of the Blessed Beauty remains as a brilliant example in the hearts of all the believers who had the privilege to meet and be inspired and illuminated by him.

The Institution of Ḥuqúqu'lláh remembering his valuable services shares its sadness with all the other Bahá'í Institutions throughout the world, and offers its deep sympathy and condolences. . . .

With deepest love,

The Trustee of Ḥuqúqu'lláh A. M. Varqá

16 November 1986

. . . DEEPEST CONDOLENCES IN LOSS . . . REVERED HAND OF THE CAUSE OF GOD AND CO-WORKER. THE BAHÁ'Í WORLD HAS LOST ONE OF THE PRE-CIOUS LINKS TO OUR BELOVED GUARDIAN WHOM HE SERVED WITH UNTIR-ING DEVOTION. HIS SPIRIT NOW FREED FROM PHYSICAL BONDS WILL ASSIST THE FAITH ALL OVER THE WORLD AND WILL BE WITH YOU IN YOUR GRIEF. OUR PRAYERS FOR THE PROGRESS OF HIS SOUL . . . WILL BE OFFERED AT THE HOLY SHRINES. DEEPEST LOVE.

INTERNATIONAL TEACHING CENTER

13 November 1986

WE DEEPLY GRIEVE THE LOSS OF ONE OF THE JEWELS OF THE FAITH, HAND OF THE CAUSE, ZIKRULLAH KHADEM BUT REJOICE IN THE YEARS AND MEMORIES WE HAVE SHARED WITH THIS VERY GOOD AND GENTLE SERVANT OF BAHÁ'U'LLÁH.

WE PRAY THAT HIS SPIRIT AND HIS STRENGTH OF PURPOSE WILL BE WITH US IN THE YEARS TO COME AS WE ENDEAVOR TO SHOULDER THE GREAT TASKS THAT LIE AHEAD OF US.

WITH DEEPEST AFFECTION,

THE BAHÁ'Í INTERNATIONAL COMMUNITY

16 November 1986

WE ALL BEMOAN DISTRESSING DEMISE FIRST HAND OF THE CAUSE WHO VISITED ASIA HAND CAUSE KHADEM. HIS VISITS AT INSTRUCTIONS BELOVED GUARDIAN BEGINNING OF 10 YEAR CRUSADE BROUGHT AN EXAMPLE TO THE COMMUNITIES IN ASIA OF FIRMNESS COVENANT AND LOVE FOR THE GUARDIAN. HIS REPEATED TRIPS BROUGHT UNINTERRUPTED RADIANT BAHÁ'Í LOVE; A SEED THAT GERMINATED IN HEARTS OF THOSE COMMUNI-TIES. EXPRESSING DEEPEST SYMPATHY LAMENTABLE LOSS ONE MORE CHO-SEN OF OUR BELOVED GUARDIAN WHO SHOWED PARTICULAR KINDNESS

AND CONCERN FOR BAHÁ'ÍS OF N.E. ASIA; WHOSE LOVE AND MEMORY IS
CHERISHED BY EACH MEMBER OF OUR COMMUNITY.

CONTINENTAL BOARD OF COUNSELLORS IN ASIA

18 November 1986

For many of us who never had the opportunity to know the beloved
Guardian, Mr. Khadem through his great love and devotion to Shoghi
Effendi brought him to life for us. This was a service of inestimable value
and will continue to be so as the Faith moves ahead towards the unveiling
in all its lustre the vision of the world civilization ordained by Bahá'u'lláh.

In addition to his love for Shoghi Effendi which inspired the hearts, the
friends were awed by his "sin-covering eye," and the fact that he seemed to
live in a state of constant prayer. . . .

. . . .
. . . Know that our constant prayers will accompany you at every step
along the way. . . .

With warm and loving greetings,

The Continental Board of Counsellors in the Americas
Ruth E. Pringle

6 December 1986

We recall his loving kindness, his deep knowledge, his staunch defense of
the Faith, and his inspiring leadership in the teaching work. We will never
forget the debt we owe him because of his stewardship with the other
Hands of the Cause during the period following the passing of Shoghi
Effendi and before the establishment of the Universal House of Justice.

While gathering under the shadow of the Mother Temple of the Pacific
in Samoa . . . with all members present we prayed for the dear Hand of
the Cause. . . .

With loving Bahá'í greetings,

Continental Board of Counsellors for Australasia
Joy Stevenson

NATIONAL SPIRITUAL ASSEMBLIES

1 November 1986

GRIEVED LEARN ILLNESS DEFENDER COVENANT, NOBLE CHAMPION UN-
NUMBERED VICTORIES, DEARLY CHERISHED, STEADFAST SERVANT BELOVED

GUARDIAN, DHIKRU'LLAH KHADEM.* ASSURE DISTINGUISHED HAND OF THE CAUSE OF GOD . . . OUR DEEPEST LOVE, OUR CONTINUING PRAYERS.
NATIONAL SPIRITUAL ASSEMBLY OF THE BAHÁ'ÍS OF CANADA

13 November 1986

Profoundly grieved passing beloved Hand of the Cause of God, Zikrullah Khadem, the indefatigable defender of the Covenant, and the exemplary, erudite, loving, gentle, humble and staunch servant of Bahá'u'lláh. We beseech the Blessed Beauty to exalt his pure and radiant soul. . . .

National Spiritual Assembly
of the Bahá'ís of Canada

19 November 1986

BAHÁ'ÍS TAIWAN JOIN OTHERS IN EXTENDING HEARTFELT CONDOLENCES ON PASSING WELL-LOVED HAND KHADEM. LOCAL COMMUNITIES HOLDING SERVICES ISLANDWIDE TO OFFER PRAYERS HIS BEHALF.

NSA TAIWAN

17 November 1986

WITH GRIEF STRICKEN HEARTS CONVEY TO YOU AND FAMILY DEEPEST CONDOLENCES PASSING BELOVED HAND CAUSE MR. DHIKRULLAH KHADEM. OFFERING PRAYERS FOR PROGRESS HIS RADIANT SOUL ABHÁ KINGDOM.

BAHÁ'ÍS OF JAMAICA

15 November 1986

WE LIFT OUR HEARTS PRAYERS BEHALF DEAR HAND OF THE CAUSE MR. KHADEM. . . .

NSA AND FRIENDS GRENADA

15 November 1986

Deeply grieved at passing beloved Hand of the Cause Zikrullah Khadem who is so fondly remembered from his visits in years past. His kind and gentle nature touched the hearts of believers young and old alike, and the memories of his visits remain very precious. . . .

National Spiritual Assembly, Alaska

---

*This cable was received during the last days of Mr. Khadem's illness.

Spiritual Assemblies, Bahá'í Communities, and Individuals

So many individuals, communities, close friends, and associates from all over the world—Bahá'ís and non-Bahá'ís alike—showered us with their love, appreciation, grief, loss, and inspiration in tender words, moving poetry, thoughtful acts, precious gifts. Many honored Mr. Khadem with sacrificial contributions to our Faith in his name as well as donations to charities and other humanitarian organizations. What follows is only a sampling of the hundreds of communications we received.

20 November 1986

Mr. Khadem walked through this life so erectly that it seemed that an invisible cord reached from the top of his head and was tied firmly somewhere in the realm above. This bearing of upright and infinite dignity combined with the courteous sentiments of respect and humility in his speech reminded us of the Biblical phrase "salt of the earth" and of the prophecy of Jesus, "by their fruits ye shall know them." We regarded him as a living proof of the claim of Bahá'u'lláh and it gave us comfort to know that he was among us and a part of our world-wide family: a leader by virtue of deeds.

Mr. Khadem was a long-suffering and self-sacrificing servant of the Cause, who, though a Hand of the Cause of God, was in our view never fully appreciated and understood by us Americans, we think, because of his formality, accent and radically different perspective on the Bahá'í Faith. It must have been a great frustration to him that his services were not better used in the public representation of the Faith. Yet his contribution was immeasurably great and the effect of his passionate words of love for Bahá'u'lláh, 'Abdu'l-Bahá and the Beloved Guardian, Shoghi Effendi, ring today in our ears and in the ears of all who were privileged to hear them. He gave our insignificant efforts meaning by analogizing them to the heroic events in our Faith's illustrious history. And he exemplified the phrase "true believer" in both deed and word. . . .

But for all his sweetness, there was also in the heart of Mr. Khadem, a tiger's ferocious spirit which was aroused instantly when he sensed that the Faith was being attacked, besmirched or misrepresented. It was fitting that he was chosen to liberate the sword of Mullá Ḥusayn from Iran. As 'Abdu'l-Bahá said of an earlier defender of the Faith, "He was a consolation to the

hearts of the believers and as a drawn sword to the enemies of Bahá'u'lláh."
p. 51 *Memorials of the Faithful.*

And finally, this pure and radiant soul who opened his eyes to the
spiritual Kingdom, also dared to see and did not turn away from the sordid
conditions from which his fellow believers were seeking to free themselves.
He listened as commanded ". . . to the midnight sighing of the poor" and
to the tales of suffering and difficulty which many laid before him. And
though he was a diffident, shy and conservative man by nature, he reached
out to one and all with understanding and love. He sacrificed his own
nature to serve others and that example is what we remember most vividly
and try to emulate in our lives.

We believe that this is how our Faith grows: that men like Hand of the
Cause of God Zikrullah Khadem arise and exert themselves ceaselessly to
be of loving service and we, inspired by their example and moved by their
prayers, strive to emulate them in our own small ways. To walk in their
footsteps and to diffuse the fragrances. . . .

Nashville, Tennessee

3 January 1987

Mr. Khadem was so deeply loved, admired and cherished by all the Bahá'ís
who knew him that every sign of illness they ever saw (or imagined) in him
in his latter years was like an icy hand clutching at their hearts. . . . Mr.
Khadem showered so much of his love . . . that we have soaked it up,
stored it up in the reservoir of our hearts, and have it to comfort us all the
rest of our earthly lives. We loved his devotion to the beloved Guardian,
and he made the Guardian feel closer to us because of that. We are deeper,
better Bahá'ís than we were before being enveloped in the warm spiritual
embraces of . . . your beloved husband.

Haifa, Israel

14 November 1986

HAND OF THE CAUSE JINÁB-I-KHADEM SINCE HIS YOUNG AGE WAS A DE-
VOTED LOVER OF OUR BELOVED GUARDIAN AND RENDERED GREAT SERV-
ICES TO OUR BELOVED FAITH. . . .

THIS HUMBLE SERVANT HAD THE HONOUR OF HEARING PERSONALLY,
OUR BELOVED GUARDIAN PRAISING AND APPRECIATING HIS HISTORICAL
SERVICES WHICH HE CONTINUED WITH OUR BELOVED UNIVERSAL HOUSE
OF JUSTICE.

NICE, FRANCE

18 November 1986

JINÁB-I-AYÁDÍ ZIKRULLAH KHADEM* TOWER OF LOVE SERVITUDE LODE-STONE OF GRACE OF ABHÁ BEAUTY. HIS PASSING GREAT LOSS TO ENTIRE BAHÁ'Í WORLD. MAY HIS VICTORIOUS SOUL BECOME CONQUERING FORCE FOR FURTHERANCE SUCCESS IN FULFILLMENT DIVINELY INSPIRED PLANS LOFTY INSTITUTION UNIVERSAL HOUSE OF JUSTICE. . . .

COLORADO SPRINGS, COLORADO

24 November 1986

We send to you our strong courage that tests the promise of reunion and only we who remain are left with the agony of absence of this giant of a man who was unique in his station amongst the Bahá'ís of the world.

For generations and light years to come it will be my humble privilege to offer prayers for his greater advancement in the next world but somehow, no matter how I dismiss it, the thought that he, Zikrullah Khadem, is now with the beloved Guardian surmounts all others.

The man whom Hand of the Cause Kházeh says loved the Guardian more than anyone; . . .

The man who suffered as the world continued thru its growing pains;

The man who all Americans really always called MISTER KHADEM because of his dignity, bearing, and special light.

We love him also;

We miss him also; . . .   Laguna Beach, California

17 November 1986

. . . he deepened our love for Shoghi Effendi and our vision of his greatness in the unfoldment of the Cause. What a reward he must be reaping now once again united in the presence of his beloved Guardian under the shadow and infinite blessing of the Three Central Figures of the Faith and in the company of the holy ones of all ages! . . .

Haifa, Israel

20 November 1986

What words can express our deepest sympathy and sorrow over the earthly separation of our Beloved Mr. Khadem.

---

*"Jináb-i-Ayádí Zikrullah Khadem" means "His Honor, the Hand of the Cause of God Zikrullah Khadem."

Thank God, on bended knees we have the words and strength of the Blessed Perfection to console us. . . .

"I picture the Beloved Guardian waiting with open arms to embrace him and that can't make me sad." "He is with his Beloved Guardian now." . . .

We will miss him terribly and we will double our teaching efforts (if God permits) in Mr. Khadem's honor. He was and will ever be a shining example of Bahá'í love, humility, and steadfastness for all Bahá'ís everywhere for generations to come. . . .

Pickerel, Wisconsin

23 November 1986

When I think of Mr. Khadem, I always remember him . . . so quiet, humble, gentle, and soft-spoken. Everyone would stand up and he would put his hands out—pushing downwards—telling us to sit, sit. It makes me smile to see him.

It is a great loss to all of us. . . .

New York, New York

Tenderly, we remember as if it were only yesterday, when mother declared to our Bahá'í Faith in . . . your home, and—Mr. Khadem, prayer book at hand, smiling his ever so warm-fatherly smile, requesting mother to read the little prayer: "Blessed is the spot, . . ."

Chicago, Illinois

5 December 1986

Our loss is indescribable as is our gain for having known him. How is it??—the heart can break and be full of joy at the same time!! . . .

Virginia Beach, Virginia

15 November 1986

The Bahá'í World is shaken to the core as it ponders and grieves the loss of your esteemed and noble husband who, during all those years in service to the beloved Guardian, has touched hundreds of thousands of hearts and quickened their souls.

. . . his words come back again and again, telling us how he always longed to be a sacrifice for the beloved Shoghi Effendi. Now he has been gathered into the Abhá Paradise, embraced by our Guardian, and bathed with rejoicing in the presence of his Beloved and the great Master.

All of you, living embodiments of all that Mr. Khadem stood for, now must surely be resolved to even more than ever, carry on the banner of the Most Great Name that he held high, aloft, during years of trials and years of victory.

In his honor, must not we Bahá'ís probe deeper into the roots of Faith, and arise to win the great victories which he so much prayed for! . . .

Lake Mary, Florida

25 November 1986

The loss of his presence will be greatly felt by all. I think what I appreciated most in Mr. Khadem was his references to the Beloved Guardian—always reminding us of the words of Shoghi Effendi, the guidance for all Bahá'ís and mankind. Mr. Khadem helped all Bahá'ís to know and appreciate the Beloved Guardian. . . .

Bonita Springs, Florida

26 November 1986

He not only was a noble, elevated soul—he was a darling man who showered love on everyone, encouraged, uplifted them. . . . I truly loved him. . . .

As I am sure is the case with you, I am joyous that Mr. Khadem's heart's desire is now fulfilled by being intimately rejoined with his adored Shoghi Effendi, and with Bahá'u'lláh and 'Abdu'l-Bahá. What rejoicing must have occurred in the Abhá Kingdom when Mr. Khadem joined them to carry on a new and even higher level of service. . . .

Conway, Missouri

13 November 1986

Our world has lost a beloved and priceless soul. His precious services to Bahá'u'lláh and to the friends are an indelible part of our wondrous heritage. He will surely have an even greater influence now. . . .

Evanston, Illinois

24 November 1986

Although we know that he has been gathered into the blessed company of those souls like his own, we feel such a deep sense of loss for ourselves, for we counted so heavily upon his touching our spiritual selves and inspiring us to live our lives more selflessly and to love the Blessed Beauty with all our hearts. I shall never forget my last meeting with him when he so moved us

delegates to the National Convention that we *begged* our House of Justice
to levy the Ḥuqúq upon us in America. . . .*
Trenton, New Jersey

February 1987
Mr. Khadem loved America and often spoke to us about the bounties and
glories of America. . . .

The beloved Guardian told Mr. Khadem that he was sending him to
America to witness all the glories of that country. . . §

He demonstrated his deep love for America and the believers in giving
them so unselfishly of his strength, his knowledge and wisdom, assurance
and inspiration everywhere he travelled. This, he did all over the world also,
but we in America have felt that he "belonged to us."

There are two "titles" relating to Mr. Khadem which will be remembered. Hand of the Cause William Sears more than once referred to him as
"the lion of the Covenant" and this was evident in all his services in the
Cause, but most especially in protecting the Faith. . . .

The second "title" was stated at the memorial service on the day of the
funeral of Hand of the Cause of God Zikrullah Khadem. His daughter
referred to him as "a mountain of a man," which . . . has many, many
meanings.
Wilmette, Illinois

16 November 1986
WORDS CANNOT CONVEY OUR ETERNAL APPRECIATION HIS LOVING EN-
COURAGEMENT OUTSTANDING EXAMPLE DEDICATED SERVICE CAUSE HIS
INVALUABLE GUIDANCE TRAINING TO US IN ADMINISTRATIVE FUNCTION-
ING AND TEACHING. WE WILL NEVER FORGET HIM. . . .
HAIFA, ISRAEL

[n.d.]
. . . It is indeed strange that many people are unaware of how severely
mankind has been diminished. . . .

. . . In 1971, . . . I was blessed to meet him for the first time. Having
only been a Bahá'í for a few weeks, I did not know who he was or what a
Hand of the Cause was. After his moving talk, every one went up and

---

*For an account of the talk Mr. Khadem gave on the subject of Ḥuqúqu'lláh at
the 1984 conference, see pp. 142–47.

§See chapter 4, p. 55, for an account of the Guardian's promise.

hugged him. Not wanting to appear rude, I followed. When he embraced me, I felt literally like an electric current flowed up my spine. He was a pure channel, as many can testify. I was blessed to see and hear him many times. . . .

The memory that will be with me in all the worlds of God is how he would take out his handkerchief and say, "The beloved Guardian . . ." How he loved the Guardian. And through his love, our love grew. . . .

Comayagua, Honduras

[n.d.]

The Hands all had their own personalities and "diffused the fragrances" in their own way to our great joy and benefit. To many of us Mr. Khadem diffused the fragrances of *reverence for the Faith* and a spiritual awareness of the station of the Guardian. In the way he spoke, in his mannerisms, he showed such a love, such humility, such respect for his beloved Guardian, that we were all enchanted, moved to tears, and felt gratitude for God's bestowal to mankind: the Guardian. Mr. Khadem . . . brought a standard of dignity and respect to all the meetings and conferences in which he participated. He, I felt, always was standing in the presence of the Guardian he loved. This pure love he had for the Guardian, and through him for the Faith, this pure channel of love, had an effect on many of the friends. That's the secret, to be a pure channel of spiritual love, to have one's heart an open conduit. He was one who had it and we are all better for having been recipients of that love.

. . . My own heart is leaping with happiness and gratitude for having had the privilege of knowing him. He has added to my life and strengthened it. For this, I am grateful. . . .

Richmond, Virginia

20 November 1986

. . . OUR DEAR HAND CAUSE MR. KHADEM WILL BE MISSED TREMENDOUSLY. . . . WE JOIN FRIENDS AROUND WORLD IN PRAYERS. AT LAST HE IS UNITED AGAIN WITH BELOVED GUARDIAN. . . .

PAPUA, NEW GUINEA

17 November 1986

DEEPLY SHOCKED GRIEVED NEWS PASSING DEAREST HAND CAUSE MR. ZIKRULLAH KHADEM WHOSE LOVING KINDNESS TO OUR FAMILY WILL ALWAYS BE TREASURED IN OUR HEARTS. . . .

JAPAN

25 December 1986

. . . it seems that Mr. Khadem visited the southeastern states twice a year, adding special luster to winter and summer schools. When he recounted episodes from the history everyone knew that each detail was as he stated. At the close of the sessions he would be surrounded by believers, drawn to him by his love and eager to drink more deeply of the teachings. . . .

Truk, Caroline Islands

14 December 1986

. . . he became a spiritual pillar shouldering the lion's share of teaching and deepening activities, all towards carrying forward the progress of the Faith in this country. We all saw him grow tired physically, while his spirit and dedication became increasingly stronger. . . .

Scottsdale, Arizona

Zikrullah, Mention of God

From the smile of Khadem,
Light filled the heart,
God's Mercy shone from his face.

From the eyes of Khadem,
The guides to the Path,
You could find the Holy Trace.

From the tongue of Khadem,
Flowed the melodies of love,
For he could see the Most Holy Place.

Now with Beloved Shoghi,
He surely can fly,
And with Martyr Ojji,*
He surely can Dance.

O thou, Mention of God,
Sit by the Tree,
    And listen to the Beauty,

---

*"Martyr Ojji" refers to Mr. Ḥabíbu'lláh Awjí, an Iranian Baháʼí who was executed in Shiraz on 16 November 1982.

Who whispers the Secret Melody,
And Reveals our Sacred duty.

You never forgot for one moment,
Of where your heart belonged.
Soar, O Dove of Certitude,
To where you have always longed.

With your flight into the Garden,
The smell of Roses fills the air,
Your wings have blown back its Sweetness
To us from your landing There.

Open the Gates, O thou Mighty Dove,
Ridvan is so close to See,
"Closer to thee than the vein in thy neck,"
Closer to thee are We!

Inhale the Air of the sweet-smelling Breeze,
And your Spirit can fly like a Dove,
Then ask your Lord upon humbled knees,
To send you Khadem's Love.

PAUL T. BAUMGARTNER

For Zikrullah Khadem

. . . .

O gentle friend, we should have learned from you.
Your radiant wonder shone on every meaning
In each small victory, and found the miracles.
Your talk began and ended praising God,
Began astonished, ended in thanksgiving.
We'll miss those words, their melody, their fire,
Your smiling kindness, the ardor of your faith
That made us see God's new order established,
Even in chaos, even in black despair.
And when our memories are history,
Our children will remember what you did,
Saying in hushed voice, "He was one of them,
Hands of the Cause, rocks in a mighty wall

Standing between His people and destruction,
Teaching us all how free surrender is
And what love's fire can fashion from a mortal."
Janet Bixby

To Daddy June

I will bathe your spirit
in the musk of joy,
from the Tent of Roses
that adorned the world.

And the Trumpet-Call
will blast your sleep
as the Banner of Light
unfurls.

And as the sun sets
on the mountain-top
you will see the shadows
in the valley below,

frantically tracing
their steps to the past,
broken and drowning in a sea of sorrow.

And with one Rose
from the dust
you will soothe their hearts
from fear of the unknown

and together they will string
the pieces of this broken earth
until the Promise of Heaven
is born.
Vanda Khadem

23 November 1986

. . . What a great empty chasm we felt and what tender loving thoughts
followed. We will never forget the example of sacrifice and complete
obedience and humility he gave us. We will always thank Bahá'u'lláh for so

precious a gift to our Hemisphere, for such a glorious love as he constantly gave each one and for a glimpse of the magnitude of love he bore for the beloved Guardian. . . .

Florida

Notes

Notes

INTRODUCTION

1. Shoghi Effendi, letter dated 8 February 1934, "The Dispensation of Bahá'u'lláh," in *The World Order of Bahá'u'lláh: Selected Letters*, 2d ed. (Wilmette, Ill.: Bahá'í Publishing Trust, 1974), 134.

2. Ibid.; 'Abdu'l-Bahá, quoted in Rúḥíyyih Rabbaní, *The Priceless Pearl* (London: Bahá'í Publishing Trust, 1969), 2.

3. 'Abdu'l-Bahá, *Will and Testament of 'Abdu'l-Bahá* (Wilmette, Ill.: Bahá'í Publishing Trust, 1944), 13.

4. Ibid., 3.

5. Bahá'u'lláh, *The Seven Valleys and The Four Valleys*, trans. Ali-Kuli Khan and Marzieh Gail, 3d ed. (Wilmette, Ill.: Bahá'í Publishing Trust, 1978), 8.

Part 1/ HIGHLIGHTS OF A LIFE OF SERVICE
Recollections by Javidukht Khadem

CHAPTER 1 / MY HUSBAND

1. 'Abdu'l-Bahá, undated tablet to Mr. Khadem's paternal grandmother, surnamed Bíbí Ján, translation approved by the Universal House of Justice.

2. From notes taken from talks given by Mr. Khadem in April 1957 in Panama City, Panama, at the Seventh Annual Convention of the Bahá'ís of Central America.

3. *The Koran Interpreted*, trans. and interpreted A. J. Arberry (New York, N.Y.: Macmillan Co., 1955), 57.

4. Bahá'u'lláh, *The Seven Valleys and The Four Valleys*, trans. Ali-Kuli Khan and Marzieh Gail, 3d ed. (Wilmette, Ill.: Bahá'í Publishing Trust), 7.

5. Quoted from Mr. Khadem's notes.

6. Shoghi Effendi, *God Passes By*, new ed. (Wilmette, Ill.: Bahá'í Publishing Trust, 1974), 188.

7. Bahá'u'lláh, in Bahá'u'lláh, the Báb, and 'Abdu'l-Bahá, *Bahá'í Prayers: A Selection of Prayers Revealed by Bahá'u'lláh, the Báb, and 'Abdu'l-Bahá*, new ed. (Wilmette, Ill.: Bahá'í Publishing Trust, 1985), 238–39.

CHAPTER 2 / EARLY SERVICE

1. Shoghi Effendi quoted in "In Memoriam, I. The Unity of East and West, American Bahá'í Sacrifices Her Life in Service to Persian Believers. Mrs. Keith Ransom-Kehler's Mission," *The Bahá'í World: A Biennial International Record, Volume V, 1932–1934*, comp. National Spiritual Assembly of the Bahá'ís of the United States and Canada (New York: Bahá'í Publishing Committee, 1936), 398.

2. Bahá'u'lláh, in Bahá'u'lláh, the Báb, and 'Abdu'l-Bahá, *Bahá'í Prayers: A Selection of Prayers Revealed by Bahá'u'lláh, the Báb, and 'Abdu'l-Bahá*, new ed. (Wilmette, Ill.: Bahá'í Publishing Trust, 1985), 147.

3. Shoghi Effendi, cable dated 9 May 1944 to Zikrullah Khadem.

4. "Persia Celebrates the First Hundred Years," *The Bahá'í World: A Biennial International Record, Volume X, 1944–1946*, comp. National Spiritual Assembly of the United States and Canada (Wilmette, Ill.: Bahá'í Publishing Committee, 1949), 181–82.

CHAPTER 3 / APPOINTMENT AS A HAND OF THE CAUSE OF GOD

1. 'Abdu'l-Bahá, *Will and Testament of 'Abdu'l-Bahá* (Wilmette, Ill.: Bahá'í Publishing Trust, 1944), 13.

2. 'Abdu'l-Bahá, *Selections from the Writings of 'Abdu'l-Bahá*, comp. Research Department of the Universal House of Justice, trans. Committee at the Bahá'í World Centre and Marzieh Gail (Haifa: Bahá'í World Centre, 1978), 51.

CHAPTER 4 / INTERNATIONAL SERVICE—EUROPE

1. Shoghi Effendi, cable dated 18 March 1952 to Zikrullah Khadem.

2. See 2 Pet. 3:10.

3. Bahá'u'lláh, *The Seven Valleys and The Four Valleys*, trans. Ali-Kuli Khan and Marzieh Gail, 3d ed. (Wilmette, Ill.: Bahá'í Publishing Trust, 1978), 34.

4. [Shoghi Effendi], *The Unfolding Destiny of the British Bahá'í Community: The Messages from the Guardian of the Bahá'í Faith to the Bahá'ís of the British Isles* (London: Bahá'í Publishing Trust, 1981), 377.

5. For information on Dagmar Dole, see Honor Kempton, "In Memoriam," in *The Bahá'í World: A Biennial International Record, Volume XII, 1950–1954,* comp. National Spiritual Assembly of the Bahá'ís of the United States (Wilmette, Ill.: Bahá'í Publishing Trust, 1956), 701–02.

6. Jean Deleuran, attachment to letter dated 27 June 1989 from Jean Deleuran to Javidukht Khadem, author's personal papers. The account has been edited to maintain the first-person narrative.

7. Shoghi Effendi, cable dated 16 November 1952 to National Spiritual Assembly of the Bahá'ís of the United States, attached to letter dated 14 June 1989 from Archives Office of the Universal House of Justice to Bahá'í Publishing Trust of the United States.

8. Shoghi Effendi, quoted in Kempton, "In Memoriam," in *Bahá'í World, Vol. XII,* 702.

CHAPTER 5 / INTERNATIONAL SERVICE—AFRICA

1. The text of the cable with interpolations is printed in Shoghi Effendi, *Messages to the Bahá'í World: 1950–1957,* rev. ed. (Wilmette, Ill.: Bahá'í Publishing Trust, 1971), 40, 41. For the full text of the message announcing the Ten Year World Crusade, see pp. 40–45.

2. Shoghi Effendi, cable dated 5 September 1952 to Zikrullah Khadem, International Bahá'í Archives, Haifa, Israel.

3. Letter to the Hands of the Cause, the Members of the National Spiritual Assemblies, the pioneers, the resident believers and visitors attending the African Intercontinental Teaching Conference in Kampala, Uganda, in *The Bahá'í World: A Biennial International Record, Volume XII, 1950–1954,* comp. National Spiritual Assembly of the Bahá'ís of the United States (Wilmette, Ill.: Bahá'í Publishing Trust, 1956), 121.

4. Ibid.

5. For a biography of the Hand of the Cause of God Dorothy Baker, see Dorothy Freeman, *From Copper to Gold: The Life of Dorothy Baker* (Oxford: George Ronald, 1984).

6. See J. E. Esslemont, *Bahá'u'lláh and the New Era: An Introduction to the Bahá'í Faith,* 5th rev. ed. (Wilmette, Ill.: Bahá'í Publishing Trust, 1980). The book has been translated into many languages.

7. Shoghi Effendi, cable dated 22 March 1952 to Mr. and Mrs. Khadem, Mr. and Mrs. Banání, and Reginald Turvey, International Bahá'í Archives, Haifa, Israel.

8. The Báb, in Bahá'u'lláh, the Báb, and 'Abdu'l-Bahá, *Bahá'í Prayers: A Selection of Prayers Revealed by Bahá'u'lláh, the Báb, and 'Abdu'l-Bahá,* new ed. (Wilmette, Ill.: Bahá'í Publishing Trust, 1985), 28.

Chapter 6 / International Service—West and East

1. See "The Guardian's Message on the Occasion of the Dedication of the Mother Temple of the West," in *The Bahá'í World: A Biennial International Record, Volume XII, 1950–1954,* comp. National Spiritual Assembly of the Bahá'ís of the United States (Wilmette, Ill.: Bahá'í Publishing Trust, 1956), 141.

2. Shoghi Effendi, letter dated 4 May 1953, *Messages to the Bahá'í World: 1950–1957,* rev. ed. (Wilmette, Ill.: Bahá'í Publishing Trust, 1971), 153.

3. Ibid., 152–53. *Yá Bahá'u'l-Abhá!* (O Thou the Glory of the Most Glorious!) is a form of Bahá'u'lláh's name, the Greatest Name, that is used as an invocation; *Yá 'Alíyu'l-A'lá!* (O Thou the Exalted of the Most Exalted!) is a form of the Báb's name that is used as an invocation.

4. For an account of Ella Bailey, see Robert L. Gulick, Jr., "Ella M. Bailey," in *Bahá'í World, Vol. XII,* 685–88.

5. Shoghi Effendi, quoted in ibid., 688.

6. For further details on the trip, see Dorothy Freeman, *From Copper to Gold: The Life of Dorothy Baker* (Oxford: George Ronald, 1984), 272–73.

7. Shoghi Effendi, cable dated 14 December 1954 to Zikrullah Khadem, International Bahá'í Archives, Haifa, Israel.

8. Shoghi Effendi, cable dated 5 January 1955 to Zikrullah Khadem.

9. Zikrullah Khadem, cable dated 24 October 1955 to Shoghi Effendi; Shoghi Effendi, cable dated 27 October 1955 to Zikrullah Khadem.

10. Abbasali Butt, "An Account of the Services of Siyyid Muṣṭafá Rúmí," in *The Bahá'í World: A Biennial International Record, Volume X, 1944–1946,* comp. National Spiritual Assembly of the Bahá'ís of the United States and Canada (Wilmette, Ill.: Bahá'í Publishing Committee, 1949), 517.

11. Details are from Mr. Khadem's diary.

12. For the text of the cable from Shoghi Effendi naming him a Hand of the Cause of God, see Butt, "An Account of the Services of Siyyid Muṣṭafá Rúmí," in *Bahá'í World, Vol. X,* 519–20.

13. Bahá'u'lláh, *Gleanings from the Writings of Bahá'u'lláh,* trans. Shoghi Effendi, 2d ed. (Wilmette, Ill.: Bahá'í Publishing Trust, 1976), 334.

14. Zikrullah Khadem, letter dated 30 January 1970 to the Universal House of Justice.

Chapter 7 / The Impact of the Passing of the Guardian

1. Nabíl-i-A'zam, in *Ayyám-i-Tis'ih* (Los Angeles: Kalimát, 1981), 336. See also Qur'án 12:30–31.

2. Translated from the Persian by Zikrullah Khadem from *Gulzar-i-Na'ím* (New Delhi, 1958), 167.

CHAPTER 8 / LATER SERVICE

1. For the cable that launched the Ten Year World Crusade, see Shoghi Effendi, cable dated 8 October 1952, *Messages to the Bahá'í World: 1950–1957*, rev. ed. (Wilmette, Ill.: Bahá'í Publishing Trust, 1971), 40–45.

2. Shoghi Effendi, letter dated 4 May 1953, *Messages to the Bahá'í World*, 153, 152.

3. Paul Haney, "The Institution of the Hands of the Cause of God," in *The Bahá'í World: An International Record, Volume XIII, 1954–1963*, comp. The Universal House of Justice (Haifa: The Universal House of Justice, 1970), 345.

4. See The Universal House of Justice, statement presented at the Bahá'í World Congress on 30 April 1963, *Wellspring of Guidance: Messages, 1963–1968*, 2d ed. (Wilmette, Ill.: Bahá'í Publishing Trust, 1976), 1–3.

5. 'Abdu'l-Bahá, *Will and Testament of 'Abdu'l-Bahá* (Wilmette, Ill.: Bahá'í Publishing Trust, 1944), 11.

6. For many passages from the writings of Shoghi Effendi on Bahá'í schools, see Shoghi Effendi and The Universal House of Justice, *Centers of Bahá'í Learning: Extracts from the Writings of Shoghi Effendi and The Universal House of Justice*, comp. The Universal House of Justice (Wilmette, Ill.: Bahá'í Publishing Trust, 1980), 1–17.

7. See Adib Taherzadeh, *The Revelation of Bahá'u'lláh: Adrianople 1863–68* (Oxford: George Ronald, 1977), 401. See also 'Abdu'l-Bahá, in Bahá'u'lláh, the Báb, and 'Abdu'l-Bahá, *Bahá'í Prayers: A Selection of Prayers Revealed by Bahá'u'lláh, the Báb, and 'Abdu'l-Bahá*, new ed. (Wilmette, Ill.: Bahá'í Publishing Trust, 1985), 65.

8. Jane Faily, talk delivered on 16 September 1984 at the Green Lake Bahá'í Conference.

9. Ruth E. Pringle, letter dated 18 November 1986 to Javidukht Khadem.

10. Lord McNair, speech to the House of Lords, 10 February 1982, *Parliamentary Debates (Hansard)*, vol. 427, no. 38 (1982), cols. 244, 247.

11. Lord Whaddon, speech to the House of Lords, 10 February 1982, *Parliamentary Debates (Hansard)*, vol. 427, no. 38 (1982), col. 254.

12. 'Abdu'l-Bahá, *Will and Testament*, 3.

13. 'Abdu'l-Bahá, *Tablets of the Divine Plan: Revealed by 'Abdu'l-Bahá to the North American Bahá'ís*, rev. ed. (Wilmette, Ill.: Bahá'í Publishing Trust, 1977), 47, 48, 38.

14. Ibid., 59–60.

15. Ibid., 48.

16. Letter dated Riḍván 140 B.E. [1983 A.D.] to the Baháʼís of the World from The Universal House of Justice.

17. ʻAbduʼl-Bahá, *Will and Testament,* 13.

18. *God Passes By,* written by Shoghi Effendi, is a survey of the outstanding events of the first Baháʼí century (1844–1944). See Shoghi Effendi, *God Passes By,* new ed. (Wilmette, Ill.: Baháʼí Publishing Trust, 1974).

CHAPTER 9 / MR. KHADEM'S PASSING

1. Javidukht Khadem, letter to the National Spiritual Assembly of the Baháʼís of Canada, quoted in *Baháʼí Canada,* vol. 8, no. 11 (January/February 1987): 2. The quotation attributed to ʻAbduʼl-Bahá is a paraphrase of a passage attributed to Him in May Maxwell, *An Early Pilgrimage,* 2d rev. ed. (London: George Ronald, 1969), 42.

2. Baháʼuʼlláh, *The Seven Valleys and The Four Valleys,* trans. Ali-Kuli Khan and Marzieh Gail, 3d ed. (Wilmette, Ill.: Baháʼí Publishing Trust, 1978), 34.

3. Zikrullah Khadem, letter dated 23 October 1986 to the National Spiritual Assembly of the Baháʼís of the United States.

4. National Spiritual Assembly of the Baháʼís of the United States, letter dated 31 October 1986 to Zikrullah Khadem.

5. See Baháʼuʼlláh, *Gleanings from the Writings of Baháʼuʼlláh,* trans. Shoghi Effendi, 2d ed. (Wilmette, Ill.: Baháʼí Publishing Trust, 1976), 319–22.

6. Continental Board of Counselors for the Americas, National Spiritual Assembly of the Baháʼís of the United States, and the Auxiliary Board members, e-mail dated 16 November 1986 to the Universal House of Justice.

7. Universal House of Justice, e-mail dated 17 November 1986 to National Spiritual Assembly of the Baháʼís of the United States.

8. Universal House of Justice, e-mail dated 14 November 1986 to the National Spiritual Assemblies of Australia, the United States, Canada, Alaska, and the United Kingdom.

CHAPTER 10 / MEMORIALS

1. Baháʼuʼlláh, in Baháʼuʼlláh, the Báb, and ʻAbduʼl-Bahá, *Baháʼí Prayers: A Selection of Prayers Revealed by Baháʼuʼlláh, the Báb, and ʻAbduʼl-Bahá,* new ed. (Wilmette, Ill.: Baháʼí Publishing Trust, 1985), 43–45; ʻAbduʼl-Bahá, in *Baháʼí Prayers,* 135–36; for an English translation of the Tablet of Visitation, see Baháʼuʼlláh, in *Baháʼí Prayers,* 230–33.

2. ʻAlí-Nakhjavání, letter dated 4 January 1987 to Javidukht Khadem.

3. Mic. 7:12.
4. The Báb, in [Bahá'u'lláh, the Báb, and 'Abdu'l-Bahá], *Bahá'í Prayers: A Selection*, rev. ed. (London: Bahá'í Publishing Trust, 1975), 7.
5. Bahá'u'lláh, *The Hidden Words*, trans. Shoghi Effendi (Wilmette, Ill.: Bahá'í Publishing Trust, 1939), Persian No. 5, p. 24.

Part 2/ OUR FATHER
Reminiscences by Zikrullah Khadem's Five Children

CHAPTER 1 / "ALL IS THE BELOVED, THE LOVER IS A VEIL"

1. Annemarie Schimmel, "Maulana's Last Letter to Shams," in *Mirror of an Eastern Moon* (London: East-West Publications, 1978), dedication.
2. Bahá'u'lláh, *Kitáb-i-Íqán: The Book of Certitude*, trans. Shoghi Effendi, 2d ed. (Wilmette, Ill.: Bahá'í Publishing Trust, 1950), 59–61.
3. I translated the passage from a book of poems by Ṣubḥat-i-Lárí, (India: Naseri Publishing Co., 1895).
4. The article, written in Persian and entitled "The Blessed House of the Báb," was published in *Payam-i-Bahá'í* in Geneva, Switzerland.
5. Bahá'u'lláh, *The Hidden Words*, trans. Shoghi Effendi (Wilmette, Ill.: Bahá'í Publishing Trust, 1939), 29.
6. Bahá'u'lláh, in Bahá'u'lláh, the Báb, and 'Abdu'l-Bahá, *Bahá'í Prayers: A Selection of Prayers Revealed by Bahá'u'lláh, the Báb, and 'Abdu'l-Bahá*, new ed. (Wilmette, Ill.: Bahá'í Publishing Trust, 1985), 7.
7. Mírzá Áqá Ján, quoted in Shoghi Effendi, *God Passes By*, new ed. (Wilmette, Ill.: Bahá'í Publishing Trust, 1974), 116.

CHAPTER 2 / IN MEMORY OF MY PRECIOUS FATHER

1. Bahá'u'lláh, *The Seven Valleys and The Four Valleys*, trans. Ali-Kuli Khan and Marzieh Gail, 3d ed. (Wilmette, Ill.: Bahá'í Publishing Trust, 1978), 34.
2. Bahá'u'lláh, *Gleanings from the Writings of Bahá'u'lláh*, trans. Shoghi Effendi, 2d ed. (Wilmette, Ill.: Bahá'í Publishing Trust, 1976), 10, 11; Bahá'u'lláh, *Tablets of Bahá'u'lláh Revealed after the Kitáb-i-Aqdas*, comp. Research Department of the Universal House of Justice, trans. Habib Taherzadeh et al. (Wilmette, Ill.: Bahá'í Publishing Trust, 1978), 107.
3. 'Abdu'l-Bahá, quoted in Genevieve L. Coy, "Illumined Faces," in *Star of the West*, 20, no. 2 (May 1929): 52.
4. Bahá'u'lláh, in Bahá'u'lláh, the Báb, and 'Abdu'l-Bahá, *Bahá'í Prayers: A Selection of Prayers Revealed by Bahá'u'lláh, the Báb, and 'Abdu'l-Bahá*, new ed. (Wilmette, Ill.: Bahá'í Publishing Trust, 1985), 105.

5. Ibid., 8, 9.

6. Ibid., 247.

7. Ibid., 238–45.

8. Bahá'ís observe the following nine holy days and anniversaries: the Feast of Naw-Rúz (the Bahá'í New Year), 21 March; the Feast of Ridván (commemorating the Declaration of Bahá'u'lláh, Prophet-Founder of the Bahá'í Faith), 21 April–2 May; the Declaration of the Báb, Prophet-Herald of the Bahá'í Faith, 23 May; the Ascension of Bahá'u'lláh, 29 May; the Martyrdom of the Báb, 9 July; the Birth of the Báb, 20 October; the Birth of Bahá'u'lláh, 12 November; the Day of the Covenant, 26 November; and the Ascension of 'Abdu'l-Bahá, 28 November. Bahá'ís also observe a nineteen-day fast each year, beginning 2 March.

9. Bahá'u'lláh, *The Hidden Words*, trans. Shoghi Effendi (Wilmette, Ill.: Bahá'í Publishing Trust, 1939), 49.

10. Shoghi Effendi, *God Passes By*, new ed. (Wilmette, Ill.: Bahá'í Publishing Trust, 1974), 165.

11. Bahá'u'lláh, *The Hidden Words*, trans. Shoghi Effendi (Wilmette, Ill.: Bahá'í Publishing Trust, 1939); Bahá'u'lláh, *The Seven Valleys and The Four Valleys*, trans. Ali-Kuli Khan and Marzieh Gail, 3d ed. (Wilmette, Ill.: Bahá'í Publishing Trust, 1978); Bahá'u'lláh, *Kitáb-i-Íqán: The Book of Certitude*, trans. Shoghi Effendi, 2d ed. (Wilmette, Ill.: Bahá'í Publishing Trust, 1950); the Tablet of Carmel is found in Bahá'u'lláh, *Tablets of Bahá'u'lláh*, 1–5.

12. Bahá'u'lláh, *Seven Valleys*, 3, 28.

13. Exod. 3:5.

14. 'Abdu'l-Bahá, in Bahá'u'lláh, the Báb, and 'Abdu'l-Bahá, *Bahá'í Prayers*, 235.

15. The Universal House of Justice, *The Promise of World Peace: To the Peoples of the World* (Wilmette, Ill.: Bahá'í Publishing Trust, 1985).

16. Bahá'u'lláh, *Gleanings*, 197.

17. The Valley of True Poverty and Absolute Nothingness is described in Bahá'u'lláh's *Seven Valleys*, 36–42.

CHAPTER 3 / THE POWER OF EXAMPLE

1. Bahá'u'lláh, in Bahá'u'lláh, the Báb, and 'Abdu'l-Bahá, *Bahá'í Prayers: A Selection of Prayers Revealed by Bahá'u'lláh, the Báb, and 'Abdu'l-Bahá*, new ed. (Wilmette, Ill.: Bahá'í Publishing Trust, 1985), 204.

2. For a copy of the photograph, see Rúhíyyih Rabbaní, *The Priceless Pearl* (London: Bahá'í Publishing Trust, 1969), facing page 148. See also Rúhíyyih Rabbaní, *The Guardian of the Bahá'í Faith* (London: Bahá'í Publishing Trust, 1988), between pages 66 and 67.

Chapter 4 / Glimpses of an Endearing Father

1. See 'Abdu'l-Bahá, *Selections from the Writings of 'Abdu'l-Bahá*, comp. Research Department of the Universal House of Justice, trans. Committee at the Bahá'í World Centre and Marzieh Gail (Haifa: Bahá'í World Centre, 1978), 70–71.

2. See the Báb, in Bahá'u'lláh, the Báb, and 'Abdu'l-Bahá, *Bahá'í Prayers: A Selection of Prayers Revealed by Bahá'u'lláh, the Báb, and 'Abdu'l-Bahá*, new ed. (Wilmette, Ill.: Bahá'í Publishing Trust, 1985), 28.

3. See J. E. Esslemont, *Bahá'u'lláh and the New Era: An Introduction to the Bahá'í Faith*, 5th rev. ed. (Wilmette, Ill.: Bahá'í Publishing Trust, 1980), 35.

4. Bahá'u'lláh, *Kitáb-i-Íqán: The Book of Certitude*, trans. Shoghi Effendi, 2d ed. (Wilmette, Ill.: Bahá'í Publishing Trust, 1950).

Chapter 5 / With Gratitude

1. See Bahá'u'lláh, *The Seven Valleys and The Four Valleys*, trans. Ali-Kuli Khan and Marzieh Gail, 3d ed. (Wilmette, Ill.: Bahá'í Publishing Trust, 1978), 8.

Part 3 / A SAMPLING OF ARTICLES
by Zikrullah Khadem

Article 1 / Pilgrimage to the Scenes of the Báb's Captivity and Martyrdom

1. Bahá'u'lláh, quoted in Shoghi Effendi, *The Promised Day Is Come*, 3d ed. (Wilmette, Ill.: Bahá'í Publishing Trust, 1980), 43.

2. The Báb, quoted in Shoghi Effendi, *God Passes By* (Wilmette, Ill.: Bahá'í Publishing Trust, 1974), 23.

3. Bahá'u'lláh, *Gleanings from the Writings of Bahá'u'lláh*, trans. Shoghi Effendi, 2d ed. (Wilmette, Ill.: Bahá'í Publishing Trust, 1976), 244.

4. Shoghi Effendi, *God Passes By*, 53.

5. Nabíl-i-A'zam [Muhammad-i-Zarandí], *The Dawn-Breakers: Nabíl's Narrative of the Early Days of the Bahá'í Revelation*, trans. and ed. Shoghi Effendi (Wilmette, Ill.: Bahá'í Publishing Trust, 1932), 309–10.

6. The Báb, quoted in Shoghi Effendi, *God Passes By*, 4.

7. See Nabíl, *Dawn-Breakers*, 256.

8. Ibid., 243.

9. Bahá'u'lláh, in Bahá'u'lláh, the Báb, and 'Abdu'l-Bahá, *Bahá'í*

Prayers: A Selection of Prayers Revealed by Bahá'u'lláh, the Báb, and 'Abdu'l-Bahá, new ed. (Wilmette, Ill.: Bahá'í Publishing Trust, 1985), 232.

10. The Báb, quoted in Shoghi Effendi, *Promised Day Is Come,* 8.

11. The Báb, quoted in Bahá'u'lláh, *Kitáb-i-Íqán: The Book of Certitude,* trans. Shoghi Effendi, 2d ed. (Wilmette, Ill.: Bahá'í Publishing Trust, 1950), 231.

12. 'Abdu'l-Bahá, *Will and Testament of 'Abdu'l-Bahá* (Wilmette, Ill.: Bahá'í Publishing Trust, 1944), 3.

13. See Bahá'u'lláh, *Gleanings from the Writings of Bahá'u'lláh,* trans. Shoghi Effendi, 2d ed. (Wilmette, Ill.: Bahá'í Publishing Trust, 1976), 14–17, or Bahá'u'lláh, *Tablets of Bahá'u'lláh Revealed after the Kitáb-i-Aqdas,* comp. Research Department of the Universal House of Justice, trans. Habib Taherzadeh et al. (Wilmette, Ill.: Bahá'í Publishing Trust, 1978), 2–5.

14. 'Abdu'l-Bahá, quoted in Rúhíyyih Rabbaní, *The Priceless Pearl* (London: Bahá'í Publishing Trust, 1969), 8.

15. See Shoghi Effendi, "The Dispensation of Bahá'u'lláh," in *The World Order of Bahá'u'lláh: Selected Letters,* 2d ed. (Wilmette, Ill.: Bahá'í Publishing Trust, 1974), 123–39.

16. See Nabíl, *Dawn-Breakers.*

17. See *The Bahá'í World: A Biennial International Record, Volume IX, 1940–1944,* comp. National Spiritual Assembly of the Bahá'ís of the United States and Canada (Wilmette, Ill.: Bahá'í Publishing Committee, 1945), frontispiece. [The Shrine of the Báb was completed in 1953.]

18. Bahá'u'lláh, *Tablets of Bahá'u'lláh,* 5.

19. Bahá'u'lláh, *The Hidden Words,* trans. Shoghi Effendi (Wilmette, Ill.: Bahá'í Publishing Trust, 1939), 27.

20. Bahá'u'lláh, in Bahá'u'lláh, the Báb, and 'Abdu'l-Bahá, *Bahá'í Prayers,* 230.

21. Ibid., 233.

22. Shoghi Effendi, *God Passes By,* 25.

ARTICLE 2 / FROM BADASHT TO SAINT LOUIS: AN EVALUATION OF THE FIRST BAHÁ'Í CONFERENCE AND THE LARGEST

1. 'Abdu'l-Bahá, *Memorials of the Faithful,* trans. Marzieh Gail (Wilmette, Ill.: Bahá'í Publishing Trust, 1971), 200.

2. Nabíl-i-A'zam (Muhammad-i-Zarandí], *The Dawn-Breakers: Nabíl's Narrative of the Early Days of the Bahá'í Revelation,* trans. and ed. Shoghi Effendi (Wilmette, Ill.: Bahá'í Publishing Trust, 1932), 243.

3. The Báb, quoted in ibid., 236.

4. Ibid., 259n. 1. The translation is from Emily McBride Périgord,

Translation of French Foot-notes of the Dawn-Breakers (Wilmette, Ill.: Bahá'í Publishing Trust, 1939), 38.

5. The Báb, quoted in Nabíl, *Dawn-Breakers,* 269; Nabíl, *Dawn-Breakers,* 269.

6. Nabíl, *Dawn-Breakers,* 292.

7. Ibid.

8. Shoghi Effendi, *God Passes By* (Wilmette, Ill.: Bahá'í Publishing Trust, 1974), 31–32.

9. 'Abdu'l-Bahá, *Memorials of the Faithful,* 200.

10. Ibid., 201.

11. Ibid., 200–01.

12. Nabíl, *Dawn-Breakers,* 294n. 1.

13. 'Abdu'l-Bahá, *A Traveler's Narrative Written to Illustrate the Episode of the Báb,* trans. Edward G. Browne, new and corrected ed. (Wilmette, Ill.: Bahá'í Publishing Trust, 1980), 4.

14. Isa. 9:6.

15. 'Abdu'l-Bahá, *A Traveler's Narrative,* 4.

16. Na'ím, *Istidlálíyyih Na'ím,* 130–31.

17. Mírzá Haydar-'Alí, *Dalá'il'u'l-'Irfán,* 156.

18. Shoghi Effendi, *God Passes By,* 32.

19. Nabíl, *Dawn-Breakers,* 352.

20. Quddús, quoted in ibid., 352–53, an allusion to Qur'án 11:86.

21. Shoghi Effendi, *God Passes By,* 33.

22. Táhirih, quoted in Martha L. Root, *Táhirih the Pure,* intro. Marzieh Gail, rev. ed. (Los Angeles: Kalimát Press, 1981), 121.

23. Táhirih, quoted in Nabíl, *Dawn-Breakers,* 295.

24. Nabíl, *Dawn-Breakers,* 293.

25. Ibid., 297.

26. 'Abdu'l-Bahá, *Memorials of the Faithful,* 201.

27. Nabíl, *Dawn-Breakers,* 293–94.

28. 'Abdu'l-Bahá, *Memorials of the Faithful,* 201.

29. Nabíl, *Dawn-Breakers,* 295.

30. 'Abdu'l-Bahá, *Memorials of the Faithful,* 201.

31. Nabíl, *Dawn-Breakers,* 295–96.

32. 'Abdu'l-Bahá, *Memorials of the Faithful,* 201.

33. From the Báb's Commentary on the Súrih of Joseph.

34. The Báb, quoted in Shoghi Effendi, *God Passes By,* 324–25.

35. Bahá'u'lláh, *Gleanings from the Writings of Bahá'u'lláh,* trans. Shoghi Effendi, 2d ed. (Wilmette, Ill.: Bahá'í Publishing Trust, 1976), 136.

36. Ibid., 16.

37. From *The Mathnaví* by Bahá'u'lláh.

38. From a poem of Shaykh Bahá'í (953 A.H./1547 A.D.–1030 A.H./

1621 A.D.), a well-known mathematician who discovered the Greatest Name of God.

39. Nabíl, *Dawn-Breakers,* 293.

40. Bahá'u'lláh, quoted in Shoghi Effendi, *God Passes By,* 101.

41. Shoghi Effendi, *God Passes By,* 72.

42. 'Abdu'l-Bahá, quoted in Shoghi Effendi, in "America and the Most Great Peace," *The World Order of Bahá'u'lláh: Selected Letters,* 2d ed. (Wilmette, Ill.: Bahá'í Publishing Trust, 1974), 77.

43. Táhirih, quoted in Nabíl, *Dawn-Breakers,* 296.

44. Nabíl, *Dawn-Breakers,* 298.

45. 'Abdu'l-Bahá, quoted in Shoghi Effendi, letter dated 30 June 1952, *Messages to the Bahá'í World: 1950–1957,* rev. ed. (Wilmette, Ill.: Bahá'í Publishing Trust, 1971), 38.

ARTICLE 3 / CARMEL: THE MOUNTAIN OF GOD AND THE TABLET OF CARMEL

1. Shoghi Effendi, *Messages to the Bahá'í World, 1950–57,* rev. ed. (Wilmette, Ill.: Bahá'í Publishing Trust, 1971), 63.

2. Bahá'u'lláh, *Epistle to the Son of the Wolf,* (Wilmette, Ill.: Bahá'í Publishing Trust, 1988), 145.

3. 'Abdu'l-Bahá, trans. by the Universal House of Justice.

4. Memoirs of Dr. Habib Mu'ayyad, pp. 19, 21, 22, 53.

5. 'Abdu'l-Bahá, quoted in Mirza Ahmad Sohrab, "Mount Carmel, the Vineyard of God," in *Star of the West* 14, no. 5 (August 1923): 148–49.

6. Shoghi Effendi, *Tablet of Twin Monuments,* 14.

7. Isa. 2:2–5.

8. Unpublished memoirs.

9. Jinábi Husayn Iqbál, letter to Shoghi Effendi; letter to the National Spiritual Assembly of the Bahá'ís of Persia.

10. Shoghi Effendi, letter dated Naw-Rúz 1955, trans. by the Universal House of Justice.

11. Shoghi Effendi, *Message to the East,* Naw-Ruz 1952.

12. Shoghi Effendi, letter dated Naw-Ruz 1955, trans. by the Universal House of Justice.

13. Shoghi Effendi, letter dated April 1954, in *Messages to the Bahá'í World: 1950–1957,* rev. ed. (Wilmette, Ill.: Bahá'í Publishing Trust, 1971), 63.

14. 'Abdu'l-Bahá, quoted in Shoghi Effendi, an unpublished daily memorandum conveying a talk by 'Abdu'l-Bahá on 3 August 1919.

15. 'Abdu'l-Bahá, *Memorials of the Faithful,* trans. Marzieh Gail (Wilmette, Ill.: Bahá'í Publishing Trust, 1971), 27.

16. Shoghi Effendi, *God Passes By,* rev. ed. (Wilmette, Ill.: Bahá'í Publishing Trust, 1974), 194.

17. Bahá'u'lláh, *Gleanings from the Writings of Bahá'u'lláh,* trans. Shoghi Effendi, 2d ed. (Wilmette, Ill.: Bahá'í Publishing Trust, 1976), 15, 14, 15, 16–17.

18. Bahá'u'lláh, *Epistle to the Son of the Wolf,* trans. Shoghi Effendi (Wilmette, Ill.: Bahá'í Publishing Trust, 1988), 145.

19. Na'ím, well-known Bahá'í poet.

20. Rev. 21:1, 3, 5.

21. Dabistánu'l-Madháhib, *Munazirát-i-Díniyyih,* 37.

22. Guldash-i-Chaman-á'ín of Zoroaster, 71; *Munazirát-i-Díniyyih,* 38.

23. Isa. 9:6–7.

24. Ibid., 11:5.

25. Qur'án 1:1 (Sale translation).

26. The Báb, quoted in Shoghi Effendi, letter dated 8 February 1934, "The Dispensation of Bahá'u'lláh," in *The World Order of Bahá'u'lláh: Selected Letters,* 2d ed. (Wilmette, Ill.: Bahá'í Publishing Trust, 1974), 146–47.

27. Isa. 11:9.

28. Shoghi Effendi, trans. by the Universal House of Justice.

29. Shoghi Effendi, *God Passes By,* rev. ed. (Wilmette, Ill.: Bahá'í Publishing Trust, 1974), 348.

30. Bahá'u'lláh, quoted in ibid., 188.

31. Shoghi Effendi, *God Passes By,* 188.

32. Shoghi Rabbani, cablegram received 5 December 1939 in "The Spiritual Potencies of that Consecrated Spot," in *The Bahá'í World: A Biennial International Record, Volume VIII, 1938–1940,* comp. National Spiritual Assembly of the Bahá'ís of the United States and Canada (Wilmette, Ill.: Bahá'í Publishing Committee, 1942), 245.

33. Bahá'u'lláh, quoted in "The Spiritual Potencies of that Consecrated Spot," in ibid., 249, 251.

34. Ibid., 251.

35. Bahá'u'lláh, in Bahá'u'lláh, 'Abdu'l-Bahá, Shoghi Effendi, and Bahíyyih Khánum, *Bahíyyih Khánum: The Greatest Holy Leaf,* comp. Research Department at the Bahá'í World Centre (Haifa: Bahá'í World Centre, 1982), v.

36. Isa. 54:2–4, 5, 7.

37. Isa. 54:11–12.

38. Bahá'u'lláh, *Tablets of Bahá'u'lláh Revealed After the Kitáb-i-Aqdas,* comp. Research Department of the Universal House of Justice, trans. Habib Taherzadeh et al. (Wilmette, Ill.: Bahá'í Publishing Trust, 1988), 5.

39. 'Abdu'l-Bahá, *Will and Testament of 'Abdu'l-Bahá*, (Wilmette, Ill.: Bahá'í Publishing Trust, 1944), 14.

40. Isa. 2:5.

41. Qur'án 17:1.

42. The Universal House of Justice, letter dated 5 June 1975 to the followers of Bahá'u'lláh throughout the world.

43. An allusion to Qur'án 55:27.

Article 4 / Bahá'u'lláh and His Most Holy Shrine

1. Bahá'u'lláh, *The Hidden Words,* trans. Shoghi Effendi (Wilmette, Ill.: Bahá'í Publishing Trust, 1939), 27.

2. Bahá'u'lláh, quoted in Shoghi Effendi, "The Dispensation of Bahá'u'lláh," in *The World Order of Bahá'u'lláh: Selected Letters,* 2d ed. (Wilmette, Ill.: Bahá'í Publishing Trust, 1974), 104.

3. Bahá'u'lláh, quoted in Shoghi Effendi, *God Passes By,* rev. ed. (Wilmette, Ill.: Bahá'í Publishing Trust, 1974), 100.

4. Shoghi Effendi, "The Goal of a New World Order," in *World Order of Bahá'u'lláh,* 46.

5. Isa. 9:6.

6. Bahá'u'lláh, *Gleanings from the Writings of Bahá'u'lláh,* trans. Shoghi Effendi, 2d ed. (Wilmette, Ill.: Bahá'í Publishing Trust, 1976), 210–11.

7. Bahá'u'lláh, quoted in Shoghi Effendi, *God Passes By,* rev. ed. (Wilmette, Ill.: Bahá'í Publishing Trust, 1974), 100.

8. Qur'án 14:5.

9. Qur'án, quoted in Bahá'u'lláh, *Epistle to the Son of the Wolf,* trans. Shoghi Effendi, new ed. (Wilmette, Ill.: Bahá'í Publishing Trust, 1988), 117.

10. 'Abdu'l-Bahá, quoted in Shoghi Effendi, *God Passes By,* 183.

11. Ishráq-Khávarí, in *Áhang-i-Badí',* 347.

12. 'Abdu'l-Bahá, *Makátíb-i-'Abdu'l-Bahá* 1:39.

13. Ishráq-Khávarí, *Commentary on Na'ím's Poems,* 468.

14. Ezek. 43:2.

15. Isa. 60:1.

16. Ishráq-Khávarí, *Commentary on Na'ím's Poems,* 471.

17. H. M. Munje, *The Whole World Is But One Family,* 3d ed. (New Delhi: Bahá'í Publishing Trust of India, 1985), 50–51.

18. *Dalá'ilu'l-'Irfán,* 156.

19. Bahá'u'lláh, *Epistle,* 140 (italics added).

20. Shaykh-i-Bahá'í, *Ash'ár-i-Parákandih Shaykh-i-Bahá'í,* 76. Translated by Mr. Khadem.

21. Qur'án 20:11, 13–15.

22. Qur'án 7:139–40.

23. Bahá'u'lláh, *Epistle,* 42.

24. Qur'án 17:1.

25. Qur'án 53:4–14.

26. The Báb, quoted in Shoghi Effendi, *God Passes By,* 94; Bahá'u'lláh, quoted in Shoghi Effendi, "The Dispensation of Bahá'u'lláh," in *World Order of Bahá'u'lláh,* 104.

27. Shoghi Effendi, *God Passes By,* 98.

28. Ibid., 97.

29. Bahá'u'lláh, *Gleanings,* 212.

30. The Báb, quoted in Shoghi Effendi, *God Passes By,* 324–25.

31. Shoghi Effendi, *God Passes By,* 69.

32. 'Abdu'l-Bahá, quoted in ibid., 293.

33. A chronicler of 'Abdu'l-Bahá's travels, quoted in Shoghi Effendi, *God Passes By,* 293–94.

34. Bahá'u'lláh, *Epistle,* 20–21.

35. Ibid., 77.

36. J. E. Esslemont, *Bahá'u'lláh and the New Era: An Introduction to the Bahá'í Faith,* 5th rev. ed. (Wilmette, Ill.: Bahá'í Publishing Trust, 1980), 51.

37. Bahá'u'lláh, *Epistle,* 21.

38. Yúnis Khán, in *Áhang-i-Badí',* no. 70, 5.

39. Shoghi Effendi, *God Passes By,* 93.

40. Ibid., 221.

41. Shoghi Effendi, *God Passes By,* 222.

42. The Báb, quoted in ibid., 97.

43. See Shoghi Effendi, *God Passes By,* 214.

44. Ibid., 222.

45. 'Abdu'l-Bahá, *Memorials of the Faithful,* trans. Marzieh Gail (Wilmette, Ill.: Bahá'í Publishing Trust, 1971), 144.

46. Shoghi Effendi, "The Dispensation of Bahá'u'lláh," in *World Order of Bahá'u'lláh,* 105.

47. Shoghi Effendi, *God Passes By,* 193.

48. Hájí Mírzá Haydar 'Alí, *Bihjatu's-Sudúr,* 517–18.

49. Yúnis Khán, *Memoirs of Dr. Yúnis Khán,* 80–81.

50. Ibid., 143–44.

51. Hájí Mírzá Haydar 'Alí, *Bihjatu's-Sudúr,* 517–18.

52. Habíb Mu'ayyad, *Memoirs of Habíb, (Khátirat-i-Habíb),* 173–74.

53. Ibid., 452.

54. Ibid., 60.

55. Ibid., 176–77.

56. Ibid., 131.

57. Mary L. Lucas, *A Brief Account of My Visit to Akka* (Chicago, Ill.: Bahá'í Publishing Society, 1905), 19–20.

58. G. L. C., "The Plain of Acca," in *The Bahá'í Magazine: Star of the West* 13, no. 8 (November 1922): 208.

59. Yúnis K͟hán, *Memoirs,* 37.

60. 'Abdu'l-Bahá, *Will and Testament of 'Abdu'l-Bahá* (Wilmette, Ill.: Bahá'í Publishing Trust, 1944), 3.

61. See [The Universal House of Justice, comp.], *Bahá'í Holy Places at the World Centre,* (Haifa: Bahá'í World Centre, 1968), 40.

62. Bahá'u'lláh, quoted in Shoghi Effendi, *God Passes By,* 3.

63. Bahá'u'lláh, in Bahá'u'lláh, the Báb, and 'Abdu'l-Bahá, *Bahá'í Prayers: A Selection of Prayers Revealed by Bahá'u'lláh, the Báb, and 'Abdu'l-Bahá,* new ed. (Wilmette, Ill.: Bahá'í Publishing Trust, 1985), 230.

64. Ibid., 232.

65. Ibid.

66. Bahá'u'lláh, *Gleanings,* 99.

67. Bahá'u'lláh, quoted in Shoghi Effendi, *God Passes By,* 109.

68. Ibid., 101.

69. Qur'án 24:35.

70. Ibid.

71. Bahá'u'lláh, quoted in Shoghi Effendi, "The Spiritual Potencies of that Sacred Spot," in *The Bahá'í World: A Biennial International Record, Volume VIII, 1938–1940,* comp. National Spiritual Assembly of the Bahá'ís of the United States and Canada (Wilmette, Ill.: Bahá'í Publishing Committee, 1942), 249.

72. Ibid., 251.

73. Bahá'u'lláh, *Gleanings,* 136.

74. Ibid., 16.

75. Shoghi Effendi, *God Passes By,* 93.

76. Bahá'u'lláh, quoted in ibid., 184.

77. 'Abdu'l-Bahá, quoted in Shoghi Effendi, *The Advent of Divine Justice,* new ed. (Wilmette, Ill.: Bahá'í Publishing Trust, 1984), 47.

JAVIDUKHT KHADEM wrote *Zikrullah Khadem, The Itinerant Hand of the Cause of God: With Love* because she wanted to share with other Bahá'ís something of the passion Mr. Khadem held for the Central Figures of the Bahá'í Faith and for Shoghi Effendi, the Guardian of the Faith. Married to Zikrullah Khadem for over fifty years, Mrs. Khadem assisted him in most of his traveling assignments, which spanned six continents. She also had the privilege of witnessing the expansion of the Bahá'í Faith under Shoghi Effendi's inspired direction and later under that of the Universal House of Justice, the international governing and legislative body of the Faith.

Noteworthy in her own right for her long years of service to the Bahá'í Faith, Mrs. Khadem has spent twenty-six years serving on the Auxiliary Board, an advisory body the function of which is the consolidation of the Bahá'í community. She has traveled widely in that capacity, addressing numerous audiences in the United States, Canada, Asia, Europe, and Africa. She has conducted Bahá'í school seminars and prepared extensive study guides on the subjects of world peace, the world order of Bahá'u'lláh, the covenant of Bahá'u'lláh, Bahá'í family life, and the education of children. She resides in Skokie, Illinois.

At Mrs. Khadem's request, her five children wrote essays about their father, each recalling from his or her unique perspective, what it was like to grow up in a family grounded in the love of God and service to humanity. Mozhan Khadem is an internationally known architect residing in Brookline, Massachusetts. Jena Khadem Khodadad, a research scientist in molecular biology, is on the faculty of Rush Medical College in Chicago, Illinois. Riaz Khadem, author of *One-Page Management,* is an international consultant in data management in Atlanta, Georgia. Ramin Khadem is the chief financial officer for Inmarsat in London, an international organization involved in satellite telecommunications. May Khadem Czerniejewski, a practicing opthalmologist, is on the faculty of Northwestern University Medical School in Chicago.